P9-DDJ-712
YALU RIVER
PEIPING
NORTH KOREA
38TH PARALLEL
SEOUL
SOUTH KOREA
TAEGU
PUSAN
YENAN
NGTZE VALLEY
SHANGHAI
NAGASAKI
HIROSHIMA
KYOTO
ISE
TOKYO
YOKOHAMA
KAMAKURA
ATAMI
JAPAN
PEARL RIVER
FOOCHOW
TAIPEI
FORMOSA
CANTON
SWATOW
MACAO
HONG KONG
VICTORIA
PACIFIC OCEAN
PHILIPPINES
LUZON
ZAMBALES MTS
SUBIC BAY
BATAAN
CORREGIDOR
MANILA
PASIG RIVER
PALAWAN
NEGROS IS.
MINDANAO
DAVAO
MT. APO
NORTH BORNEO
NEO
ESIA
BALI
GUADALCAN
N
W
E
S

THERE IS NO ASIA

THERE IS NO ASIA

by

DWIGHT COOKE

KENNIKAT PRESS
Port Washington, N. Y./London

THERE IS NO ASIA

Reissued in 1971 by Kennikat Press by
arrangement with Doubleday & Company, Inc.
Library of Congress Catalog Card No: 79-118487
ISBN 0-8046-1404-0

Manufactured by Taylor Publishing Company Dallas, Texas

ESSAY AND GENERAL LITERATURE INDEX REPRINT SERIES

To the hospitality and friendliness and understanding
which uncounted people all over Asia
gave one American abroad

PREFACE

Today the best that can be said is that we have not yet lost Asia. If we go on as we have been going, we will lose it to communism. And the whys and wherefores of our danger swing around the fact that there is no single entity in the Far East called "Asia." Unlike "America," or "Europe," or even the "Middle East," there is no Asia.

The nations of the Middle East or Europe have far more in common than we realize. Certain basic words in every culture of the West have the same meanings: good, evil, dictator, profit, economics, vote, individual, dignity, co-operation, freedom, God. The only things the nations of Asia have in common are negative. They are not white. They are not well fed. They do not trust or admire the West.

Asia includes one third of the world's land and one half of the world's population. It includes the highest and lowest points on the globe, the wettest, the loneliest, and the most crowded. The eager, wretched, proud, fledgling nations of Asia, which swing a great arc from Japan and the Bering Sea down around to Pakistan and the Arabian Sea, are a seething mass of vastly different and totally separate civilizations. Each of them must be helped to a non-Communist stability with different methods.

Therefore, this is not a book about the great truths of the incredible cultures of Asia, nor is it about the myriad ways in which the United States should learn from the East and so enrich itself. This is a book about the ways and delays in the path of Asia toward the benefits it is hell-bent on getting for itself from the twentieth-century technology of the West. And it is about the ways and means whereby the United States can safeguard itself and the rest of the non-Communist world from the spread of political slavery in the East.

August, 1954

CONTENTS

THERE IS NO ASIA

POINT OF RETURNS:

The Philippines

Everywhere in Asia, East and West are coming together. But in most countries the result is a head-on collision from which both parties pick themselves up with a curse, gather together the scattered pieces of their own precious civilizations, and vow more caution the next time their paths cross.

Only in one country of Asia do West and East really join hands, in the Philippines. This archipelago, which swings a thousand-mile arc of islands down the Pacific from Formosa to Borneo, is the only country in Asia which was ever ruled by Americans. Our proudest achievement as a world power is the existence of twenty million free Filipinos who have built for themselves the most enthusiastic democracy outside the Atlantic Community and who have, in their dramatic national election of November 1953, proved themselves to be the most advanced practitioners of freedom in Asia.

Since these islands occupy the strategic center of the western Pacific, their increasing political maturity is a protection to the rest of the free world. From their volcanic-tipped mountains can be felt the cold winds of communism blowing across from the great land masses of China and Manchuria. Luzon, the northernmost island of the Philippines—about the size of New York State—reaches up near Formosa and points on toward Seoul, Tokyo, and Vladivostok, farther north. The island of Mindanao, far to the south, lies across from Malaya and above Indonesia. In between these two largest islands, the other seven thousand islands of the Philippines sprawl out almost parallel to Red China and the free world's most crucial area, rich, vulnerable, and divided Southeast Asia.

Thanks to the unique mutual relationship between the Filipinos and the Americans, the United States is developing in these islands the most significant cluster of military and psychological bases we have anywhere in the Far East, plus one of the largest governmental staffs in any foreign country. And they are all welcomed here. Nowhere else in Asia could this be said.

The potentially rich and prosperous Republic of the Philippines, which has been in existence only since July 4, 1946—and even the date selected has an American flavor—has been suffering from the tribulations of a devastating war and the disorders of a new republic. The islands were smashed to pieces by the Japanese occupation of World War II and the American liberation in 1945. After the war the Filipinos put down a serious communistic terror and civil war. Today, under the reform administration of President Magsaysay, they are tackling the problems which spring out of war ruin, lack of experience, long-standing social evils, a poor peasantry, and a minuscular industrial system.

In what they do and the way they do it, the Filipinos are not only a first line of defense against communism in Asia, they are America's illustration of a promise kept, a democracy in action. If you have seen none of the rest of Asia, these people seem very unlike us; when you have known other Asians, you find yourself halfway home when you come to the Philippines. Economically our years of occupation made the Filipino, poor though he may be by American standards, richer than any other people in Asia. Culturally the Filipinos are making themselves into an Asian reflection of our virtues and our vices. They are the living symbol, the observable evidence of what our twentieth-century democracy can accomplish in the ancient, fantastically different, and furiously revolutionary new republics of Asia.

Only thirty-six hours after the arid orange-cream plains and mountains of northern California have fallen away behind the tail of your Asia-bound plane, the rugged purple mountains and green jungles of Luzon rise up out of the blue Pacific ahead of you, jagged mountain ranges and jungles of massed coconut palm trees, their upper branches spreading out from the center of the trees in regular designs so that there seems to be a canopy of flat dusty brown snowflakes covering the jungle below your plane. Close in to Manila, you pass Mount Banahaw, double-peaked and cloud-capped, and as the plane loses altitude, the lime-green of the young rice paddies begins to alternate with the deep mahogany-rust patches of burned-over rice paddies.

These two colors are set off by small circles of turquoise water, not lakes but bomb craters from World War II.

When you land at the Manila International Airport and step out into the soft moist air, you know you are in the Asian tropics. In the distance are bamboo clumps, palm trees, and the omnipresent water buffalo, the carabao, plowing the wet mud of the rice paddies. There is a blazing sun above your head, and moving in a leisurely, courteous tempo around you are people with warm brown coffee-with-cream skins which make yours seem a pasty white.

In a modern limousine, driving in from the airport along Dewey Boulevard, you see the characteristic Philippine combination of East, West, and War. During World War II, the Japanese converted this boulevard into a landing strip for their fighter planes. As you wind on around the bay, on the land side, house after house is still pockmarked with shell holes. Many of the fences are made from rusted Swiss-cheese squares of iron with which the American Air Force converted jungles and deserts into landing fields. But on the other side of Dewey Boulevard a group of Philippine women with crude clay jars on their heads move with a dancer's gait as they carry drinking water to their husbands. The men, clad in sun-faded diapers, are fishing in the bay as they have for one thousand years, hauling in the great brown-black lengths of their nets. And beyond them, the huge circumference of Manila Bay, one of the best harbors in the world, is broken by peculiar little red-brown rusted volcanoes, the hulks of the Japanese battleships and cruisers sent to the bottom by American pilots in the last days of the war.

Manila is crowded and crammed and teeming with Filipinos, most of them in Western clothes. Its main streets are lined with Western buildings. Western merchandise fills its stores, which are rarely more than two stories high, with arcaded ground floors so Manilans can walk through most of the downtown area and come out in the hot sun or rain only when they cross the streets. Billboards scream of cola drinks and American cars; the department stores sell everything from chlorophyll toothpaste to falsies; you can buy American magazines or malted milks.

The most popular sport of the islands is basketball and the favorite entertainment is American movies, which keep Manila's movie houses packed from morning to evening. One of the most amazing things about today's Asia is that no matter which civilization you visit, no matter what the background or religion of a country, its people are passionately fond of American movies. The gooey pink marshmallow dreamworld of Hollywood is the chief way, and often the only way, millions of Asians learn about the United States, which to them is therefore a potpourri of western sheriffs, Chicago gangsters, and scantily clad blondes preferred by young and handsome millionaires.

In the big cities or in the barrios, the country villages of the Philippines, everybody wants American things. They represent success. If you cannot be successful, you can at least learn English, so half the people speak English and there is no place where an American is likely to go in the Philippines and nothing he is likely to want, from palm juice, the murky, varnish-red drink of the countryside, to prostitutes as expensive as New York call girls, where English does not serve perfectly. In Manila the other languages are Spanish and Tagalog, the principal dialect of Luzon Island and one of the eight major dialects of the eighty-seven spoken in the islands.

Manila is only fifteen degrees north of the equator, but it is no steam bath. Any resident of Philadelphia or New Orleans could come here and cool off from his own home-town summer. This is a country where you do not need glass windows because the only time you want to keep out moving air is during a heavy rain, and then an overhang above the window frames, or wooden shutters to pull across them, does the job. The dining room and ballroom of the grand old Manila Hotel have no windows at all, just tall and wide graceful concrete arches opening out on terraces leading to palms and coconuts on the edge of the harbor. Where you find glass windows it is usually to keep in the coolness of air conditioning.

In the first months after the Japanese were driven out of Manila, people from the countryside moved into the city, where the American Army could protect them from Japanese soldiers and could feed them from the stores the Americans had brought in. As everywhere else in the world, once having tasted of city life, they do not want to leave it. Many thousands still hang around Manila, hoping to find white-collar jobs. One of the things the Filipinos have not learned about Americans is that we are proud of working with our hands. They associate success with a classical education and they sacrifice and go to night school for the shoddiest versions of our university courses. Many of the houseboys of Manila are university graduates, and the schools continue to turn out thousands more, hopelessly untrained in the technical skills their country so urgently needs.

The citadel of Philippine education is Manila's Santo Tomás University, founded in 1611. It is a beautiful group of formal brown-gray buildings enclosing courts in the Spanish style with separate staircases leading up from them labeled "males" and "females." In front of Santo Tomás is a large park fenced off from the main street. The Americans were interned here by the Japanese during the war and many of them were kept from death by Filipinos who risked their own necks to smuggle in food.

Today the park is green again, but in the center of its front fence, right where you look up the stately avenue to the central arch of Santo Tomás, there is a gas station. The Filipinos seem to prefer the ugliest modern designs to their own beautiful old native buildings, like the balconied two-story wooden houses adapted from Spanish styles. Once in a while in one of them, you see a wonderful old sea-shell window; each pane, about the size of four checker squares, is made not of glass but of shells: soft, warm, translucent, textured creams in age-softened, grayed wood frames.

Incidentally, the adjective "native" is the first word to take out of your vocabulary when you are in Asia. Americans use it as an affirmation of our own pride in ourselves: native Texan, some wonderful native southern food, native-born; in Asia it is a word of insult which has always separated the people of a country from their foreign rulers.

It is weird to see banners with Chinese ideographs flapping over the shell windows down on Ongpin Street in Manila's Chinatown, a mixture of blaring records and odors, stores, restaurants, and workshops spilling people out onto the sidewalks. Ongpin Street is the headquarters of the three hundred thousand Philippine Chinese whose immensely rich and immensely powerful leaders rule their own quarter their own way: "If you are Filipino and make trouble in this place, you be killed."

The Jews are not one tenth as powerful in the finance and commerce of the West as the Overseas Chinese are in Asia. South of Japan, no possible combination of economic and financial power in any country could compete with the Overseas Chinese. They start with nothing and become financial moguls. At least 40 per cent of the stores in the Philippines are run by Chinese; in Southeast Asian countries the figure runs up to 90 per cent. And they never miss a chance. One Manila street, Gandara, is solidly lined with two-story Chinese warehouses filled with American spare parts bought from the United States after the war as military surplus for a few cents on the dollar and now being sold for more than list price.

On Gandara Street or on Manila's main thoroughfare, Rizal Avenue, two things about the Philippines make an immediate impression on you. In the first place, you do not see more than one white in every fifty faces. Yet you never feel yourself an outlander anywhere in the islands, for everyone smiles at you and, if you will let him, accepts you as an equal. I had not thought this would happen in Asia; it rarely does. The other thing you notice is that everyone wears a wrist watch and nobody is on time, not even, and this is the acid test, engineers in radio studios. Whether because of the easygoing tropical climate, lack of training, non-interest in efficiency, or just plain irresponsibility, appointments are kept by guess and eventually, or not at all.

The good side of this indifferent approach to time is the very different tempo of life even in the big bustling city of Manila. Building goes on all around you in this Phoenix of the Pacific, but not at breakneck speed. I saw a modern neo-Greek bank building of heavy stone still being repaired from the war's damages, but the scaffolding was made of bamboo lashed together and the workers clambered up and down their undependable netting like constructive spiders. There is all the hectic noise of an American city, newsstands and taxis and traffic, yet on the crowded sidewalks people seem pleased to make way for you. You may have to leap for your life if you cross a street against traffic, but the truck driver who slams on his brakes gives you a friendly grin and a wave of the hand.

Two different passenger vehicles in Manila, the jeepney and the calesa, underline the two main influences which have shaped the urban life of the islands. The Filipinos solved their postwar transportation problem by buying up surplus U. S. Army jeeps, screwing a plank down along each side of them, hanging up an awning, and going into business as bus operators. Today's modern jeepney models are as up to date as American cabs, but in miniature, individually decorated and named, still with seats along the sides, still cramming in ten passengers.

Moving slowly among the jeepneys and bicycles are the calesas, romantic relics from the days of the Spanish rule. The calesas are picturesque high-wheeled carts with elaborate rigid tops like Victorian hansom cabs, but vividly painted and un-Victorianly hung with Chinese brass ornaments and drawn by the Filipino version of the Mongolian pony, a tiny horse any Victorian nana would have said was too weak to draw a children's cart.

Another symbol of the culture of the Spanish who ruled the Philippines for almost four hundred years is Malacañan Palace, once the palace of the Spanish viceroys and now the White House of the Philippines. Malacañan is a beautiful, long, and rambling two-story white building, Spanish in general feeling but proudly Philippine in its red mahogany windows and doors and the lush green of the palm trees and lawns and foliage around it. Under former presidents, the Filipinos at Malacañan receptions always wore the white tie and tails of the West, but President Magsaysay has brought the barong tagalog, the unique Philippine evening costume, back into fashion.

This evening shirt shows how the Filipino, resilient as his native bamboo, has learned to adjust to pressure. In the old days only a Spaniard had the right to wear his shirttails tucked into his trousers; the inferior "indios," even in full formal dress with cloak and top hat, were required to leave their shirttails out. Result: the Filipinos invented the barong tagalog. It is made of piña cloth, a pineapple fiber, soft and transparent with the lustrous texture of a slightly starched sheer silk. Cut like an American sport shirt and worn outside the trousers, it comes in pastel colors with pearl buttons, starched collar, and embroidered shirt panel, collar, and cuffs. A tie is never worn with the barong tagalog, but if the collar is unbuttoned the barong is a dinner coat; button the collar and it becomes the equivalent of white tie; either way, it is the coolest, most comfortable men's formal wear yet invented.

The Filipina's evening dress is equally distinctive. To a smartly cut Parisian gown she adds ruffled fanlike wing pieces which fit over the shoulders in a butterfly effect. In the old days these pañuelos were keep-away-from-me signs, heavily starched and suitable to the strict Spanish morals of the period; to caress the lady of your desire required more than the average Filipino's arm reach. Now, *O tempora! O mores!* the design has been altered. The pañuelos are made of soft material, unstarched, quite small, and detachable.

Filipinos consider their women the most beautiful in the world: "European women are beefish, American women mannish, and the other women of Asia too flat-faced." The Filipinas have been among the most suppressed women in Asia because under Spanish law they were placed in the same category with children and idiots; a woman could not leave her home without her parents' consent until she was twenty-five or married, and, once married, her husband had control over her. The double standard continues under the republic because the old Spanish Catholic sentiment still prevails in the islands.

A Filipino girl seldom goes out on a blind date and she is expected to have a chaperone until she is formally engaged. The older married women, asking very few of the rights American women demand, "serve their husbands in all things." The younger women of Manila, who have been exposed to the ways of the West, yearn for our "freedom from inhibitions and dogma and traditions and all that." But, although the old custom of families selecting their sons' wives is dying out and young men now marry for love, the Filipino has not altered his superior view.

In things sexual, most men of Asia think only of their own pleasures. This might be one reason the Asian women respect Americans as great lovers. It comes as a startling compliment to the American male to discover that in this part of the world he, poor fumbling amateur in Europe's eyes, is regarded as the Don Juan of his own fond dreams. This may be in part due to the American's appreciation of a woman as an equal partner. The Filipinas say, "You do things with mutuality."

The most important reason may be psychological. There are many indications that the nervous system of a Filipino, like that of other Asians, reacts differently from ours. Perhaps this is because their nervous systems have never been subjected to the strains we are used to; anyway, their nerves do not seem to be able to stand the extended tensions of the West. Halfway through the most dramatic sequence in an American movie, a Filipino will begin to giggle, not in amusement but as a nervous release. If there is an extended kissing sequence in a Tagalog movie, he laughs before it is over, again as a nervous release. And in things sexual, it is said the Filipino has an over-enthusiastic, almost uncontrollable, nervous system.

Incidentally, on a related subject, here is a legal point a Philippine judge still has under advisement: an ardent young Filipino was arrested because on a crowded street he had caressed the beautiful bosom of a Filipina; brought into court, he swore from his own first-hand experience that the girl had been wearing falsies, "therefore I committed no misdemeanor because I touched nothing real."

One of the most important influences on the pattern of Philippine life is the system of family relationships and responsibilities called the *parientes* system. This is a private family method of social security, an informal income tax levied by society on its more fortunate, an

Asian arrangement of family ties and responsibilities which the West has abandoned. Here, if you have money and your second cousin's widow needs a home or money to educate her children, she brings them to live with you and you pay the bills. Every family takes this as a matter of course; it is an instinctive pattern of responsibility which extends out to fourth cousins. And they cannot understand why Americans do not feel the same way. "I guess in the American character you don't have these deep profound drives that are almost instinctive."

At first glance, this parientes system seems a fine way to cushion unemployment; if you are out of work, you always have some relative, some *compadre*, who is working. And the system works even where there is no financial want. A wealthy family from the provinces would not think of staying at the luxurious Manila Hotel if they have relatives with extra beds. But the parientes system also has drawbacks. There is not much point in trying to save money if your cousins and nephews-in-law by the double dozens come to stay with you and eat it up. And in the first years of the new republic many a family gained while the nation lost. "If you had a lot of pull in the government, you made sure your compadres, efficient or not, got good jobs too."

Such an orientation around the family is one of the profound differences between East and West. Once true of feudal European societies, it has lasted in the colonial countries of Asia because for hundreds of years "government" has meant "foreign conqueror" and there has been no reason to develop loyalty to that central foreign power.

Whatever its side effects may have been, the parientes system has shaped a more integrated and more affectionate family life and the Filipino has badly needed such strength to face his postwar problems and rebuild his smashed country. When MacArthur's armies liberated Manila in 1945, it was a twisted mass of bombed bridges, buildings, and houses; with the exception of Warsaw, it was the most devastated capital city of World War II. More than 7 per cent of the entire population of the islands were killed. In the heart of Manila, within the old moss-covered adobe walls of the old city, the Intramuros, not a building remained except for parts of one small church and a fort.

Today the Filipinos, called indolent by so many people, have successfully rebuilt their islands. They have even listened to Japan's pleas to forget the past and re-establish trade exchanges of food and raw materials for Japanese manufactured products. A third of the Philippines' foreign trade is carried in Japanese ships which again ride at anchor in her harbors, but the Japanese sailors tend to stay on board; when they come into the cities, somehow many of them seem to disappear.

The struggles of returning to normalcy are nothing compared to the backbreaking problems the Filipinos must now overcome before their islands can feed and clothe them adequately, and protect them from internal and external communism. The largest set of these unsolved problems swings around land, who owns it and how it is used.

It was land that provided the fuel for a Communist insurrection in the Philippines which nearly wrecked the government. The Hukbalahap, Tagalog for People's Army Against the Japs, are the native Communists of the Philippines. During the war these Huks joined the guerrilla forces fighting the Japanese and then these hard-core fanatics began agitating among the young guerrilla idealists, trying to persuade them to hate their own government and the United States. And after liberation, the postwar facts of life in the new republic gave the Huk leaders powerful arguments.

There were only two main classes in the Philippines, divided by an enormous gap. There was a small privileged class of less than 10 per cent, the wealthy hacienda owners, government officers, small industrialists, Chinese traders; and then there was the great mass of *taos*, the peasant farmers living out in the barrios. At least sixteen million of the entire twenty million people in the Philippines are farmers. Around 40 per cent own no land, and few farmers have more than twenty-five acres.

Until the administration of President Magsaysay, the internal history of the Philippines had been the usual sorry story of the exploitation of the landless. Not only did the wealthy landlords hang onto their rich blocks of land, but since land had always been a good investment, yielding around 25 per cent a year, the small professional class of Manila put their savings in absentee-owned farms. The Liberal Party and President Elpidio Quirino, in power during the most dangerous period of the Huk insurrection, represented the wealthy classes and were gentle with the landlords: their land was assessed at 10 per cent of its selling price and taxed at about 1 per cent a year. The sharecropper was kept over a feudal barrel. He paid up to 70 per cent of his crops as rent and, in a poor year when he could not pay his rent, he could get a loan from a moneylender, almost always a Chinese, for 200 per cent interest. Thus exploited, many of the tenants were in debt until they died from malnutrition or tuberculosis.

The Huks took full advantage of this setup. From among the brave and idealistic ex-guerrillas who had been fighting for their country's freedom, they had gathered forty thousand armed Huks by 1949. Typical of these recruits was Manuel Cayod. He was eleven years old when his parents were killed by the Japanese invaders and he fled to the hills. In 1945 he was a seasoned veteran of fifteen: "I can't remember how many Japanese I killed." During the war the Huks turned him into a Communist and after the war he organized other idealistic, battle-seasoned high school classmates into Communist cells.

At nineteen he was back in the hills as a Huk company commander, "killing unnecessary civilians and government employees." As chairman of the National Finance Committee of the Philippine Communist Party, Cayod used direct methods to collect money: "I had six hundred armed men, so we went to Santa Cruz and took all the money away from the banks and the merchants." When a train with a government pay car came along, "we made a fight with the train security guards. We killed them and exploded the safe and sent the pesos to the Central Committee."

Supported by thousands of Cayods, by 1950 the Huks were becoming a second government of the islands. Pounding home their promise to "divide our country among the peasants and give it an honest government," they were in control of great sections of central Luzon. They set up a Stalin University, printed a newspaper, and even had a Politburo hidden away in Manila. The Philippine Government was blind to the need to reform its land policy, and the men of the constabulary and the Army were inefficient and corrupt, many of them thieves and rapists. The Huks saw their opportunity to make another Indo-China of the Philippines.

Then, barely in time, a new factor entered the equation. Not an idea, but a man. When immediate change comes in today's Asia, the odds are a hundred to one it comes not because of an idea's fertility but through a man's leadership. The man in this case was Ramon Magsaysay, President Quirino's new Secretary of Defense. He saw the perils to his country, saw the possible solutions, and drove forward. Before the Huk guerrillas could be blocked, the Philippine Army had to be revitalized, so Magsaysay gave it a shake-up spectacular in extent and effect. "It took a lot of reforming. I had to fire two generals, the Chief of Staff of the Army, and the chief of staff of the constabulary, and I had to put in jail many of the officers."

But ex-guerrilla Magsaysay knew that cleaning up the Army was only the first step. To kill guerrillas you have to fight them their own way, a fact the French could not learn in eight years of costly fighting in Indo-China. Secretary of Defense Magsaysay promptly set up a new unit of the Army under a famous anti-Communist fighter, Colonel Napoleon Valeriano, also the handsomest man in the islands and married to one of the beautiful Filipina screen stars. Valeriano assembled a detachment of volunteers at a secret training base and taught them Huk ways. They went barefoot, no shaves, haircuts, or baths; they were indoctrinated in the Huk code words, contractions, and slang; they were furnished with fake names and captured credentials. Then, on a rainy night Valeriano secretly transported his men to a mountain in Huk territory. At dawn he led a detachment of the regular Philippine Army in a sham attack against his anti-Huk group. "We pretend to beat them, they withdraw up into the hills, they are accepted as real Huks, they infiltrate, in time they tell us who and where the Huk leaders are."

All this time Magsaysay was making broadcasts and sending letters to the Huk leaders pointing out flaws in the Communist arguments and guaranteeing his personal protection and help if they would surrender. He met one Huk leader alone at three o'clock in the morning. "They planned to assassinate me, but their car broke down, so they thought God was preserving me and surrendered." Manuel Cayod, now disturbed by the Communist leadership of the Huks and offered an alternative hope for his country in patriots like Magsaysay, surrendered and revealed Huk secrets to the government. Many other Huks followed Cayod's example and helped the government fight their former comrades.

Next, Magsaysay and his Philippine and American advisers went to work on the rank-and-file guerrillas who had become Huks because they were landless: "Give them land of their own and they become the best possible anti-Communist propaganda." Thus was born Edcor, the Economic Development Corporation, one of the most successful devices to eliminate communism yet found in Asia.

I flew down from Manila to inspect a new Edcor camp being hacked out of the virgin jungles of Buldon on the southernmost of the large islands, Mindanao. Eight minutes from Nichols Field, we were over one of the hottest Huk sections in the Philippines, the mountain terrain around the same double-peaked Mount Banahaw, which seemed so placid and beautiful when I flew into the Philippines. As we droned south, the Filipino flight sergeant, in American nylon overalls, read about movie stars in *Life*, and Magsaysay's aide ruffled through *Mutt and Jeff* and *Tarzan*.

When we crossed Guimaras Strait and were over Negros Island, he looked up from his comic book. "I used to walk from one end to the other of that." In World War II he was a guerrilla, helping to bring supplies to American headquarters. Tons of supplies were secretly landed by American submarines and then carried on men's backs over the two hundred miles of rugged mountains to the northern tip of Negros: "We never figured distances in miles, we just said, 'It's a four-and-a-half-day walk.' "

The plane flew on over more straits and islands, over the mountainous jungles of Mindanao, around a bend in the hills, and we were at Urandang, a tiny air strip, about the size of a carrier flight deck, hacked out of the jungle. Urandang had a swamp at one end, two low hills at the other, and sharp mountains on each side. Its operations building was a bamboo, matting-sided, thatch-roofed hut, its wind sock a cone of bamboo hung on a tree whose branches had been hacked off. The swamp at the far end of the field serving as a brake for the plane, we slewed way around and stopped beside a waiting jeep and a war-surplus American troop truck loaded with armed soldiers.

We bumped away into the jungle, very pleasant-looking and not too overgrown. After plowing and lurching along for an hour, we arrived at Buldon. Magsaysay started the project, saying, "Rush, rush, put it up in two months." The major in charge said okay, lost forty pounds on the job, and was carried out to the hospital as the first settlers arrived, exactly two months later.

Buldon points up how poor the average *tao* is in his barrio, for by tao standards Buldon is luxurious. The houses, of rough wood frames on wooden stilts, open on all sides, have two small rooms furnished with bamboo matting for beds and for side walls to be let down against the rain. On a tiny wooden porch—the kitchen—is a heavy rough-hewn wooden table supporting a thick slab of slate where charcoal is burned. Over the fire, a couple of iron pots sit on top of three stones. Near them are two cooking utensils, a flat spatula, and a big wooden ladle, plus the only dishes, several chipped plates and cups. These are the entire furnishings of a Buldon house except for the shrine you always find in each of these devout Catholic homes. Sometimes it is only a religious picture with a candle under it, sometimes a backdrop of cheap gold satin with side hangings of red satin and colored lithographs and a tiny paraffin lamp to burn before the Mary.

Everybody and everything neat and clean, and in front of each hut a little flower bed, usually of bright zinnias. The washing and bathing are done at hydrants spaced along the streets, one for every ten or fifteen houses. And, symbol of the conjunction of old and new, in one corner of the little open-sided wood hut that was the town meeting hall, a modern white porcelain refrigerator run by bottled gas standing next to an ancient red clay water cooler.

No ex-Huk who has come to an Edcor camp has wanted to leave, and as soon as the first contingent raised a crop, they petitioned to pay back more of their loans so there would be money available sooner for more Edcors. Having so little makes no difference in the hospitality of these people. The minute I arrived they brought me a heaped platter of their carefully hoarded corn, and they kept urging me to eat more. Later there was a feast in their mess hall, a crude building literally no more than plank floor, screen sides and roof, one table, and a few old chairs set on very clean gray-blue and red linoleum. Lunch was an old chicken, very tough but served with great pride because it was home-raised, some rice, local fried fish, and gelatin pudding made from jungle plants and served with sweet squash sauce.

When you read of the famous cuisine of an Asian country, it is food that no more than 5 per cent of the people of that country have ever tasted. These Edcor settlers never eat the famous delicacy of the islands called *camarón rebosado*, tiny shrimps in a rich clear sweet-sour sauce with garlic and small pieces of ginger and tomato; nor have they tasted the famous *macapuno* ice cream, made from a special kind of coconut, the macapuno, whose meat is gelatinously soft with a very delicate coconut flavor.

But just as this food would seem Lucullan to the settlers of Edcor, so most of the taos would have considered the Edcor lunch a fine feast. For breakfast they eat rice, left over from the night before and fried with dried salted fish; with it, they drink *salabat*, ginger boiled in water with sugar, and sometimes, on feast days, they have a little coffee or chocolate. Lunch is fresh boiled rice and a fried green called *cangcong*, a spinach rich in calcium. Dinner is more of the same, plus a few ripe bananas or a pineapple. If the family is well off, it may keep a few chickens or have a small fishpond for protein food.

Thanks to Magsaysay, the revitalized Army and the anti-Huk corps, Buldon and the other Edcor projects, the threat of the Huk terrorists is no longer serious. But how to prevent the creation of new Communists is still the crucial question in the Philippines and in every other new republic of Asia. Each is saddled with the terrible problems left over from war or colonial occupation and with the threatening presence of trained native Communists. Local communism is like tuberculosis: once the germ has been walled off from the community, the immediate danger may be over, but the infection remains, ready to break out again if the organism becomes weak because communism in these countries is far less a foreign infiltration than a domestic revolt against inefficient or corrupt governments that do not give their peoples a better life.

The principal slogans of unrest, in the Philippines and in Asia, swing around the word "land." Four out of every five peasants in Asia are landless; therefore, they have nothing to lose by overthrowing the existing order. They have never known any political freedom or democracy, so they are not worried about losing it. Land, getting some land for themselves; this is the prime appeal to most Asians, and token land reforms will not appease them. Every new government of Asia has sweeping new land-reform laws on its books. So has the Philippine Republic. The test is how well a government enforces its land reforms and it was at this point that the pre-Magsaysay governments of the Philippines, including that of the Americans, failed miserably.

The greatest good fortune and economic strength of the Filipinos is that they have acres of undeveloped land and therefore need not undergo the heartbreaking struggles of India or Pakistan or China or Korea or Japan, where no matter how beneficent the government, there will never be enough land to go around.

The Philippine Islands, if they utilized their land as does Japan or Java, could support four times their present population. The greatest reservoir of immediately available land is on their second largest island of Mindanao around the principal city of that island, the raw, vigorous, and lusty frontier town of Davao, dominated by the 9700-foot volcanic Mount Apo, highest peak in the Philippines.

The second-floor terrace of Davao's principal hotel, the Apo View, is open on three sides, with bare green masonite walls, glaring neon signs, thick hot sliceable air, and happy mosquitoes. Juke boxes play "The Little White Cloud that Cried" and "Kiss of Fire." A sign on the wall reads, "The Davao Rotary Club Meets on Thursday at 12:15"; another, over the reception desk, "Check Your Firearms or Bladed Weapons Here."

Across the street from the hotel a line of rickety, tilted Filipino houses swarming with tiny, dirty, and happy children, most of them in little sweat shirts but no pants. A jeep rolling down the road with music blaring and signs advertising *Valley of the Eagle*. The children pay no attention. The jump from primitive times to the postwar world has been so rapid that machines are looked upon as equally magical and therefore no mechanical miracle is less likely than another; if Martians with seven-foot antennas suddenly materialized out of an opalescent globe, the Filipinos, children or otherwise, would give them a friendly smile and go on with whatever they were doing, or not doing.

Around Davao there are over two million acres of fertile virgin land, or green land as the Filipinos call it; here, where the green jungle is forever encroaching, green means wild, untilled, useless. There are hundreds of thousands of land-hungry Filipinos who would give anything to take the green off these acres, but until the new reform government of Magsaysay, the landless were blocked by red tape, government inefficiency and corruption. The tao, emigrating to Mindanao, could not find out ahead of time what land was available. If he found land to homestead, he was often unskilled as a farmer and he could not find out how to raise successful crops. If he could not do a good job, the Chinese moneylenders took over his land; if he did a good job, he would find someone with money and political influence contesting his title and taking his land away.

This is typical of the vicious circle that confronts the illiterate peasants of Asia and their well-meaning political leaders. But from his first campaign speeches, candidate Magsaysay focused on "building up the barrios, we will open for settlement our vast and fertile public land." And now President Magsaysay and his administration are taking the interlocking actions necessary to begin cleaning up the Philippine land problems. Agencies are being set up to screen applicants before they leave Manila and send them to the areas that best fit their backgrounds. New land-title laws are being passed and government agencies established to which the tao can go for legal aid if his title is contested. The government has already allotted $10,000,000 for better roads to open up land for the farmer and bring markets nearer his produce.

This, of course, is only a beginning. The inexperienced farmers must be taught how to farm, what crops to plant, and how to fertilize them. Agricultural schools must be opened, irrigation projects started, safe water found for drinking. American agencies, private and public, are helping the Philippine Government start this job. The Japanese had smashed the Los Banos Agricultural College, largest in the islands, so the United States and the Philippines, on a fifty-fifty cost basis, have erected a new college; the dean of Kansas State College was in charge of the rebuilding, and six men from Cornell University are teaching there now. Soon Los Banos will turn out three thousand agricultural technicians a year, enough to take care of present Philippine needs. Add to this, 4-H Clubs in most of the provinces plus various kinds of help from the U. S. Department of Agriculture, from American state agricultural colleges and other agencies, from private enterprises like the International Harvester Company of the Philippines, which underwrites field-crop projects.

Add still another boost, the gift of the Lions Clubs of California and Nevada, which, incidentally, will pay back its cost several times in good will. These ordinary American farming folk got together a million-dollar cargo of farm machinery, clothing, books, household utensils and sent them as an anti-Communist weapon to the Philippines. Everywhere in this rich country of the United States, private organizations could find struggling people somewhere else in the world who need something we could spare. By sending it, we would not only learn more about the world around us and gain much satisfaction, we would show how, at a small cost, private citizens can fight communism without armaments and without casualties.

In our efforts to help the governments of these new countries do their jobs, we had better realize that progress will be very slow. Even the most modern and efficient of these new nations, like the Philippines, do not possess the wherewithal to do what we have done in the United States; they have not available one tenth of the needed trained personnel, land lawyers, scientists, agricultural specialists, or even clerks. Therefore, everything depends on the decisions of the central government and its executives. There is barely enough skill left over to carry out their instructions at the local level. If Magsaysays do not lead, the countries go nowhere, except toward communism.

But another of the paradoxical and bewildering facts of Asia is reflected in the Philippines. If honest government and efficient methods can increase the food yields of the country and raise its health levels, this automatically creates the most powerful and deadly of all the weapons communism can use against freedom: overpopulation. Before Western public health technicians came to Asia, it was a land of high death rates where populations remained in balance with food supplies. Now Western science keeps more people alive to share no more food. In the Catholic Philippines, with no birth control, the birth rate has quadrupled since 1935, adding one million more Filipinos each year.

Pushed by the implacable, impersonal pressure of more and more people, the Philippine Republic is confronted with two massive problems. First, it must find enough land and feed all these mouths. And second, it must find enough jobs and enough goods to provide for all these people. As land reform is step one in the blueprint of every new republic of Asia, so sufficient industrial production is step two. To the extent that the Philippines can build factories of their own, they will not have to buy factory products abroad. Then they need not sell so much raw material abroad to get foreign exchange. And then they can keep more food at home and their factories will be providing more goods and more jobs.

In undertaking step one, land reform, the Philippines are lucky because they have so much green land; in undertaking step two, industrial production, they are fortunate again. In all Asia, only the Japanese have more industrial know-how. This is because, while the United States ruled the islands, we showed the Filipinos how capitalism could contribute to their own development and we encouraged American industry to set up plants in the Philippines. No other colonial power did this. The Dutch in Java and Sumatra, the French in Cochin China and Tonkin, the British in Burma and Malaya, all suppressed industrial development in their territories and prevented their subject peoples from learning how to operate an industrial system.

As a result of our tutelage, the Filipinos today are eager to attract foreign capital; in fact, they do more to encourage and protect it than does any other country, or combination of countries, in Asia. They have two tests for the value of any new industry: does it save dollars by producing something for which they must now spend dollars, and does it produce more dollars by creating products they can sell abroad.

So much could be done by the right kind of understanding and financial support. Take the most famous producer of beer in Asia, the San Miguel Brewery of Manila, which is owned and operated by Filipinos and the Spanish-born American citizen who helped President Quezon escape from the islands during the war, Colonel Andres Soriano. It cost San Miguel too much foreign exchange to import beer bottles from the United States, but there were no glass factories in the Philippines and no known deposit of sand suitable for glass-making. So San Miguel surveyed the islands until it found the right kind of sand on Palawan.

Boats were built to haul the sand to Manila, and new trade was developed so that the boats would not go back empty. Soon a glass factory was producing bottles for other concerns as well as San Miguel. Next, the brewery found it was paying too much money for cardboard beer containers, so it surveyed for suitable wood, found it, started a carton plant, and went on to a larger factory to turn more wood into pulp for newspapers and wrapping paper; each step making jobs and saving dollars.

To the Philippines, a factory is as much a part of freedom as any clause in a constitution. When a new factory opens, there are front-page articles in the Manila papers, the factory gives a reception, and all the guests come in evening dress to watch the machines begin to turn. Going through any such factory, you see trained Filipinos operating the most modern American equipment. A man of one civilization can operate a machine as well as a man of any other if he really wants to, and if he has been able to get the proper training. The Philippine Air Lines' repair shops, manned by Filipino mechanics trained by Americans, in six years have established such a record of efficiency that they now overhaul American Air Force planes.

To strengthen the economy of the Philippines, President Magsaysay has started a five-year plan. Over half of its cost will come from private sources, and one of its objectives is to create jobs for the 20 per cent of the labor force who have been unemployed. This would provide a sounder economy which in turn would attract more foreign capital. But about three quarters of the foreign trade of the Philippines is with the United States and they have nowhere else they can sell their raw materials except possibly to Japan, which is already embarked on a postwar program of economic imperialism and hopes to increase its trade with the Philippines until it can turn the islands into an economic and international pawn. This would have highly dangerous consequences for the United States.

Philippine trade with us is regulated by a special treaty, the Bell Trade Act, which, granting them favored status for the first years of their independence, now provides for a gradual withdrawal of that aid. That treaty was drawn up in the days before the cold war and the Korean war; if we now insist on holding to that treaty and not granting the islands a few years' extension of the favorable-imports clause so they can build up a strong anti-Communist economy, we may gain a few dollars, but we will lose much strength in that part of Asia.

Magsaysay is doing his best to create conditions where American capital will want to enter and help develop the country. If we wish a strong and self-sufficient Philippines, it is up to American capital to do its part through trade pacts and other economic devices. In our modern economic self-sufficiency, Americans often forget that our capitalism was once a young and weak plant that needed huge European investments to get it under way. Today younger nations hope that we will remember our early days and realize that capitalism cannot degenerate into a stationary force and survive. The Philippines cannot achieve economic stability unless American capital flows in, so American businessmen have a free choice: they can help build an oasis of free enterprise here off the shores of the Socialist-Communist mainland of Asia, or they can take the consequences of their own stupidity.

There is no better way to measure the economic freedom or the political freedom of a nation than to see how much freedom of speech its press exercises. The freest press of Asia is in the Philippines, where there are over five hundred publications and no government censorship. The variety of the seventeen Manila daily newspapers, in Tagalog, Spanish, Chinese, and English, underlines why these islands are so hard to portray in sweeping terms. Like the American culture upon which it patterns itself, the culture of the Philippines does not come into focus at a few points as does that of Japan or Thailand or Indonesia. Here, all kinds of individuals are doing different and often overlapping and contradictory things. Perhaps one of the best signs of a functioning democracy is that it is not sharply focused on one or two lines of activity laid down by a dictator or oligarchy.

The Philippine free press chases every sort of story and pleases any kind of reader who will buy papers. It models itself on the great American reform newspapers, copying their flamboyant methods to dig up government corruption or graft. One of the favorite leads for a crusading editorial is "Something Must Be Done Right Away." But the press lambastes Americans just as sharply as its own people. When some American GIs raced army trucks through the center of Manila, a leading editorial commented: "The terrified people must have thought war had been declared, until they realized the American drivers, who had just given such a superb exhibition of fast driving through heavy traffic and who had shown how easily Philippine laws could be broken, were hurrying back to camp to perfect plans for the defense of democracy in this country."

Like the press, the Philippine Constitution patterns itself on the American model, providing for three branches of the government and a president to be elected every four years. Philippine democracy has had another lucky break because it chose an American type of constitution, the only such document in Asia. The other new republics adopted European constitutions with all-powerful parliaments able to overthrow prime ministers at will. Unfortunately in new republics where political patterns and party policies have not jelled, the parliamentary system too often leads to parliamentary bickering, dickering, and inaction as helpless prime ministers struggle to preserve their parliamentary majorities. None of the other constitution writers of Asia seems to have realized how much more efficiently new republics can be run by duly elected presidents.

A side effect of an American type of constitution is the drama it brings into national elections. Instead of voting for members of parliament, the citizens go to the polls to choose their leaders and therefore have a much more personal identification with the election. The Filipinos have learned to approach their own elections very much as Americans do. "Popular government is just like a swimming pool. You have to change the water every so often, otherwise it would no longer be a pleasure to take a swim in it."

On November 10, 1953, the Filipinos changed every drop of water in the swimming pool of their government and staged the most enlightened election Asia has ever witnessed. All of the Philippines' neighbors want freedom too. But Malaya and Indo-China are still colonial possessions. Thailand and Formosa, although presenting façades of democracy, are dictatorships. Burma and Korea have been limited by wars. The governments of Pakistan and Indonesia chose to get along without any national election for the first six or seven years of their respective republics. While India, although deserving the world's applause for its first election in which over ninety million Indians voted, still did not have an election in the true American sense because a high percentage of the voters were illiterate and there was no other national candidate of comparable standing to Nehru, the liberator.

The Filipinos have had an election every two years since independence, each time learning more about how to run an honest one. In 1953 the five million men and women electors, all literate, could read the newspapers during the campaign and were thus able to make up their own minds between two major political figures and two major political parties, Elpidio Quirino and the Liberal Party or Ramon Magsaysay and the Nacionalista Party. Every issue, every aspect of the rival records was publicly debated.

In the 1949 and 1951 elections there had been considerable fraud and terrorism at the polls and so, while observers from all over Asia looked on, the Filipinos organized themselves to prevent a repetition in 1953. All the leading civic groups, from the Philippine League of Women Voters and the Rotarians, to the Lions, YWCA, and the Knights of Columbus, joined together into NAMFREL, the National Movement for Free Elections. Backed by the press and radio, they poured out pamphlets, broadcasts, cartoon books, billboards, booklets of advice and admonition:

"PEOPLE DESERVE WHATEVER GOVERNMENT THEY HAVE"

"WHO WANTS IT, LETS IT; WHO LETS IT, GETS IT"

"BEWARE BAD COMPANY AT THE POLLS"

"STAY AND WATCH THAT OTHERS VOTE PROPERLY"

"WATCH FOR VOTERS WHO TRY TO VOTE MORE THAN ONCE"

"DO NOT ALLOW YOURSELF TO BE FRIGHTENED AWAY FROM THE POLLS"

Catholic nuns and priests escorted timid souls to the polls. American newspaper reporters were rushed to towns where violence was expected; when they arrived, the goons disappeared. Radio station DZBB in Manila stayed on the air forty-eight hours so that when anyone telephoned in from anywhere in the islands it could broadcast a report of violence or corruption at the polls; the army jeeps were tuned to the station and rushed straight to the polling place to investigate.

When November 10 was over, Asia had seen its first truly modern election and the Philippines had chosen a new leader. By a majority vote of 85 per cent, Quirino and the Liberals were swept out of power and Ramon Magsaysay, the most vital young leader in Asia, became the third President of the Republic of the Philippines.

The son of a poor farmer and blacksmith, he had an ordinary high school education, studied a little law, and then worked as a mechanic. In 1941 he took to the mountains to fight the Japanese and emerged at liberation as one of the best guerrilla officers of the war. He then served two terms in the Congress before he burst on the political scene as Secretary of Defense.

Magsaysay makes no pretenses of being a thinker or intellectual; he is the man of action, big, solidly built, husky, and supercharged with energy, always doing something, or just talking to people. He would be a perfect star for television because his face and body are always animated. When he talks with you, he has a characteristic pose: he thrusts his right arm straight out in front of him in a dramatic reaching gesture to emphasize a point while he steps forward on his left foot and then rocks back and forth as he gestures.

He hates air-conditioned rooms and stays out of them no matter how humid it is. He always has a comb in the pocket of his shirt, but he never bothers to use it. When he can, he dresses casually in loud sport shirts. He does not drink or smoke, loves people but hates parties as a waste of time and money, never celebrates his own birthday: "It isn't worth the time." He tackles every problem head on. When an army truck in which he was riding bogged down in the middle of a creek, Magsaysay jumped out and started pushing it. He was not thinking of a headline: there were no press men along. It was his natural way to attack an obstacle. Another time when his jeep had engine trouble, Magsaysay began tinkering with it. He discovered that although it was supposed to be a brand-new jeep it had a number of old parts in it, so he started an investigation and found that thousands of dollars were being made by selling new parts from government jeeps and putting in secondhand parts.

He forbids members of his family to ride in government cars, and when he was Secretary of Defense he would not permit soldiers to do any chores around his house at Camp Murphy. Before the 1953 political campaign, when he had to have his appendix out, he flabbergasted the Filipinos, who were used to having their leaders line their pockets; Magsaysay had to borrow money from his brother for the operation. While he was recuperating from this operation, he promised me a broadcast from Corregidor. Although just out of the hospital and still running a fever, he tried to make the twenty-mile trip with me by launch across the choppy bay from Manila to Corregidor. Having promised, he refused to turn back when the sea began bouncing him around and was quite annoyed when we did go back.

Perhaps his most outstanding trait is a combination of idealistic zeal and hard-boiled realism. His favorite motto is, "Get the right people and you have no headaches"; then he added to me with a grin, "But check up on them once in a while." When he was a congressman, a group of men brought him their month's salaries as a gift. He said, "No, thanks, give it to your families. But be sure you do, because I'm going to write your wives about it to make sure you don't spend it in Manila night clubs and then pretend you gave it to me."

When he was reforming the Army, he established a special complaint post where anybody could send in complaints. He arranged a special price of twenty centavos to send a message to his complaint post from anywhere on the islands and he assigned five special officers to check up on the messages, publicly warning the Army that if any complainant was mishandled or beaten, everybody concerned would be fired, but if the men who had caused the complaints admitted their mistakes and corrected them, he would forget the matter.

During the height of the Huk insurrection, when an army post heard there were Huks in the neighborhood, often the officers ordered troops out to kill the Huks and then went back to their mah-jongg game. The troops, in turn, went off for a day's outing of swimming and picnicking. At dusk they fired off some ammunition, butchered a pig, sprinkled its blood on some old rags, and then they reported back to their officers that they had killed a lot of Huks, showing the bloody rags as proof.

Magsaysay changed this. He called his officers together and told them that each one who could kill ten Huks in a year would be promoted. They were very pleased until Magsaysay went on, "But it won't be simple any more. I've bought thirty-eight hundred cameras. Take them with you when you go Huk hunting. Never mind telling me you've killed ten Huks. Send me photographs of the ten men. And don't try to use the same body twice. I'm keeping a file of the pictures."

Magsaysay's policy toward communism is another example of his combination of zeal and shrewdness. He believes that communism is at least 75 per cent the result of the "cesspools and quagmires in our countries, like disease, starvation, and land-tenancy problems." But the other 25 per cent are hard-core Communists directed from abroad. So, publicly and privately, he offers Filipino Communists a choice of surrender and rehabilitation, or attack by the Army, and he has created the best anti-Communist slogan the free world has yet produced: "We offer communism all-out force or all-out friendship."

The Philippines today carry out this same realism in a foreign policy which in most important aspects parallels that of the United States. Although they are close to the threat of Red China, the mainland being only seven hundred miles from Manila, they permit us to maintain some of our main Pacific bases on their soil and they are thus irrevocably tied to our international fortunes. They speak out against Russian and Chinese aggression. They were one of the few Asian nations who sent troops into Korea to back up the United Nations. They refuse to recognize Red China until "it proves it is the legitimate ruler of China." Formosa, only two hundred and fifty miles above northern Luzon, is of prime importance. If the Communists ever controlled that island, it would be an easy jump over to Philippine soil; therefore, Manila has the warmest relations with the Chinese Nationalist Government on Formosa.

They part company with the United States on Japan. Harboring a fear of Japan very similar to that of France for Germany, they oppose Japan's re-emergence as a first-class power, and they did not admire American foreign policy during the first years of the Indo-Chinese civil war. Vietnam, only a thousand miles to the west, would be the gravest threat to them if it were Communist. They have always opposed the Vietminh Communists there and were willing to permit the United States to operate an air lift between Indo-China and its Philippine bases as soon as it was necessary. In the years before the partition of Indo-China they were unsympathetic to the French government of Vietnam. Like every other ex-colonial people of Asia, they looked upon the Indo-Chinese war as a struggle for independence against the French and they considered the Vietnamese Chief of State, Bao Dai, as a French puppet with "no international personality."

The Philippines try to get the United States to realize that her greatest self-protection and the fastest elimination of the threat of Communist aggression in Asia will be achieved by the same action: the development of trained and armed, free, Asian man power. "The Western democracies have a vast inferiority in man power. One man, backed up by American air and naval power, must now plan to fight one hundred Communists." Filipinos think this is a perilous and stupid way to win a war when there are millions of men in Asia who are not Communists. "Convince these men that freedom for their countries coincides with the defeat of communism and you have power on your side."

Their chief criticism of our role in foreign affairs is that we have not firmly picked up the nettle of world leadership. "You just allowed it to get thrust in your lap." They want us to realize that we are the centrifugal force and power center of the great whirling mass of the free world. As we waver or shift slightly in our orbit, our friends and dependents swerve and veer; if we go round in hysterical circles, the force of that hysteria can throw them right out of our orbit and away from our friendship.

At the present time, in our attempt to try to shore up areas of strength off the continent of mainland China, the United States is arming Korea, Formosa, and Japan. Each is an ally, but none could be depended upon to act to our benefit if it should not be to theirs. Outside the Philippines, our only dependable base is Okinawa, powerful, useful, but on an island only seventy miles long. But the Philippines, about midway between Korea and Southeast Asia, are an invaluable military ally for the United States. Their widespread area allows us to have dozens of harbors, hundreds of airfields, defensible in depth. If we should have to abandon our Philippine bases, we would be forced to retire down to Australia and back to Alaska and Hawaii.

Quite aside from our spiritual or economic investments in the islands, we have a huge military stake and military investment. Our new naval base at Cubi Point on Luzon is costing $60,000,000 as we scoop out jungle swamps and shove mountaintops into the sea to carve out some of the Far East's longest runways, ammunition dumps and storehouses. Cubi Point is one tenth as large a project as the Panama Canal. From Cubi Point and our naval base at Subic Bay and our air bases at Clark Field we are within reach of any trouble spot or danger point in Asia: Manchuria, Korea, Japan, Formosa, the whole length of the China coast, Borneo, Malaya, Indonesia, Thailand, Indo-China, and Burma; all are within a fifteen-hundred-mile radius. It is these bases which could enable us quickly to set up an air lift to any crucial area in Southeast Asia. And the American naval and air bases in the Philippines are today the only barrier to communism's military control of the South China Sea, whose waters wash South Vietnam, Thailand, Malaya, Indonesia, North Borneo, the Philippines, and Formosa. Across from the Philippines, on Hainan Island and at Haiphong in North Vietnam, the Chinese and the Russians are already busy building powerful new air and submarine bases.

The Voice of America has built one of the world's most powerful radio transmitters in the Philippines, twenty times as powerful as the largest United States domestic broadcasting station. The United States Government has the largest staff outside the United States here, including the military personnel, between twenty and thirty thousand people. In Manila there is a U. S. Reproduction Service Plant, which services all of Southeast Asia with printed materials, publishing over sixty million items each month.

But because the Filipinos have been under Western rule longest of any Asian people, because they can speak English and understand our ideas, because they are willing to be our allies, it does not follow that Americans dare check this country off as a sure thing and go on to more urgent problems. Nor can we treat them as equals when we choose and as children when we do not.

In the first place, Americans need to adjust to the fact that these are Asians, living in an enervating climate. They want to work and produce, but it is folly to assume they will do so at our tempo. In spite of what they can accomplish, it would be grossly inaccurate to depict the Filipinos as a vigorous, hard-driving people like the Japanese and the Germans, the Chinese and the Americans. One of their prime characteristics is indolence and lack of initiative. The Americans in the Philippines recognize this, the Spaniards talk about it, the Filipinos agree with it. They have an expression like the Mexican "*mañana*": "*bahala na* [let God take care of it]," and they often show a characteristic which, judged by American measures, is close to laziness and shiftlessness. They are charming, they smile, they laugh, they can work hard, but they do a great deal more loafing than we do. The different tempo of the tropics, laziness, a wiser way of life, or the colonial heritage from four hundred years under Spanish bosses who discouraged their initiative; whatever the reason, here where the weather is warm and the land fertile, the Filipinos, along with their fellow Southeast Asians, think it is foolish to work too hard or too long.

It does Americans no good to criticize them for this or try to push them where they will not go, as some of our diplomatic representatives or businessmen try to do. A country's friends take as cautious handling as its enemies. Even in the Philippines our friends need consideration. The Congress is controlled by the Nacionalista Party, but a bloc of anti-American ex-collaborators with the Japanese, led by Claro Recto, are trying to swing the country away from the United States.

Stupid Americans have given them valuable ammunition. In the case of one important consular officer who was insulting the Filipinos who applied for visas, Washington took no action for two years. Since most of the Filipinos who can afford to apply for visas to the United States are important, he did us a great disservice. And the wife of one of the diplomatic officials in our mission at a formal diplomatic dinner delivered herself of a remark the islands can now quote: "The Filipinos should return to the trees."

It would take very few such incidents to lose legislative support for Magsaysay's policy of American co-operation, and, if we should allow such stupidities to occur frequently enough, we could lose his friendship. President Magsaysay is the first really important pro-American leader Asia has produced. Of our other allies, Rhee and Chiang are old men, and the prime ministers of Japan and Pakistan are influential only at home. Until the last Philippine election there had been only two men of international importance in Asia: the leader of the Chinese Communists, Mao Tse-tung, and the leader of the Asia neutrals, Jawaharlal Nehru. Now for the first time there is a third leader, and a friend of the United States, Ramon Magsaysay.

He has the opportunity to accomplish wonders in the countries around him. It is one thing for an American to point out to a suspicious ex-colonial brown Asian that he is doing something the wrong way. It is quite another thing when a brown-skinned ex-colonial Asian shows how a different way pays off better. Before he became president, Magsaysay went to Cambodia to confer about better methods to rid that country of its Communist guerrillas. He questioned the King of Cambodia and his generals and found out that when their troops went into the jungle no high officer checked on whether or not they actually fought the Communists. No white man could have told them they could not trust their own troops, but Magsaysay, the Asian, could. Once the point was accepted, the Cambodian Minister of Defense went into the jungles to check on his men and the incidence of Communist guerrillas went down.

There are many ways in which Filipinos could serve as a bridge between their suspicious neighbors and the strange new twentieth-century civilization of the West. Asians do not deny that our way works for us, but they are not convinced that our methods would pay off in their very different situations. There is no reason why a Voice of Free Asia could not be set up, by the Filipinos and their allies, to do most of the information broadcasting to Asia that American transmitters now undertake. It would be immensely more impressive if the suspicious or Communist people of Asia heard Asians developing anti-Communist arguments on transmitters not managed by whites.

There is a dramatic phrase, unfortunate in its wording but pregnant in its possibilities, that is used over and over to describe the Philippines: "the showcase of democracy." It sounds condescending, like a large American patting a small Filipino on the head and saying, "Be a nice little showcase of democracy." And it is a misnomer. The Philippines are not a showcase, nor a come-on sales window for our ways, nor a pretty exhibit at an international fair. They are a functioning democracy, an example of what a people can do for itself with a democracy that is its own indigenous creation.

We and they should forget this silly "showcase of democracy" phrase. The Philippine experiment should be presented to the rest of Asia for what it is, an independent culture that has taken what it chose to from the American democracy and then gone on to create its own individual democracy. Most Asians do not realize this.

The agencies of the American Government pay to bring young Asians to the United States to learn about the American way. It is a fine-sounding idea, but consider the shock to a gentle, easygoing yellow-skinned Buddhist Cambodian when he is suddenly dropped down in the twentieth-century pressure, noise, dirt, and racial discrimination of an American skyscraper city. It would be wiser and less self-centered to help these future Asian leaders learn more gently some of the things they want to know by sending them to the Philippines. The Malays and the Indonesians are blood relations of the Filipinos. And the other South Asians, the Cambodians, the Burmese, the Thais, the Vietnamese, and even the Indians and the Pakistani, would at least be in a familiar climate and among Asians.

True, three months in westernized Manila would still be a major shock to most of them, but it is a halfway station where they could become acclimated and where they could see for themselves how American methods can be adapted by Asians. They would see all sorts of American things, from democratic newspapers to small modern assembly plants or shoe factories. They would learn to like the Filipino better, which would bring them closer to understanding Westerners. And, most important, they would be able to study Asian democracy in action.

We would be helping the Filipinos learn to shoulder more responsibilities and take a more active role in inter-Asian affairs. It would cost the United States less money than its present exchange programs because it would be far cheaper to send Asians to the Philippines. The dollars we would spend on such activities would also furnish the Filipinos valuable foreign exchange to help them strengthen their economy.

In addition to all the selfish reasons why we should co-operate with the Filipinos, there is another reason. We Americans have made a lasting moral investment here. No matter with whom you talk in the islands, "I like and trust Americans and I want to be more like them" is a common theme.

In World War II, when Corregidor fell and a few American army officers beat their way out of Bataan up into the Zambales Mountains, they were afraid of what would happen when they encountered Filipinos after having failed so thoroughly to defend the country. And they knew that to harbor an American guerrilla would mean death to an entire Philippine village. Yet when they approached the first barrio, the people came out to meet them and carried them to shelter and food, and the chiefs of all the nearby barrios came in to a meeting and asked, "How do we help now?"

Philippine volunteers went down from the mountains to work for the Japanese in radio depots to help remove short-wave tuners from all Philippine sets so that broadcasts from America could not be heard. After reconditioning the sets, the Filipinos smuggled stolen parts through the Japanese lines to American guerrilla camps to build the short-wave sending sets that guided the MacArthur campaign of liberation.

By the time American forces struck again at Manila Bay, Filipinos were manning outposts all around it. American aviators were advised of the safe areas in which to crash-land, and the Filipinos hid them and smuggled them back to contact points where they could board American submarines. You hear about these stories only from American guerrilla leaders. The Filipinos take their heroism for granted, and if you ask them why they did this for Americans, they answer, "Why not?"

In the Korean War, the Filipinos again backed up their friendship with acts. Up at their training camp at Makati, on a warm, sunny, tropical plateau northeast of Manila, men who had never known a frost trained for the sub-zero cold and grim war of Korea. Yet with typical Filipino happy-go-lucky resiliency they mocked our huge

Pentagon with a tiny six-sided pavilion of bamboo posts and thatch roof they solemnly labeled "The Hexagon." The commander in chief of the Army, General Vargas, told me that every man there was a volunteer and that he had ten times as many as he could use: "Our boys believe that where an American soldier stands with a gun and bayonet, a Filipino must stand side by side with him for the safety and defense of democracy."

We have made of the Philippine democracy an imperishable monument to American altruism, an island of conviction in the vast sea of Asian doubt and disbelief. The Philippines are our best friend in Asia. For ourselves, for them, and for Asia, it now remains for us to live up to their firm conviction that "America is ready to go venturing for the best."

INSECURITY INC.:

Japan

The kingdom of Japan, like the Republic of the Philippines, is a group of islands, spread out in the Pacific about six hundred miles off the coast of mainland Asia. Also like the Philippines, Japan is learning Western ways and its people have yellow skins. These three facts begin and end the similarities between the two nations. As is true of the other countries that make up the theoretical entity called Asia, their backgrounds, their civilizations, their religions, their costumes, their politics, their economics, and above all their psychologies, are not only different, they are irreconcilably disparate.

Where the Philippines are friendly, easygoing, and not absorbed in business profits, the Japanese are hard-going and determined, tireless traders. There are over eight hundred ports in the Japanese islands, and no spot in the land of this trading people is more than one hundred miles from the sea. In contrast to the warm climate and rich land of Southeast Asia, Japan endures the harsh extremes of the northern temperate zone in a country which is principally thin soil and the sides of mountains.

But there is another difference of far more importance to the United States. While it is a pleasure to have the Filipinos as friends, it is a necessity to have the Japanese as allies. It was by no fluke that their sturdy, well-disciplined Army was able to conquer all of Asia from Korea and North China down to the islands of Indonesia and on across Southeast Asia to the approaches to India. Of the countries of Asia, Japan alone had the industrial capacity to support and supply an army in the field. Should any other Asian nation become involved in a war, whether it be Korea or Vietnam, China or India, the armaments and supplies for that war must come either from the

United States and the West or from Russia and her satellites. It is this unique military-industrial base that makes Japan such a valuable Asian ally, either to the democracies or the Communists, and a partial counterbalance to the man power of Red China. With Japan on our side, the most important aim of American foreign policy must be to detach China from Russia. Equally, with China on their side, the Communists' principal Asian objective is to detach Japan from the United States.

In the immediate future we can keep the power of Japan out of the Communist bloc because China and Russia are her historic enemies and the Japanese Communists have had little success in their own country since the war. But there are more ominous possibilities ahead. The chaos in some of the other countries of Asia is more obvious, but the economy of Japan is appallingly unsound. There are about eighty-six million people penned in on a group of poor, resourceless islands the size of Montana. As a result of the defeat in 1945, they have lost all of their colonies, many of their factories, most of their raw materials and markets. In the meantime, an oriental birth rate and an occidental death rate every day add more thousands of hungry mouths in this ancient kingdom so firmly imprisoned on its physical islands, so fantastically proud of its peculiar feudalism, and so frantically self-trapped in a psychological prison of do's and don'ts, principally don'ts.

The Cherry Blossom Festival is the first picture that comes to an American's mind when he thinks of Japan: the deep blue skies and the dark greens of the fir trees, the perfumed white and pink of the cherry blossoms falling gently around a joyous and laughing people as they celebrate their release from the jail of another Japanese winter to the beauties of nature which they, more than any other Asians, love and merge themselves with. But far more true to the unhappy lot of the Japanese is the picture of their life along the highway between their two great modern cities of Tokyo and Yokohama at dusk on a midwinter afternoon.

It is a scene of bustling activity; Yokohama has been rebuilt from the bombed ruins of 1945 to a great port that handles ten million tons of shipping a year. The equally wrecked capital, Tokyo, is also full of postwar buildings. But electricity is still too expensive to light many of the streets, so the main boulevards are a dotted design of lanterns marking wartime holes and craters. Drivers swerve around them, paying no attention to other cars or pedestrians doing the same, and throw their headlights in everybody else's eyes, sending wide fans of mustard-yellow light through the thick smog veil over the cold dampness of the streets. Every sort of car, in every condition but new, crowding and jamming and honking: rattling jeeps, bicycles, motorcycles, little three-wheeled motorcars. And pedestrians in clogs, shoes, sandals, Western clothes, kimonos, tags of Japanese or GI uniforms and rags wound around hands or throat or feet to keep in a little warmth.

Everybody has pinched faces, running eyes, red noses, for Tokyo in winter is smoggier than Los Angeles, dirtier than Akron, colder than Detroit. The people hurrying along seem tenser and tighter than in the United States. They move through the streets in a short, shuffling half run, the slap of their wooden clogs sounding a curious high lament, somewhat like the clopping of horses' hoofs on cobblestones but a sharper clack that the sounding board of the damp air spreads out to the off-pitch sounds of a wooden xylophone.

The pedestrians scurry in and out between the cars. None of the easygoing traffic jams of Manila or the lighthearted recklessness of Paris drivers who give you a sporting chance and swerve at the last minute if you cannot make the curb. This is grim, callous, I'm-on-my-way-get-out-of-my-way driving, and the cars seem to make no attempt not to hit the pedestrians.

Nobody smiles, nobody wants to smile, nobody has time to smile in these desperately poor islands of postwar Japan, still recovering from the American bombing which laid waste over a third of their sixty largest cities. Watching these people work so hard to rebuild their country, seeing how little they have today and, compared to the industrial might of the United States, how little they ever had, it is impossible not to pity them. Because their stupid police state had matched them only with third-rate powers before 1941, they believed themselves supermen when they attacked the United States at Pearl Harbor. Even if they had won at Guadalcanal or Midway, defeat was always ahead of them. As they struggle back to their feet, it is still impossible for Americans to fathom whether they blame their own leaders and their own gods or the United States for the worst defeat in their history.

There are no electric signs or neons on the stores along the Yokohama highway. A few gas-station signs in English, a few painted signs in the Chinese characters, which Japanese use for their written language as we use the Latin alphabet in English. The stores use cloth banners with characters painted on them to advertise the goods for sale. Usually five or six long black rectangles are hung in a row like flags fluttering across the front of the store. The writing is in red or white, beautifully spaced on the black, and there is usually some very simple line drawing which runs across the whole set of flags, tying them together into a single artistic design.

The small and rickety houses along the way are built of unpainted wood that ages into muted natural colors harmonizing restfully with the grayish rocks and the black-greens of the fir trees on the hills. The outer walls of the houses are covered with bark strips or small lengths of contrasting woods laid in simple vertical and horizontal patterns which bring out the beauty and grains of the wood. Each house seems to have put roots down into the Japanese earth.

Store banners or building materials—all around you are examples of this people's superb taste in the limited and constantly expressed love of nature. So beautiful and so earth-bound. None of the sloppy exuberance of the Filipinos, whose favorite colors are bright rice-paddy greens and warm bamboo creams. The Japanese prefer elephant grays or earth greens or the deep grayed purple which is their favorite color for dignity and reserve and strength.

Tokyo, the third largest city in the world, is far more Western than even Manila, and the only truly westernized city of all Asia. Much of it would not be out of place in northern United States. The modern office buildings and hotels are skyscrapers in Japan but rarely over five stories high anywhere else in Asia. There are streetcars, busses, telephones, railroads, factories, industrial din, and all the other paraphernalia of the industrial West. Tokyo has Western newspapers, a great deal of radio, and little television.

This grim city of seven million people, deliberate imitation of the West, powerhouse and all-powerful ruling center of Japan, is a good symbol for one side of this people's life and character. To see the other side you must go to one of the old cities, a holy city like Kyoto or Kamakura, or even better a resort city like Atami. A combination of Atlantic City and Niagara Falls, Atami is the famous honeymoon town of Japan whose popularity is built on its hot springs. In this country, so cold so much of the year and able to afford little wood for heat or warm water, hot springs are supreme luxuries. The hotels of Atami offer small suites and meals at cut-rate honeymoon prices, which include rosy-pink tiled bathrooms with hot-springs water. And they add a special bridal touch; at one end of the shallow bathtubs are two headrest indentations, and the tubs are just wide enough so that the bride and groom can take the waters side by side in connubial companionship.

Everything in this charming, happy, childlike town, with its cheerful bunting-hung lanes winding up and down the hills, carries out the mood of honeymoon happiness. As the train pulls into the Atami station you hear a sound unduplicated anywhere in the world; the barkers for the various hotels greet the happy couples with a "Hello, honeymooners," in Japanese a wonderful long-drawn-out ululating sound. It is one of three unique sounds in Japan. The other two are the slap of the hurrying clogs and the tap-tap night sound of the fire watchers. These watchers patrol every city in this country of dry, wood dwellings, carrying two blocks of wood which they tap together in a slow-slow, fast-fast rhythm; when you hear this any-o'clock-and-all's-well sound come and go past your house, you know you are safe from fire.

Whether in Atami or Tokyo, relaxing is one of the serious pursuits of the Japanese. No other civilization in Asia spends time and money and energy on relaxing, for no other Asian people drive themselves hard enough or get so tightened up they need to pay for relaxation. But, like the Americans, the Japanese have made a large business out of entertainment. On Christmas Eve, over a million and a half people go to Tokyo night clubs. The Japanese get a tremendous kick out of liquor without needing to drink much of it. A couple of scotch highballs, the most socially acceptable drink because it is expensive and because important Americans drink it, and they are released. In the late evening a Tokyo main street would be oddly empty without pairs of drunks reeling happily along, grinning at everybody as they hold each other up.

Most capital cities of Asia have no night clubs unless they have been opened up because American army forces are near by; Tokyo has hundreds of bars and dance halls patronized by the Japanese. In appearance they are much like New York night clubs, except that there are bright neon lights everywhere and each club has its tokonoma, the ever-present niche decorated with a scroll and a small vase of flowers.

In the night clubs most of the women are dressed in smart Western gowns, but none of them are wives. Entertainment in the Japanese system is for husbands only. The wives are still caught in the trap of the old feudal arrangement of life. For instance, instead of rugs the

Japanese use padded *tatami* mats of bamboo, and many of them think that a wife should be like a tatami mat, "soft and clean and always useful." Recently there was a Women's Week in Japan and one husband was honored for showing himself to be a Number One husband because "he picked up his own quilt every morning and folded it neatly and put it away." At home, wives may sometimes be the dictators of the family, but in public, if they get out in public, they are meek and obedient. They have been trained to please their husbands, a highly desirable trait from a male point of view, but "from a woman's point it is getting rather hard."

The women you see in the night clubs were liberated by the GIs during the American occupation. Having tasted the sweets of freedom, they can never go back to Japanese family respectability. Yet they are young and attractive, with intelligence and courage and drive. A little westernization is a dangerous thing; if their society cannot move forward and accept them, communism will find them invaluable recruits and spies.

A less influential class of postwar girls is found on the side streets of Tokyo, the streetwalkers. They are another creation of American GIs, but they bear no grudge. They make from seventy-five cents to a dollar and a quarter per customer, far better pay than they could earn in a factory, and they consider it easier work. The Japanese press is whipping up ill feeling against the Americans because of these girls, but nobody attacks the Japanese police who allow the traffic to continue, or the girls in it.

In the night clubs there is a great distinction between the girls who cater to Japanese and those who cater to foreigners. If a girl changes to foreigners, there is no resentment on the part of her former lovers; women are easy to find. But the girls have their own firm code. If a man goes with one girl, none of the others in that bar will have anything to do with him beyond being pleasantly courteous. If he tries to approach another girl, he will be called one of their worst names, "Butterfly."

Today the young Japanese, dancing to American jazz, have the happy, out-of-this-world absorption in the music that American youngsters have; and if they can afford it, they wear the same kind of clothes, drink the same soft drinks, and have picked up the same slang from American movies. As in Manila or Delhi or Rangoon, our movies are always enjoyed and understood.

But there is one side of Japanese night life where the two civilizations meet, and then go in opposite directions: the burlesque shows, which are packed seven nights a week with American GIs escorting Japanese girls, and with Japanese men with no girls. The usual strip-tease routines: feather girls, balloon girls, fan girls, but principally just girls. The Japanese insist that the strip tease was introduced by American GIs, but in fact it was introduced by a French troupe in 1932. The Japanese figured that if it was French it was culture and so they imitated it. They believe they are like the French, classical in their tastes. But they really like the romantic side of Western art; their music stores are full of white plaster busts of Beethoven and their favorite occidental composers are Wagner or Liszt, never Bach or Mozart.

When it comes to imitating the French strip tease, the Japanese are unique; whether it is classical or romantic depends on your point of view. Bras come off at the point where our teasers are taking out their hairpins. The Japanese G strings are barely "." strings. Yet kisses are never allowed; on the stage or in the movies, no performers' lips may come closer together than an inch apart.

In a culture of co-ed public baths and casual nakedness, the Japanese find the strip-tease part of the burlesque shows rather dull. They come for the entertainment. You can turn your back to the stage and from the reactions of the audience tell what is happening where. If the GIs are looking at stage left and the Japanese are watching stage right, you know there is a naked girl at the left and a comedian or a hoofer on the other side.

Where our strip-teasers dance to put their erotic zones in motion, the Japanese beauties dance for dancing's sake. Most Japanese are minus our kind of rhythm, but they dance to our kind of music, more or less, and the result is rather odd. A Japanese girlie line in French costumes do a Parisian cancan, out of time, to "Ta-ra-ra-bom-der-e," while an eight-piece orchestra plays weird harmonies that would drive Schoenberg into melody. And in the background, a group of stark-naked girls with towering headdresses of stars drape themselves over a staircase.

How the Japanese blend Minsky and Tin Pan Alley is trivial but illuminating. When Westerners try to understand foreign civilizations they tend to assume too much or too little; although we are all human beings with similar brains and hearts and nervous systems, a Japanese does not react in the same way an American does to nakedness or other stimuli. Yet to fall into the opposite trap and believe the

Asian is the inscrutable product of an incomprehensible culture is equally absurd.

Each Asian civilization converges on ours and separates from it at different points. The Filipinos are relatively easy to understand in spite of their Malay background; for four hundred years they have been ruled by Westerners and, having become Catholics, they share with us the most important of a civilization's frames of reference: God, religion, ethics, right and wrong. This can be said of no other people in the mélange of Asia. Each has its own and varying standards and none of them are ours. Therefore, to get a glimmering of how a people reacts and why it will or will not appreciate us or work with us, you have to search for psychological guideposts: politics, food, economics, sex, art, or religion.

Of the Asian countries, Japan is not the most foreign to the West. No people who have absorbed so much of the Western industrial revolution could be completely different, but this westernization does not mean the Japanese are like Americans. The American who is acknowledged by the Japanese to be our leading authority on their culture has lived in Japan for twenty years, loving and studying the people. But he came to Japan because "I traveled all over the world and I settled down here because nowhere else did I find a country as different from the United States."

The Japanese words for "yes" and "no" furnish an everyday example of our differences. "Yes" is *hai,* pronounced just like our "hi" of salutation. "No," is *ie,* pronounced something like "yeh." But, and this is the significant clue, when the Japanese say these words *hai* is loud, firm, proud; *ie* is short, swallowed, almost a shameful word. Compare this with the loud, strong words for "no" in Western countries.

Or study the way the Japanese react to rules and regulations. If a Filipino does not like a rule, he smiles sweetly and breaks it. Not so a Japanese; he insists both he and you follow each rule to the letter. As I drove from Yokohama to Tokyo, my guide insisted I stay exactly with the posted speed limit. If I went half a kilo faster, he objected, "Sign says forty kilometers. Must be forty kilometers." But in South Yokohama when I was almost out of gas, he was sure there was a gas station twelve kilometers along the highway. I trusted him and ran out of gas; it was thirty kilometers to the station. When I taxed him with this inaccuracy, he excused himself, "Only difference in figures.

Not important." This time there was no rule involved, so the figure did not matter.

The minute you dig into Japanese behavior you run into the central theme of paradox and contradiction in their own values as well as in yours. They are obsessed with the tiniest points of regulation or obligation, but this lives next door to one irresponsibility after another. In the Philippines I learned not to take the time set for an interview too seriously. I might be late or my guest might be late and an hour is not important one way or the other. But when a Japanese says didactically, "I can spare you twenty-five minutes at exactly one o'clock," he may not appear until two o'clock and then he shows no concern and makes no apologies. But just reverse the setup and be late yourself. Here, as almost anywhere else in Asia, you are considered rude and insulting, deliberately underlining your white arrogance.

If ever there was a determined people, it is the Japanese. They are determined when they attack a Pacific atoll, or when they charge on and off a train, or when they pick themselves up from an earthquake or a war. But again a paradox. Courageous, determined, and tireless, the Japanese worker will do a task over and over and over again, but that does not mean he is efficient. One famous Japanese industrialist said: "Deliver us from teaching workers to be efficient; if we did, everything we need could be done by 10 per cent of our labor force and we'd have ten times as much unemployment."

At the Foreign Office I asked one man to make an appointment for me with a statesman; he rushed off willingly. When he could not find the phone number of the cabinet minister, he brought me back a biography, in Japanese, of the man I wanted to talk to. When I found the phone number and told him to ask in Japanese if I could have an appointment, he hung up and said, "He says maybe you can." So we started over for the third time.

They do not look a situation over first. They dive in anywhere or do exactly what they are told. How could they have ever thought they could conquer the United States with these methods; and yet, in the long run, can anything stop a people who will try so doggedly over and over again?

Maybe "negative" is a good first word for them. But not "negative" in the sense of weakness but as a word of force, fully as powerful as the "positive" of the American. They are negative in the quiet colors they prefer. They are negative in their relations with each other. On trains there is no sharing of anything with the people near by, they eat by themselves out of little cardboard-box trays and they talk to no one else, of their own race or foreigners. Like the English, they pretend the other passengers are not there.

This does not mean the Japanese are cold or unfriendly. Their civilization is more repressive than almost any other in the world. A psychiatrist immediately sees here the reason for the wild paradoxes in their character and the constant contradictions in their actions. They are trained from childhood to hide their feelings. They are always eying you, but when you look around, they give you a blank look. They are acutely curious about everything, but they believe it is unseemly to show inquisitiveness. One day when I went out I left a bottle of assorted pills on my washbasin, some red vitamin capsules on top. When I came back they were mixed up with the other pills, but my hotel boy insisted he had not touched them. In the Philippines, conditioned by a freer and easier system, my hotel boy had picked up this same bottle and brought it into my bedroom: "What's matter? You sick? What are red pills for?"

In Japan, secret watching only. They are taught their faces must stay blank, show no emotion. A man comes to his employer to ask for the day off: "My mother died. I hope it won't inconvenience you." Then he titters a little in nervous release as he tries to conceal his anguish and live up to the inhuman behavior pattern his civilization imposes on him.

But in a different civilization, psychological modesty does not necessarily imply physical modesty. In the public hot-spring baths of Atami I was warm for the first time since I had come to Japan but I was not exactly at ease. I was led into a big room lined with small wooden lockers. Men and women both use this same room to undress in and the same big tiled pool to bathe in. You are issued towels about the size of a small handkerchief, and if a woman wishes to indicate that she is truly decorous, when she passes you in the bath she claps her towel against her skin, but she aims it for no particular spot; as long as the towel hits somewhere between breastbone and knees, conventions have been observed. The men do not bother with towels; they observe the conventions by holding themselves when they cross the threshold from pool to locker room, but not from locker room to pool.

These concealments are for decorum's sake, not modesty's. The Japanese are uninterested in naked bodies. They reserve their modesty for the inner side of man, his thoughts. To blurt out your true emotions in front of someone you do not know is more of a shock to them than stripping your clothes off at a church social would be to us.

Yet this is an acquired characteristic, the pattern into which the mores of centuries force them. You almost never see an unhappy child in Japan. Until they are seven years old, the boys spend a happy and free life with the women in the family, spoiled, petted, allowed to do as they please. But at seven the training process is reversed. Suddenly and violently begins the instilling of self-importance, pride, self-control; the father steps into the picture, and iron suppression closes down on the child. The Japanese have a famous proverb: "There are three great misfortunes in life—earthquakes, fires, and your father."

The Japanese father does not want to lose the love of his son, yet his culture says it is part of his duty to enforce harsh discipline. What a traumatic experience for the affectionate and pampered child; Western psychology knows that if you do not wish a child to evolve into an integrated adult with faith and strength in himself, you need only destroy his conviction that he fits and is loved. The Japanese system may create obedient followers for the state; a more efficient way could not be devised to set up lifelong frustrations and instability.

In time, the child becomes a young man, having been taught for years that the most important do's are the don'ts, that he must struggle to be good because his instincts would make him bad, uncontrolled, and without dignity. Good training for a follower who must fit into the cramped society of Japan; poor conditioning for a voting member of a new democracy. It is difficult for a young Japanese to prepare himself for self-reliance and the initiative of democracy when "mustn't" and "don't" are the operative words in his culture.

Where the father leaves off, the state takes over. The Japanese ethical code is not a written one like the Ten Commandments, but a series of personal relationships resting on the credo that your superiors tell you what is right and fitting. It becomes second nature to a Japanese to think of his relations with everyone else, whether family or friends or business associates, as fixed on a vertical scale of superiors and inferiors.

Japanese society rests on the relationship between the *oyabun*, the superior or more powerful authority, and the *kobun*, the inferior, the less powerful or assistant, the servant. Thus, hierarchy is present everywhere, a very live relic of the old feudal centuries when Japan was a feudal society far more rigid than Western Europe in the Middle Ages, its relationships inherited, its classes rigidly separated. The warrior, or samurai caste, could do no work and the farmers were not permitted to fight. Until a hundred years ago, when Commodore Perry burst open an unwilling society, the Japanese fiefs were still independent states with borders and customs barriers; until Pearl Harbor, no farmer's son could aspire to serve in the Imperial Navy.

The Japanese culture has always been feudal, delayed, and isolationist. When nearby Chinese art was in one of its most brilliant periods and medieval art was flowering in Europe, the Kamakura art and armor of Japan were still primitive and semi-barbaric. Yet then, as now, the Japanese were trained to believe theirs is the most superior of all races, to be carefully guarded from pollution by lower groups.

Today they still adhere to the oyabun-kobun system of relationships. In Japanese there is a different phrase to be used for friends, or for inferiors, or for superiors, when you ask them to be seated. In a bow of salutation or farewell there is a different genuflection. In a room full of people you have never seen before, you can instantly tell which are the more important; they bow very slightly, a gentle inclination of the neck and a slight, almost inaudible inhalation of the breath. The kobun in the room bow from the waist with their hands placed flat on their thighs above the knees, inhaling a long, loud hiss of respect. The gradations in this simple salute are infinite and delicately balanced.

Of course every society has some caste system; in our business conferences in America, it is easy to pick out the higher ranking by the way they are respectfully yesed or not interrupted. But in Japan the duality operates in every relationship: Emperor-people, employer-clerk, husband-wife. It operates in a family, from top oyabun, the father, down through eldest son, younger male children, male relations, husband's mother, wife, female children, female relations; each has his proper place. The good man or woman suppresses his feelings and welcomes opportunities to demonstrate that he knows his place in the society.

The supersensitivity of the Japanese ceases to seem psychotic when you understand this system. A too casual interruption of a speaker, a sharp question, even a slight turn of the head, indicate to the other man that you have assumed the oyabun position; if he does not think your status rates it, the implied assumption becomes a deliberate slight.

There is another significant word in Japanese, *on*. Roughly it means your responsibility or a debt to be repaid at all costs. Few Japanese plays have happy endings because so many of their problems of living revolve around repayment of *on*. The Japanese happy ending comes from carrying out your *on* even though you die unhappily in the process.

If you help a man who is run over in the street, both oyabun and *on* are involved. By helping him you have become the superior, whether he thinks you rate it or not. Either he grudges you the supererogation or he must accept both his inferior position and the *on* or debt you have placed upon him. Incidentally, if you help him, Japanese law recognizes you as his oyabun, but in an unpleasant way: under the law you become responsible for him. No wonder people walk right by when a child is knocked down and injured by a car. "Pick him up? You think me crazy?"

So these people are very fussy about accepting *on* from others as their phrases for "thank you" show. *Katajikenai* means, "I didn't deserve it, I am ashamed"; *Kino doku* implies, "You make me feel guilty because you have placed an *on* on me"; *Sumimasen* says, "All this doesn't end here, I must pay you back."

Taking this matter of obligation so seriously and making it a center of their way of life mean it is not more blessed to give than to receive. Therefore, if you go out of your way to perform some little action of generosity to a Japanese, you may actually be offending him. He does not want to accept an *on* from you; if he does, he is obligated to you and formally recognizes you as his superior. Believing in this set of values, it becomes hard for the Japanese to begin to understand the central set of values of our democracy: giving, unselfishness, group co-operation. You obey or you command; but to do neither or both at once, that is not Japanese.

There is another connotation for Americans in this oyabun-kobun relationship. The oyabun has the right to demand absolute loyalty from the kobun, and in turn he must be responsible and provide for the kobun; he has a right to demand loyalty only so long as he can protect. In protecting and guiding Japan as the United States has, we think of ourselves and Japan as partners against communism, but that is not the way the Japanese look at it. As their postwar protector and mentor, we are their oyabun. This in turn means that they are obligated to live up to agreements with us only as long as we carry out our responsibilities to them via international protection and economic recovery. If we fail to live up to our part of their hierarchical bargain, they owe us no gratitude or support. Or if we attempt to deal with Japan as we like to think we do with all other countries, on a basis of sovereign equality, by so doing we cease to act as an oyabun and thus confuse the relationships.

A people so hemmed in and hammered down would go irrevocably berserk if they could not find some release. The Japanese have found one in an area completely foreign to us. We think of sexual repression as the cause of most of our neuroses and psychoses. There is no better way to underline how differently the Japanese and the Americans approach life than to realize that sex is the one vital drive in which the Japanese are completely and relaxedly uninhibited with no holds barred. They approach sex openly. The crammed living quarters and paper walls of a Japanese house would make sexual shyness an anomaly, but that is not the main reason for their attitude. About the only real relaxation allowed the Japanese by their code of living is enjoyment of sex.

When a young man approaches his first sexual experience he gets no more help from his elders than do most Americans, but for a very different reason. In Japan anything important is carefully instilled in the boy, but sex is not important enough for anyone to bother about. He picks it up himself as he goes along or he waits until he is married and then consults the elaborately and explicitly illustrated "marriage books" handed down from generation to generation, standard operating procedure under every bride's pillow. In Japan sex falls into the same category as tempura cooking or flower arranging, a proper pleasure to be explored and enjoyed.

It is startling to an American to find an advanced civilization like Japan's making literally no connection between morals and sex; even the voluptuary of Paris has a lingering memory of some moral code he is transgressing. After a business conference or golf game, a Japanese takes his friends to some pleasant house on the outskirts of Tokyo. There they have a few drinks and then separate to have relaxing hot baths in big wooden tubs; girls get into the tub to scrub tired backs and massage tired muscles.

Do whatever you want as long as it does not interfere with the fulfillment of your duties to society. A Japanese praises the accomplishments of a good cook and talks with as explicit detail and just as unarousedly about the accomplishments of a good mistress. There is nothing a wife can or would think of doing about a mistress as long as the husband fulfills his responsibilities to her, not by loving her but by getting her pregnant. That accomplished, the man may turn where he pleases, as long as these minor pleasures do not interfere with his earning a living and serving the state.

The Japanese girls who go with Americans, like their Philippine sisters, rate them as gentle and considerate. The Japanese male wastes no time thinking about the woman and "Japanese he exhausts so fast." It is hard to be sure why Americans are considered superior. It may be because of a better diet, greater strength, or just a differently triggered nervous system; perhaps like liquor, sex, so to speak, goes to the Japanese head.

Japanese and Americans also have contradictory approaches to art. For us, artistic expression means the unlimited, the soaring, the divine fire. They are inspired by the limited and the miniature; theirs is a breath-taking ability to express themselves in the meager. Give a Japanese three little pieces of straw and you get something beautiful; give him a haystack and he will be confused.

In every Japanese room there is a tokonoma, an alcove set into a wall about six inches above the floor. Within the alcove one scroll is hung and under it a vase holding a sprig of flowers, or a piece of interestingly formed rock. Art, to be beautiful to them, must be subdued. The scrolls and the ornaments of the tokonoma are varied, depending on mood or time of the year. In spring, at the time of the cherry trees and the Doll Festival, it may be a few cherry blossoms and a scroll of a beautiful maiden. In summer, a branch of fir and a scroll showing crystal water falling over rocks; at New Year's, a dwarf-pine tree symbolizing strength, and a gray-and-white scroll of two cranes, the symbols of long life. This custom helps you bring nature into your house and offers you beauty at so little cost.

Like the tokonomas, poetry is another wonderful example of the Japanese art of limited things. And is it so limited? They are very fond of short epigramlike poems like the *tanka* with its five lines restricted to five or seven syllables. These poems are often about nature, and one tanka can pack in a page of Wordsworth. It is difficult for an American city dweller to understand the extent to which nature is part of their lives. A single descriptive word evokes dozens of images for them: "plum" will remind them of the taste of the ripe plum and the sun-warmed juice, of the clear deep pink of the flowering plum blossom and the spring winds that blow it, of everything in their own lives that happened at the time of the plum.

Or, if you will grant that cuisine is a branch of art, there is the

Japanese *tempura*, a revelation in how much can be done with how little. I was introduced to it by Japan's most famous tempura artist, Shioya, at his home-restaurant in the Mamiana section of Azabu prefecture in Tokyo. His address gives no street or number, for the Japanese may love efficiency, but it never occurred to them to have street signs or numbers until the American occupation; why should anyone know how to find his way to your house if he did not know you so well he needed no specific address? Fair enough as a social point, but it does not make for efficiency.

Mrs. Shioya, in a subdued moss-green kimono, unlaced my shoes at the door, slipped fresh straw slippers on my feet, and I padded upstairs to a clean open room, its walls a light framework of sliding paper screens. In most Japanese houses the floors are covered from wall to wall with padded tatami mats of two-inch-thick soft rice straw, covered with a simply woven design of cream reeds. These tatami mats are woven in only one size, six feet long and three feet wide. The floor space of Japanese houses, huts, or mansions has always been designed in combinations of this basic measurement. Every sliding partition is three feet wide and the drawers in which cloth is stored are the same unvarying width. The introduction of one out-sized piece of American clothing or furniture into this rigid system would upset everything. Shioya chooses to keep his floors bare: clear, polished wood without a mar or scratch. The minute I was inside the room, Mrs. Shioya knelt at the door and repolished the threshold.

The tempura master, all in white, was ready at a long, darkly varnished table, about a foot off the floor. He had one long fingernail for opening foods or scooping them up. Around him, stacks of simple, clean wood trays, containing the raw foods; in front of him, a wide upside-down coolie hat of tin, his stove. The courses of the tempura are dipped in thin egg-yolk batter, fried lightly in deep fat, set to drain in a little rack in front of you, and eaten with chopsticks. I had thirty-seven courses, each consisting of one tiny piece of food no bigger than a fifty-cent piece.

The opening course was a bright green cooked cucumber, like a tiny green summer squash, touched with mayonnaise and served on a small flat plate, dark cream-colored with cross bars of blues, olive, and Chinese red. And the courses which followed were improvised by Shioya as he watched my reactions to what I was eating.

A potato-like root with a bland nutty flavor. Three little acorn-sized nuts tasting like sweet chestnuts, delicious. Very sweet shrimp, to be eaten fins and all—"The prawn swims with his fin; the taste and the strength are there." From the flatness of the root to the sweetness of the shrimp, the variations in flavor subtle and deliberately calculated. White fish, delicate and less sweet than the shrimp. A repeat of the prawn theme. A spinach-like vegetable with a pungent undertaste like *orégano*. A lotus root cut in disks like a wheel with spokes. A piece of rubbery squid. Mushrooms. A prawn. Sharp cold pickled roots to clear the palate. A bowl of rice mixed with half a teaspoon of salt, sweet shrimp, and half a cup of green tea. Strong, dry, tart, it was a wonderful preliminary to the final course of ground nuts, dark, plum-colored, and with a maple-syrup flavor.

To make a magnificent dinner of roots, nuts, leaves, and small bits of fish, how much discipline and adjustment are demanded before it comes naturally? The Japanese are trained to fit into their environment, never to rebel against it. This characteristic fits in with their ability to imitate. The Filipino imitates Americans because he admires them and wants to be like them. But he can only do it so far, and he only wants to do it so far. Not so the Japanese; he puts no premium on originality; quite the reverse. "Adjust yourself to your surroundings and imitate them till you are at home in them. That is good."

So it becomes easy and desirable for them to do the same thing in other fields. It is a cliché that they have borrowed their language from the Chinese, their ceramics from the Koreans, their beer from the Germans, their ships from the British, their factories from us. The Japanese is proud of it. When he sees something he wants, he is not envious, he adjusts himself until he can imitate it and thus get it for himself.

These people have immense ability to adjust. They have had to adapt to floods, fires, earthquakes, every sort of catastrophe, including World War II. They have protected themselves from some of the worst consequences of their national pride by their ability to adapt: what can conquer is superior, and therefore no status is lost by yielding to it.

Thus they could adjust to the Americans coming in to occupy their islands. One American who stayed in Japan during the entire war and occupation saw only one time in that period when the people could not adjust. "The Japs were okay as they watched the Yanks parade into Tokyo until a group of armored cars came along. A young GI was putting on a big show of nonchalance in the driver's seat of the leading car. He drove with only one hand on the steering wheel and kept the car right in line. The Japs appreciated this until he slouched back in his seat and started picking his nose with his other hand. It's the only time I thought the Japs would blow their tops. It was okay to be licked by Yank machines and GIs, but when they were callow kids who picked their noses, how could this be explained to the ancestors?"

It is his ancestors who are the final oyabun and control over a Japanese. His dead grandfathers are gods and censors of the present via the religion of Japan, Shintoism. One of the satisfying experiences for a Japanese is to make a pilgrimage to a Shinto shrine like Kamakura, ancient capital of the first shoguns, the Mayors of the Palace who ruled Japan for so many centuries. Here, overlooking the sea and the sandy, stunted-pine shores at the foot of the mountains, in air with the crystalline exhilaration of Maine, are some of Japan's most sacred Shinto and Buddhist shrines.

Shintoism is a weird combination of folklore and totalitarian propaganda put together centuries ago by the feudal rulers of Japan to rally the people behind the state. It teaches that you get prosperity and do good in this world by doing your duty to your ancestors and the Emperor. When pilgrims come to these holy places they show neither hushed worship nor exultation. Their faces relax, they breathe and walk more slowly. They get "a wonderful peace of mind" while they are there. Again this negative quality of the Japanese. Religion is not for inspiration but to help you relax a little.

The Shinto shrines are a series of pagoda-like courts, covered alcoves, and small buildings open on all four sides, their beams supporting elaborate eaves painted clear red and inlaid with bright colors, very pleasing against the massed fir trees and gray rocks of the mountains around them. Inside the shrines, nothing but some object believed to be a dwelling place of one of their gods, or *kami*. There are "eight hundred ten thousands of kami." Almost any force, clouds, tornado, flood, wind, can be a kami in Shintoism; almost any exceptional man is a kami too, certainly the Emperor and leading men of the kingdom.

God is only an approximate translation of this word kami. It really means anything outstanding or unusual. The Emperor is a kami because he is worthy of worship. An unusual tree is a kami because it is superior, worthy of special respect; a Japanese puts a straw rope around it, bows to it, believing that when it dies its spirit will remain.

The greatest of the kami is the sun goddess, from whom the Japanese believe they descend. They worship the sun as only people can who are so often cold; farmers at dawn clap their hands with joy to the rising sun. The people are taught to believe they are literally gods and that theirs is a bright character worthy of the sun.

In every Shinto home there is an altar where water and food are left for the ancestors. And the Japanese are very practical; if you give a Japanese girl a stick of peppermint candy for Christmas, she will take it home and give it to her ancestors. That is, she lays it on the altar for them. When the kami have enjoyed it for a couple of days, she eats it with a double pleasure.

Perhaps the best of all possible indications as to whether democracy is really going to take hold in Japan will be found in how much of a kami the government will now make of the Emperor. For a while after V-J Day he was treated as a human being, and he renounced his divinity by imperial rescript. Now the court is building up his kami character again. Last year his favorite brother, Prince Chichibu, died of tuberculosis. Much as Hirohito loved him, he did not see Chichibu during the last period of his illness because the prince was too sick to come to the palace and it was not fitting for Hirohito to go to visit his brother. The Emperor is above all ordinary men and cannot demean himself by visiting anyone.

Shintoism teaches that your ancestors remain around you. They were superior or they would not have been Japanese ancestors; that makes them kami and immortal. Thus the wonderful phrase of Shintoism, "Every living being is the grave of his ancestors." And with your honorable ancestors keeping their eyes on you, the most important single Shinto rule is to be worthy of them. Over the centuries this has been craftily manipulated to mean, "Be worthy of doing what your leaders and the Emperor tell you is right." The Russians did not invent all the tricks.

The Japanese are caught in a terrible trap, the trap of the centuries. The Filipinos are lucky. They had the Spanish conquistadors for four hundred years and the Americans for forty; the Japanese have been under the conquering heel of their own countrymen for two thousand years. And how they will release themselves no one knows. There is a Japanese adage that "a fog cannot be dispelled with a fan." It remains to be seen whether feudalism can be expunged with nice hopes.

In the past the Japanese have reacted to pressures not by violent explosions but by the slow rock-flow method of adaptation. Left to themselves to adapt to a modern democratic world, having a model under their eyes in the free and equal ways of the American Occupation Forces, they might have managed slowly to wriggle loose from their feudal trap. But today there is a new pressure upon these unhappy people; its urgency will force violent changes not in centuries but in decades.

Of all the great industrial nations of the postwar world, Japan is in the worst short-range and long-range position. Thanks to hard work and to bloody conquest, she beat out for herself the highest standard of living in Asia and the only one comparable to that of the West. With the greatest concentration of people per square mile in Asia, in spite of the poorest land, she has enjoyed the lowest death rate, the lowest infant-mortality rate, and the largest number of doctors per capita in Asia. She has had the lowest illiteracy rate and the highest rate of power consumption in her part of the world. But today the main indices of her economic life are ominous: rising population, falling food supply, falling exports, rising imports, a run-down factory system, and an unbalanced budget.

She has too many people and, as in every other country of Asia, they are increasing faster than they can be fed, far faster on the Japanese islands where there is no possibility of raising the food yield. There is no religious or social objection to birth control, and abortion is legal whenever the birth would endanger the mother's life, or whenever a poor family thinks it would not be able to feed an extra mouth. That is almost never. A Japanese wants to have babies; he loves them and they are his best form of social security, for they will shelter and care for him in his old age. And since the adults are used to an inadequate diet, they do not worry much about whether their children have enough food: "If you own your own house and rice paddy, don't worry about how many children you have to feed."

Thanks to these attitudes toward children, Japan has an oriental birth rate. But unfortunately for Japan's future, thanks to Western medicine and the lowering of infant mortality, she has a sharply falling death rate. Result: the islands are becoming more dangerously overcrowded every year: in 1945 there were 72,000,000 Japanese; today there are over 86,000,000. True, Japan's rate of population increase is falling off more rapidly than that of any other modern industrial country; nonetheless, her population, increasing 2 per cent a year, will soon reach 100,000,000.

This would be explosive enough if she were trying to live on the land she had before the war. Instead, her Co-Prosperity Sphere has been reduced to a group of islands about the size of Montana. Because no land can be spared for grazing, half of the farmers have no livestock; even India has four times as much cultivated land per capita.

Japan has only 15,000,000 acres of arable land in all the islands. Compare this with the United States, where 15,000,000 acres are planted in peanuts, one of our smallest and least important crops. Or put Japan's tragic situation another way, in terms of human beings. Where our farms have 160 acres, the average farmer in Japan has about two and a half acres of land. The yield from it must feed him, his wife, his children, and his dependents. That same two acres must also yield enough extra food to cover taxes and to exchange for everything else he needs.

Only by exporting billions of yen of manufactured products each year can Japan pay for extra food to keep her from starvation and for the raw materials without which she cannot manufacture. She must buy abroad a great deal of her coal, 90 per cent of her oil, and 100 per cent of her cotton, wool, and nickel, and she can get the foreign exchange for these purchases only by selling her manufactured products abroad.

Before the war she did all right. She possessed a conquered empire from which she could import cheaply most of the raw materials which her industries needed. And then she could sell back her artifacts at high prices, both the trade and the price levels enforced by bayonets. In 1936, 20 per cent of her trade was with conquered Manchuria and China and another 20 per cent with her colonies of Korea and Formosa. Today she has half as much land, no colonies, and no empire.

Before the war she had an up-to-date industrial machine; today much of what was not destroyed is obsolescent. Textiles used to be her best money-maker. Now the other countries of Asia are trying to build textile mills of their own and she is exporting less than half as much as she did. Britain is determined to grab more of the world textile market and as a result, two of Japan's biggest customers, Indonesia and the Commonwealth, have reduced their yen-buying by 30 per cent. Right behind the competing new plants of Asia and the competing old plants of Britain is the latest threat to Japanese industrial exports, the rebuilt, revitalized factories of postwar Germany, which have quadrupled their exports in four years.

For some years Japan has been buying twice as much as she sells;

each year this imbalance has pushed her into more inflation. As the value of the yen goes down and she must pay more for raw materials, her manufactured prices go up and she prices herself out of more markets. Up to the end of the Korean War, there was no threat of bankruptcy because of American purchases in Japan; in 1952 and 1953 we spent some $800,000,000 there and thus made up her trade deficit. Now we have cut our spending down to around $500,000,000 a year and so provide that much less support.

Japan's economic predicament is the most urgent economic problem the United States faces in Asia today, and there are only four possible ways out of it. One way is for the United States to fill much of this trade gap with Mutual Security funds given to Japan for her rearmament, but the number of years the American taxpayer will foot such a bill is limited. A second way is for the United States to let volumes of cheap Japanese goods flood our markets, but it seems unlikely that the American Congress would vote for this. Both of these means of American assistance are being used, but too restrictedly to bear the whole burden of the Japanese deficit.

One or both of two other very different types of economic activity will have to do the job for Japan. One is for her to return to her prewar pattern of trade with China; the other is to increase greatly her trade with Southeast Asia.

There is no doubt that Japanese businessmen want to, and intend to, go back to trading with China. Their publications and papers are full of agitation for it; in mid-1953 their House of Representatives passed a unanimous resolution calling for more trade with China. They have been selling less to the Communists than do the British or the French or the Italians or even the Belgians, but now Japanese trade is increasing each month. They have signed a trade treaty whereby they will deliver to China $100,000,000 of steel plates and machinery in return for coal and iron they can purchase far more cheaply on the Asian mainland than in the New World: "We would rather shop in the nearest stores than go to far-off ones by hiring a taxi."

Simultaneously, Russia has been offering this starved economy tempting exchanges like lumber in return for building the Soviets some freighters. It is far cheaper for Japan to get her lumber this way than to buy it from the United States, but, to Americans, the Japanese are supping with the devil when they have no long spoon. In the old days China trade was very profitable and today the 480,000,000

Chinese are desperate for manufactured goods, but this time the Japanese have no army to back up their traders. Today the hard-boiled Communists buy via state barter deals. If they could once bring Japan into their economic orbit, the Japanese would have to sell on Communist terms or see their markets cut off; and once this was the choice, the Japanese could not long remain anti-Communist.

The one hope the United States has of preventing this is to promote the only other big trade outlet for the desperate islands, Southeast Asia. An economic wedding between the heavy industry and skilled man power of Japan and the overflowing raw materials and yearning markets of the backward countries in the southeast sounds wonderfully logical, but it is costly to work out and it brings forward a new set of dangers.

Japan was the loathed conqueror of Southeast Asia. The Southeast Asians want neither to see again nor to become dependent upon this "cruel race." Moreover, most of them now have little purchasing power, so Japan, the United Nations, and more especially the United States, would have to advance huge sums of capital to get this trade under way. And by doing so, we would build more Japanese industrial power and more competition for our other allies, the British and the Germans, unless the purchasing power of Southeast Asia can be immensely expanded.

The Japanese are going ahead as fast as they can without our help and investing hundreds of millions of yen in Southeast Asia. They are signing trade pacts and building factories in partnership with the nations of Southeast Asia. When their ex-conquests demand billions of yen in war reparations, Japanese diplomatic missions maneuver to switch these demands from yen into trade pacts whereby they loan technicians and erect factories in the countries. As they succeed, they tie the economies of these nations to Japan's.

And here again comes a complicated set of decisions for American foreign policy: how much help for the Japanese in Southeast Asia is enough and not too much? They must have our help to make a go of north-south trade. If we will not underwrite their advance south, we can look forward to inevitable economic alliance between Japan's industrial machine and the armies of the Chinese. But the other horn of the dilemma is just as lethal. If Japan succeeds too well in the south, we will have helped her establish the Southeast Asia Co-Prosperity Sphere for which her armies fought in World War II.

But that is a far-off predicament which most American policy makers ignore as they consider the most immediate dangers. Our statesmen are pressuring the Japanese to rearm and take off American shoulders the burden of protecting their islands from Chinese and Russian threats. According to the terms of the constitution drawn up under the American occupation, Japan bound herself not to rearm, and all the parties of the left, including the non-Communists, remembering back to Hiroshima and thinking forward to armament costs and new wars, are against rearmament. They agitate, instead, for more trade with Russia and China and more money to be spent on public works. But the men who rule Japan want their country to be powerful again, and they would be fools if they overlooked the threats of Russia and Red China. Rearmament is coming: how fast depends on how much of the bill the United States will pay. It is good politics for them to feign reluctance and thus maneuver us into taking over a larger share. And, in fairness to them, we must recognize it will be a terrible economic burden on top of all their other financial problems.

But some eight years from now it will remain to be seen whether we acted wisely. When Japan possesses a modern army, navy, and air force, when Japanese bombers and guided missiles are sitting a few miles away from Alaska, we may or may not be glad we financed this rearmament. There are three questions no one can answer today about this people: will they be able to resist internal communism, will they turn their country into a modern democracy, and will they remain our friends?

During the American occupation they wasted no time hating us, they put up with us, watched us, and learned from us. Since they were not permitted publicly to criticize us, many Americans assumed they loved us dearly. They do not and there is no reason why they should; like most peoples, they love only themselves.

We read reams of American prose on how the Japanese people admired and appreciated General MacArthur. Maybe so, but in 1952 a campaign was launched in Japan to collect funds to build a MacArthur Memorial Hall. After months of high-pressure publicity, for which $62,000 was spent, according to the Japanese newspapers, the fund managed to collect a grand total of $39.

The Japanese are beginning to use Hiroshima and Nagasaki as propaganda to build Asian sympathies for themselves at our expense. Stories out of Tokyo for other Asian newspapers report that citizens of Nagasaki may sue the United States Government or Truman or

Marshall for the explosion, thus suggesting by implication that the dropping of the A-bomb was an illegal act. Baseball is Japan's favorite sport, and a baseball team has been traveling around Asia building good will and playing demonstration games. But it is a team from Hiroshima, and when it is greeted by an Asian head of state, it presents him with a silver rice scoop and a set of pictures of the atomic devastation the United States wreaked on Hiroshima.

This does not imply that the Japanese are turning again into enemies of the United States. There is a considerable substratum of favorable sentiment toward us and most GIs remember experiences of Japanese friendliness. But it is by no means established that our two nations from now on are to be fast and mutually dependable friends.

More and more Japanese newspaper stories are attacking the United States; public-opinion polls in 1952 showed 48 per cent of the people wanted to keep American troops in the country; by 1953 this figure had fallen to 27 per cent. It is increasingly difficult for American businessmen to stay in business in the islands, which are returning to the slogan, "Japan for the Japanese."

But their decreasing friendship for Americans does not mean that, judged strictly on present data, they are turning toward the Communists. Only Pakistan and Formosa have less successful Communist movements. The Japanese attribute this to their own superior secret police and civilization. It could more accurately be called an accident of geo-history: the two chief proponents of communism today happen to be Japan's two hereditary enemies, China and Russia. Also, as is true in the rest of Asia, the Communist Party of Japan has been run from the Kremlin and manipulated exclusively for Russia's national gains.

Sanzo Nosaka, who studied under Mao of China and accompanied him to Yenan, has been the philosophical leader and the brains of the Japanese Communists. Nosaka preached the peaceful development of communism and worked to identify his party with the strivings of the little man for a better life. As did his associates in Europe, he wanted to join with the Socialists and secure a popular-front government in which his better-disciplined group could gradually take over the power. This did not jibe with Russia's intentions to make trouble for the American Occupation Forces and to block Japanese rearmament, so the Cominform journal came out with a virulent attack labeling Nosaka as a Tito. He was forced to resign, go underground, and carry out a Kremlin-dictated campaign of violence, giving the Japanese people clear evidence on who pulled the strings.

It would be hard to conceive any Japanese becoming a follower of a Russian-controlled system. But unfortunately for the West, that is not the only road to communism. As Nosaka knows from firsthand observation in China, Mao Tse-tung threw out the Russian-dominated Communists in his own country and turned his party into a force still 100 per cent Communist but wholly Chinese. It was this alignment of the Chinese Communists with the Chinese peasants which gave Mao his victory.

Sooner or later Nosaka or someone else is going to realize this and pull away from Russian domination. The party will not then be based on the farmers as Mao based his, because the Japanese have handled their land problems wisely. During the occupation, the United States guided Japan through a land-reform program that has taken the strength out of the Communist appeal, so successful in Asia, of urging the landless farmers to unite and throw out the landlord class.

But, if the Japanese Communists can find a program which promises the oppressed laboring man in the big cities a better world, and if they can find a shrewd leader able to base his appeal on a conglomeration of typically Japanese exhortations to frugality, discipline, and the building of a better Japan, then communism can become a most serious threat, especially since it will be appealing to the same class in society that powered the Russian Revolution in 1917, the proletariat.

Today the Japanese Communists are infiltrating the labor unions and they are working for a united front with the other left parties of the proletariat. The largest labor union, the Teachers and Schoolworkers Union, is called *tancho-zuru*, the name of a Japanese crane with a red comb, because of its pro-Communist leadership. The amalgamation of unions formed under the American occupation, Sohyo, the General Council of Trade Unions whose three million members comprise more than half of all Japan's organized workers, is another tancho-zuru. The General Council has swung so far over toward communism that a new anti-Communist setup, the Japanese Trade Union Congress, is being organized to fight it. But if the economic situation does not drastically improve, the tancho-zurus could become Japanese communism's springboard to political power. And in the interim period, through these unions, communism could slow or stop Japan's industry in an emergency like a war with China or Russia.

The balance of power between Japanese capital and labor is an Achilles' heel. Industry has no American history of gradually evolving co-operation between capital and labor; its pattern was imposed by the state when the rulers of Japan realized they must have modern industry for international power and decreed its creation. The government turned the job over to a few families, the Mitsui, the Mitsubishi, the Sumitomo, the Yashuda. Thus, industry has been dictatorial and paternalistic, never bothered by anti-trust laws.

The industrialists, ultraconservatives, are determined to weaken the occupation laws which granted labor unions the right to strike. The workers, having had no reason to consider themselves partners with the factory owners, have been enthusiastically trying out their new weapon, usually in a tentative and non-violent form. In a typical strike, you may see a government building or a factory with a long, temporary platform thrown up in front of it. On this, a long row of men lying next to each other, rolled up in quilts against the cold. Banners over the platform explain the men are on a hunger strike, refusing to eat or move until their demands are met.

Suppression is the only way employers can prevent these strikes in a time of so much inflation and rising prices. It takes a half month's salary for a professor to buy a subscription to one American scholarly publication. Gas bills are fantastic: $250 a month to heat a four-bedroom house in winter. The average worker with four children makes about $52 a month. His family's minimum food costs alone run to at least that much, and so the only way to support themselves is for the wife or children to go to work too. Women and children get lower wages and much of the time they work under wretched conditions similar to those in British factories in the early nineteenth century.

It is from such economic wretchedness and from political suppression that a strong Communist Party could arise. If we cannot guarantee Japan enough trade for a better standard of living, her people will rebel against the system and turn gradually to Communist ways; if the leaders of Japan will not lead their people toward more freedoms and more participation in their government, communism will have more and more appeal for the young.

There are many sides of the Japanese conditioning which fit well with a police-state communism. They yearn to be constructive under guidance, they have a masochistic love of discipline, they reach for *esprit de corps* in the conformity meaning of the phrase, they have always been trained to follow the leader and take orders from above.

There are ominous portents on the horizon. Japan is having the greatest student unemployment in its history because businessmen are reluctant to hire students for fear they are Communists. If the young intellectuals are riddled with communism, again it is the old story of young brains rebelling against a wrong world. In Japan they have nowhere to go except to communism. There are no leaders on the horizon like Magsaysay to give the young idealists hope and faith.

Compared with the Philippines, where people are always talking about what they are doing before they do it and always displaying their power before they get it, in Japan you hear very little about her secretive bosses, no less powerful because they do not flourish their powers. They were the only trained brains of the old prewar regime. Put on ice during the occupation, they are craftily taking back the reins of power and permitting no liberals to come into prominence.

These men will never understand the creeping threat of communism; they put their faith in their policemen, the *hanchos: han* for group in general or civil district and *cho* for chief. There is a sentry box with a policeman in it every two city blocks in Tokyo, and the hancho keeps a sharp eye on everyone in his district. There have been other countries that depended on secret police to protect them from native Communists. They are now Communist states. Communists have ways of getting around police surveillance, survival-of-the-fittest ways. They set up small cells of revolutionaries. If the police catch one cell and kill the revolutionists, too bad; if not, the leader of the successful cell is promoted and uses the same tricks to protect a group of cells, and so on up to the Politburo of the country involved.

When Communists are of the same race and country, police cannot do a very good job. It takes a positive program of reforms. But the democratic leaders of Japan are old-guard die-hards who regard communism as a novelty, something new for youth to dabble in. "In Parliament, in the labor unions, and in the so-called intelligentsia, there are many Communist people; young people are fond of new things, you see, so there you are."

Turning their backs on the danger, these old men are applying subtle pressures to direct their country back to prewar arrangements when there were only two political parties, the Seiyukai and the Minseito, both conservative and differing only in their leaders. Today the majority in the Diet is made up of the same kind of parties, now called Liberals and Progressives. In last year's elections, they captured about two thirds of the seats. Their leaders are prewar conservatives like Yoshida or two of the men the Americans banished as war criminals, Hatoyama and Shigemitsu. The other important bloc of parties is the Socialist group that agitates for strict neutrality between Russia and the United States. But they have only a quarter of the seats in the Diet and are splintering on the rock of how far to make common cause with the pro-Communists.

The zaibatsu, the monopolist industrial barons, are back on the scene reassembling their combines again and the military are reviving Nihou Seishin, the Spirit of Imperial Japan. In the meantime, Japan is turning its back on the liberal reforms made during the occupation. The leaders are junking local self-government, building up the power of the central government, re-creating the old cartels, redeifying the Emperor, and refurbishing the national Shinto shrines. The popular slogan, "correction of occupational mistakes," is used as a pretext to pass laws re-establishing a unified national police, and the infamous neighborhood associations, which were used as a method of thought control by the prewar Army, are coming back to life. These repressive policies of the Right are causing an ever deepening schism which forces the Socialists nearer and nearer to a common front with the Communists.

It takes more than a flood of decrees by a foreign occupation, or a yearning for freedom by an occupied people, to turn as ruthless a dictatorship as Japan's into a modern democracy.

The present machinery of parliamentary government is crude. Its Diet does not well understand its role of responsibilities to the people. The Sohyo, the General Council of Trade Unions, got up a huge petition against some pending labor legislation. They staged a very orderly parade through the streets. Their scroll of protest, with its thousands of signatures, was so heavy it had to be drawn on a horse cart up to the Diet building. But the Diet members refused to open the main gates and the horse cart could not get through an ordinary doorway so the petition was never presented. The Diet saw no reason why it should open the gates to receive this petition from the people.

But there are many favorable portents, too, on the horizon. Since V-J Day, with our help, the Japanese have made longer strides forward than was believed possible: they have given suffrage to their women, who are far more democratically minded than the men; in the economic field they are rigorously enforcing the land-reform laws; on the industrial front labor unions are in force; and in the cities the young are more and more Americanized. Each of these actions required a radical change in their thinking; each is causing significant changes in their society; each is creating its own new forces to help resist a return to old patterns.

Americans, for their own safety, must be realistic about the dangerous instability of the Japanese system, but we need also to have sympathy for these people, trying so hard, bedeviled by so many don'ts, caught in so many traps.

And we had better realize that although we so desperately need their strength and support in a postwar Asia dominated by Communist China, we cannot force this people in any direction. We can only do whatever we can to improve their economic lot, while in every possible way, privately and as a government, we must encourage them, teaching and showing them what democracy is and how it works.

It is impossible this soon to know how the drama of these eighty-six million courageous and enduring people will end. They are now a defeated second-class power and they have adapted to this status. But it may be a positive adjustment, a learning from their defeat to break the vise of their old system and move into a way of wider individual freedom; or it may be another negative adjustment, a waiting until the catastrophe passes and then going back to work for the same old objectives.

I came upon my own symbol for the Japanese people in a Tokyo night club on Christmas Eve. At the top of the entrance staircase, lit by cruel bright lights, was a little songbird in a glass cage and someone had put a sprig of fresh flowers into the cage for the bird to enjoy.

The Japanese are a race superb in the arts of the limited and limiting. No people in the history of the world has ever done more with less.

THE PEOPLE WHO NEVER HAD A CHANCE:

Korea

If the Japanese are trapped, it is in a trap of their own making and sprung by their own leaders. The Koreans have been trapped down through the centuries by geography and in spite of themselves. If the Japanese play is an unfinished drama building up toward its climax, the Korean play is a long tragedy whose curtain was rung up for another pitiful act when the North Koreans crossed the 38th parallel on June 24, 1950. In three years and thirty-two days of fighting, the dynamics of the Communist sphere and the free world met, struggled, and recoiled to the status quo, leaving South Korea to count its losses: 257,000 combat casualties, 1,000,000 civilian war deaths plus 1,000,000 wounded, 8,000,000 refugees, 4,000,000 Koreans on relief, 300,000 war widows with no way to make a living, 15,000 amputees, and 100,000 orphans. Twenty million desperate people living and suffering in the hunger, desolation, disease, and chaos of a peninsula more devastated by war than any other place in the world.

Korea is today a country with no future save what the great powers give it or take away from it. Looking to the United States for protection and rehabilitation, South Korea has been our responsibility since V-J Day. Our armies occupied it as the Japanese moved out. The man selected by our military leaders, Syngman Rhee, became its first president. Our bombers in the course of repelling the North Koreans were responsible for much of the country's physical damage. It now costs the American taxpayers about $1,000,000,000 a year to support the Republic of Korea in its economic rehabilitation and to build up its Army.

Today the logical solutions to Korea's plight are impossible; the possible solutions are no solutions at all. The 38th parallel is only a line on a map, the land looks no different on one side than on the other. The five to six million North Koreans and the some twenty million South Koreans are the same people with the same religion and customs and language and a thousand years of the same history. Their two economies are complementary: natural resources, minerals, and water power in the North; agriculture in the South. Separate, each must be supported from abroad.

Perhaps there is no better scene to portray this unhappy country, so ironically called "Land of Morning Brightness," than its wretched, although never bombed, principal port, Pusan. This southern city may once have been a beautiful town whose tile-roofed houses leisurely climbed the tree-clad hills above the clear blue waters of Pusan Bay. But that was in another world. Now the hills are sere and desolate and there are over a million refugees crowded into postwar Pusan. Desperate for fuel to keep from freezing, they have cut down the fir trees and left the earth bare for the rains to wash down into the bay, and for the mainland winds of Asia, bitter and crackling dry, to raise into a haze of yellow dust. The town lies in a couple of pockets in the hills and smog now dims the brightness, the less light the kinder for Pusan. Squatters and refugees have crowded into miserable settlements on the edges of filthy creeks. Any kind of shelter is a house, its walls of old splintered boards and rusted pieces of corrugated tin, its roofs of beer cans pounded flat for shingles. Every so often a candle or lamp falls against some flimsy shack wall and looses a wind-swept fire to roar down a mile or two of packing-case hovels, leaving families to sift the ashes for something to trade for wood or food. Multiply by a hundred the worst Squatters' Row you have ever seen, add hundreds of thousands of people, cold, miserable, dirty, dazed, milling about: Pusan.

Yet the Koreans try to keep life going on as usual. Tumbled-together shacks are piled against the hills. Outside them men, women, and children hawk their wares: open frying pans pounded from the aluminum of burned planes or canoe-like slippers from U.S. tires found on a junk heap or stolen from a careless supply sergeant.

The asphalt-paved main streets are far cleaner than Fifth Avenue. A mother nurses her child on a curb in a temperature about four above zero. A baby toddles along dressed in one pants-leg of GI khaki. A boy, not ten years old, struggles up over the frozen ruts of a steep hill, the frosty air turning his wheezes into puffs of white like the smoke ads on Broadway; his *chi-ge*, a frame carried by loops over his shoulders, is loaded with broken bricks. Two little girls jump rope with incredible speed, the rope is an old dirty piece of woven straw. A child looks fascinatedly into an empty beer can while other children lined up behind him jump up and down waiting their turn; a few holes have been punched in the bottom of the can, some colored pebbles dropped in, and it is now a kaleidoscope.

In today's Korea a woman works just as hard as a man. With a large baby on her back, hung like a papoose by two broad bands crossing over her breasts, a mother plods along with a hundred-pound sack of rice balanced on her head. Heavy-set girls, who look as if they could hold their own in a wrestling match, direct traffic. Their platforms are half oil drums painted with white diagonal lines, they wear white helmets, and flowing out from under the backs of the helmets are long braids that proclaim they are unmarried. Other women kneel at every irrigation ditch or puddle of water in the city, no matter how dirty it may be, washing clothes, bathing babies, preparing their roots and rice. When their hair is done up in a knot on the top of the head, it shows they are married.

The battle-maimed and the jobless mill about during the day and at night until it is too cold to stay out. Where there are few jobs or relief agencies, men steal to stay alive; women, if they are remotely attractive, have to work at the oldest trade.

The Koreans have a realistic proverb: "What looks like blossoms on the dead tree turns out to be only the white mold of decay." They are now watching to see whether we, their Western allies, will help their near-dead country bud into a livable land. Otherwise, out of sheer desperation, it must become covered with the red mold of communism. All depends on how much the West is willing to do to repair what the Korean War did to this land as the fighting seesawed back and forth between Taegu and the Yalu.

The United Nations has pledged some $245,000,000, of which the United States will pay two thirds. On its own the United States has already promised another $1,000,000,000. And this does not count the possible private aid and charity the American people could donate. If forthcoming and spent wisely and quickly, this aid to Korea can not only save the life of a people but also be a demonstration of the might and charity of the free world, far more impressive than a hundred Berlin air lifts.

The sums involved may seem a large amount to expend in one small country about the size of Minnesota; it is little measured against the needs. We are not only committed to the world's largest rehabilitation project, we are also involved in a direct competition with what the Communist bloc can do in North Korea. Both China and Russia have pledged amounts far higher in proportion to their total wealth than we have promised. China, the more generous, has canceled all the war loans she made to North Korea and has given an additional quarter of a billion dollars of economic aid. Russia has promised another quarter of a billion dollars, but she has been a little less open-handed; she specifies that in addition to being used for aid, this money must repay some of North Korea's war debt to Russia.

The Eastern European satellites are sending technicians and machinery to rebuild North Korean industry. Besides training North Koreans in China, Peiping is sending in Chinese settlers to strengthen the country and help build a powerful military force in the North. The Communists are taking no chances of a Rhee push to reunite the peninsula by force of arms. Except as a side result of another world war, it is unlikely Korea will be a single nation in our lifetime.

South Korea herself is not as fortunate as her two war-smashed neighbors, Japan and the Philippines. Japan has an industrial plant and a trained people to do her work of rehabilitation; the Philippines, protectorate and protégée of the United States, has had our guidance, our technicians, and hundreds of millions of American dollars. Also, the Filipinos and the Japanese had been trained for half a century in the ways of the West, but Korea until the end of World War II was a Japanese colony permitted no industry or training in self-government. In the most literal sense the country must be rebuilt from the ground; the Koreans have no industry, little transportation, little fertile land, few schools or hospitals.

The most urgent problem is homes; over six hundred thousand homes were destroyed during the bombardments and at least a million are needed today. The magnitude of this figure can be measured by comparing it with the maximum number of houses the rich and industrialized United States has ever been able to build in a year which was a million and a quarter. In Korea homes do not mean modern workers' apartments, or even modest bungalows, but only "the most basic of shelters, four tight walls, a good roof, and a floor that can be kept warm against the freezing cold." Homes and a minimum of consumer goods, food and blankets and shoes and medicines, to keep the people alive while production is starting up, "above all, to get industrial projects under way as soon as possible."

Only industry can provide employment and begin to raise living standards and lower charity needs. Coal mines to be put back in operation for fuel and power; tungsten mines, some of the best deposits in the world, to be opened up for foreign exchange. Both need transportation, roads and some railroads. Hydroelectric power, dams and dynamos and wire, all must be imported. Textile mills and rubber-goods plants to fill minimum needs for clothes and shoes. Fertilizer plants for food. Dredges for the heavily silted rivers and harbors. Boats and ice plants and fish canneries for what could be one of Korea's largest industries. All kinds of materials to be imported for the reconstruction of thousands of blocks of wrecked buildings. Irrigation and flood control and dikes to prevent erosion; at least half a billion saplings to rehabilitate Korea's forest land. Now so largely denuded, this land releases floods to erode more acres of South Korean farm lands.

And Americans do not have to sit back and wait for slow-moving national and international agencies to fill the needs. There are so many places we could, as groups and as individuals, demonstrate to Asia what private enterprise and individual responsibility mean. We believe in private enterprise. Korea gives us a fine chance to demonstrate it in action. Many private groups have already helped in Korea. American universities have found extra technical books from their libraries for Korea. When they build a new laboratory, they can send their old equipment to a needy Asian nation. Farm organizations can send tools, seed, or livestock. One group has sent rabbits, bees, goats, and two hundred million fertile hens' eggs to Korea. Religious councils conduct dispensaries and rehabilitation clinics. And, of course, any individual can give a few cents to his favorite charity to help the underprivileged peoples.

Private technical assistance on a far larger scale would be such a dramatic and fruitful way to help Korea. Any single private project costs so little and can be checked and supervised by the private group that supports it. Surely every great university in the United States could send one graduate technician to help out somewhere in Korea. He would learn his own profession by practicing it; as he worked, he could transfer his knowledge to the people there who have none; he would understand the world better as he did so, and thus later he would be one more wiser American to help shape wiser policies.

Any willing American club could pay for one expert to teach young Koreans the rudiments of administration; they would not be able to run a General Motors a year later, but they would be invaluable in the government of Korea. So little of ours would accomplish so much.

And they have so little. No one who has visited one of the orphanages of Korea will ever forget it. I wanted to do a broadcast from an orphanage while I was in Korea, but I had seen too many tragic sights so I asked to be taken to the most cheerful orphanage in Pusan. We went to the Happy Mountain Orphanage which was originally started by American GIs in 1951 and is now supported by the Korean Government.

It was pitiful beyond description, a collection of hovels and shacks put together any old way and falling down a hill next to a pile of broken pieces of boards and debris as high as the shacks. The Happy Mountain dormitories were rooms built of old packing-case boards rescued from army crating. Up under the eaves of the rooms, some of the boards were too short and left openings for the arctic winds. No desks, nothing to write with. A few tattered books and a few teachers as ill-clad as the children and equally happy.

Inside, the orphans go barefoot on the icy boards, which have been scrubbed smooth by the older children. The older girls have little rooms of their own, each one named for a flower, with old pieces of canvas for doors. Each of the shacks has a small tin basin with a handful of charcoal burning in it, warmth for twenty-five small orphans. If they are lucky, they have a couple of Christmas cards some Americans have sent with a gift, and these are pasted up in the middle of a bare wall, brightening the dormitory. There are no beds or cribs and only one thin worn blanket apiece. The smaller children sleep curled up next to each other, a mound of orphans keeping each other warm.

When I was there, the children had one uniform each, sewed together from donated old pieces of wool: a little jacket, which came up around the neck, and a pair of thin pants or a skirt. Maybe straw sandals, a thin sweater, or middy blouse. The kitchen was an open lean-to with two huge vats of barley steaming in it. The orphans do not get enough proteins or greens, or enough calcium to grow decent bones and teeth. In each dormitory there was a plain board nailed to the wall and ranged along it, in perfect order and exactly the same distance apart, was a long row of little wooden toothbrushes. The orphans brush their teeth carefully twice a day.

The hospital and dispensary was a separate shack presided over by a young Korean doctor. I counted the bottles of drugs on his shelf:

eight. A sharp kitchen knife or two, a pair of scissors, no surgical instruments, a pile of clean rags; his complete equipment to care for three hundred young patients a week. Very few orphans I saw were without some kind of sore or infection.

At that, the children were luckier than the older people. Down in the city of Pusan the refugees line up at the door of a clinic at dusk so they can get medical care the next day. Eighty per cent of the hospitals of Korea must be rebuilt from the ground. To care for one million civilian war casualties there are less than ten thousand hospital beds in the whole country. Thirty per cent of the people have tuberculosis, 80 per cent have some intestinal parasite. In the last year of the war there were eight hundred cases of smallpox. A cheap quick inoculation could have prevented this outbreak, but there were no medicines.

Outside the office shack of Happy Mountain, some of the children were playing tag on the frozen orange earth and others were clambering around on the big junk heap, prying frozen boards loose to use for charcoal. One little girl about eight, red-nosed and red-eared, slid down the slope below the junk pile to fetch water from a well. She took hold of the wet pulley rope with her bare hands, held on tightly, and threw herself backward onto the hard frozen ground. This hauled the bucket up a few feet. Then, like a sailor climbing a rope, she pulled herself erect again and repeated the process until the bucket was out of the well and she could drag it up to the cook shack.

When I was ready to broadcast from a schoolroom of the orphanage, I asked one of the teachers to try to get a few of the children to sing outside the shack. Describing what I had seen, I managed to keep my voice steady until from outside I heard the voices of at least a hundred children singing a folk song for the American guest. And as I looked out to the orphans, over their heads I could see a crude wooden arch of three beams nailed together; on it in English:

> THE FUTURE OF KOREA LIKE ANY OTHER NATION
> IS DEPENDENT ON THE EDUCATION AND WELFARE
> OF ITS CHILDREN

From the orphanage I went to record Korean singing and music at their radio station. It had two modern Western studios and control booths. But the musicians, their costumes and their music, were Eastern and so was the audience who had come to hear the recital. The walls were lined with waiting people; children sat in a row on top of an old piano, the control-room window was solid with faces peering in from every height and angle, a montage of faces on the glass.

The instruments for Korean music are bamboo and ancient, handed down from generation to generation. For percussion, there is a *chang-goo,* a sort of hourglass drum as big around as a large wastebasket. Lashed to it at each end is a tautly stretched membrane that gives out a dull flat thud when the player's curled fist hits it in the center, and a snare-drum clack when his fingernails snap against the rims. The Korean harp-violin is a *hai-gum,* which looks like a pipe, and along from the bowl of the pipe, extending up the curved stem, are strings of gut. As in most Asian violins, the bow is inserted between the stem and the strings to draw out a tight, wailing, oboe sound.

Each of the instruments showed off separately and when a big flute hit a clinker and blew a sour note, everything stopped in the studio and the audience turned into impassive orientals. The musician was vastly disgusted. Not a wrinkle moved in his face, but he laid his flute down with deliberation, stood up, rolled his bamboo mat together, put his flute in its case, bowed gravely, and started toward the door. No one moved until he reached it, then everybody, musicians, chorus, audience, engineers, burst into a tornado of Korean exhortation until he was persuaded to come back.

The chorus sang the same folk song the orphans had sung, the unforgettable "Ari-rang," which tells of a girl watching her lover climbing Mount Ari-rang as he deserts her, but, like all Korean women, she is realistic and knows her temperamental male will not go far: "Over Ari-rang hill he is going; he who goes out deserting me will have foot sores within a mile."

Unlike our mawkish laments, "Ari-rang" is haunting but also full-blooded and lusty. When Koreans get to work on any art, some of their fierce pride, their harsh country, their own direct drive comes through. You feel the same impact in their songs or in an antique Korean vase. They took the urbane and flowing symmetry of Chinese ceramics and irregularized it so that their pottery has an out-of-balance, reaching quality as if the artist saw the vision whole in his mind and then had to fly at the clay.

More than half of the singers were refugees and every one of them had been personally hit by the tragedies of the war, but their voices rolled out, powerful, full-throated, exultant. This is the people whom our generals had to hold back in battle, they wanted to charge forward no matter what the casualties; this is the people who, facing an invasion from Japan back in the sixteenth century, promptly invented the first ironclad war vessel in history, shaped like a tortoise with a fierce dragon's head, and then rowed it out in Pusan Bay and sank the Japanese Navy.

Korea's former conquerors, the Japanese, call the Koreans "lazy, lawless, and dirty." Lazy, no; there is no such word in this cold climate and poor country. If you loaf, you freeze.

Lawless, yes and no; this people have had no training in social responsibilities and were forced to be a nation of guerrillas for the half century of Japanese occupation, and they do not pay much attention to a law unless there is power behind it. In Tokyo, you are told half the crimes of the city are the work of Korean refugees. You are impressed until you suggest going to a "number one hancho" to count up the Korean names on the police blotter; then the subject is dropped.

Dirty, yes; who can be clean in a country where hot water or soap are luxuries for the few wealthy people. Like their fellow Asians, Koreans are dirty only when they are too poor to afford soap and water; only on the Indian subcontinent do you see people who seem to prefer to remain dirty.

It is typical of the stubborn national pride of the Koreans that even in their filthy and poverty-stricken cities they wear their national costume. Old men move slowly along, dressed from head to foot in their ceremonial clothes of white, pulling on long bamboo pipes with amber bowls, their two-tiered horsehair hats tied under their chins. The women wear small wrap-around blouses of white or light-colored silk and widely flaring velvet skirts, which come up to a narrow waistband high under the breasts. On their feet are white socks and flat slippers, like ballet slippers, but coming up only an inch around the foot and slightly turned up in front of the big toe.

These are the costumes they wore back in the forgotten days when the Koreans lived peacefully in their peninsular civilization. Only two dynasties ruled them for fifty decades. Three hundred years before the French scholars thought of it, Korean scholars had compiled an encyclopedia. They had a spinning wheel, movable type, a compass, and observation balloons, before Elizabeth Tudor became Queen of England. They built a suspension bridge three hundred years before Brooklyn thought of it. They have kept scientific records of rainfall since before the American Revolution, and they were one of the first countries in Asia to set up a public education system.

But in modern times the Koreans have been conquered by one people after another. Cursed by geography to be a dagger pointing either at the industrial heart of Manchuria or the teeming islands of Japan, Korea has been whipsawed by the fears or ambitions of her bigger neighbors. "Happy is the country that has no history." The Mongols invaded Korea in the thirteenth century. Three centuries later when a great Japanese Army came to conquer the mainland of Asia, the Koreans stopped that dream of conquest, but their peninsula was overrun, their cities destroyed, and they withdrew from international relations for three centuries to try to rebuild their country by themselves.

But "a shrimp's back is broken in a battle between whales," and at the turn of the century the whales of Japan and Russia fought over Korea and the Japanese won. They seized the wealth and resources of the country and turned the people into peons. Three fourths of the farmers of Korea became sharecroppers, seldom paying less than 50 per cent of their crops to their absentee Japanese landlords; often they paid up to 80 per cent. With no exposure to Western ways, the Koreans remained a typical, backward, Asian peasant society, saddled with debt and using antiquated farming methods, with little social responsibility in the privileged classes, with rice production rising very little between 1900 and 1940 while the population was almost doubled.

The Japanese allowed no more than a third of the Korean children to receive any education. No teaching of Korean history or language was permitted, and there were twice as many police stations as public schools. No skilled jobs were open to Koreans, even locomotive firemen had to be Japanese. No Koreans were allowed in the top administrative echelons of the Japanese Occupation Government. The Koreans fought back as best they could, so hostile to their foreign rulers that the Japanese would allow only one kitchen knife for every three farmers. Until V-J Day, one out of every ten young Koreans became a guerrilla fighter or fled into Manchuria or Siberia.

At the Cairo conference the United States, Britain, and China promised Korea its independence, but in 1945 its leaders returned to a country divided at the 38th parallel, with the minerals, hydroelectric power, and heavy industries of North Korea cut off from the ricelands on the other side of the parallel. But the South Koreans went to work with what they had: "To make mountains you must carry every load of earth." In spite of so few and so inexperienced leaders, in three or four years they almost doubled their educational facilities and on-the-job training; 80 per cent of the children were in schools. The government of this country with the largest percentage of Christians in Asia had broken up the absentee-landlord setup and was distributing land among the farmers. It was making plans for industrial development in South Korea. Then came June 24, 1950, and Korea again became a battlefield.

Today it would seem that the best this people can hope for is the limited independence they had in 1945. The Communists will not consent to neutralizing the peninsula, setting up a demilitarized zone near the Yalu, withdrawing all foreign troops, and arranging for a single, unified Government of Korea via a plebescite supervised by the United Nations. There being nearly four times as many South Koreans as North Koreans, an anti-Communist government would win in a fair election and we could safely withdraw our troops. It would hardly be to China's and Russia's profit to allow a free anti-Communist government to rule a peninsula that they consider so vital to their own strategic safety.

In the days of land armies and short-range planes Korea was of vital military importance; but, with the development of atomic weapons and intercontinental bombers, with the age of the flying missile coming around the corner of history, Korea becomes of secondary and negative value, to be kept out of your enemies' hands. However a cold war or a cold peace evolves during the next few years, Korea will most probably continue to be a tragic house divided against itself and simmering with hatred, intrigue, and propaganda, two indivisible halves of a country permanently divided, supported and financed by the antithetical powers of Communism and the West.

Today, as both sides push forward to strengthen their spheres of influence on the peninsula, the United States is gaining one powerful advantage, the South Korean Army, which we have built into one of the world's powerful fighting forces. In the early days of the Korean War these troops were a brave but untrained and undependable fighting force; by the war's end they held two thirds of the battle line. We pay 95 per cent of the costs of equipping and training this Army, which we have promised to enlarge to a full twenty divisions.

The maintenance of the Korean Army costs us three quarters of a billion a year. In a period of international tension, it is hard to conceive of money better spent. It creates a more and more powerful force in being in South Korea that will soon be strong enough to repel anything but an all-out invasion. The men in the Army are taken off the streets of Korea and given jobs and education and training, thus decreasing the danger of internal Communist appeals to the desperate and unemployed. As the soldiers become trained, they release American troops to return home. And it is immensely less expensive to pay for a native army than for American troops abroad; twenty Korean soldiers cost considerably less to maintain than one American GI.

In Korea, where we carried forward what we had learned from experiences we had in training the Greek Army, our military men found they could train and equip an Asian Army for a fraction of the cost of a comparable American Army; Asians do not expect the luxuries to which the American GI is accustomed, even in Army training camps. Such radically lower cost figures offer the West a very encouraging opportunity. It offers us at least the practical possibility that if we must, we can afford to raise a sufficient number of divisions along the periphery of China to at least deter Communist expansion.

There is a further gain from American action to flesh up Asian divisions. It would mean we do not have to spread thinner our small supply of soldiers. And it could also mean that Asians would be equipped and prepared to fight for themselves and their countries. In recent years, only the presence of white men in Korea and in Indo-China has kept these countries from being conquered by the Communists. The day no white man is needed on any Asian battlefield, the Communists have lost their best Asian propaganda weapon against the West.

The gradual rise of a group of anti-Communist native armies, well trained and well armed, is one of the emerging forces that might in the long run stabilize Asia even if China remains the enemy of the free world. In the foreseeable future, as the United States can complete their training and furnish them modern armaments, the combined armies of the South Koreans and the Chinese Nationalists on Formosa can become in their own right a strong deterrent to Chinese expansionism. Add to that the eventual rearmament of Japan and Pakistan, then also add the emerging forces of the Philippines and Thailand. You begin to have strength which, if united, could make Chinese aggression a costly operation. Such a defense alliance will have to come slowly and the United States will have to pay billions upon billions to create and sustain it. Whether it is needed, whether we can avoid these costs does not depend on us; it is dictated by what happens in China: how firmly the Communists can hold the government and how thoroughly they remain the ally of Russia.

Given the productive power of the American industrial machine, the arming of free Asia is not an insupportable burden. But this is not the end of our responsibility. There is still a more arduous assignment: the nurturing of modern, national, workable systems of democracy in these new republics and old kingdoms. It is easy to take a peasant of Asia and train him to march and shoot a gun; it is quite another order of difficulty to wed the ballot box and the Bill of Rights to ancient agrarian systems based on little intercommunication and absolute monarchies.

One man has held postwar Korea together and given it cohesion and unity, the aged ex-schoolmaster, President Syngman Rhee, who is more of a figure of controversy to Americans than any other Asian but Chiang Kai-shek. Irrespective of the arguments over his intentions and methods, irrespective of whether or not he has used strong-arm methods to preserve his power, the fact remains that there is no other top-ranking national figure in Korea.

He is a small, slight, quietly moving old man, with wrinkled skin but a very alert eye. His hands are gnarled, not only from age but from the jailers of the last Emperor of Korea. Even in his early youth, before the Japanese conquest, Rhee was fighting against tyranny at home. Captured by the Emperor's police, his fingers were spliced between wooden sticks and the bones twisted out of shape as a means of persuading him to reasonableness.

With the conquest of his country by the Japanese, he fled abroad to beg President Theodore Roosevelt in vain to grant his country independence in the Treaty of Portsmouth. For the next forty years he fought and worked in exile for an independent Korea, which no man could have believed would ever arrive. Having fought against the Japanese so long, having watched them wreck his country for so many years, having been smuggled out of their country in a coffin with a corpse on each side of him, Rhee is no friend of the Japanese. Next to their hatred of communism, all the leaders of South Korea hate most and fear most the renaissance of Japanese power in the North Pacific.

Every attempt of the Americans to rebuild the Japanese economy is viewed by the Koreans at least as antagonistically as France does the revival of German power in Europe. Many American officials find the Koreans a most difficult and unreasonable people with which to deal. Certainly, from Rhee down, the Koreans are intractable on Japanese questions. Although maintaining a Korean embassy in Tokyo, they have permitted no Japanese mission in Seoul. And many Koreans are convinced the United States favors Japan. It still rankles that we ran the Korean War from American Army headquarters in Tokyo, and it is impossible to convince them that during the Korean War it would have been infeasible to shift the complicated machinery of command and supply operations over to hard-pressed, under-supplied Korea.

Korean-Japanese hostility will not lessen. Korea is using American naval units, which have been turned over to her, to fire on Japanese fishing boats that come within sixty miles of her coast. If we give Japan naval units to strengthen her defenses against China and Russia, she will also use them to strike back at the Korean ships. Already Japan looks suspiciously at our military aid to Korea. As we finance the Japanese rearmament, Korean hostility toward us as the friend and ally of her old enemy will add more intensity to Korea's patriotic and single-minded national intransigence. When and if the United States ever weaves together an all-Asian defense force, the greatest headache of its supreme commander will be to persuade Korean and Japanese units to fight side by side instead of face to face.

It is an impossible assignment for American diplomacy to eliminate this mutual hostility; the best we can do is alleviate it where we can and scrupulously remain unprejudiced and impartial between their conflicting claims. Every cent of Korean reconstruction funds the United States spends in Japan to buy factory products for Korea will be bitterly resented by Koreans; they want the money expended directly in Korea even if it means building new factories there. Yet we have only so much money to spare; some of it can work twice by buying goods in Japan for Korea and thus shoring up the islands' economy as well as rebuilding the peninsula, and some of it will purchase needed materials far more cheaply in Japan than anywhere else.

President Rhee received me in his combined cabinet room, reception room, and living room. It had a long table in the middle, an oil stove on a box of sand at one end. Over the unused fireplace—wood being too expensive to waste for heat—was a Korean scroll, a symbolical painting on silk of the Korean peninsula. What the eagle is to Americans, the tiger is to the Koreans; the wildcat is their symbol for the Japanese and one of their favorite proverbs runs: "Wildcats will be self-important where there are no tigers." In Rhee's painting, the

Korean peninsula had been turned into a fierce old tiger clawing at its enemies, its hind claws pushing away Japan, its spread out front paws challenging Manchuria and Siberia.

While I was waiting for the President, a small woman with hazel eyes and a serene face came quietly into the room: Madame Rhee. Not the least of the unusual things about Rhee is his wife, Francesca Maria Barbara Donner Rhee. A Viennese by birth, she has been married to Rhee for twenty-five years. Because so few trained people are available, she works as his personal secretary. Some people say she is the power behind the throne; meeting her, you do not feel this. She has a selfless devotion to him and to the cause of Korea. She insists on staying in the background and refuses to make public appearances.

In the long years of exile from Korea she had gradually collected paintings, furniture, and books, and when a free Korea was established, she brought them to Seoul with her to the first permanent home she had known in twenty-five years of wandering.

It was permanent for less than five years. The first North Korean bombing of Seoul destroyed everything the Rhees owned. When I asked her if she missed these things: "I kept seeing how beautiful they would have looked on the bare walls of any house we lived in, but now I don't want them back—principles are more beautiful."

The night before my appointment with the President, the Korean Office of Information had insisted I submit written questions for my interview. Madame Rhee scolded me because the questions had arrived so late her husband had spent much of the night working on answers. Then, hearing him coming, she slipped quietly out of the room. He came in with a sheaf of answers in his own handwriting, underlined and worked over. After we had read his material, he asked me if I thought what he had written made the position of Korea clear. When I said no: "Then we will start over." He tore his manuscript in half and threw it in the wastebasket. Many Japanese and many enemies of Rhee in Korea picture him as an egotistical frozen-minded old man, verging on senility. Yet, thinking only of the use my broadcast with him might be to his country, he was willing to discard all the words he had so painstakingly written out.

During our broadcast I asked the President what he thought about freedom. Speaking without a script, in a language not his own, he answered:

"Whenever you have a sufficient of something, Mr. Cooke, you do not feel the need of it. For instance, a watch, you take it for granted. You lose it, and then you miss it. Koreans lost their liberty forty years ago. Then they turned around and thought, we cannot live without liberty, our lives are not ours. So when our country is reborn, we say we won't let go of freedom again. That's why when the Communists came down and camped in Seoul we stood up to say let them come and kill us all. Everybody who's had the bitter experience of losing freedom knows its value. That's what binds us together through this unbearable suffering and deprivation."

Freedom to Koreans, with such a different background from Americans, cannot possibly mean exactly the same things it does to us. Freedom from a conqueror they must have, but freedom from outside control does not necessarily mean a burning desire to bestow complete internal political freedom upon every Korean. One of the things Americans are going to have to accept about other parts of the world is that because a people is passionate for freedom, it does not follow that theirs will be a model and orderly democracy with the protection of individual rights we in the West have learned to include.

Korea's internal political situation is confused and fiercely partisan. Measured by Western standards its democracy is a limited one. In the old days when most of the governing was done on a local level by the village elders, national consciousness was very limited. Then forty years of Japanese rule liquidated even the local self-government. The five years of postwar freedom brought interminable wrangling among the Korean political leaders who had been exiles for forty years. They had had no chance to learn to rule and they were fiercely divided by the irreconcilable ethics and politics of the countries in which they had spent their exile, China or Russia or the United States. And the Korean War's three years of bitter fighting against conquest by force and infiltration, plus the coincidental terrorism and bribery of Communist agents in South Korea, have given the leaders little more chance to acquire political skills. As they put it: "Thread must go where needle takes it."

The result is that Korean democracy has been rough, tough and full of violence. Acts of intimidation, bully boys, and youth corps have been used by every political faction on the peninsula. The days just prior to an election in Korea are not a time for political leaders to go about unescorted. As in most new republics, squabbling and often corrupt politicians make up much of the national assembly. Power here, as everywhere else in the world but in the Western democracies, lies in the hands of the few who can apply force: in Korea, as in most of the rest of Asia, this can only mean the Army, the national police, or the President or Prime Minister, as the case may be.

In a new democracy like that of the Republic of Korea, the police are far more powerful than in the Western democracies. They are the law-enforcement agency, the public health department, the forest rangers, and often the county agricultural agents. They furnish the postal services and control the wire as well as the road communications; all these function while protecting the villages from Communist guerrillas or infiltraters. No wonder that in today's Korea control of the police now rests in a three-man commission personally responsible to the President. The only other power group that can balance out the police is the Army. It could thwart any attempted police dictatorship and its leaders having been hand-picked and trained by the United States, its weight is likely to be thrown behind law and fair elections.

The third force today and tomorrow in Korea is that of the President. As long as Rhee is alive and in office, that force will be decisive. Ever since he returned to his country as the protégé of the American Army in 1945, Rhee has been the real boss of Korea. More than once his forces have arrested candidates on election eves or forced them to hurry to an American hospital for protection. He has declared martial law and used the police against national assemblymen when he believed they were not heeding the wishes of the people. But this does not make him a fascist. Political actions must be judged in the political context in which they take place; without such actions, Rhee would not have been able to ride the confused and often corrupt whirlwind of Korean politics. Marquis of Queensberry rules come later in new democracies.

Rhee has also shrewdly practiced the art of most political leaders, to make certain no other figure rises to equal prominence. As one waxes in Korea, in due time Rhee reduces his prestige. Lee Bum Suk for years was Rhee's closest associate and finally tried to become Vice-President. Lee Bum Suk's principal strength coming from his youth corps, Rhee first amalgamated it into his own group and next abolished all such corps in favor of a Home Guard, which reports to the Minister of Defense whom Rhee appoints. General Paik Sun Yup, whom most Koreans believe "is a good man and a lucky man," was the American-supported Commander in Chief of the Korean Army; Rhee in due time shifted him to a field command; rotating generals makes good military sense and it also prevents one man from becoming too famous.

Cho Bong Am was Vice-Chairman of the Korean National Assembly and a leader of the Democratic Nationalist Party, the largest opposition party to Rhee's Liberals. In the 1952 presidential elections, Cho Bong Am received 770,000 votes; in the 1954 Assembly elections, he could not find 101 Koreans to sign a petition for his candidacy. With the Democratic Nationalists claiming coercion was used against them and the government insisting that the elections were entirely honest, a new Assembly was elected in which the Liberal Party has a two-to-one majority.

The final result of President Rhee's use of power is that, through the turbulent years of Korean political violence and war, he has maintained a continuity of leadership and unity invaluable in the entire free world. Moreover, most Koreans, even when they are political opponents of Syngman Rhee, will tell you that in any popular election held in Korea Rhee would win by a large majority.

In our future relationships with the Republic of Korea, as with other new nations in Asia, we must spend less time condemning the flaws in their democracies and more time appreciating how far they have been able to progress. We Americans are so used to democracy we assume that such a political order is natural to man, that the minute he is allowed to follow his instincts, man immediately creates the immensely intricate pattern of mutual co-operation and extended unselfishness we call democracy. But few people in Asia have had a chance to develop a sense of close human relationships with other people who are not their own blood relations. Our Western conviction that we are, in the widest social sense, our brothers' keepers, has shown us how to expand our sense of family responsibility out to the wider spheres of community and national responsibility. This is where we go most wrong politically in dealing with new Asia. When we get holier than thou and condemn these peoples for working out an order less good than we want. It may well still be the best order they can understand and achieve now. It will be a long time before all Asians can learn to function together for the enrichment of the individual instead of the unit, be it family as in Korea, the state as in Japan, or the proletariat as in communism.

Within the United States we have developed a system that, with all its errors and weaknesses, and with all our abuses of it, remains a system of great political beneficence. We hope we know better than to abandon it for any leader, no matter how wonderful he might seem in a moment of crisis. But many of the new republics of the world have never known such a system. They have always been told what to do, by sultans or emperors or foreign conquerors. It is childish for American idealists with no knowledge of Asia to expect the United States to be able to take civilizations that for a thousand years have combined agrarian family systems with autocratic central governments and turn them overnight into twentieth-century republics.

The Communists know these facts of political life. In each country they search out and develop native leaders with the ability to rule people and to lead them to communism. Whether we like it or not, we too had better recognize that varying degrees of force, even some degree of personal dictatorship, may be an ingredient in the first stages of democracy. In Asia, the forms of democracy do not lead necessarily to the content of democracy. It may well take a leader to guide an inexperienced people to its full freedom.

Of course, wherever they exist, governments under law and with all the checks and balances of democracy, must be supported by the United States, otherwise we undermine our own future. But where there is no choice, where they do not exist, where complete democracy has not yet been realized, the United States must still help by searching out the best possible elements in such governments and backing them with American influence. Only after that, gradually and patiently, may we be able to help other peoples realize fuller political democracy in their countries.

In the eyes of Korea's leaders and its people, as well as in the eyes of Asia, Korea is still America's ally and our responsibility. We cannot determine the fate of Japan, although we may be able to influence it; but the fate of Korea is up to us, militarily, economically, and politically. If we can gradually accomplish in Korea what we have done in the Philippines, we shall have two enthusiastic working democracies in Asia, both of them our friends, both believing in the same way of life we do. Such allies are our only insurance in tomorrow's unforeseeable world.

And any American feeling complacently superior about all this might remember that the present democratic goal of a Republic of Korea is our creation. Syngman Rhee spent most of his exile in the United States and his government was brought into being by the American Army. We might ask ourselves why, in the ten years we have been the principal supporter of Korea, more has not been done to teach and lead Koreans to more political democracy and better administration of it.

Military considerations had to come first, but out of the billions spent in Korea, surely a few more thousands could have been devoted to the mechanisms and the trainings of personnel for self-government: "You Americans told us we were too stupid to learn to do anything for ourselves. But when you had to have us, you trained us to be good soldiers and now you say we fight well. How could we have known how to fight your way before you showed us? Now you complain about our poor government and you don't believe we are capable of doing better."

During the Korean War American military missions of every sort, from communications and training to psychological warfare, provided the military with the most elaborate of materials, but very little was made available to the civilian government of Korea. We picture ourselves as a great and peace-loving democracy with skills in the arts of peace; much of Asia sees us as a great military power: "That is what really matters to you and there is where you spend the money and take the pains."

UNSINKABLE AIRCRAFT CARRIER:

Formosa

The immense dissimilarities of the nations of Asia are high-lighted once again by the contradiction between two countries both conquered by the Japanese for approximately the same length of time: the wretched people of the peninsula of Korea and the lucky people on the island of Formosa. Never trampled down by the Japanese or by the Chinese Nationalists, who fled to Formosa when China fell to the Communists, the Formosans now enjoy almost unlimited American aid and almost the highest living standard in Asia.

The island of Formosa, named Beautiful Island by the Portuguese, and Taiwan, Terraced Bay, by the Chinese, lies in a strategic spot in the western Pacific. To the south, the Philippine Islands are less than 250 miles away, about half an hour's flight by fast bomber. To the north, two hours' flying time would put the great American air installations at Okinawa under a plane's bomb sights, and another two hours' flight would take the bomb bays over the main cities of North China or Japan or South Korea. Most important of all, directly to the west of Formosa, a few minutes' flight by jet planes or a few hours by ship, lies the weak and exposed bulge of Central China.

On Formosa sits the exiled government of the Chinese Nationalists, hated and feared by the Chinese Communists, ignored and disliked by Asian neutrals like India and Indonesia, recognized and supported by Korea and the Philippines and Thailand. Most important of all, the Nationalists are the present ward, friend, and military ally of the United States against Red China. When Free China collapsed, some two million mainland Chinese, including Chiang Kai-shek, his government, and an army of about half a million and some five thousand veterans of the Chinese Air Force, fled to Taiwan.

Also on the island are nearly seven million more Chinese, the Formosans or Taiwanese, a people of Chinese extraction ruled by China until the island was taken over by the Japanese in 1895. The Nationalists yearn for the day they can reconquer the mainland of China. The Taiwanese yearn for the day the load of the Nationalists will be off their economic backs, but it is not established how willing they would be to fight on the mainland to achieve that end.

Formosa's importance to the United States is measured by juxtaposing two opposing facts, one unfavorable and the other favorable. Taking the negative first, even after adding the Taiwanese to Chiang's Nationalists, there are only half as many people on Formosa as in the Philippines or Burma or Thailand or South Korea; there are only one eighth as many as on the Japanese islands and only one thirty-seventh as many as in India. Putting the man-power weakness still more pessimistically, there is only one Chinese on Formosa for every fifty on the mainland.

On the other side of the equation, Formosa is the base of the government-in-exile of Free China, the only rallying point in the world for the millions of mainland Chinese who want to throw off the Communist shackles. Also involved here are about thirteen million Overseas Chinese who have emigrated to Hong Kong, the Philippines, and Southeast Asia. These Overseas Chinese are not only greater in number than all the Chinese on Taiwan, they are also the financial moguls of Southeast Asia. If they, scattered and divided as they are both politically and geographically, should ever throw their full weight behind Formosa, it would be a real nightmare for the Chinese Communists.

For these reasons, the United States is building up the military power-in-being of the Chinese Nationalists as a threat to our present enemy, Red China, and we are raising the standard of living of the island as an example of the benefits the starving millions of mainland China might get for themselves if they abandoned the Communists, and as a plea for the Overseas Chinese to support Free China.

Formosa is about two hundred and twenty-five miles long and eighty miles wide, a rich, fertile, and fully developed island. Three quarters of it is mountainous and every acre of arable land is used. The south is dry, but in the north the island gets up to two hundred inches of rain a year. Its temperature soars to 130 degrees in summer, but in winter it is close to freezing. The western side of the island is like a slightly green San Fernando Valley, but over on the east it is a damper Puerto Rico, with tall fern trees. Geology adds another confusion; the island lies on a main earth fault and is shaken by a thousand earthquakes a year.

Around the cities are flat plains and rice fields dotted with rice-straw piles in a characteristic Formosan pattern. The straw, stacked in piles like haystacks, rises to twisted, round tops that look like mandarin buttons. Out in the country the rice paddies start far up on the folded mountainsides and terrace down to the plains in neat, bright green cascades. Along the roads are eucalyptus trees and neat cemented ditches for irrigation or to drain off the rains. The Taiwanese, busy but not driving themselves, friendly but reserved, stalwart and healthy, pedal along the roads on bicycles or stroll along beside their water buffaloes, the work horses of Asia.

In every country from Korea to India you see these lumbering ungainly water buffaloes, or carabaos, with thick wrinkled hides, long tails ending in a tuft of coarse hair, and long curved horns. When they get the chance, they submerge themselves in any pond to get away from the sun, letting just their eyes and the tips of their horns and noses show above the water. In contrast to the faster-moving, jittery horse of the West, the water buffalo, always mild, patient, and affectionate, plods along no faster than a man can drag his feet. The Asians, being 90 per cent farmers, have all through the centuries moved at the tempo of their slowly changing seasons and their slowly moving water buffaloes. They have never learned to move any faster. There would be no point to it; carabaos would not plow faster, rice would not ripen faster, seasons would not change faster.

If a Taiwanese leads his buffalo any distance along a cement highway to a new pasture, he binds rough straw sandals over the carabao's feet to protect its tender hoofs. The peasants are usually barefoot, wearing a cone-shaped bamboo straw hat tied under the chin, faded blue coolie jacket, shorts, and neatly folded umbrella tied over the shoulder.

The Japanese conquered Taiwan three years before the United States took possession of the Philippines, and in the first half of the twentieth century they turned it into a model colony. They planned the island as the capital of the great empire they were going to build in the Pacific. To keep the Taiwanese contented, they left them their rich fertile lands and built for them one of the best road systems in Asia. They constructed large hydroelectric installations, brought electric light to the peasants' homes, and vastly increased the rice yield.

And the Japanese did all this without pouring much money into the island; quite a comparison with the Philippines where, after all our help and money, the Filipinos are still trying to balance their budgets and straighten out their land problems. Some people say the difference is due to American errors in the Philippines: "You Americans taught us how to spend, but not how to earn." Others say it was because the Formosan birth rate was so much lower than in the Philippines where there are always more people and more hungry little mouths.

Perhaps climate is the more significant factor. You find the same qualities of industriousness and energy among the Formosans as in the northern climates of Korea and Japan. Formosa is as hot as the Philippines in summer but quite chilly in winter. Perhaps if you wish to have Western energy and concern for order, a cool climate is necessary to push people on; certainly none of the peoples of hot Southeast Asia have this sort of drive. But if climate should turn out to be a strong determinant of national characteristics, Americans had better begin to take it more into account and change their expectations and timetables of help as we go south in Asia.

Another thing that gives Formosa such a different appearance from the Philippines or Korea or Japan is its clean, uncrowded villages and houses. There are many brick and cement plants on northern Formosa, and so instead of the typical flimsy wood and bamboo structures of most Asian villages, the Taiwanese houses are of cement and brick with an open wall facing the street, with folding wooden doors to close across it at night.

When you come into Taipei, the capital of Formosa, it looks the way you would expect a Japanese city to look; neat and orderly, it is by all odds the cleanest capital in Asia, far cleaner than New York or Paris or Rome. The highways and city streets are broad, open, spacious. There is little begging, and, day or night, it is perfectly safe to wander about.

Bicycle rickshas are the taxis of Taipei, usually with canvas flaps over the passenger's seat because it rains so much. As the hoof-like clatter of wooden clogs is associated with Tokyo, so the typical sound of Taipei is a soft musical jingle of bicycle bells floating through the misty rain.

The houses and stores are two or three stories high, of stone or brick. As in the Philippines, the second floor is built out over the sidewalk, flush to the street, and part of the ground floor thus becomes a sidewalk arcade to keep out the sun or rain. In the arcades, vendors with movable stands sell everything from fruit to fountain pens. As in the Philippines, a wild mixture of East and West and a mélange of merchandise in the stores. A box of Kotex on a pile of Chinese brocades. A chemist's shop with old Chinese blue-and-yellow plates, one plate piled with Chinese drugs and starfish-like brown roots, on the next a neat box of Vitamin B Complex and a bottle of aureomycin. A bookstore with a row of Chinese classics, leaning against them a picture book, *The Beauties of Two Worlds,* featuring a Reubens blonde stretching out in a Bikini bathing suit.

You miss the color and the individuality of the national costumes of Korea. Most of the Chinese wear Western dress, not because it is cheaper or more practical, but because the West has become associated with importance and power. Whether it is Americans and Chinese eating together in a restaurant, or sitting together in joint meetings of one of the American commissions in Taipei, or working together on rural reconstruction somewhere out on the island, the Chinese Nationalists have made common cause for common ends with the Americans and have learned to function together with Westerners more closely than any oriental people has ever done.

Since it is vital both for the United States and for the Nationalists to create more fertile fields and a more prosperous and healthy Taiwan, together we have formed a Joint Commission on Rural Reconstruction, the JCRR, to raise living standards on this island, one sixth the size of Minnesota, containing far less arable land and supporting three times its population.

The JCRR has set up over three hundred health centers on Taiwan. For the initial stage of each center, the JCRR draws up the plans, the Chinese supply money from the Formosa budget, the Taiwanese select the location and provide volunteer trainees, and the United States donates the medical supplies. In the second stage the local communities take over part of the burden of support. Eventually they pay the whole bill.

These health centers have excellent supplies of drugs, good laboratories, and hospital equipment. There were more equipment and drugs in one room of one of these health centers than had been available for all the orphans of Pusan. The Korean civilians were not of direct military value, therefore we could leave orphans without medicines; but if the Taiwanese are not kept healthy and moderately contented, they would not produce the food for the Chinese Nationalist

Army on Formosa. Then the United States would have to spend a great deal more money sending food to Formosa, or else there would be too little food to keep the Chinese soldiers strong and they would cease to be a threat to the Chinese Communists. If only the orphans of Pusan could have fired guns.

The Chinese and the Americans on the Joint Commission on Rural Reconstruction also co-operate in every sort of agricultural improvement. In vocational schools, Chinese children start with stories like "The Fox and the Grapes" and soon they can read our Department of Agriculture pamphlets. American 4-H Club experts teach 4-H Club procedures to the Chinese children who learn them with gusto. I saw one classroom with a group of dovecotes nailed up over the doorway. The cotes were made from American beer cases, hammered and sawed with American tools, painted white with American brushes and paint; the children had nailed together the beer-case dovecotes to form big wooden letters spelling out "4-H Club."

The Chinese household gods still stand in the place of honor in the farmers' houses, but across the room from the altar there will be a large American poster pasted on the whitewashed mud wall, showing how to plant and fertilize rice. Out in the fields the farmers plant new strains of rice seeds imported from the United States. When the rice is harvested, it is taken to the Taiwanese Farmers' Association Co-operative, originally built from American plans with American help and now underwritten by Chinese and Taiwanese.

The Government of Formosa itself is tackling the usual Asian headache of land ownership. It is limiting private ownership of land to about seven acres and it is selling public lands to the peasants. It buys the land from the landlords with bonds payable in farm products or with shares in the state-owned corporations seized from the Japanese. The peasants in turn borrow from the government to buy their land and repay the loan over ten years, again in farm produce.

The Chinese are proud that the top rent any landlord can now get from a farmer is 37 per cent. It used to be 60 or 70 per cent. But to find out what the Taiwanese peasant pays in taxes to Chiang's government is another matter. The Nationalists are bland and vague; it seems there are household taxes and defense taxes and police taxes and many other taxes, varying according to the farm, peasant, and village; they "guess a Taiwanese tenant farmer does not pay more than 7 per cent taxes."

Politically the government on Formosa is a *de facto* dictatorship with the trappings of a democracy. Since ideology is the only difference between the two million Nationalists and their countrymen who stayed in China to become Communists, the problem of detecting Communist spies is difficult. The rulers of Taiwan do not allow individual rights to limit the freedom of action of the secret police in their search for suspected spies. The Kuomintang, the single party that rules the Chinese Nationalists, has created a Peace Preservation Corps, the *Pao An Szu Ling Pu*. In theory it reports to the provisional government of Formosa, but in fact it is kept under the sharp and suspicious eye of Generalissimo Chiang Kai-shek. The Pao An Szu Ling Pu has the responsibility of discovering anyone who is not in favor of preserving peace, that is to say anybody who has the slightest Communist leanings, anyone who has the slightest doubt of the wisdom of the decisions of Chiang and the ruling clique. The Nationalists believe devoutly that they will be the saviors of China and, therefore, the only people who would not want to support them are obviously enemies of China who do not wish to rescue it from communism.

While the Peace Preservation Corps goes about its business among civilians, there is a separate secret police to investigate treason and subversion in the Armed Forces, the Political Department of the Army. Chiang, like any other dictator, is well aware that the one group he must be able to depend on is the Army. In China after V-J Day, American pressure forced him to abolish the Political Department and he is still convinced that a main reason the Communists were able to take over in China was the absence of a secret police to insure the loyalty of the army officers.

Therefore, Chiang is going to take no chances a second time; the reconstituted and all-feared Political Department is bossed by his eldest son, Chiang Ching-kuo. When the first American military mission arrived on Formosa, it found 25 per cent of the training time of Chinese soldiers was allotted to political indoctrination. Strong American pressure cut this in half, but Chiang still thinks it was an unwise move and he will tolerate no more interference with his police.

Both the Political Department and the Peace Preservation Corps, after due investigation, and torture if necessary, turn their cases over to the Military Prosecutor's Office. After secret trials, the sentences go up to the Generalissimo himself for a final okay and thus Chiang keeps the final power in his own hands.

There is a strong parallel in organization between the Kuomintang

Party and the Communist parties of China and Russia; each rules a theoretically democratic state based on free elections, but behind each is a one-party dictatorship backed by secret police; Formosa bans *1984*: "It is not a constructive book"; and it also bans *Brain-washing in Red China,* the book that tells in detail how the Communists established thought controls over the mainland Chinese. And every month, a number of Chinese are executed as Communists. No one outside of the small group who rule the island can find out what these men were accused of or how it was proved they were guilty.

However, the official American observers on Formosa insist that there is immensely more humanity and give-and-take here than under a Communist system. Also, it is very easy for an American living thousands of miles away from violence and death to repudiate such secret-police measures, but, as was the case in Korea, Formosa is a country at war, with Communist subversives seeking to overthrow the government and assassinate its leaders.

The personal dictatorship of Chiang and the reactionary Kuomintang clique is quite another thing. It repels the Overseas Chinese and it weakens the Nationalists' cause throughout Asia. The Overseas Chinese have always been deeply suspicious of the Kuomintang and the Chiang clique is doing little to change their distrust. Chiang's youngest son, Chiang Wei-kuo, is a Major General formerly in command of the Chinese National Armored Force; his eldest, Chiang Ching-kuo, is undoubtedly the second most powerful man on the island.

With his political control of the Army plus his own forcefulness, Chiang Ching-kuo is a good candidate eventually to succeed his father as dictator, probably not coming into the spotlight as President but running things from behind the scenes. His deputy is the actual head of the dreaded Political Department of the Army; his supporters control about three quarters of the Central Executive Committee of the Kuomintang; and he is still head of the Youth Corps, another of the key power points in any dictatorship. Chiang Ching-kuo probably knows more about Russia and Communists than any other man on the island for he is married to a Russian and he was sent by Chiang to spend some years in Moscow studying the Russian methods of dictatorship. He is reputed not to be especially entranced with the usefulness of a democratic system for Formosa or China.

Until recently, at the other end of the political spectrum, a group of American-educated liberal Nationalists, who were convinced the old-type, one-party rule must yield to a modern and at least semi-democratic government, rallied around the leadership of the West's best friend on the island, K. C. Wu. Heavy-set, bland, with a ready wit and a quick smile, a graduate of Grinnell College, with a PhD from Princeton, Wu was the only man on Formosa who dared criticize the regime. Mayor of Chungking and Shanghai, Vice-Minister of Foreign Affairs, Minister of Information, and a loyal Chiang man, he had been sent to Formosa by the Generalissimo long before the Chinese mainland fell. Chiang saw the disaster coming, and sent generals, gold, and administrators to Formosa to build up a place for his government-in-exile.

Wu was the first Governor of Formosa; as such, he was identified with reform by the Taiwanese and he became their favorite Chinese. In 1950 he began democratization in the Taiwanese villages, and in the city and district councils, until three quarters of the municipal councilors, magistrates, and mayors were Taiwanese. Wu and his supporters had two compelling reasons why this turnover of power to the islanders should go on.

In the first place, they knew that before the Nationalists could count on the support of the Overseas Chinese and those living on the mainland, the Kuomintang would have to prove it could bring freedom as well as a higher standard of living. The strength of the Army was also involved. There are less than half a million Nationalist troops. For replacements and enlargements they must be augmented with Taiwanese. Out of a population of nine million, Wu estimated nearly a million more soldiers could be found if the Taiwanese felt it was their government and their fight.

Unfortunately for Formosa and for its principal supporter, the United States, Wu has been stripped of all his offices. He has been expelled from the Kuomintang and is in voluntary exile in the United States while the party machinery in the last outpost of Free China tries to turn the islanders against him. In a recent intelligence test given by Chiang Ching-kuo's Youth Corps to the students of Formosa, one question ran: "Who is the real traitor to China—Mao Tse-tung, Li Tsung-jen, or K. C. Wu?" Li was the former Vice-President of China who sought to appease the Communists. The correct answer, according to the Youth Corps, was "K. C. Wu."

In the February 1954 elections, held by a species of rump assembly, but the only one that could be assembled while the mainland is in the hands of the Communists, the party machine worked smoothly. The anti-Chiang former Vice-President, Li Tsung-jen, was ousted from his position, Chiang Kai-shek was re-elected as President for another six-year term, and Premier Chen Cheng, a moderate but a faithful follower of Chiang who has always gone along with the reactionaries, was selected as the new Vice-President. Like Chiang, Chen was born in Chekiang and studied with him at Paoting Military Academy and still speaks no English. He is a former Chief of Staff and Minister of War who prepared Formosa for the Nationalists. He is also the man who introduced land reform on the island. Chen would take over Chiang's office if he died; it is anybody's guess whether he would be able to, or would dare try to exercise the Generalissimo's powers.

Formosa goes on trying to rally the Overseas Chinese to its cause with impressive statements and anti-Communist National Salvation Conferences. But Wu in exile is a mute refutation of Formosa's claims to truly democratic government. The Overseas Chinese are not flaming liberals, but many of them think they still see on the island the old familiar pattern of Kuomintang clique rule for its own aggrandizement instead of for the good of China. America's Asian friends, as well as the Asian neutrals, may well ask if this is the kind of government we would be prepared to support on the mainland.

We claim to the world that we believe in democracy and freedom, but we have not clearly proved this on Formosa. Behind the façade of diplomatic phraseology, Formosa is the ward of the United States and the KMT has no future if we withdraw our support. With all our power, our friends have not seen us put real pressure on Chiang to permit his people political freedom. If it takes a secret police and a military dictatorship to maintain his government on an island where two million loyal Nationalists live, the government would seem to have little chance of regaining the support of the vast subcontinent of China. And as long as we tacitly, by virtue of our partnership with the Nationalists, condone this totalitarian government, we are going to find it hard to convince Asians that Western democracy guarantees the political freedoms communism scorns.

We can effect considerable political changes on Formosa if we are determined to, but we will not be able to do it all at once because the Nationalists know that we need them as an ally against our common enemy, Red China. And reactionary or liberal, it is to our advantage to go on strengthening the Nationalists and their army on Formosa.

All year round this Army trains and maneuvers up on the high plateaus of Taiwan, and theirs could not be a more austere life. They build their hutlike barracks of clay plastered on a bamboo frame, whitewashed, and thatched with rice straw. Dirt pounded hard by the men's feet makes the floor, and the windows are openings without glass. Inside each barrack are two long wooden platforms, between them room for one man to walk. The soldiers sleep side by side on these platforms, with their feet toward the middle of the room. Each soldier has a thin straw mat two feet wide, his bed. When I asked the commander what happens when a man wants to turn over, he said, without a trace of humor, "He doesn't."

Each soldier is issued a helmet, a gun, a thin comforter, a rice-husk blanket, a thin cotton uniform, some heavy underwear, a cap, puttees, and a pair of sneakers. He gets a minimum diet with barely enough protein. The officers of the Army live exactly as their troops do, wearing the same kind of uniforms, and eating the same kind of food, a startling change from the Army class system of old China.

I went out on a cold wind-swept plain with an officer-candidate squad to watch training maneuvers of three squadrons against a stronger enemy force. If and when these soldiers ever land on the mainland, they will face superior forces and so their training concentrates on showing them how to fight when outnumbered.

Blackboards were set up on a little ridge and an outline of the salient points in the maneuvers, mimeographed in Chinese on rice paper, was distributed to us. With the aid of diagrams on a blackboard, the instructor went through the operation before we saw it unfold on the plain below us: "Never let the enemy know where your main reserve is and never engage him until you have drawn him into your area of maximum fire power."

There was no field-communications equipment available, or sufficient arms, so each of the three squadrons had different colored flags to indicate their units: tanks were yellow, bazookas, green. The machine gunners had bamboo tubes; they beat on them lightly for small arms, hit them heavily for big guns. Once in a while one round of live ammunition was fired, representing fifty rounds. It was strange to be standing in the clear mountain air on a tea plantation on the top of a plateau while peasants and carabaos placidly went about their business below, paying no attention to the deadly play acting that went on as if in another dimension.

The squads in their places, the bugle blew and the flags were raised so we could see the position of every group. Then step by step, with explanations and comments from the instructor at each move, the maneuver unfolded until the outnumbered attackers coaxed the superior force into the center of their area of concentrated fire power. The only time the officer candidates broke their grim discipline was during the final simulated bayoneting of the enemy; then they jumped up and down, threw their caps in the air, and cheered.

That same afternoon the officer candidates went back to their barracks grounds to go over what they had seen, to criticize and suggest changes, and to raise questions. Then the next day, the maneuver would be repeated with slight but fatal alterations so that this time the attacking force would be defeated.

The training group concentrated single-mindedly on its business until the instructor politely invited me to criticize the day's maneuver. The officer candidates, knowing I was anything but a military strategist, assumed impassive looks, eyed me without expression, and waited for my answer. When I hit upon a small error, they were as delighted as children, grinned, pointed at the spot, argued about it among themselves, and laughed at their instructor. What a difference from the way a group of Japanese would have reacted; the Chinese are animated, frankly curious, and when not on their ceremonial best behavior, they show their emotions as frankly as we do.

Ninety-seven per cent of the men in the present Chinese Army on Formosa have come from the mainland; 75 per cent have had actual combat experience. There are also several thousand seasoned pilots in the Nationalist Air Force, who are learning to fly advanced American planes. Incidentally, we Americans have always thought we were so much better at high-speed operations than Asians, but our air force generals have found that Chinese or Koreans, when properly trained, can handle jets as well as Americans.

The Chinese Nationalist Air Force is a good example of the results of the tug of war between Russia and the United States. Up to 1950, Chiang's fliers had about the same number of planes as the Chinese Communists and about as good ones. When the Korean War started, the Russians supplied their Chinese allies with far more modern planes and jets until by 1952 the Communists had a superior Air Force. Now we in turn are giving the Nationalists newer and better planes to keep them ahead of the Chinese Communists. And so on, *ad atom*.

The average Chinese soldier, until he came in direct contact with combat-training teams from the United States, believed that the

American soldier was a playboy. This notion is being thoroughly unsold by MAAG, the American Military Advisory Aid Group on Formosa. American teams live with the Chinese troops; they train and get down in the mud and rain beside them.

It is difficult to teach American standard-operational procedures to Chinese soldiers who have been without knowledge of mechanical technology. MAAG and the Chinese High Command are training them to function together in large combined operations and amphibious landings. As anyone who has been in a modern army knows, this is impossible unless there is a book of rules and everybody follows it. This seems natural to us, but it is not the way the Chinese have fought their wars. The commander in the old mainland setup was usually a feudal-minded war lord. When he was shifted to another division, he took his retinue with him; when he attacked, his corps or division did it his way. Nobody knew what a division would do next in a battle unless he was familiar with the specific methods of the specific general in command. No wonder the trained and regimented Japanese conquered so much of China.

In the Far East today, we have enormous military prestige because we took on the two greatest professional armies in the world, the German and the Japanese, and beat them with a civilian army. Our techniques are admired, taught, studied, and followed all over the East. It may be described as Asian desperation or American imperialism, the result is the same; an incredible shifting of methods of doing things from old folkways to new methods. An irresistible force has been set in motion.

It is amazing the way our techniques can be successfully taken over by a civilization theoretically so different from ours. In Asia, teaching has been by rote, and very dull work. When MAAG arrived, it began teaching Chinese GIs via American methods, to the horror of the more conservative Chinese. The reading of a contour map is very hard to explain in words, and almost impossible to translate into Chinese, but very necessary for Chinese soldiers to understand. Our trainers had the answer; they taught contour markings, as they had back in the United States, with a large drawing of a naked woman on which to plot the locations. The Chinese sparked to it just as fast as the GIs.

What is happening on Formosa seems to prove that, as in so many other areas, the "Old-China hands" did not know what they were pontificating about. On the mainland, China was supposed to be able to digest or spew forth the Chinese Communists; there is no evidence that either is happening. On Formosa, the so-called rigid and resistant-to-change Chinese are adjusting themselves to an entirely foreign set of mechanisms. Some of the credit goes to the flexibility and wisdom of the Chinese and some to the patience and deftness of the Americans. Most of it goes to necessity, not only the Mother of Invention but the ancestral Matriarch of the House of Change. When other peoples in other lands want to change themselves as passionately as the Chinese have here, the immutable East will mutate as rapidly as any American prairie town.

There is one overriding purpose behind everything the Chinese do on Formosa: to get back to the mainland. The Nationalists look across the hundred-mile-wide Formosa Strait to the bulge of South China between Canton and Foochow. The Communists have only two main railroads and highways with which to supply this huge coastal bulge and both of them are north-south supply lines; in the two provinces that lie across from Formosa, Kwangtung and Fukien, there are no main roads or railroads running east-west from the interior to the coast.

It is the ultimate hope of the Nationalists to land somewhere along this bulge, block off a beachhead from the rest of China, and drive inland somewhere above Canton to cut communications between North and South China by slashing the Peiping-Canton railroad. If they could gain this kind of victory, they are convinced anti-Communists from all over China would flock in to reinforce their beachhead. South China has always been a different nation from North China, speaking Cantonese instead of Mandarin, eating rice instead of wheat. The Chinese Communist Government, a North Chinese regime, does not trust the loyalty of the South and is planning no large industrial developments there. If the South Chinese helped them, the Nationalists could then capture Canton, and the days of the Chinese Communist supremacy would be numbered.

Chiang Kai-shek constantly exhorts his men to prepare for an invasion, but he has never committed himself to a specific timetable. His own life and death is a central factor in invasion calculations. The available evidence indicates that the people of China are not anti-Chiang, that the oppression of the Chinese Communists has built up a greater friendliness for him, that the mainland's fear has always been of the Kuomintang and not of Chiang. These things being so, his death would leave the Chinese Nationalists with no leader whom the mainland Chinese know or respect.

From now on, what happens on the island of Formosa, or what happens from the island of Formosa, involves the United States in a complicated Asian gamble. Win, lose, or draw, our future and our safety are directly and very complicatedly involved. But for once in Asia, we can at least partially take the kind of action we choose rather than that which is forced upon us. In Korea, aggression forced American armies to fight on the peninsula. In Indo-China, all along we were faced with the sour choice of losing Southeast Asia or being prepared to step into the breach with American fighting men. On Formosa, neither the Communists nor the Nationalists but the United States decides whether or not there shall be an invasion of the mainland. Chiang's forces are dependent on our aid for military hardware, jet planes, naval support, and even food supplies; if we do not release enough of the right materials from our own arsenals, they have no chance for a successful landing.

Our present military and economic aid runs up toward five hundred million dollars a year and financing an all-out attack would cost us billions more. But, in view of the hostility to us of the Chinese Communists and their alliance with Russia, an all-out attack could, if successful, solve our Asian problems. But once the operation has been put into motion and it is too late to back out, there are three possible outcomes: the Nationalists win, the Nationalists lose, they become involved in a long-drawn-out civil war.

If the Nationalist invasion were sensationally successful, the Chinese Communist Government would be overthrown, Russia would lose her chief ally, and a fresh start would be possible in Asia. A consummation devoutly to be wished, but, according to most experts, distinctly unlikely in the near future. Too many of the younger mainland Chinese are in favor of the Communists; too many of them distrust or hate the Kuomintang. Even among the Free Chinese, many leaders believe that the Chinese Communists cannot be overthrown without a third world war.

The second possibility is that the Nationalists could gain a beachhead but not extend it. Such a limited Chinese success would be a great victory for the United States. A continuing Chinese civil war would have immense repercussions in Asia. The Chinese Communists would lose their freedom of action and their military power to menace Korea and to support the North Vietnam regime or the insurgents in Burma and Laos. Communism would cease to be a military threat in Asia. Therefore, if we could be sure a mainland invasion would have even a limited success and if, a very important if, we could be certain we would not later be forced to send large American land armies into China to prevent a collapse of the anti-Communists, the United States should assign our highest priority to the gamble.

But, while it might not be possible for the Communists quickly to bring their troops into the beachhead, they would unhesitatingly throw in their thousands of jet planes against the threat to their very life. So in its opening stages, the invasion would require an enormous umbrella of air power to be provided by the United States. If the success of the beachhead hovered in the balance because of air power, or anything else, the United States could not afford to withhold whatever additional military help was necessary, including American man power. At first this would probably be extra pilots and aircraft carriers, but later, if necessary, we might be forced to land American troops to prevent a catastrophe. And then we would find ourselves in the middle of a land war on the mainland of Asia against half a billion Chinese.

The third possibility, of course, is that the invasion would fail at the start. This would be a most serious defeat for the United States. We would have to find a new foreign policy in the Pacific and the only peace we could have in Asia would be Communists' peace. Sometimes the wisest decision a nation can make is to make no decision. The greatest strength of the Communists in today's world is that we do not know what they are going to do next or where. Formosa offers the free world a rare opportunity to present the same kind of uncertainty to the Communists.

Conceive of an unsinkable aircraft carrier two hundred and twenty-five miles long and stationed less than ten minutes by jet plane from Philadelphia and Atlanta; fill this aircraft carrier with troops who are the sworn enemies of the United States and arm them with the latest military equipment: this gives an approximate idea of the way the Chinese Communists must regard Formosa. An armed Formosa limits the amount of aggressive action in which the Communists dare involve themselves anywhere in Asia; they would be in a very awkward position fighting simultaneously in Indo-China against the Vietnamese and their allies, in Korea against Rhee's armies, in South China against the Nationalists, not to mention the American Navy and Air Force.

We should exploit our tactical position in the Formosan affair and we should continue to expend millions to increase the threat. It is a sound investment against the military threat of communism. Also, our dollars go farther spent on Asian man power than on our own military.

And whether Americans approve of the politics, the police state, or the past record of the Kuomintang, we must not lose sight of the central point that the Nationalists are an invaluable ally because our objectives parallel each other. The United States must give first priority to allies who want to fight the Communists, who are able to fight the Communists, and who have no choice but to fight the Communists. Every country and every power group follows its own needs, and we cannot expect any country in Asia, or for that matter anywhere else, to back our policies because we want them to. Like the South Koreans, the Chinese Nationalists have nowhere to go except against the Chinese Communists. Their own future and the freedom of their country depend on the defeat of the Chinese Communists. Therefore, unless and until we are able to reach an ironclad agreement with the Chinese Communists, we would be insane not to support South Korea and Formosa.

Supporting the Chinese Nationalists means more than military and economic assistance; it extends into the field of psychological encouragement to them and psychological warfare against the Communists. The Nationalists, although defeated and driven into exile, are the only legitimate standard to which the anti-Communist Chinese can repair and no other is likely to arise within the efficient police state on the mainland. No group of Chinese off Formosa can command the power, the reputation, or the prestige to rival Chiang or his eventual successor. But to hold this position and continue to be a counter to the Communists, the Nationalists need every bit of encouragement and international prestige they can get. And that includes their place in the United Nations and their seat on the Security Council.

But if the tactical value of a free Formosa is apparent to us, its threat must be equally obvious to the shrewd political realists who run Red China. Now that their military strength has been extricated from the wars in Korea and Indo-China, Formosa automatically becomes their prime military target. Unfortunately, most of the other nations of Asia look upon this island as a purely local, Chinese problem; therefore Formosa is the one place in today's Asia where Peiping can safely use force without branding itself in Asian eyes as an aggressor. And so Mao Tse-tung, Premier Chou En-lai, and General

Chu Teh have publicly committed themselves to the speediest possible elimination of the Damocles' sword of the alternate Chinese Government on Formosa.

If the Chinese Communists mean what they say and this island becomes the next storm center in Asia, the United States will have no excuse for not deciding ahead of time where we stand and how far we are willing to go. So far, our defense of Formosa has been painless; we have sailed the Seventh Fleet up and down in Asian waters and we have buttressed Chiang's regime with money, advisers, armaments.

But when the Chinese Politburo has accumulated enough Russian submarines and bombing planes, it can confront us with a terrible predicament and a crucial decision. On the one hand, we can limit our help to matériel, and if that be insufficient, we can let the Chinese Communists eliminate the threat of Formosa. Or, on the other hand, as a consequence of shielding Formosa with American sailors and aviators, we can involve ourselves in a sea and air war with China, which has the largest population in the world.

As is true in so many other situations in Asia, the alternatives which would confront us as the result of an invasion of Formosa are not happy ones. But China, firmly anti-American and pro-Communist, gives us no others. We can only continue to work for some kind of balance of power and some kind of peace in the Pacific with what is available, not with what we would like.

THE CHINESE QUESTION MARK:

Hong Kong, Macao, and the Overseas Chinese

The pivotal center and present enigma of Asia is China. Indisputably, the half billion Chinese who live in or out of Communist China are the most important single group in all Asia. It is impossible today for an American to travel inside mainland China and find out for himself how the Communist regime is working. But around the periphery of the mainland live over twenty million Chinese who know a great deal about what is happening behind the Bamboo Curtain and who are as powerful an ally, either for the Communists or the free world, as any nation in Asia.

In addition to around nine million Taiwanese Chinese and Nationalists on Formosa, there are some ten or eleven million Overseas Chinese living in the islands of the Pacific or in Southeast Asia. And, where the Pearl River rolls down ninety miles from the great Chinese city of Canton to spill its yellow silt past two watchtowers of the West, the rock of British Hong Kong and the peninsula of Portuguese Macao, there are three hundred thousand more Overseas Chinese living in Macao and another two million or more clinging to the territories of Hong Kong and its city, Victoria.

This city, 99 per cent Chinese, yet the largest British city in the Far East, is an anachronism without peer, perched in South Asia. Everything about it is exciting, including the approach by air. Flying in over the ocean, you come upon small and rather pretty islands dotting the sea, with high-fingered hills something like those of northern Maine or a more barren Hawaii. Winding down past their peaks and around a couple of turns, there, spreading out below you, is the harbor of Hong Kong.

Modern apartments perch on improbable hills around the native city. The whites and yellows of the concrete modern buildings give way to dark yellow-gray masses tumbling in tiers down the side of a mountain, something like rice paddies, but they are the squatters' huts of the wretched Chinese refugees. You round another sharp angle, swoop down over a couple of flat apartment-house roofs and land with a precipitous thump on the shortest, trickiest runway in the world. There are a few hundred feet of narrow concrete straight ahead of you, with a mountainside at the end; on one side is a four-lane concrete highway, on the other, the harbor. If the fog has come in or it is dusk, it is too dangerous to land; your pilot turns around and flies back to Bangkok or Okinawa or Manila.

From the airport on the peninsula of Kowloon, a ferry runs across the harbor to the eleven-mile-long island, the rock of Hong Kong. This is the storied East. A Chinese junk lumbers by, her tattered sail billowing out above the ancient grandmother who stands at the tiller. The junk is made of dirty gray wood, its sides streaked with opalescent harbor oil, the elongated tiller a bright Chinese lacquer red where it comes out of the swirling dirty chartreuse water. No men to be seen. Grandma, in coolie rusty black, with a cigarette glued to her lower lip. Mama, with long black pigtails swinging, strains against a huge sculling oar. Two medium-sized children swing from the hoisting sheet as they raise the billowing mainsail, a soft faded ocher patched with beautiful grayed-purple rectangles. Under bamboo-matting awnings, down in the open middle of the junk, a tiny baby lies on its back, kicking its feet.

Just beyond the junk is a small coastal steamer; from its deck, a woman in red silk pajamas waves at the baby. Canopying both boats, the distorted sound from the steamer's loud-speaker: Bing and Dinah crooning "Let's Do It." Past the steamer, a small French gunboat. Further on, a huge American aircraft carrier, sailors at the stern tossing pennies to Chinese boys in tiny sampans. And scattered over the far reaches of the harbor like a handful of colored marbles tossed out on a piece of glass, every size, shape, and color of Chinese fishing junks.

Victoria, the city of Hong Kong, is a wild mixture too. Small English autos on the streets dodging Chinese pedestrians; rickshas; the unique Hong Kong streetcars, double-decked and dark green, a little like the old Fifth Avenue busses but higher and very narrow. Some of the buildings are Victorian edifices; others are colorful Chinese apartments jammed next to each other like New York brownstones, but four stories high, with balconies on each story facing the streets, each balcony flapping with varicolored laundry; all with Chinese characters painted on the side columns. A blaze of movement and design.

The higher the floor you live on in tropical Victoria, the cooler it is and the higher the rent. The famous Gloucester Hotel has its lobby, cocktail bars, and dining room on the top floor. One of the glamorous sights of Hong Kong is the view at night from a roof garden, looking up the mountainsides to the houses and apartments floating on the darkness of the hills, and looking down across the pools of red and green neons of the town to the lines of blue neon lights along the harbor and the bobbing yellow lights of the ships at anchor in the bay.

In Victoria, ricksha boys still run on inch-thick callused soles, which flatten like suction cups against the road. At a main street corner a group of rickshas, their upholstery a deep red, the long bars by which they are pulled resting on the pavement, under a huge billboard of Jane Russell as Montana Belle. Just around the corner from Russell and rickshas, the Red Star of China floats over several buildings, for the British recognize Communist China. There are over ten thousand hard-core Communists in Hong Kong, more than there are Britishers, and there are many bookshops filled with Communist publications.

These stores are neat, clean, carefully organized. Outside, big placards advertise Chinese translations of Russian best sellers: to the Communists of this part of the world, Russia is the elder brother setting cultural and economic styles, and Red China is the vigorous go-getter younger brother. Inside, the shops are filled with smartly designed modern pictorial magazines and books. There are stacks of comic books, each telling the story of a brave guerrilla hero or a woman who turned out three more gears a day in some Russian or Chinese factory; all of them having been tortured or raped by some capitalist group before they were able to lead their compatriots toward the glorious future depicted by the glittering rays of the Red Star.

The Communists are doing diabolically shrewd propagandizing in every country in which their publications are permitted. The bookstores are full of earnest young students; if they cannot afford to buy the books, they stand by the hour reading them. Communist pamphlets, costing as little as five cents, or even two cents a copy in poor countries like Indonesia or Burma, are far cheaper than most of the

Western publications and aimed at a far more serious level. In the Western bookstores of Hong Kong, a good third of the publications are sex displays and there are never a third as many students in these stores.

If they wished to, the Chinese Communists could almost take the British Crown Colony of Hong Kong by telephone. By doing so, they would certainly involve themselves in a war with the British that might widen into a third world war. But there is no reason why the Communists should now wish to risk a war. Hong Kong is very useful to them. It is a useful window on the West and it is an outlet for banking and export and trade. Also, China, by supplying the food for this city, as large as Philadelphia, gains invaluable exchange and holds a terrible weapon in reserve. If China closes down on food supplies, it can slowly starve the city, or it can force Hong Kong into desperate straits if it must import food at high prices from other lands. And if the downward trend of Hong Kong-China trade continues, either because of allied embargoes or Chinese barriers, the city's predominantly Chinese population will become worse and worse off and thus more and more likely to go over to Mao Tse-tung's side.

The British themselves go about their business seemingly unruffled by the perennial threat of Communist action against their rock. Colonizing Hong Kong was a farsighted British move, for it has the best harbor along a thousand miles of the East Asian coast. And, in spite of a tiny airfield, it is one of the key air termini of the world, an easy short trip by plane north to Shanghai en route to Japan and Manchuria, or east to Manila and on to the United States, or southeast to Indonesia and on to Australia, or southwest to Bangkok and on to India and the Middle East.

Having selected this barren rock back in 1841, the British genius for combining law and order, cleanliness, and a good commercial profit, made it not a Western colony in the East but a British sanctuary for those who wished to flee from China. After experiencing the present government of China, more than a million refugees have fled to the eighty-odd islands and the overcrowded three hundred and ninety-one square miles of this British colony. Its population has increased from one million to almost two and a half times as many, creating the most formidable refugee problem of any place on the globe. And the government of Hong Kong has had to fit these miserable squatters into its economy at a time when UN boycotts on trade with China had reduced its income a third. But the British carry on, trying to treat all the refugees with equal fairness and to find them some sort of work.

These hapless men and women without a country are not only pitiful human beings, they are a terrible waste of anti-Communist material. By the very fact that they fled to Hong Kong, they are among the more adventurous and intelligent Chinese. Yet there are no places and no jobs for them in Hong Kong, and from here there is nowhere for them to go; no other country will permit them to become citizens.

The free world cannot afford to waste the strength, convictions, and knowledge of the million and more Hong Kong refugees, or the additional hundreds of thousands who have fled from the Iron Curtain countries of Europe. Since the United States must continue to fight communism, it would be hardheaded common sense, as well as Christian charity, to create some kind of twentieth-century Freedom Legion in which these refugees could enlist.

Turning away from the wretched problems of these men without a country and from the precarious grandeur of Hong Kong, it is a short trip across the mouth of the Pearl River to the other watchtower of the West, the tiny port-peninsula of Macao, most romantically colorful spot left in our mechanized world. As your steamer pushes its way through the glassy gray-green waters, as Hong Kong fades into the distance and its white houses on the hills become swatches of unreal snow, you move deeper into the world of the Chinese.

Just as in a Chinese painting, mists begin to veil out the low mountains, leaving only the softened wavery outlines of their peaks. In the middle distance, giving perspective, the firmer outlines of junks float across the darkening water. One, drawing closer, shows in its ocher patched sail, about five feet above the steersman's head, a perfectly round hole, a shell hole, made by a Communist gunboat or a British destroyer or a Kuomintang armed junk.

Macao is a placid little town clinging to a couple of low hills around a shallow bay that is the perceptible outhouse for the most crowded single spot in Asia. Over three hundred thousand Chinese live on a peninsula three miles long and one mile wide. Macao, Europe's first outpost in the Far East, was settled by the Portuguese in 1557 and about four hundred years later, seven thousand Portuguese still follow their country's tested pattern of colonialism, a limited laissez-faire administration, which interferes as little as is consistent with keeping its sovereignty and profits.

Today Macao is a mad texture of the centuries and civilizations—of modern American cars, pure eighteenth-century. Portuguese buildings and customs—mixed into the most Chinese city outside of China itself. Macao's streets are jammed with the restless hustling busy Chinese and their shops and goods spill out onto its sidewalks. Outside the restaurants are big jars full of variegated and indescribable Chinese delicacies packed like stuffed olives. Next to them, fish in tanks, birds and cats and snakes in cages. You pick out your main course for dinner before you go inside; it is caught or netted and taken into the kitchen to be prepared as you prescribe.

Down here in the South the food is much like that which you get at good Chinese restaurants in the United States: rice, soft noodles, and combinations of Chinese vegetables, nuts, and fruit lightly fried in oil. But at a Cantonese dinner in Macao there is an addition; a charming attendant is assigned especially to you. She keeps your teacup filled, brings warm, scented towels when your hands get greasy.

The Chinese insist they can tell much about a man's character and background from the way he holds chopsticks. If he holds them far down, he is a peasant with no sense of delicacy. If he holds them far up near the ends, and thus makes them long, he shows he is greedy, because at a Chinese dinner the food is served in platters and each one uses his chopsticks to reach out for what he wants. The farther the chopsticks reach, the more delicacies from the other side of the table.

In a Chinese dinner, the final course, after all the heavily seasoned foods, is often a clear, hot, duck or fish broth flavored with lemon and black pepper. Odd as it may seem to Westerners, soup is a satisfying end to a meal, cleansing and refreshing the mouth. There are so many exchanges possible between civilizations if each is not convinced it alone possesses the boon of culture. Marco Polo brought Shanghai food back home with him to Europe and the Italians called it ravioli. One of the present-day Shanghai versions of this, served on Kowloon, is *tang-pao,* a dumpling filled with a piece of beef and a rich sweetish broth. Very treacherous for the chopsticks amateur to try to hold the dumpling between his chopsticks and bite it open without showering himself with the fatty liquid.

When I ate tang-pao, there was a Chinese couple with a little baby at the next table. They watched me with obvious delight as I tried to handle my chopsticks, roared with laughter when I had a spectacular failure, yet I was sure they were not laughing at me but at the human ludicrousness of the situation. Along with Americans, Filipinos, Thais, and Burmese, the Chinese have a kind but lusty sense of humor. This ability to laugh at yourself, or not mind other people laughing at you, is not shared by the Japanese or the Koreans, the Indonesians or the Indians.

After their dinners, the Chinese like to gamble; they are incurable gamblers, betting on anything. The biggest hotel in Macao, the Center Hotel, has three floors of casinos devoted to fan-tan. In this game, the croupier claps an inverted brass bowl down over a mound of white buttons, covering an indeterminate number. Bets are then placed on how many buttons will finally remain after the croupier has removed them four at a time until there are only three, two, one, or none left. With four possibilities, the winner is paid off at odds of three to one, quite a house percentage.

Each round of fan-tan is prolonged almost unbearably. The croupier carefully lifts off the brass bowl, picks up a narrow bamboo stick, carefully divides the heap of buttons into two parts; delicately he arranges four buttons in a neat line with his stick and pushes them slowly aside, repeating this process, four by four by four. Hundreds of different faces and expressions changing in the half light, half shadow around the table, the planes of the faces sharpened by neon overhead lights bouncing off tile floors and tiled columns.

Each floor of the Center Hotel caters to a different economic level of gambler, ranging from the poor coolie on the first floor who can only bet a cent or two and hopes to win a pipeful of opium, up to the rich Chinese on the third floor who is waited upon by beautiful Eurasian girls and hopes to rent two or three for the night with his winnings.

After dark in Macao, iron shutters are pulled down over most of the stores and away from the main boulevard drenched in the moldering light of blue neons, the town is fitfully lit and full of shadows. The streets are only about six feet wide, paved with round stones, and always going up or downhill and maybe around a bend at the same time, everything on a slant or slope so that the light from a street lamp away down the street and halfway around a bend makes pools and twisted Picasso-like breasts of light. The buildings lean with age; many of them are two-storied, with narrow shuttered Iberian windows on the second floor, through which shafts of broken light fall across the mist. And the open ground-floor fronts are covered at night with vertical planks set in slides at the street level. At their tops are shuttered openings through which faces peer, framed in chinks of streaming yellow light.

The characteristic night sound in a Chinese quarter of any Asian city is a sharp clap and clatter, like ivory hail on an enameled roof, the sound of the mah-jongg players who play on a shiny hard table shuffling the ivories with a clatter and slamming down each tile with an individual crash.

Every so often on the darkened streets, you come upon a meat vendor trying to sell a single covered plate of food or a bread vendor carrying two cases like glass medicine chests, one at each end of a yoke. Or you hear the plaintive singsong cry of a sugar-cane vendor. He has a yoke carried front to back. There is a weighted chest of some kind on the back, and on the front a broad, four-foot-wide, thick metal tray turned up like a shallow cone and hung from thin wires fanning down from the wooden yoke. Sections of sugar cane ten inches long, their stripes and knuckles arranged in clean orderly patterns, radiate out from the center of the tray. And in the very middle of the sugar cane, a candle sits in a sheltering glass tube, throwing shadows.

There is at least one shop open for business on every block. In them, at one or two o'clock in the morning, Chinese workers are cobbling shoes, sewing shirts, working or laughing or eating together. Once in a while there are temples with barred bronze doors and gilded figures of gods and dragons; on their porches skeletonlike beggars curl up at the bases of cinnamon and gold pillars. And for a final touch of incredible color, an empty square, with shallow steps at its end, leading up to the arched portico of the Cathedral of St. Paolo etched in clean moonlight. But it is only a façade; behind its front, empty darkness.

Throughout the city of Macao, the Portuguese, although keeping a firm rule of law and order, have left the Chinese to live their own lives, neither proselytizing them nor condescending to them. Laissez-faire is their secret of rule by so few over so many; across the bay in Hong Kong, the British colony practices this same live and let live principle. It is a principle we Westerners do not employ enough in our dealings with the Far East where people are in violent transition from their todays, our yesterdays, to their tomorrows, our todays. The less we try to push them, the more willingly they will move, in their own time and way. Here on the Pearl River, the British and the Portuguese have learned that the least amount of outside interference, even when it be assistance, builds the greatest stability.

And alone of the non-Communists who deal with the Communist Chinese, the Portuguese are able to get along with them. When they want to strike a bargain with the mainlanders they send couriers a few days ahead explaining what they will want to talk about. Thus the Chinese, suspicious of the intentions of all Westerners, have time to think out their own positions and do not feel that something is being sprung on them. When negotiations start, the Portuguese never put their cards bluntly on the table but let points gradually emerge, if possible not until the Chinese bring up a subject; they never allow their adversaries to lose face, helping them out of any position in which they would be trapped. This is essential to satisfactory bargaining with the face-conscious Chinese.

Similarly, the Portuguese never base an argument on principles but on bargains; when they must refuse Chinese terms, they never say the offer is unfair and that they will stand on their rights. This is a silly argument to oriental minds; they believe disagreements must be negotiated to a mutually profitable conclusion. Instead the Portuguese say they cannot accept an offer because by so doing they would destroy themselves. This is an objection that the Chinese immediately understand; it involves no contradictory and incomprehensible collision of ethics but the simple fact of self-preservation. An American believes a test of his strength of character is his willingness to fight for his rights even if he loses by doing so; a Chinese believes: "A man who cannot put up with a small wrong ends up with disaster."

It is very hard to be sure what the Chinese people are really like. Even if you could lump any half billion people together under general headings, it is especially difficult today to analyze Chinese motivations when it is impossible for a Westerner to travel inside China. Here on the periphery of China, observing and talking with the Chinese of Macao and Hong Kong and Formosa as well as the British and the Portuguese, a pattern begins to emerge.

When you see the ordinary Chinese in their own surroundings, it is impossible not to like and admire these people. They are friendly, outgoing, and full of humor, ready to join in with you in anything you are doing, or to pretend they cannot see you, if that is what you wish. And in spite of the fierceness of their competition, they practice toward each other loyalty and consideration, the "Confucian twins,"

twins because "Confucius teaches considerateness is habit in loyalty." They believe this is a trait they share with the Americans, while the Japanese are "loyal but not considerate." The Chinese also think that in spite of our differing systems we and they have in common the same foundation in life: humanism, the belief that the individual is central and the state only a means to an end.

The only place the Chinese abandon their emphasis on the uniqueness of the individual is in their system of family relationships. A Chinese family shares the food and money of its members in a more embracing arrangement than the parientes system of the Philippines. Affections are focused within the family and Confucianism teaches the central goodness of filial respect for elders and parents. Children are necessary to your afterlife happiness, for only your own sons will make the sacrifices that will help your departed spirit. In contrast to the Japanese, the Chinese do not shore up their own superiority by admiring their ancestors, but they are always conscious of their ancestors being around them and sharing their lives. The most obscene curse in Chinese is one similar to the Spanish, "I obscenity your mother and her mother to the eighteenth generation."

The purpose of marriage being progeny, in Korea or Japan or China, or for that matter in most of the Far East, romantic love becomes a silly concept and erotic love is a respectable emotion to be proposed without Western circumlocutions. A famous Chinese movie actress is as much an object of love desire as any Hollywood beauty is in America; but a Chinese sees nothing insulting in sending the actress a letter specifying the amount of money he will pay to enjoy her favors.

The old system of keeping a mistress under your roof and calling her a concubine being outmoded, and housing being expensive, few Chinese can afford to keep a mistress in a separate apartment. But this realistic race finds that no great handicap; a number of men get together and support one mistress in a co-operative apartment. Incidentally, there is a small hotel in Kowloon, very modern, with steel casement windows, but still a glorified bordello; the newspapers never mention it because every so often the proprietors give the reporters an "overnight press conference."

In and out of mainland China, the women are breaking loose from the rigid mold of past centuries. The wife, in her brocades, hobbling along on bound feet has disappeared. So have most households with three or four wives. The Chinese wife is becoming her husband's equal, slowly outside Communist China, much faster inside. The Communists have enacted modern marriage laws, set up modern divorce courts and even decreed equal pay for equal work; another of the reasons why many young people in China go along with the Communists.

Some of the Chinese on Formosa who have known our civilization say the special status enjoyed by women in the United States comes from our frontier period when there were too few women to go around: "Your women still think of themselves as the only virtuous women in a frontier town." The Chinese have always had an oversupply of women, but they absorbed it with dignity by creating their concubine system and providing that the children of a concubine were legitimate. In China your first wife was always your equal. Compare this with the inferior, feudal position of women in Japan. The Chinese insist a test of a civilization's maturity is equal status for both sexes: "Husband and wife should respect each other just like guests in the same house."

Sometimes in the simplest reactions of a people a clue can be found to the whole complex of psychological-sociological differences that separate civilizations. Such a clue can be found in the most used of all Western words, "yes" and "no," and you see the difference most sharply in the Chinese, the most polite and ceremonial of Asian peoples. Only in the Philippines, another example of how westernized they have grown, are these words used as we use them. China and the rest of Asia, as well as the Middle East, approach them from a very different point of view. They have the same essential angle toward "no."

In the dramas of these civilizations, the loud voice and the flat negative are only used by clowns and buffoons. Polite people use indirect methods to say "no." In Chinese, if you want to disagree, you say *bu* followed by the phrase you disagree with; this indicates you are somewhat dubious of the statement, but it does not approach what is, to an oriental mind, the impoliteness of the Westerner's flat "no." In Thailand, you must hitch a similar negative suffix onto the verb of the question asked you and even then it is rude. In Burma, when I asked for "no," they said, "This is quite a question. Maybe you could add *ma* to your question and get an approximation."

If the difference seems trivial, remember that the peoples of Asia and the Middle East, because of the past interferences of Western nations in their countries, are suspicious of our intentions and alert to evidence of our lack of breeding or unfriendliness; our blunt "no," gives quite a jolt to Asians.

Conversely, "yes," gives Westerners a false picture of Asian honesty. In our system the word means exactly what it says, again a flat indisputable agreement; if you say "yes" and do not mean it, you are a liar. Not so in Asia. Take the *duei-li* of Chinese, the *saya* of Indonesia, the *houkke* of Burma; although they can be translated as "yes," they can have quite a different set of connotations and infinite shades of meaning, depending upon the situation. They may mean exactly what we mean, an unhedged agreement, but a considerate man will also use them to save your face; he expects you to realize that he is being polite and really means "no," not "yes," by them.

They are also used to cover up the fact that the Asian does not follow your English; many of their officials are not fluent in English and use "yes" just as we do in polite conversation when we cannot understand someone's accent or reasoning; it would be rude to say, "your English is not clear," and face-losing to say "I cannot follow it." A safe rule in Asia: whenever you get a "yes," rephrase the point to its contrary and see if you get a second "yes."

The most subtle meaning Easterners give the word is in its connotation of maybe, we'll see. An oriental expects you to know when you are proposing something that would turn out to be a loss to him; even then, to turn you down with a flat refusal would be insulting. So he says "yes," meaning, "Maybe, I'll see whether it is to my advantage to do what you propose, and naturally you understand that until I have tested this out I cannot be certain I will go along with what you propose, but for politeness' sake, and to indicate my mind is open, I'll explore the matter."

But just as the oriental thinks you have the low mentality or consideration of a clown for your flat "no," so you are in danger of thinking him Machiavellian or irresponsible because of his flat "yes." There must be dozens of other submerged icebergs floating around in the sea of international understanding.

There is another profound difference between Eastern and Western mentalities that stands out most clearly in the Chinese: the difference between our absorption in the objective, scientific method, and their subjective, unscientific thought and behavior patterns. Here is the reason why this people, who knew the principles of science so many centuries before we did, are today so far behind us in scientific development.

Two thousand years ago Socrates and the Greek philosophers turned their thoughts toward the outer world of mathematics and physics while Confucius and the wisest Chinese were interested in the problems between man and man; the Greeks "ventured high in the sky and deep down in the water and tried to learn how a bird flies and a fish lives. We Chinese we are interested in how people live together peacefully."

Focused away from science, the Chinese civilization remained agricultural and efficiency remained a foreign word: "what's the use to save a few minutes? The rice will grow by seasons not by minutes. You cannot push the rice up to grow or pull it up to ripeness." Our Western efficiency grows out of modern technology, modern science, and modern industry: when we take a train, if we miss it by half a second, it is gone; but the Chinese go by rowboat: "You miss half a day, the boat will be waiting for you." And if you object to this reasoning and ask if it does not depend upon what you wanted to do with the half day you have missed—"Well, I wander around and see the frogs and fish and birds and trees."

Or the difference in our two civilizations can be viewed from the angle of perception and how differently we regard the world around us. The oriental looks upon each experience as separate and unique. A frog on a lotus petal is a moment in time and beauty to contemplate and to meditate upon. Like the Japanese, the Chinese somehow stay close to the phenomena of nature, whereas the West has developed what one of China's wisest living men, Chiang Mon-lin, calls the "all-piercing intellect," which from Plato on has sought to create an abstract or generalized pattern that would fit all frogs on all lotus petals. Involved is the difference between the idea and the ideal. The Chinese feel that they reach the ideal through contemplating any one example, while we believe we reach the idea through an intellectual synthesis of many examples; the oriental believes each person or thing is unique, while we try to make of each an illustration of some universal thesis.

This approach has consequences in politics as well as in philosophy or art. If each person is unique, it is absurd to try to write a rule which will apply rigorously in every case and so Eastern law leans on common sense to settle disputes. It is hard to realize, until you have been in the East, how much the pattern of modern Western life rests upon the general laws of cause and effect. It is because we understand as a general law that there is friction between moving metal parts that in the specific case of our car we keep it properly greased. In larger social mechanisms we are able to function together as a society only because we understand as a general law that if we do not carry out our obligations to remote members of our society who are not our blood relations, we cannot depend upon their promises to us.

Perhaps the highest reward from the Eastern concept is the spiritual enrichment and serenity the oriental receives from his contemplation of the frog on the petal; perhaps the contribution of Western law is that millions of people can dependably function together for the common good. How to combine these two sets of good, so far incompatible, is the largest challenge to both sets of values.

When it comes to their conception of the value of the individual and their appreciation of work, the Chinese have an approach more like an American's. Where the Japanese believe the state is the end and the individual a weapon of the state, the Chinese believe each individual has his all-important dignity and rights, "even the right to be too individualistic for his own good." They have a zest for work that only an American or a Scandinavian shares and a pride of workmanship now vanished in most of the West. In Hong Kong a Chinese tailor made me a suit in fourteen hours, from the first selection of material to a final fitting in the men's room of the airport. And it was the Chinese tailor, not I, who insisted, in the last ten minutes before I boarded a plane, on ripping out one last seam and correcting an almost imperceptible wrinkle. He had worked all night, he had already been paid, he would never see me again; but he wanted it right.

Necessity has made the Chinese the shrewdest traders in Asia; if they were not, they would have starved to death long ago. And the implacable pressure of the Chinese overpopulation has forced them to spread out from their homeland to the rich young countries of Asia. These communities of Chinese who emigrated from their homeland to settle in Hong Kong, the Philippines, and Southeast Asia are called the *hua-chiao,* the Overseas Chinese.

The hua-chiao, the uncaptured prize of today's Asia, number almost as many people as dwell in many countries of the Far East. Exactly how many there are is anybody's guess in this part of the world where there are no dependable censuses and where Chinese families increase rapidly. Also, Formosa sometimes wants the figures to be larger; individual countries sometimes prefer to underestimate their hua-chiao.

Appraising the varying figures as best one can, the main centers of the Overseas Chinese are distributed as follows:

Thailand	2,500,000–3,500,000
Hong Kong	2,000,000–2,500,000
Macao	250,000– 300,000
Federation of Malaya	2,300,000–2,900,000
Singapore	700,000– 900,000
Indonesia	2,500,000–3,500,000
Vietnam-Vietminh	900,000–1,200,000
Burma	250,000– 350,000
Philippines	250,000– 350,000
North Borneo-Sarawak	250,000– 300,000
Cambodia	200,000– 250,000

So, not including the nine million Free Chinese who live on Formosa, perhaps the most accurate statement is that there are somewhere between twelve and sixteen million hua-chiao.

But the figure is misleading because it does not indicate the amount of power these Overseas Chinese control. They are the merchants and the bankers along the whole arc of the Pacific from Japan to India. From 50 per cent up to 90 per cent of the business and commerce of the Philippines, Indonesia, Malaya, Laos, Cambodia, Thailand, Vietnam, Burma, Hong Kong, and Singapore is in the hands of these tireless traders. Dominating the wealth of the countries to which they have emigrated, if they threw their full strength behind either Peiping or Taipei they could become the most powerful revolutionary underground the world has ever seen, able to determine not only the future of the Red regime in China but the success or failure of communism in Asia.

But so far, the hua-chiao are no third force in Chinese affairs and no entity in anything except commercial prowess and racial background. They have had very little political power, they are traders and in most of Asia traders are regarded as second-class citizens, ineligible for high political office. The Chinese went overseas as visitors, to work, make money, and then to go home and die in their ancestral villages. They had no political interests: "We don't care who holds the cow as long as we can milk it." Their loyalties were first to their sons and families, then to their pocketbooks, and finally to their relatives back on the mainland to whom they used to send large remittances.

They have been tolerated in the countries to which they immigrated because of their usefulness, but they have been hated and suppressed; they are outlanders, their status strikingly like that of the Jews of medieval Europe; they have been persecuted, limited in citizenship, and frequently restricted to living in special districts. In Indonesia, for years they could not travel into the country without a special permit; in Malaya they are restricted in voting even when born there; in Thailand they pay a special alien-registration tax; they are similarly discriminated against in Burma and in Indo-China.

The hua-chiao have had their own schools and newspapers and they have not been subject to military service. Many of their children never learn to read any language but Chinese and know nothing of the history or traditions of the countries in which they live. They watched the struggle for China without political conviction and with a calculating eye, waiting to see which bandwagon to clamber aboard.

After so many kinds of oppression the Overseas Chinese learned that the way of self-survival is to bend to the storm: "We can tolerate what we must." To sacrifice for a faltering cause would be an idea foreign to them: There is a famous Chinese saying: "The snow that falls on your neighbor's threshold, why should you want to sweep it off?" They had no intention of finding themselves on the losing side of the Chinese fight. They did not dare. These millions without a country depend on the Chinese ambassadors, representing the power of their homeland, to protect them from repressive measures in the countries of Southeast Asia, and they still are not certain which ambassador, Peiping's or Taipei's, will be able to protect them better.

The Overseas Chinese watched the disintegration of the once noble Kuomintang Party in a China it ruled more and more corruptly and wretchedly. When the KMT fell, it had few overseas admirers. Even in the strongest pro-Formosa community, the Chinese of the Philippines, there are not over 10,000 Kuomintang members and the KMT's most recent shenanigans toward K. C. Wu and its own liberal wing have given the realistic Overseas Chinese no reason to feel reassured.

When Mao came to power in Peiping, the Chinese abroad swung toward the victor. The most important focus of power in a Chinese community being the chamber of commerce, in Djakarta and Bangkok and Singapore, these groups began electing pro-Communist presidents. The Red flag was flown over their headquarters. Their children, in the special Chinese schools, began learning pro-Communist doctrines and overseas contributions to Communist causes took a big jump.

Then the Communists began to kill this golden goose. The Overseas Chinese were sending money home to their relatives that was valuable foreign exchange. The Communists began threatening or torturing the families in China to extort larger remittances. As this became clear to the hua-chiao, their attitude changed and finally they forced themselves to a step as hard as any a Chinese can make: many of them have now cut themselves adrift from their homes and families in China, ceasing to write to them or to send them money. And, because of these personal reasons and because they saw what was happening to business under a Communist regime, their hearts began to harden against the Communists.

Too late, Peiping realized its blunder. Now its Commission for Overseas Affairs, a powerful comintern and secret-police force, is using money and threats, trying to swing more Overseas Chinese back into the Red orbit, and the Chinese Nationalists are also struggling for their loyalty. Remembering how Sun Yat-sen once organized the Overseas Chinese behind him, collected three hundred million dollars from them, and overthrew the Manchus, Formosa is desperately trying to rally them to its support. It realizes they can make the difference between success and failure: there is an Overseas Chinese Commission on the island; the Nationalists held an anti-Communist National Salvation Conference in late 1953; and they are working out ways whereby the hua-chiao will have representatives in the National Assembly.

It is difficult for a foreigner to penetrate far into the underground activities of the various Overseas Chinese. Each of the groups is jealous of the others and there is no single attitude evident among them. In each country it varies according to how close they are to China and how successful the Communists are in international affairs. As far as can be ascertained, they have no international organization today and it seems unlikely they soon will have one. American notions of dealing with them as a unit against communism are not supported by actualities; in different countries of Asia the attitudes of the hua-chiao are quite different.

The Philippines Overseas Chinese, less than 2 per cent of the total population—and among the richest and freest of their people—are the strongest supporters of the Chinese Nationalists. Because the Philippine Republic is firmly pro-Formosa and anti-Peiping, so are most of the Philippine Chinese; they are ready to back Formosa with money and even with some volunteer man power. The Chinese of Hong Kong, almost 100 per cent of the population, are on the fence; apprehensive of the power of Mao, suspicious of the Kuomintang. Again, they parallel the position of their rulers.

In Malaya, the hua-chiao make up over 50 per cent of the people on the peninsula. So far, they are reorienting themselves away from both Peiping and Taipei; those in Singapore are agitating for a Chinese university and those in the Federation of Malaya are pressuring the government for citizenship rights. If they support Formosa at all from now on, it will be only after the island has shown itself to be stronger than it is now. Likewise, the hua-chiao of Indonesia, less than 4 per cent of the people in the East Indies, have very little interest in the Chinese Nationalists. But Red China enjoys immense prestige among the Indonesian Chinese. Indonesia has been on the best terms with Peiping of any Asian neutral and the Chinese ambassador in Djakarta is easily the most influential Chinese in the islands, maintaining an elaborate embassy, spending money openly for Communist propaganda and meetings, providing teachers, textbooks, and scholarships to China for the most promising young hua-chiao.

In Thailand, where almost 20 per cent of the people are Chinese, the government is an ally of Formosa and an enemy of Red China. But while this has so far kept the Thai Chinese from being much help to Peiping, it has not automatically turned them into strong supporters of the Nationalists; they do not trust the Kuomintang and although Bangkok has permitted funds to be exported, the Thai Chinese have sent very few ticals to Taipei. Thailand, exceedingly wary of her Chinese and gravely apprehensive of Red China's power or intentions in Southeast Asia, handles its hua-chiao with the shortest of reins, intending that they shall keep their noses entirely out of international concerns. And in Burma, pressured by three different fanatical Communist parties and by a central government determined to take no sides between Red China and Free China, the less than 2 per cent of the people who are hua-chiao are desperately trying to sit on the fence.

The United States would like the Overseas Chinese as an ally in Asia, but it is absurd for us to hope that American money and some propaganda by American Chinese will swing the Overseas Chinese into a position contradictory to that of the country in which they live or contrary to their own self-interest and safety. And if we want them to put their influence or their man power behind Formosa, we and the Nationalists must demonstrate two things to them.

First, they must be convinced that Formosa is going to continue to be a force in existence and will continue to speak for China in the world. This brings in Nationalist prestige and their seat in the United Nations. If the United States should recognize the Communists as China's representative in the United Nations, in effect we say to these Overseas Chinese that we are going to do business with Communist China.

Second, the Overseas Chinese must become convinced that the Chinese Nationalists on Formosa are able and willing to be a noble champion of freedom for the unhappy people of China. The young Overseas Chinese are as idealistic as any other young group and they do not admire dictatorship by the sons of Chiang, or small Kuomintang cliques keeping themselves in power via a secret police.

For Americans it may be desirable to have the Overseas Chinese solidly behind Formosa, but it is vital that their power and wealth do not work for the Communists as a fifth column and a most dangerous undermining force. If they turn their backs on both Chinese governments and reconcile themselves to becoming Indonesians or Thais or Malays, they will contribute greatly to the stability and future of their adopted countries.

But to repudiate Peiping is only safe if Peiping is going to lose. No prudent trader, Chinese or American, turns his back on the future. And the free world is far from having convinced the hua-chiao that communism is going to lose the struggle for world supremacy. In Malaya one of the wisest of the Chinese asked, "Why do you fear the thing of the future?" Few Overseas Chinese today have faith that the free world will protect them from Red China's eventual revenge. Every Communist victory in Asia, like the debacles of the West in Vietnam, convinces more hua-chiao they had better get on the Peiping steamroller, while they can.

Where they will stand, whom they will support five years from now is impossible to predict. Only one thing is certain: the Overseas Chinese are the most powerful uncommitted force in Asia.

On the periphery of mainland China much can be found out about what is happening behind the Bamboo Curtain, but you are faced with many contradictions. On Formosa, the Nationalists and the United States Mission give a picture of weakening Communist internal power. In Hong Kong and Macao, the Chinese, British, Portuguese, and Americans all join in an estimate far less cheering to the free world, and their pessimistic appraisal is supported by much of the information that comes from the Overseas Chinese in the rest of Asia.

Internally, in their first period of rule, the Red Chinese have successfully been riding a wave of nationalism and land reform. They have been busy smashing outmoded customs, rooting out corruption in government, and generally modernizing the old order of Kuomintang China. They have driven forward along the lines of reform that they promised the Chinese people before they came to power, and so far they have done a more efficient job than the experts on China told us was possible.

Their first step was the familiar one Communists follow wherever they come to power: to make sure no one else has the means to take away that power. The Chinese Communists took all weapons away from civilians, even the homemade pieces of the farmers. Then they made sure their own administrators were dependable. In the first stages of the revolution, the civil governors were Communist guerrillas who for years had been doing the fighting against the Nationalists; fighting behind the lines, suffering more than the Red Army, they had learned to organize and to lead. Within a year or so, these men were jailed or liquidated. Their places were taken by thoroughly indoctrinated hard-core Communists from North China, particularly from Manchuria and the far eastern provinces.

With these men in control, the party began its brainwashing, searching out potential threats to the regime, killing any possible focuses for future anti-Communist revolutions. This is by all odds the most dangerous technique of the Communist states, their carefully worked out technique for finding and eliminating all potential opposition leaders. We Americans assume that, under the right circumstances, any man could become the leader of a revolution. The Communists know better. Only a few in any society have the particular kind of ability that makes leadership. If these few are weeded out, the dough of discontent is without yeast. Communists do not hesitate to kill an extra few hundreds of thousands of people to be certain no anti's are left alive.

Like the Russian leaders, or like the KMT leaders, the men who run Red China constantly double check on the ideological convictions of the Armed Forces. They remember that a large percentage of the men with whom they defeated Chiang Kai-shek were deserters from the Nationalists, and they have no intention of allowing men to remain in positions of army authority if there is the slightest question about their loyalty. Peiping is confident it would have no trouble smashing a Nationalist assault on the mainland if their armies remained loyal.

To keep the mass of the people loyal, the skillful propaganda machine of the Reds controls all sources of printed or spoken or pictured information. It tells the Chinese how the white imperialist Americans keep China from becoming rich, and how happy peasants in other parts of China already are, always people over the hills, some place else. Those who are keen enough to detect the falsehoods are subject to the three F's: fraud, false accusations; fear, of torture; and force, of prison and death. In their interrogations, brainwashings, and trials, the Red Chinese again follow the Russian pattern, taking months and elaborate psychological third degrees to force pro-American Chinese to recant publicly.

Experts in Hong Kong believe the Reds have not yet been able to destroy the peasants' respect for China's old friend, the United States. Strange as it may seem to some Americans, it is not our military power but our record of friendship with China that most worries the Red Chinese. While they fear large-scale war with the United States, they believe that we fear it still more and that our Army is less of a threat to them than Japanese military power will be. And, although apprehensive of American atomic energy, the Chinese Politburo seems to believe a few atomic bombs dropped on China would do more good by uniting the people against the United States than the destruction would do harm. Also: "The Soviet Union will take care of the atomic bombs."

The first stage of Chinese communism seems to have been fairly successful. The masses wanted the elimination of war lords and landlords plus some kind of internal political and economic security. This the Communists have supplied, enacting sweeping land reform, taking the properties from rich landlords and thus gaining land to divide among the peasants and money to spend for public works.

The Reds staged a nation-wide "Three Anti's" movement: anti-corruption, anti-waste, and anti-bureaucracy. Each of these provided new categories of wealthier Chinese to be stripped of their profits from earlier regimes. Next came the "Five Anti's": anti-bribery, anti-tax evasion, anti-government-contract gouging, anti-stealing from the government, anti-profiteering. The five anti's were an excuse to expropriate the wealth of the middleman and the city dwellers.

Now there are no more fatted calves to be butchered and inflation is rising in China. Their problem from now on is one of production, which means that, since there is so little urban or factory production in China, the burden of supporting the state will fall back on the shoulders of the farmers. The Chinese Communists are bearing down hard on the Chinese people today: "We have to work all day and then attend classes in communism at night; we get up by bugles, and if we oversleep, we are counterrevolutionaries." The next thing to watch for is how well the men who run Red China can hold the loyalty of these same peasants who gave Mao Tse-tung the power to overthrow the Chinese Nationalists.

There are some indications that the Red Chinese are not going to have as easy a time from now on. More and more people are trying to get out of China as the purges and persecutions spread. But this is not necessarily a gain for Formosa. A while ago, ten thousand fishermen fled from China en masse, but they remained in Hong Kong unwilling to join the Nationalists. Like their countrymen in China, they had heard little about the present-day economic reforms on Formosa and still judged it in terms of its action during the days when China collapsed. Formosa has "got to do much more in political field before it convinces China it would do good for Chinese people."

To put a stop to mass migrations or disloyalties, the Communist Chinese have revived an old Chinese custom, the "mutual-guarantee society." This is a diabolical arrangement by which fishermen, educators, or any other class that needs watching, is registered in groups of ten, each member of a group being responsible for the other nine; if one rebels or flees, the other nine are punished. Then each group of ten is also registered as one unit of a group of one hundred, and so on, a vast system of men spying on each other because they are personally safe only by making sure their fellow workers do not rebel.

There is one more factor to be added to the balance of Communist strength, the youth of China who bring the balance well out into the Red. The Red Chinese have worked through step one, the liquidation of all opposition leadership, and through step two of a Communist revolution, the terrorization of the masses, and on to step three, the creation of a broad base for the future of their system, the indoctrination of the young. In today's China, that supposedly irreversible Chinese attitude of respect and obedience to the old has been upset and the conservative elders, whom the experts on China were so certain would block Red domination, have been by-passed as if they were not there. The Communists kill the old if they get in the way, let them alone if they stay quiet, and concentrate rewards and the state's first attention on the young.

They search always for the youngster with a little more intelligence or a little extra energy. Then they train him and keep him under close surveillance to be certain he remains a staunch Communist; if there is any doubt, he is liquidated. As a result of this system, the younger generation are the elite of China; to them go the best educations, the best jobs, the chance to rule and to share in the reshaping of their country. They are today the real strength of the new system. Enrolled, indoctrinated, furnished with guns, they police the country and watch for defections. Against them, the older Chinese who might wish to throw out the Reds, have little chance to rise up. Among the youth the anti-American propaganda is having the most success; they know little of what has gone before, follow what is told them, are willingly deceived and fanatically convinced.

On the surface, China is entirely ruled by its own Communists. There is no data to show that the Kremlin is even trying to dictate policy; the Moscow men stay in the background, functioning as friends and advisers, and the Peiping leaders use their help. There are said to be today more Chinese students in Russia than those of any other foreign country. The Moscow radio has recently announced a mass translation of Soviet textbooks into Chinese so that students in China can study the same lessons as scholars in Russia.

Mao Tse-tung, one of the two or three most able and powerful leaders in the world, is no Tito. He is both the Lenin and the Stalin of his revolution and has run it his way since he overthrew Russian control of his Politburo back in the twenties. And there is no data available to indicate that he is likely to collide with the Kremlin.

If Mao dies, next in line to rule Red China are his two principal assistants, Liu Shao-chi and Chou En-lai. Both are shrewd and able; both, like all the rest of the top Chinese hierarchy, are comrades of thirty years of revolutionary struggle. There has never been an important purge in the Chinese Communist Party. Liu is the Chinese Malenkov, controlling the party machinery, the Vice-Chairman of the Politburo and the Secretary of its Central Committee, the party's chief theoretician and close to Mao. Chou, a more charming and tactful Chinese version of Molotov, is the Premier and Foreign Minister of the Chinese People's Republic, chief salesman abroad, and the star of the Geneva Conference which partitioned Vietnam.

Partly counterbalancing Liu's greater domestic power, he is married to Teng Yung-chao, who runs the Chinese women's party organization.

Liu, as boss, having far closer ties with the Kremlin than Chou, might follow a firmer Russian alliance but there is no evidence that the present Peiping-Moscow axis brings displeasure to Chou En-lai.

In the long run there are many potentialities for friction between Russia and China, but today this alliance of sovereign states with common goals and enemies is paying rich dividends as Russia concentrates on Europe, the Middle East, and the Western hemisphere, while Red China works for control of East and Southeast Asia. Together the two Red powers are extending bases and soldiers and jet planes into the territories from Korea over to Afghanistan. Correlating their pressures and actions, they can step up trouble or reduce pressures anywhere in the world.

While the Kremlin may be at the end of an aggressive stage, there are many indications that China is in the prologue of her aggressive development. As Stalin and Company once talked of a Greater Russia, so the Chinese Politburo now talks of the renaissance of the Mongol Empire when Chinese power extended all the way to the East Indies and India. The Chinese Reds are taking over the Communist parties of South Asia, which had been Russian directed and not very successful. They can be enormously more destructive under Chinese direction for Mao's men understand the psychology and needs of underprivileged Asian peasant populations like their own.

Mao himself has been one of the world's greatest masters of the guerrilla warfare, which, as the war in Indo-China has proved, is the most dangerous military weapon available to the Reds in South Asia. The only counter is well-trained, equally fanatical, native guerrillas in each country threatened by native Communists. And that takes a lot of doing and billions of American dollars. When all the fine talk is over, the Communists of Asia plan to win through their secret weapon: "pour out blood, the more we pour out, if we keep on pouring it out, we are sure to conquer everyone." Too few non-Communist Asians are yet convinced that the alternatives to communism are worth pouring out their blood.

For that matter, too few Americans are yet convinced of the wisdom of any specific course of action in the Pacific. Peace and freedom for Asia is a fine slogan. But whose peace? And what freedom? Any sensible American must contemplate with great uneasiness the looming question mark of present-day American foreign policy: what to do about Communist China.

Two facts about Communist China are today incontrovertible: their rule in China gives no indication of collapsing and their successful collaboration with Russia gives no more indication of collapsing.

Now add a third fact: there is no foreseeable combination of countries in Asia whose power and prestige can possibly equal that of the half billion indefatigable Chinese. Peiping's economic pull on Japan has just begun. Their nascent military machine fought us to a standstill in Korea and keeps that peninsula an armed camp costing the Allies billions a year. Formosan policy is determined by events in China. And from Peiping, rapidly becoming the powerhouse of Asian communism, a web of invisible wires carries dissension and destruction to South Asia; the Huks in the Philippines, the Communists in Indonesia, the terrorists of Malaya, the three Communist parties in precariously balanced Burma, the threat to Thailand, the guerrilla wars in Laos, Cambodia, and Vietnam—all have been guided and supported by the Chinese Politburo.

There is no safe and satisfactory policy available for the United States against China. We are confronted with the same kind of schizophrenic conundrum we had with Russia: to fight, to give up, or to hang on. We are not able to live in peace with China, but we will not start the horrors of an atomic-biological war to destroy the Communists. So we are left with the uncertainties and costs of coalitions against China.

European coalitions have brought us moderate success. NATO and its attendant arrangements have blocked direct Soviet aggression there. But conditions are not parallel in Asia. Europe's basic unities of intention and belief do not exist in the disconglomerate of the Far East. Whether we call it a Pacific or a Southeast Asian Pact, a PATO or a SEATO, it is highly unlikely we can forge together any pact equivalent to the North Atlantic Treaty Organization. The best we can do, and the least we must do, is to rally our friends and allies together and simultaneously try to persuade the neutrals of Asia to come with us part of the way along the road to anti-aggression arrangements. The United States can count on some aid from the white nations concerned with Asia: Great Britain, Australia, New Zealand, and perhaps France.

But the presence of white soldiers on Asian soil would be almost a net gain to the Communists. Already Chou En-lai and his fifth columns in Asia are agitating for "mutual respect, mutual non-aggression, peaceful coexistence, and Asia for the Asians." No pact will work unless Asians are willing to fight for the independence of Asia; so far, few are. We shall have to depend on our present military allies: Korea, Formosa, the Philippines, Thaïland.

Pakistan can be counted on if we equip her army; but, by so doing, we give the Communists a propaganda weapon to use against us on Pakistan's neighbor and enemy, uncommitted India. The future of the Associated States of Indo-China is shrouded in uncertainty. Japan, as she rearms or is threatened by China and Russia, may join in our defensive arrangements; her presence will not help us make friends among the peoples of Southeast Asia. And the Asian neutrals, India, Burma, and Indonesia, will never come within signing range of an anti-Communist or an anti-Chinese alliance unless they have been invaded by China. Thus our pacts in Asia are likely to be principally with weak countries who have little industrial strength.

As a short-term policy, weak or not, for our protection and theirs we must build and support such alliances against the aggressive dynamics of China, exerting whatever restraint we can upon her. The reinforcement of Formosa is one weapon. Blocking what we can of profitable trade with the Communists is another.

But this will not be too successful a tactic because our allies desperately need more raw materials, more markets, and more commerce. Whether the United States likes it or not, the best it will be able to do is to block exports from our allies of key strategic materials; non-strategic trade with China is bound to increase. How much we should or should not try to interfere will be a tactical question of ability to act and the gains or losses involved.

The other tactical question is the one which has stirred up so much argument among ourselves and with our allies: should Communist China be admitted to the United Nations? It would be wiser if we thought of the question a different way: do we or do the Communists gain more by the admission of Communist China to the United Nations? As long as we are helping the Nationalists remain a military threat to the Reds and an alternate choice for the Chinese of Asia, it is hard to see how we can vote for Communist admission. If an arrangement were worked out for two Chinas in the UN, once Peiping was in the Assembly, it would try to throw Free China off the Security Council. Or, on the other hand, is there some possible arrangement whereby we could gain more than we would lose by her admission? Either way, our answer must be based on broader frames of reference than admission as such.

In addition to political and economic pressure on China, we shall be forced to expand our propaganda pressure on the Chinese. Our actions in the hundred years before Mao have left us an immense repository of good will on the mainland. Through the Nationalists, through Chinese Americans, through the Overseas Chinese, through our allies in Asia, and through our own efforts, in every possible way and at great cost, we must try to keep our cause alive and gradually convince the Chinese people that we are opposed to all repressive regimes in their country and want a strong, independent, democratic China to take its rightful place in the councils of the world.

But to protect ourselves and bring peace in Asia, we must follow a policy of limited short-range enmity to China while we search for a way to detach it from its Russian alliance. Attainable dream or hopeless mirage, an entente between China and the United States would change the history of the world, free the United States to guarantee political stability in Europe, and free Asia to catch up with the benefits of the West and bring a decent living to her wretched billions.

Conversely, the long-range consequences of an anti-China policy in Asia are so grave that we cannot afford to leave any possibility unexplored, no matter how small. China is, and will remain, desperately short on industry, fertilizer, food, and drugs. If the United States and/or the free world offered the rulers of China a loan or gift of tens of billions of dollars' worth of materials, would Peiping consider this a better bargain than Moscow offers her?

Russia and China have a history of hundreds of years of rivalry in Manchuria, Sinkiang, Mongolia, and other areas along their border, the longest border in the world. Is there the slightest possibility that the facts of great power politics can begin to pry the two powers apart? Could it be worth the Allies' while to consider taking the pressure off China and offering her an alternative of political friendship and industrial aid? Is there the slightest chance China could be shown that she has a brighter future as a neutral with the free world helping her peaceful development than as an enemy in an aggressive Russian alliance?

These questions, so far, would have to be answered in the negative. But are these, must these, be the final answers? If so, the choice we are forced to make in this area is not a happy one. And it has profoundly pessimistic connotations for the future of the free world.

Therefore, the most important task for American foreign policy and for the rest of the world, neutral or free, is to search for some conceivable way to move China out of the Russian orbit.

In the meantime, the United States had best face up to a far heavier burden and a far harder task in Asia than we now envisage. We shall need every friend we can find. We had better begin by understanding better the forces and events that play upon Southeast Asia, the great uncommitted arc of countries from Indonesia to India who do not know us and do not love us.

COLONIALISM IS AN EMOTION:

Indonesia

In the eight hour plane trip from Hong Kong to Indonesia, you leave behind the temperate zone of Northern Asia, pass over the jungles of North Borneo, and approach a vast and foreign area of the world, Indonesia and the other countries of Southeast Asia. Hurrying into the twentieth century, they are little known to Americans and know little about Americans.

Indonesia is the modern name for the fabulous East Indies, which Columbus set out to find. Rich in rubber, tin, tea, coffee, spices, it was the home of man at least forty thousand years before the birth of Christ. It is the world's largest archipelago, over three thousand islands, Sumatra, Java, Bali, and all the others, stretching across the southern Pacific from Singapore to Australia, a distance farther than from New York to San Francisco.

Today Indonesia has a population of almost eighty million, nearly as large as Japan's and about equal to the combined populations of Korea, Formosa, the Philippines, Malaya, and Burma. It competes with Pakistan for the honor of being the sixth largest nation in the world and the world's largest Moslem country; expert guesses here, where censuses are non-existent or undependable, put it just ahead of Pakistan in sixth place. Its *merdeka*, its political freedom, was won the hardest way; alone of the new republics of Asia, it had to fight a violent and bloody revolution against its colonial master, the Dutch.

Having won its independence, Indonesia has not been able to reap the advantages of freedom. It has been a country running downhill faster than any other in the Far East. Five years after independence, it cannot control all of its own territory or eliminate bandits and guerrillas. Its economy is in very bad shape and in spite of their idealism and sincerity, its leaders are a confused, divided, poorly trained and almost psychotically suspicious group of men who suffer from that most destructive complex of frustrations and inferiorities, the afterimage of colonialism.

Djakarta, the capital of Indonesia, is not a beautiful city. The Dutch called it Batavia and made it the administrative center for the East Indies when they ruled here; Djakarta or Batavia, it still looks like a Dutch town. Its principal avenue, Djalan Gadjah Mada, parallels the most distinctive feature of Djakarta, a shallow, slow-moving canal about twenty feet wide, which winds through the town. On each side of the canal is a wide one-way street lined with palm trees and unattractive white or dull egg-yolk yellow stucco buildings of Dutch design.

On this main street are the two best hotels of the capital, government-owned but very different from the modern air-conditioned hotels of Manila. Each has a small two-story building on the main avenue that houses the dining rooms and lounges, plus small dance floors where in the evenings bad orchestras play interminably saccharine waltzes. Indonesians trudge past the open front of the building and watch the Europeans, sweating and red-faced in the heat of the equator, ponderously whirling round and round and round.

Behind the main building is a long paved street, flanked by the plaster and white stucco living quarters of the hotel that are broken up every fifteen feet into apartments of four narrow rooms, one behind the other like railroad flats in the brownstone houses of New York. Behind a porch is a small dressing room, and its back wall is a partition of screening with a small screen door in it that serves as the front wall of your bedroom. Thus you sleep fenced off from the mosquitoes, but much cooler than under mosquito netting. Your bed consists of one sheet over a mattress and that most useful object, a Dutch wife, a long bolster over which you throw one leg so you will not perspire so much during the breathlessly hot still nights. When your room boy makes up the bed, he sweeps the sheet smooth with a little broom.

At the back of your bedroom is another screen door into the bathroom; you dodge mosquitoes in this big wide room with a couple of openings near the ceiling but no window screening.

In one corner is a shower nozzle aiming down at the tile floor; it has only one faucet because in the tropics the water is always warm. In another corner is your toilet, without lid or seat; as in Japan, you squat over it. There is no toilet paper, but an old gin bottle filled with water is convenient to your hands.

Tap water is heavily chlorinated, used only for washing. Every day your houseboy brings you a bottle filled, you hope, with boiled water for drinking and, unless you are willing to gamble with dysentery, you use this even for brushing your teeth. Boiled water is not too appetizing, but neither is the hotel food a foreigner gets in Djakarta, and unless he prefers the one or two small restaurants, he eats hotel food or he does not eat.

If the everyday food is mediocre, the famous old Sunday dinner of the East Indies, the *Rijsttafel,* is little better. You eat in an old-style Dutch dining room with high walls of dark wood paneling, pieces of Dutch stained glass sprinkled around here and there, spotted tablecloths, swarms of waiters in black velvet fezzes and once-white uniforms with high collars. A big soup bowl is placed in front of you and the waiters come by in a long parade, two dishes to a boy. Although the Rijsttafel is only half what it used to be, it runs to twenty courses; including peanut fritters and bananas fried in greasy batter, shrimps dripping in fat, tired beef on skewers with congealed peppery greasy peanut-butter sauce, fish in greasy sauce, red chili peppers in a tepid mush, fried beef black and hard like shoe leather, an old piece of chicken with skin and many pin feathers in another greasy chili sauce. Everything is tepid; the travel booklets say: "Foods are served at something less than body temperature."

Next to the Hotel der Nederlander is the Presidential Palace, a handsome neo-Georgian building right out of The Hague. There, a lucky visitor gets a chance to see a performance of one of the great ancient arts of the Indies, a *wayang,* or shadow play, in which all the characters are the shadows of flat puppets moving against a white screen. The performance is given in the beautiful ballroom of the palace, a pure white eighteenth-century-style hall with highly polished floors, fluted white Greek columns, and clusters of crystal chandeliers. The men and the Western women sit in bamboo armchairs on the puppet side of the shadow screen; the women and children of the Indies on the shadow side.

The shadow curtain is like a movie screen, but with red silk ruffles at top and bottom. On a narrow stage in front of it, the narrator sits cross-legged under a bright light, manipulating his puppets and talking in a different voice for each one. He gives foot-slapping signals to the musicians and chorus who sit cross-legged around him. The wayang has been performed ever since the Hindu conquest of Java and the musicians follow the familiar thread of the story, improvising to suit whatever new embroideries of plot the narrator weaves.

The shadow puppets are flat, made of leather no thicker than cardboard, gilded and colored, beautifully carved, and elaborately pierced to filigree the light shining through them. On the shadow side of the curtain the effect is somewhat as if you outlined very delicate filigreed iron against a white-plastered wall. The faces of the puppets are of different colors; gold or black for the good nobles, red for the nobles who have been misled, blue for stupid but not vicious men, and white for the funny men, the dupes or court jesters. All the characters have long thin and wonderfully articulated arms and hands. There are dancers and comedy characters like Abbott and Costello or Baccaloni; court ladies, elephants, horses, mountains, waves, walls and gates of towns.

With a backing of wild music, a noble, his elbows flying akimbo, his horse neighing, gallops against the wall of a fortified town; he forces the wall, and the enemy warriors atop of it to retire into the distance. Eighteenth-century coaches, pulled by four proud horses with flying manes, dash out through the wall and ride down the sides of hills like stylized conical leaves with all the material taken out except the fine veins; silhouetted in rococo filigree are the tiny princes and harem ladies inside the coaches.

After about four hours of the shadow play, your eyes begin to fall out of your head from watching the intricate designs, and your eardrums begin to fall in from the odd music and singing that accompanies it. Going outside, you can cross one of the little arched bridges that span the canal. About fifty feet away is the dazzling white-pillared palace, and looking back through the portico, past a crystal chandelier, you see the patch of white screen and the puppets of the wayang. In front of the palace, a neat patch of lawn, dazzling green in the floodlights and cut off from the street by an ornate iron fence punctuated by square sentry boxes with natty troops in half boots, khaki uniforms, white gloves, and helmets. On your side of the fence, a streetcar line with dun-colored overcrowded cars grinding along on rusted rails. In front of the tracks, cars with the steering wheels on the right, being driven along the one-way road. In front of the cars, Javanese in their batiks strolling on the narrow concrete sidewalk beside the muddy canal.

The canal is about twenty feet below the level of the sidewalk, separated from it by a three foot parapet. A vendor of balloons was sitting on the parapet, and the reflection of his balloons, red and white for the national colors of Indonesia, waved and rippled in the saffron-yellow water. The canal is shallow, slow moving, and very dirty, with bubbles and islands of putrescence and slime.

At intervals there are stone staircases that go down beside the wall to the water, very much like those to the Seine or the Tiber. On one flight of steps, a man was standing up to his shoulders in the canal, vigorously shampooing his hair, the bubbles of soapy foam on the water weaving a visual counterpoint around the reflected balloons. He scooped up a little soapy water on the flat of one finger and brushed his teeth. He was wearing a sarong and when he had rinsed his head, he unwrapped his sarong under the water, rinsed it out, twisted it back around his waist as he stepped out, thrust his feet into a pair of sandals, pulled a white sweatshirt over his shoulders, and he was done simultaneously with his laundry and his bath.

On another flight of steps a woman was sitting up to her hips in the canal, washing clothes. She soaked each piece on a step, wrung it dry of suds, flailed it down on the steps eight or ten times, making a series of staccato reports. Then she rinsed out the tough cotton and started over again. Two friends were crouched up on the parapet near her, one man wrapped in a sarong of watermelon pink, the other in a plaid of deep green and black-violet.

About sixty feet away, upstream from the washers, bathers, and toothbrushers, a man crouched over the water at the bottom of another flight of stone steps, defecating. This, the chief canal on the central boulevard of Djakarta, capital and most important city of Java, most modern of the islands of Indonesia.

The new republic has gigantic problems of health and human suffering. Where the United States has about one doctor for every six hundred Americans, and England, the Netherlands, and Japan have about one doctor for every thousand, and even India has one for every six thousand; Indonesia has only one doctor to care for every sixty thousand human beings. Most of the people go to *dukun-dukun*, doctor-dentist medicine men who can pass hands back and forth in front of a peasant's face and then painlessly pull out teeth with their fingers.

With the exception of British-administered Malaya, bad health conditions are the standard pattern in the agrarian backward civilizations of Southeast Asia, but nowhere are they worse than in Indonesia whose rich and fertile islands are full of tuberculosis, dysentery, malaria, and starvation diets as low as those in the Nazi concentration camps.

Like the other peoples of Asia, most of the Indonesians are peasant farmers; there are only two million city workers. Most of the people refuse to move to unsettled land on Sumatra and the outer islands, preferring to huddle on Java, which has some fifty million inhabitants and one of the heaviest per-square-mile populations in the entire world. Out anywhere on the island of Java, there is never a moment when there are not at least thirty people in sight, working, riding, walking, or just sitting. Along the roads are many Indonesian country carts with two huge wheels holding up a small traylike cart in which two or three dozen people ride, piled up together.

Central Java is a lovely lush land with fertile red soil, its trees and shrubs richly larger and far greener than those of the Philippines. Fruit trees, rice paddies, tapioca roots, soy beans, rubber plantations, all in a wild confusion next to each other and all growing enthusiastically and profusely. Beyond the terraced rice paddies and the rows of shrubs of the tea plantations, cloud-shrouded mountains loom up like Bali Hai's. The richer farmers live in huts with clay-tile roofs to protect them against the sun, and bamboo-matting sides to let the air in. Everybody wears the cone-shaped straw hat of the Asian equatorial countries where the sun is directly above the head all year around.

And every so often in this land you come upon a new reminder that men were erecting their monuments and temples here long before Europe had come out of the Dark Ages. One of the most beautiful is the group of old Hindu temples at Prambanam, built long before the time of the Moslem conquest, which brought Islam to this land of many religions and many histories. The temples, pyramids of ancient gray stone dappled with copper-green verdigris, sit on a low plateau and below them, in the soft grayed-violet light of the rainy season, spread out miles and miles of the clear yellowish-green of the new rice sprouts and the darker green of the high coconut trees and the shorter clumps of bamboo. In the farther distances are deep dark violet mountains.

The people live primitively, as they have for a thousand years. There are at least six children in the average family; "We have one pleasure only." If the farmers can make a little money, they do not invest it or add to their land or put it away for their old age, but spend it for some celebration, like a circumcision fete for their oldest sons.

The Indonesian family is organized almost as hierarchically as a Japanese family, with the status of every member of it defined and limited; thus there is no general term for sister or brother in the Indonesian language, only specialized terms like "older sister," "younger brother." But while they are so definite in their family obligations, they have the tropics' indefinite attitude toward time. To an Indonesian, time is not important enough to be built into the language. Instead of saying, "I went" he says, "I go yesterday" and his favorite word is *belum,* roughly equivalent to *mañana.*

The Indonesians have light to dark brown skins, straight jet-black hair, and faces that, although of Mongolian cast with wide cheek bones, are finely chiseled. They are slender, small-boned, and much shorter than Americans. A man of five feet six inches is a tall man in Southeast Asia.

The women wear their hair tied in a kind of bun at the base of the neck, showing their ears. They use little lipstick, some powder and mascara, but heavy makeup on eyebrows and eyelids, a residue of the Moslem Hindu influences. On ceremonial occasions, both sexes on Java or Bali or Sumatra dress in their native costume, the batiks, very durable cottons dyed in formalized repeated patterns. The batiks are not cut to fit the shape of the figure, but are long rectangular pieces of cotton that men and women alike wrap around themselves and knot at their waists.

Everywhere in South Asia, except in Burma and India, Western clothes are crowding out the older and colorful national costumes. In the cities of the Indies the men of all but the lowest classes now discard the batik for shorts and some kind of sport shirt. The traditional colors of the batiks are deep orange-browns and blue-black indigos printed on the white of the cotton, unbecoming colors for the white-and-pink Western complexion, but flattering to the Indonesian skin. Rarely does a Southeast Asian wear blues, he much prefers the more flattering greens or browns or reds. The word for pink in Indonesian means young red; old red describes maroon.

The poorer women wrap their batiks around them just above the breasts. Women with more money wrap their batiks below their breasts and wear light printed chiffon blouses something like Western blouses. But none of them think of design and color the way we do. With a deep orange and black batik, a well-dressed Javanese woman will wear a pastel pink blouse and carry a bright green leather bag.

In Asia, any color seems to go with any other color. Perhaps to Asian eyes the bright sun makes all colors soft.

In many countries there is a very noticeable difference between the people you see in the capital city and those you see out in the countryside, but this does not seem to be true in Java. From the people on the streets, you cannot tell whether you are in Djakarta or Bandung or up in central Java in Djokjakarta, the first capital of the Republic of Indonesia and its leading educational center.

Djokjakarta is a small quiet university town, a Cambridge or a Princeton where everybody rides bicycles and there are very few autos. Its wide main street is called Maliboro; the Dutch at the end of the eighteenth century named the street in honor of the Duke of Marlborough and Maliboro is as close as the Javanese could get to such an outlandish foreign name. At night all the bicycles on Maliboro have small oil lamps on them and the vendors who spread their wares out on the sidewalks under the mellow moon have more little Aladdin lamps to light their wares; a beautiful sight, but there is a semihaze around each oil lamp, not mist but mosquitoes.

Here in Djokjakarta is the great Gadjah Mada University with its five thousand students, an accomplishment of which Indonesia has a right to be very proud. Yet I was told that over three thousand of the students in the university are studying law. Like the Filipinos, the Indonesians do not seem to understand that an economist or a technician or a man who understands land cultivation and fertilizer formulas is a thousand times more valuable than a lawyer to a new country struggling under a terrible burden of poverty. The leading men of Indonesia tell you: "We need to be helped and we want to learn your technical crafts." If you then tactfully ask why they don't cut down on their law students: "You are here to visit our country, not criticize it!"

Indonesia has the merited reputation of being the hardest country in the Far East for whites to adjust to. There are three reasons for this. First, the Indonesians, like all the other peoples of Southeast Asia, have a sublime disregard for time. Since they also have far fewer ulcers and nervous disorders than the Westerners, perhaps they have the better part of the bargain. But when you combine this disregard for time with the lack of training and the inefficiency of the Indonesian public servant, and then you raise this double irritant to the nth degree of aggravation by adding their antagonism toward whites, you have a combination calculated to drive the man who wants to do business here almost out of his mind.

When I arrived in Djakarta, the Information Ministry gave me a typewritten sheet showing my reservations for the trip up to Djokjakarta. When I went to the offices of the Indonesian National Airline, Garuda, to buy my ticket, I found they do not cash travelers checks. So I went over to the State Bank; they open at eight, but they did not cash checks until eight-thirty. When I got back to Garuda with the money, they had no reservation under my name. I tried to phone the Information Ministry. No one knew its telephone number. When I got that straightened out, I discovered no one had booked a return seat for me. They were not allowed to phone Djokjakarta and a cable and answer took two days. They looked at me with a combination of blankness and inability to act, a glazed-eyeballs expression you find all through Asia: sometimes with a very attractive smile attached, as in Thailand; sometimes with a slightly supercilious expression, as in India; sometimes with a satisfied expression as in Burma; sometimes with disinterest attached, as here.

This return-ticket problem was serious because planes are so crowded that without a state priority you wait a month to get a seat. So I went back to the Information Ministry and we finally found my reservation. Then back again to the Garuda office to get the tickets: "Oh yes, there is a reservation, but it is for an open date." Back again to the Information Ministry because I had to return to Djakarta in two days for an interview with President Soekarno. Back again to Garuda where I discovered the reservation had been made through the Government Travel Office and so Garuda could not make out the ticket without a special form from that office. By the time we got it, it was too late to cash more travelers' checks. In most countries hotels are permitted to cash them, but the government-owned hotels of Indonesia cannot; only the government banks. The banks stay open until two in the afternoon, but they stop cashing checks at eleven in the morning. Why?—glazed eyeballs.

Or take the case of one of the very few American educators who can speak Indonesian fluently. At the invitation of the Indonesian Government, he had come to Indonesia at this particular time to inspect English teaching projects; an American foundation had given him a grant and his university had released him for the period. But when he got to the islands, he discovered the schools were out of session during the first half of his stay. So for the last couple of weeks he planned an exhausting air trip around the far-flung islands to check on as many schools as possible. The Ministry of Education sat in on his planning and agreed to get his tickets. When I left Djakarta, he was still waiting; the Ministry had not bothered to reserve his space.

From such irritations and evidences of wasted opportunities it was a pleasure to turn for one evening to old Indonesian dances for which Java and Bali are so renowned. The dancing was given in the palace compound of the Sultan of Djokjakarta. As in Europe in medieval times, the Sultan has his own dance troupe and chorus and *gamelan* orchestra, their training schools attached to his court. There were a few chairs for the guests of honor in front of a wide pavilion, tile-floored, with bamboo walls and roof, broad and beautifully proportioned. Farther back, hundreds of Javanese were crowded behind an open bamboo fence, children on their shoulders. In the hot clear darkness their whispers were a background for the whole performance.

When we were all settled down, the leader of the gamelan orchestra picked up a mallet and rapped on a wooden box. A woman dancer came on, wearing a long, figured and jeweled silk gown, split at the ankle, fitting tightly around the knees, with long trailing sashes. On her head was a golden dove with a small crown of brilliants and white plumes, and behind her ears she wore red roses. Her slow dance featured wonderfully controlled foot movements. Her bare foot came forward, the toes stretching out and writhing up; then she came down on her heel, pivoting her foot in a cross line to her body, she set her toes down, one by one; and then she danced very slowly, yet almost as high on her bare toes as a Western dancer in her ballet slippers.

The accompanying music featured women's voices chanting in strange keys, high and nasal. With them was the gamelan orchestra, the traditional music of Java. Its music is far more subtle and sophisticated and intricate than what composers of the West have devised, yet it is never noisy or clashing; the instruments are wood or bronze and their plucked, pulled, and softly struck notes hover in the air without jarring the listener.

Gamelan music is played on special kinds of instruments. Rebabs, violin-like with copper strings, giving melancholy and oboe tones. Horizontal harps with high-plucked arpeggios like harpsichords. Other strange stringed instruments with running figures, making a bass accompaniment. Once in a while a huge hanging bronze gong tapped with a felt hammer and giving out more of a shimmer in the air than a sound. Wood and metal xylophones and small gongs or drums like tambourines playing a long soft serpentine melody. You could sense the melody was there, but with Western ears you could not quite find it. A number of instruments running quickly up and down scales, not quite together, but never jarring. The total effect like hundreds of musical raindrops. Music, voices, and the movements of the dancer's body and hands and feet, all intertwining in a flowing cohesive pattern.

The final dance was a *ketoprake*, a musical play. Two male dancers and fast music. One, an evil king in maroon velvet brocades hung with royal jewelry, roared from behind a horrible red mask. His opponent, defending the people, was a monkey god in sharp blue velvet with a monkey mask of blue and black. They danced and roared, rising on one foot and fluttering gloved hands and gloved toes to indicate annoyance with each other. Finally they fought a long battle, while the gongs and strings crescendoed at high points in the pantomime, whamming away like syncopated Boris Godunov chimes. At last the evil king was killed, and out in the darkness the children sighed with relief.

It was odd to watch these ancient dances, performed in thousand-year-old costumes and set to age-old music, while attendants placed peanuts in cellophane bags and bottles of orange drink near you on the front of a stage set with modern microphones so that the people farthest out beyond the compound could hear everything.

Later, thinking back to the gamelan and the wayang, the ancient dying arts of Java, how marvelous were their intricate sophisticated patterns, and how many years of musical training and discipline it must have taken before forty or fifty illiterate peasants could learn to function together in these arts. If only the leaders of Indonesia, who so appreciate their beautiful dances and music, could understand that politics, economics, and government are at least as complicated as gamelan or wayang, that to conduct modern business successfully requires as precise interlocking as any dance.

Because they do not understand this, Indonesia's economic and political situation is exceedingly precarious. Its governing class means well and rules badly. This is the result of two forces: inadequate training for leadership, and neurotic suspicion of white men, their methods and their intentions. Both are the end product of the Dutch colonial system.

The Republic of Indonesia has been in existence only since December 27, 1949. For over three hundred and fifty years before that, the East Indies were a Dutch colony, run exactly as the Dutch chose to run it; during those years, the Indonesians were educated or trained exactly as the Dutch wished them to be. The Dutch did what they could, according to their lights; they protected the Indonesians against losing their lands to moneylenders and against exploitation by their own aristocracy; they gave the islands Western law and protection from guerrillas and bandits. They did not tax the people heavily, less than 10 per cent of the crop of an average farmer and certainly no more of a burden than was being carried by the Dutch at home. But they left the Indonesian people with pitifully few public health facilities and permitted even less educational opportunities.

The Dutch were in the Indies on business and they looked on the Indonesians, as did the other colonial powers of their time on other colonial peoples, as subjects from whom they could cheaply buy and to whom they could sell profitably. The French were pursuing almost as selfish a policy in Indo-China, and the British, although helping their subject peoples a great deal more, were still profiting from them. Truly unselfish administration by an occupying power was not seen in Asia until the United States occupied the Philippines.

Whatever contributed to their economic warehouse of the Indies, the Dutch did willingly and thoroughly; transportation, irrigation, roads, ports, these things the Dutch gave to the Indies, or rather to their own investment. Most of the income of the islands went home to enrich Holland; by 1850 it was paying over one third of the total Dutch budget. But it was a factory not a charitable institution the Dutch were running. They kept the supervisory jobs for themselves. They wanted no native business competition, and so they did not permit any Indonesian trading class to grow up, nor would they train their subjects to become their rivals in government.

This in turn led to the least admirable page in Holland's record in the Indies. Since the Dutch wanted their subject people to produce goods and buy goods, they saw no reason why Indonesians should be educated. When the Republic was created, at least 93 per cent of its people were illiterate, as bad a record as that of France in Indo-China and a terrible burden for a new democracy to carry. Under Dutch rule, only a few sons of the aristocratic class got a chance at a European education. A farmer could send a child to school for thirty-six gulden a year, which may sound reasonable but, having five or six children and a total income not running over one hundred fifty gulden a year, few could afford it.

The Dutch played the role of stern father; the Indonesians were carefully permitted no responsibilities. As late as 1941, according to the Indonesians, there were only about eight hundred doctors and sixty engineers. Of the twelve hundred secondary-school teachers, less than thirty were Indonesians and only five Indonesians were professors in the universities, one in Indonesian law, one in Moslem law, and three in medicine. Less than three hundred students were graduated each year from the high schools of the Indies.

And under Dutch rule, intentionally or accidentally, the Indonesians came to believe they were inferior in mentality to the Dutch, too inferior in abilities to aspire to managerial positions. Most Dutchmen you talk to in Indonesia still insist this is so. However, out of a group of sixty Indonesian pilots who recently went to the United States for training, fifty-eight passed the course; but when Indonesians go to Holland, only about half of them pass the courses.

Visualize yourself living under such a colonial system, or visualize yourself as a harassed ill-trained leader of post-Dutch Indonesia forced to struggle with the consequences of such a system, and you begin to see what a vicious and destructive emotional force the after-image of colonialism is and how it prejudices the peoples of Asia against the West. Perhaps Indonesia is the most vivid example of colonialism. It is not the only one. Every country of Southeast Asia, and India and China too, have been exposed to it in greater or lesser degree. It has etched hatred or suspicion or inferiority, or all three, into most Asian leaders of today.

Thus in one sense, Indonesia is a combination of the weaker sides of Japan and Korea; it has been as badly prepared and educated to rule itself as Korea and, thanks to the repression of the Dutch colonial system, its people are as neurotic and suspicious as the Japanese. One American official told me that in the last two years he, and the man who had the same job before him, had entertained at least five hundred Indonesians in their homes. Only three times had they been invited to Indonesian homes.

The attitude of the islanders cannot be explained by a special hereditary or racial background. It is worst on Java, which knew the Dutch best; it is considerably less virulent on Bali, which knew them less. And other people of the same racial stock, the Malays across on the Malay Peninsula or the Filipinos to the north, are friendly, hospitable, and outgoing.

Since most Indonesians are uneducated or have traveled very little, they assume all whites are made in the Dutch image, and impartially distrust Americans or English or Dutch. In most of Asia one of the pleasant things is the friendliness and outgoing character of the ordinary people in the streets. On Java, although the children smile at you as sweetly as anywhere else, the adults do not. They are apt to look away from you or look back at you blankly.

Until I met this reception, it had not occurred to me how free and easy the Koreans and the Javanese and the Chinese had been. Not that their faces promptly became wreathed in smiles when they saw you, as in the Philippines; but they never looked unfriendly. And in Japan where the people are reserved, they at least gave you curious side glances as they walked by. But Indonesia was one of the two places in Asia where I felt the people to be hostile. The only other place where I had such a feeling was in Vietnam, another country with a bad colonial history.

The consequences of colonialism and a backward people weaken Indonesia politically and economically, in her domestic affairs and in her foreign affairs. Although patriotic and full of good intentions, the government of the islands is ill-trained, inexperienced, and un-united. Thanks to colonialism, there are plenty of Indonesian Communists, Socialists, Marxists, and anti-American blocs, but there is no pro-American, pro-democratic or pro-Western party to stand up and remind the Indonesian people that a friendly and generous United States has granted them $22,500,000 in direct aid since 1951 as well as a $100,000,000 loan.

As in Dutch times, the islands are controlled and directed by a small central bureaucracy in Djakarta. Indonesia adopted a constitution in 1950 that guarantees substantially the same political rights as our Constitution and Bill of Rights; but their constitution set up a mechanism of parliamentary government parallel to that in France. The result has been a fragmentated chaos of parliamentary parties as bad as what France produces.

During the first five years of the new republic, it was ruled by a parliament for whom only one man in Indonesia had voted, its revolutionary leader and first president and most powerful political figure, Soekarno. In 1950 he selected and appointed the parliament, using as his criteria his own judgment of the contribution to freedom that had been made by the various groups in Indonesia, plus his own guess as to how the people would have acted if they had elected representatives. In fairness to Soekarno, it would have been impossible in this new, almost entirely illiterate nation, still convulsed with the results of the war against the Dutch and against guerrillas, to have held adequate elections in 1950.

In the first years of independence, no clear-cut division of parties with concrete programs has developed. There are four main groups in Indonesian politics, but each is actually an unstable coalition of interrelated and interantagonistic individuals. To make things harder for a foreigner to follow, three of the major groups have similar initials: the PKI, PNI, and PSI, not to mention minor groups like the PIR and the PSII. No party can count on 20 per cent of the votes in parliament.

From left to right, first comes the Communist bloc led by the PKI. Numerically they are not too powerful. They dominate the Communist-controlled All Indonesian Federation of Labor, but this is also not too important because the proletariat in the Indies is small and almost 70 per cent of the people are conservative Moslem farmers who own their own land. The PKI men are a shrewd well-indoctrinated group that plans to come to power by joining in coalitions with other parties and then gradually infiltrating until they can set up a Communist police state.

The PKI is fought bitterly by the next group on the left, the liberal Moslem PSI, the Socialists. Anti-Communist and anti-capitalist, the PSI is Indonesia's version of the British Labor Party. Its leaders are disgusted with the degeneration of their domestic affairs and are beginning to talk about the need of a dictatorship to make the people do what is good for them. An able and strong-minded man, Sutan Sjahrir, is their leader.

The center group, well to the left of center by American measurements, is the PNI, the Nationalists, founded by President Soekarno. The PNI has the largest proportion of the intellectuals and important civil servants in its ranks. Like the PKI and the PSI, it is Marxist-neutralist and anti-capitalist.

The PNI has assembled a working majority in the parliament by the very dangerous practice of joining in a coalition with the Communists. In 1953 the Communist PKI joined a cabinet under Prime Minister Ali Sastroamidjojo, a PNI man. Then the PKI, trained by Moscow in how to take over power, slipped in a Kremlin-trained man, a member of the unsuccessful Communist coup against the republic, Iwa Kusuma Sumantri, as defense minister. Then Iwa proceeded step by step to "reorganize the Army High Command" by decree while the PKI kept steady political pressure on the PNI for closer relations with Peiping and Moscow.

The best protection against such a drift toward communism is the fourth of the political parties of Indonesia, the Masjumi. Farthest to the right but well to the left of liberal American Democrats, the Masjumi stands for a Socialist, Islamic state. Appealing as it does to the peasants, it has been numerically the largest party but too subdivided to command an operating majority in the parliament. One of the leaders of the Masjumi describes it as "an elephant with beriberi"; that it may have been, but because of the unholy coalition of the Nationalists and the Communists, its leaders are now trying to forge a more powerful anti-Communist organization. Simultaneously in the mosques and in the religious schools, the Islamic holy men, the mullahs, are preaching the dangers of communism. If Indonesia can be kept from drifting into communistic hands until the middle of 1955, there may be a political change for the better after the first national election in the islands' history. Then the Masjumi may emerge with a commanding leadership in the new parliament and be powerful enough to steer their country away from neutralist-Communist sympathies.

For most of their adult lives, the leading men of Indonesia have fought and struggled for their merdeka, their political freedom, but they still do not realize that economic freedom requires just as hard a fight; they have assumed it inevitably follows political freedom. If the present non-totalitarian and non-Communist leaders of Indonesia cannot do better for their people than they have done so far, sooner or later the people will repudiate them and follow some efficient leader who will tell them what to do and shoot them if they do not do it. Already, many liberals in the islands are saying democracy is hopeless: "It takes too many trained people and we haven't got them, so a few men must do it for us."

Each of the parties vies for the support of the Army's quarter of a million soldiers; drafted, badly trained, poorly equipped, they are the only police power extant. The Army has been fully occupied trying to put down rebellions around the islands, and Djakarta has broken it up into seven corps under separate and jealous colonels. Let these men become sufficiently disgusted with lack of progress, let them form a junta, and they could rule this weak, confused, divided country.

Economically, Indonesia is in no better a position than it is politically. It produces less than it did under the Dutch; true, a good many production facilities were wrecked during the Japanese invasion, but other countries of Asia, like Japan and the Philippines and Malaya, have been able to rebuild their facilities and have brought their production back up. Another red light in the economy is its poor export record. Being an agrarian economy, it must buy abroad most of its consumer goods or capital goods, and it can only pay for them by selling its agricultural products abroad. Like other great Southeast Asian producers of raw materials, Malaya, Burma, and Thailand, its economy has been seriously weakened by the steep decline in rubber and tin prices that followed the end of the Korean War. Rubber gives Indonesia almost half of her foreign exchange.

The combination of lowered raw-material prices and inability to increase production means that Indonesia's international purchasing power has fallen. And this in a period in which the rising birth rate is adding another million people a year to the islands. The result has been a huge budget deficit and rising inflation.

Such a decline is unnecessary. There are plenty of raw materials in Indonesia that other countries need, there is plenty of unused land on which to raise more raw materials, there is an oversupply of labor available; but they are not being put together. The Western techniques and advisors necessary to halt this economic downslide are available to Djakarta, as they have been to Manila and Taipei and Seoul. It is obviously to our advantage to help build stable governments that can withstand Communist blandishments. But the Indonesian leaders will not accept the help of capitalists; instead they are hell-bent on erecting a pure Socialist system of government ownership and operation, sincerely believing this is the only way a people can raise its standard of living.

The Chinese and the Dutch are responsible for this phobia. First of all, in a characteristically Southeast-Asian attitude, like the Burmese and the Thais and the Malays, the Indonesians have never been interested in business. The Dutch kept them out of finance and the approximately three million Overseas Chinese of the islands, conducting their businesses with typical Chinese vigor, exercise an almost complete domination over retail trade that the Indonesians do not seem interested in challenging.

Hated and discriminated against by the earlier Dutch regime and the present republic, the Indonesian Chinese have shown little interest in deepening their connections with the country in which they live. Even when Indonesia, finally seeing the folly of isolating these powerful hua-chiao, offered them the rights of citizenship, less than 10 per cent were interested. Red China enjoyed great prestige among them long before the dazzling Communist victories in the Indo-China war.

Now, more than ever, the Indonesian hua-chiao wish to keep on the good side of Peiping; that does not make them an influence for political stability in Indonesia.

Also, the Chinese have always been the moneylenders of Indonesia, frequently at exorbitant interest rates. The islanders, knowing capitalism only through the exploitations of the Chinese or Dutch, have seen only the evil side of capitalism and so now they want their government to protect them from it by setting up a socialist system. And the government is equally convinced that its people can defend themselves from capitalistic monopolies only by means of a central government operating the economy. Therefore, Djakarta, with no clear conception of the economic processes involved, rules, regulates, decides, and extends government operation. Result: more and more burdens for the government and more and more wrong decisions.

It is characteristic of ex-colonial countries that when they get their freedom they keep some of the worst features of the colonial government. Djakarta, like Delhi or Rangoon, founders in colonial red tape. In Indonesia you are required to go through customs again when you go from one Indonesian island to another. The government ministries pay customs charges on everything they import, down to inkwells; the Ministry of Defense paid customs charges on the guns they bought. True, it was money taken out of one government department and put into another, but it made more paper work for everybody concerned in a capital with few skilled clerks. Why?—glazed eyeballs, again; but this time I could recognize it as a relic of the days when the Dutch imposed these duties, and then the money, a neat form of concealed taxes, went into the Dutch administration budget.

But far worse than the inherited red tape is the socialistic blundering of the Indonesian Government. Take housing conditions in the overcrowded city of Djakarta. Houses are not hard to build here, where you need no foundations. There are plenty of men who need jobs, plenty of wood in the forests of Java to supply materials, and plenty of customers eager to rent rooms. Yet little is being done.

The hotels of the city, all owned by the government, are jampacked. It is impossible to get a room without reservations months in advance because many of them are held on a semi-permanent basis by government officials who cannot find housing anywhere else. But foreign capital would not consider coming in to build a hotel because it would go bankrupt as a result of the low price ceilings imposed by the inexperienced housing authorities. My own half of a small suite, plus three meals, plus early morning and afternoon tea, plus all the laundry I wanted washed in this hot climate, cost me a total of $2.70 a day. The Indonesian officials are eager to have private enterprise help ease the housing shortage, but when you try to show them that it is an economic impossibility, they seem to stop listening.

The same pattern of economic ignorance applies in industrial projects. At Tandjong Priok, the harbor of Djakarta, is the Indonesian Motor Service Company, the first government-owned assembly plant in Indonesia, where American jeeps, Dutch trucks, and English autos are assembled. In spite of the loss in efficiency, the government deliberately uses machines from three different countries because they are afraid if only one foreign company was used, "it would get a hold." Similarly, German companies are hired for hydroelectric projects, Japanese for mining, and Dutch for dredging.

The Government of Indonesia set up its own assembly plant because it wanted to learn about assembling and selling motor cars; the foreign dealers in Indonesia "won't give our people dealerships because they don't think we're good enough at it." Since there were no Indonesians with capital and since the government could not very well select an Indonesian at random and lend him the money to start a plant, it had to build the plant itself.

There was a startling contrast between this assembly plant on Java and plants I had seen a few hundred miles north in the Philippines. There, the plants were partly owned by Filipinos and the workmen were Filipinos, but American private enterprise experts were partners and teachers in the ventures. The Philippine plants had been spotless. In the Indonesian factory, the cement floor over which the workers pulled heavy pieces of machinery, was littered with several banana peels and some broken pieces of wood, a good opportunity for industrial accidents or wrecked machines. I watched some Indonesian workers swing an auto body into place over a chassis; four men were doing their best, but they pulled in different directions, above them the chain holding the body was twisted, and they jammed one of the fenders while lowering it onto the chassis.

If he is well trained, a Javanese is no less able to handle his job than an American or a Filipino. But this plant had only one foreign technician and its workers had never been to high school or had a chance at any mechanical training.

With Indonesia in its present situation, state socialism cannot do an adequate job without money or foreign trained technicians. Yet the leaders are so distrustful of foreigners and capitalists they offer little reason for foreigners to come in and they make life almost impossible for them when they get there. One private firm, after months of petitioning, was allowed by the government to have a single phone for its one hundred and eighty employees; the government considers the company very unappreciative because it is still complaining. Government regulations forbid outgoing calls before one o'clock in the afternoon, and on Java business starts at eight in the morning and finishes for the day at two.

It would be easy for businessmen to show this country what is wrong and teach them how to right it. But the Western world is not dealing with data here; it is dealing with an emotion, a blind spot of psychotic proportions. The anti-capitalist bias has been burned in, not by communism, but by colonialism. The handful of men who rule Indonesia grew up under a colonial system that was also a capitalist system; whenever they saw a colonial master they saw a believer in capitalism: therefore, the two are inseparable and equally evil.

At the same time, the young intellectuals were searching for an alternate philosophy of life that would condemn the system which taught them to believe they were unalterably inferior to the whites. They found this in Marxism with its neat logical explanations of history that preached the evil of capitalism, and taught that it would disappear; two comforting thoughts to a yellow-skinned downtrodden intellectual.

This Marxist bias conditions the thinking of every important leader in the Indies or in Burma, and it pervades every university in this part of the world. Nothing the leaders or the young intellectuals have since learned has altered this approach. No Indonesian better illustrates this Marxist bias than the combination Washington and Jefferson of Indonesia's hard-won revolution, President Soekarno, the most powerful and popular political figure in the islands. On holidays, one hundred thousand Indonesians mass in the park in front of his Palace to cheer their *Bung Karno,* their brother Soekarno.

In 1945 Soekarno gave an impromptu speech, The Birth of Pantjasila, outlining the five principles on which to base the new republic. The Pantjasila is the equivalent for his people of our Declaration of Independence and the Preamble to the Constitution. In it he pictures the Soviets as liberators of their country from the yoke of the Czars: "within a Soviet Russia did Stalin set free the hearts of the people, one by one." And later on he talks about democracy and the United States: "Is it not in America that the capitalists are dominant? . . . what is called a democracy is merely political democracy; there is no social justice and no economic democracy at all."

Incorporating these convictions in the basic enunciation of Indonesian political principles, associating whites with colonialism and capitalists with exploitation, it is not surprising that the men who rule Indonesia are less friendly to the United States, and more friendly with China and Russia, than any other government in non-Communist Asia.

At best, they pursue a neutral foreign policy. They have exchanged ambassadors and missions with Peiping and Moscow and they dislike America's allies, the Formosans and the Koreans. They saw us as trying to extend colonial power in Vietnam and, "South Korea is a reactionary government set up by the United States to get colonial control of all Korea." They have a very different picture of Russia's role in the Korean aggression: "Oh, Russia is not a colonial power; she gave her people economic freedom."

From Indonesia's point of view there is no reason why she should choose sides. She sits off by herself, separated by water from the mainland of China. She has too little military or industrial strength to be valuable in war. She knows Russia and Red China would not bother her until they had won the rest of Southeast Asia; she knows the United States would not invade her. So she chooses to sit tight and sell raw materials to whoever will buy them. She will sign no kind of Pacific pact useful to the United States. If one could be constructed so meaningless as to be able to be signed simultaneously by Communist China and the United States, Indonesia's signature would be there just below India's and Burma's.

Much as she needs money and more financial aid, Indonesia will not take it from us if it has the remotest of military strings attached to it. One government had to resign in 1952 because the foreign minister signed a Mutual Security Agreement with the United States. And this quatrain from the *Times*, the largest newspaper in English in Indonesia, shows their point of view:

Foreign aid's a fat spider's kindness
For under-developed nations
Without capital and technical fineness
That is to say, for fly-like Asians.

Today there is little the United States can do to influence the immediate course of events in Indonesia. If it is going to drift into economic chaos, dictatorship, or communism, we cannot prevent it. It is, and will remain, a non-effector nation. In our time it is not going to change the history of the world or swing the balance of great powers. If China conquers Southeast Asia, Indonesia will become part of that bloc; if free Asia gradually strengthens itself, the islands will remain uncommitted.

If the United States wishes to help change Indonesia, we are going to have to do it indirectly, through countries she does not distrust. Pakistan understands the strengths of capitalism and knows it is a far different kind of thing from that which Karl Marx described; Indonesia respects and admires her fellow Moslems to the West; perhaps gradually Indonesians may listen to their advice. Another long-range influence is her northern neighbor, peopled with fellow Malays, the Philippines. Today, because the Filipinos respect the United States, Indonesian leaders are not enthusiastic about them, refusing to think of them as Asians: "It is not that their way of thinking is Western, it's just not Eastern; it may not necessarily be bad, but it doesn't attract us." Many of their editors scorn the Filipinos as lackeys of the United States, seduced by American temptations to spend and be corrupt. The corruption of the Quirino government helped them get this impression. But as Magsaysay and his administration can shape their islands into a modern country bringing longer life and more benefits to its people, Djakarta is bound to be impressed.

Already, English is the second language in the schools and each year a few more American teachers lecture in the classrooms. A few American business firms have been recently employed to make surveys of Indonesian administration and commerce. And some young Indonesians are beginning to wonder if their Marxism is such a sound prescription for twentieth-century progress.

The United States should let time work for it instead of trying to rush things. We cannot rush this people or this part of the world; we can do little in Indonesia and we should do it with exaggeratedly scrupulous regard for their suspicions. Our missions and information services should constantly stress that our progressive, socially responsible capitalistic system is ready and willing to help Indonesia work out its future, but only on a mutually advantageous basis, not by giving them something for nothing. No Asian understands this kind of help so he promptly begins searching for concealed power fish hooks in what he thinks is bait.

Most of all, these leaders of Indonesia are patriots whose heart is in the struggle to make their freedom work. Little by little, through our friends in Asia and with an adult patience toward an adolescent who has been psychologically wounded in childhood, we can help these men realize that making an economic system work is a job that requires thousands of trained experts who have graduated from the school of capitalism. Then they will appreciate and make these technicians welcome in their country. Once they and we work shoulder to shoulder in the same plants and power stations and public health wards, mutual respect will grow. But it is going to take a long, long time.

ASIAN MELTING POT:

Malaya

Over and over again, geography is deceptive in Asia. Geography books show the archipelago of the East Indies as one color because the Dutch made a single administrative area of these very different islands. But that did not make a national unity out of this diversity, as the bedeviled leaders of Indonesia are discovering. In Indo-China, the French made an administrative unit, called Indo-China on the maps, out of three countries which had nothing else in common. The Republic of Burma is trying to weld together a nation from dissimilar and antagonistic tribes which a single British administration had ruled.

The same lack of wish or will for national unity distinguishes another Southeast Asian geographical unity, the Malay Peninsula. It is a long pendant of tin and rubber that dangles down from Burma and Thailand to the Strait of Malacca only fourteen miles away from the coastal islands of Indonesia's Sumatra. Four fifths jungles and mountains, smaller than England and Wales, this Malay Peninsula is the conglomerate supreme of Southeast Asia. It is a federation of nine Malay states and two former settlements, plus the colony of Singapore. An accident of geography placed both on the same peninsula; an accident of colonial conquest placed both under British rule. The Federation of Malaya is ruled by a High Commissioner and a Federal Legislative Council, and Singapore is a Crown Colony ruled by a governor.

Singapore, prize port and naval base, meeting place of two oceans and crossroads of the world, was founded by the English and has been settled by the Chinese, who have made it one of the greatest Chinese cities of Asia and who make up 80 per cent of its population. The

Federation of Malaya is a mixture of three races with no one of them having a workable majority: three million Malays, two and a half million Chinese, and two thirds of a million Indians who are Tamils from South India.

Singapore, at the southern tip of the peninsula, is a flat swampy free port, an ugly harbor, and trading center half the size of Hong Kong. It is a mixture of things British and Chinese: Westminster chimes in cupolas, Victoria Memorial Halls and cricket on the water front; miles of drab streets shimmering in the equatorial heat and teeming with busy Chinese; lined with the regulation two-story Chinese buildings waving with laundry and banners, opening their fronts on arcaded sidewalks. Garages, small stores, bicycle repair shops; a semi-mechanized and wholly Eurasian setup where East and West are bedded down as roommates for a couple of itinerate nights. Not a vigorous and Victorian Hong Kong who has taken a comely Chinese concubine to his bed; just a small-minded and industrious clerk, out for the night.

The Federation is a land of jungles, mountains, and wild rivers. Two raw products, tin and rubber, create 70 per cent of its jobs and wealth. Its capital, Kuala Lumpur, is like an English town set in the foothills of the Ardennes with the summer climate of Florida, mosquitoes and all. Singapore is hot dark ocher-oranges; Kuala Lumpur is deep cool greens and mountain purples. Along the roads, the best ones west of Honolulu, are hundreds of neat English villas with English flower gardens. These gradually change into Chinese houses and stores crowding up to the administrative center of the Federation on Jalan Raja Street. A collection of buildings with improbable Indian and Arabic architecture, a conglomeration of Islamic arches and domes built by the British in the late nineteenth century, and the whole mass is topped by properly unlingamal minarets most unelevating to the enthusiastic realism of the fertile Malays and Indians.

In Malayan, *kuala* means "mouth of the river" and *lumpur*, "a muddy place." Perfect descriptions of today's Malaya, muddy delta of three great rivers of people and their accumulated silt of social behavior and psychological patterns; a confluence, confusion, and cross rip of contradictory and unreconciled cultures.

Across from the west, from the Bay of Bengal and South India, flow the tamils with their sloppy dirty clothes, dirty bodies, dark skins, and their dark cruel gods. Down from the north flow the vigorous currents of the Overseas Chinese with their yellower clearer tighter skins, their Confucianism, and their absorption in their families and their businesses. From the east, across the Strait from Sumatra and Indonesia come the third stream of peoples, the Malays, their faces soft brown and unlined, Islamic, indolent living, fun loving.

And, presiding over them all, buffeted by everybody, disliked by everybody, but clutched onto by everybody, the British river superintendents, floodgate openers-and-closers supreme. Hopefully preparing schemes to coax the cross tides of race and religion to subside into a placid Victorian pool of democracy, all the British ask in return is the preservation of their nineteenth-century British-controlled free enterprise: their rubber plantations, tin mines, trade, banking, cargoes. And, of course, their profits.

Today these profits are gravely threatened by two internationally caused forces that neither the British nor Malaya could prevent: international communism and falling world prices of raw material. The Malayan Communist terrorists have sabotaged tin mines and rubber plantations, killing white managers of both, and forcing the government to spend hundreds of millions of dollars for internal defense. Simultaneously, the fall of world raw-material prices since the end of the Korean War has undermined the finances of the federation. This same influence is undermining the economy of every raw-material producer in Southeast Asia: Burma, Thailand, Indo-China, Indonesia, the Philippines, Malaya; they all depend on exports of raw materials to give them financial strength to raise their living standards.

As world prices fall and their chief customer, the United States, buys less for less, inflation grows in these countries, their Communists are strengthened, and the United States ends up with new expenses for mutual security programs. Since we buy so much of their materials, if the Western democracies could get together on a price-stabilization program, it would do much to help these countries, enabling them to know what they are going to earn and to be able to plan accordingly. By themselves, the British in Malaya can do little as the prices of rubber and tin fall and the deficits of the federation soar. A rubber plantation cannot be closed down and a tin mine has huge capital investments in machinery that you cannot afford to leave idle, so you must produce, profitably or not; also, if you stopped, employment would fall and the Communists would have a new weapon.

So the great piles of modern western machinery, the tin dredges, go on their clanking way, one of the more incongruous sights in the scrubby jungles of Malaya. A seventy-foot-high, five-million-dollar

Gargantua of corrugated steel, pipes, buckets, and gears is assembled on a piece of dry land over the tin ore. The tin dredge is moored by long braided steel ropes to cement blocks five hundred feet away. Then a river is diverted, makes a small lake around the dredge, and is returned to its old channel. Giant winches aboard the dredge slowly reel the guy ropes in or out, and the tons of machinery slowly start their ponderous progress, moving through the lake only a few inches a day, flinging out behind the sand extracted from the tin ore. This sand builds new dry land behind the dredge and thus the lake is always being pushed along with the inching of the dredge, a liquid brood around a mother monster.

At the front of the dredge is a long chain of cast-iron buckets, each weighing three tons. They grind down into the water, and on down for a mawful of the tin-bearing sand. Slowly they grind back up a full seventy feet above the water to the top of the dredge. The dumped wet sand then starts back down, seventy feet of cascading mud falling from one separating chamber after another. Three stories of great spouts spew forth the regurgitated water and sand as it is diluted, shaken, strained, separated. Finally, far down in the innards of the dredge, a few tubes, like small stovepipes, dribble out a few grains at a time, the black, gritty, heavy tin ore that is the profit of the whole operation.

A few miles from such a dredge will be Chinese-owned tin-mining operations, and they are several centuries different. A rickety scaffolding of bamboo, lashed together wherever it threatens to collapse, leads down into an open pit where a dozen Chinese coolies flush the sand loose with fire hoses. A chain of small buckets carries it up to the top of the bamboo scaffolding and dumps the mud into a long rough-wood trough. At the other end of the trough, six or eight old Chinese women in rusty black push the residue into bamboo trays and carry it off on their heads to the separating room.

The workers do not have to be driven in cars to the mines as the western-style miners are to the dredge lake; their shacks are put up right beside the scaffolding. The Chinese owner of the tin mine would think himself a bad manager if he could not pull a 30 per cent profit out of his mine each year. And the Communist guerrillas in Malaya would think they were pretty poor terrorists if they could not threaten or beat a useful donation out of these Chinese mine owners.

The other prime source of profits and government revenue in Malaya is the beautiful modern rubber plantations. The groves of rubber trees have very much the same aura as the sequoias of California: tall, straight, clean, their trunks are gray-green and earth-brown, with small clear leaves on a few lateral branches high up on the trees, and every branch reaches upward, seeming to enfold and soften every sound into a spell of serene quiet.

On well-run plantations, the trees are planted in neat straight rows and the underbrush is kept cleared. There is a feeling of clean spaciousness as the light from the humid tropical sun filters softly down between the rows and along the aisles. The rubber-yielding sap flows best at dawn, and so when the golden light washes out the cool blues of sunrise, down the rows of trees Malays and Indians collect the latex, working quietly in their colorful sarongs faded by sun and washing.

Peaceful as they may appear, these plantations have been besieged blockhouses in the costly terrorist war that a handful of Communists have been waging in Malaya. If the terrorists could smash the tin mines, slash the rubber trees, and kill the few thousand skilled supervisors and managers, almost all whites, the economy of the peninsula would fall apart. Around the manager's house and the curing sheds of these peaceful-appearing rubber plantations are high barbed-wire fences and guardhouses with perimeter lights that burn all night. When the managers go out on their daily inspection of the groves, they ride in jeeps with guards, for out of these peaceful trees at any moment may come a shot and there will be one less manager. This is part of what the Communists call the "peaceful life of the big-business exploiters of the proletariat."

The Achilles' heel of the Communists in Malaya has not been a peasant reaction to their vicious terrorism or the military and propaganda warfare of our side. It is food. A Communist cannot live in the jungle, where no British plane can find him, and still raise his food; if he steals it, he gives the British a clue on where he is operating. He has had to terrorize the workers into smuggling him food and so these Indians or Malays or Chinese plantation workers, with their little earthen pots full of latex, may have food concealed under their bras or up their sarongs. Even the water they carry may be saturated with sugar which they plan to leave at some spot where the jungle comes down to the trees and the terrorists can come and get it.

By keeping a close eye on the workers, by resettling peasants where the terrorists cannot intimidate them, and by an elaborate arrangement of patrols and road blocks, the British have managed to win a limited success against the Communists. But controlling terrorists in a country where the virgin jungle flows down to the edges of every plantation, mine, or settlement, has been an extremely costly and arduous success.

And the internal Communist threat, although less ominous today, has terrifying connotations for the free world. Working in small groups and slipping away into the jungle between raids, the Malayan Communists have done so much with so little against so many, and it has cost such a disproportionate amount of effort to neutralize them.

There are probably not more than fifty to a hundred hard-core Communist fanatics in the whole movement. Yet since 1948, the measures against them have cost the governments of Britain and Malaya $250,000,000; 40 per cent of the fit male population on Malaya is under arms and, besides the 245,000 members of the Home Guard, the government has needed 40,000 troops from other parts of the British Commonwealth, from Africa to the Fiji Islands, including some 25,000 land troops and navy and air force men from Britain itself. All these, plus 7000 Malay troops, 25,000 regular police, and 40,000 auxiliary police, have barely won out against some 5000 ill-trained, ill-armed, ill-fed terrorists who got hardly a penny and few guns from China, nothing from Russia. Worse, they were able to create their enormous havoc at a time when their supporters, the Chinese Communists, were weak and preoccupied far to the north. Now that Peiping need no longer sustain a war in Korea, she can divert more and more strength to the south and support her fellow believers in Malaya.

With the partition of Vietnam, the Malayan Communists took new heart and stopped surrendering; they realize that, as long as Red China remains the enemy of the West, they and their fellow terrorists in the rest of Southeast Asia are worth many times their weight in instructors and pamphlets from Peiping. Not to mention old guns and cheap bombs.

If the Communists were assembled in one place, it would be easy to destroy them, but there are few communists and many hilly patches of jungle in Malaya, and since no one can tell from which hill or patch the terrorists will come, the anti-Communists must spread out over the whole country. This jungle guerrilla warfare tactic is the real threat to Southeast Asia. There will never be trained maneuvering Communist armies here like those of North Korea. The threat in Indo-China or Thailand or Burma or Indonesia or the Philippines is essentially the same kind as in Malaya; and an immensely more difficult tactic for the free world to counter than Korean warfare.

To see what kind of everyday, undramatic job was involved in this Southeast Asian warfare, I went out with a squad of the First Battalion of the Queen's Own Royal West Kent Regiment on a routine jungle patrol. It is hard to get used to the fact that the jungles of Asia are so little like the jungles of central Africa or Brazil. The first part of our patrol, through light underbrush, was a beautiful walk past firs and palms in a soft thin early-morning fog. The special jungle boots of the patrol and my rubber sneakers crushed down jungle wild flowers, delicate pinks like wild asters, small pale blue heather flowers, and vines with apricot-colored verbena blossoms. A few birds sang in the mist and once in a while there was a little clear stream bubbling over rocks.

It was almost impossible to realize that we were hunting for Communists. From a distance you might have thought we were bird watchers, until you saw that the men had their guns out of their holsters. Now and then there would be a slight clink, as a grenade at one of the men's belts swung against his canteen or belt buckle. Behind and in front of me, other men walked along with their Bren guns. When we talked, it was in slow whispers. When one man stopped, everybody stopped, always staying thirty feet apart so that if a Communist from behind some tree or clump of brush shot one of us, the others could get under cover before he could swing his gun to a new target.

As we went deeper in the jungle, the growth got wilder, the swamps got deeper, and it began to steam. We watched for snakes, and when we came out of a swamp we pulled up our trouser legs to look for leeches. The jungle-patrol lieutenant wanted to lead me around the next swamp and back to the highway because he thought I was "a bit mature for this sort of thing."

But away across one more valley, on top of a small mountain was an old bandit camp. There had been whispers from some Malays that the Communists were back there. The troops were itching for a chance to get near a Communist after all their waiting and slogging. So we set out across a long valley to the mountain. We were now spread out fifty feet apart because high up on the top of the mountain was a tree that made a perfect observation post for Communist snipers.

Two valleys back, this had seemed exciting. Now, marching along in the bright sun, I was certain there was a Communist rifle propped in the crotch of that tree, waiting for me to get within range. I was wearing light gray trousers and a white shirt; not only did my white shirt make a nice target, but to a Communist the civilian clothes in the midst of the army troops would label me as a political commissar and therefore the prize target. The jungle suddenly felt much hotter.

Finally we came to the foot of the little mountain and started straight up, pulling ourselves from one tree or bamboo thicket to the next. Dense cover all around us. Anyone could be watching three yards above us. When I slipped and a branch broke with a loud snap, I could see the shoulder muscles of the men in front of me tighten. Half an hour on up the mountain we stopped on signal while the lieutenant and one other man went to the top to reconnoiter. A long tense pause. The other men ready to charge on up; me, gunless and more than ready to leap out of their way. Then a single bird note from the top of the mountain, the all-clear.

When we got to the crest, the lieutenant said, "You are the first journalist who has wanted to come this deep." I felt pleased until he added a reward: "Wouldn't you like to climb the lookout post, sir?" The lookout tree was forty feet high and hung out over the sheer drop down to the valley three hundred feet below; its ladder was cracked pieces of bamboo lashed together with grass. Climbing, I hoped I seemed fairly nonchalant, even when a bamboo crossbar gave way under my weight. Halfway up I took a couple of quick looks down into the valley, put a big show of satisfaction on my face and started back down. The lieutenant was still helpful: "No view from there, sir. Try it from the top, it's quite fair." I suppose it was, but I did not enjoy it.

The bandit camp had been a luxurious one for important leaders. There was one little platform of branches, three feet off the ground, with a couple of bamboo supports for it, and poles above with a grass thatch. This was the Kremlin of the camp. Nearby, an old rubber sneaker with some blood dried on it and some little yellow cardboard boxes that had held camera film; again this was a proof that some important Communist leader had been there because "the big blokes are rather vain, they're always taking pictures of themselves in brave positions."

There was nothing else on the mountaintop except a crude table without any thatching above it. At night the guerrillas lie on the ground and pull the leaves of a small palm tree down to cover them.

On the other side of the camp were some rough steps cut in the side of the hill and reinforced with bamboo. They led down to a concealed pile of stones with a little charred wood on them, the kitchen. A small stream flowed near by: "Find the water and that's where the buggers are." We found four other ways down from the hilltop, all through nearly impenetrable growth.

It takes a special kind of bravery to stay steady under the unending discomfort and tension of these daily jungle patrols, sometimes going for months without firing a gun and sometimes being killed on your first day out. As the lieutenant of my patrol put it: "When you've been on patrol all day and you basher up at night, well, it just hits you and you are exhausted, but you grip yourself and get prepared for the next day." These men serve out here for three-year terms.

Cold is probably more uncomfortable than damp heat or mosquitoes, snakes, and leeches, and certainly more Americans died in Korea than British here on this peninsula. But here in Malaya the young British soldiers seem to realize they are doing the same kind of dirty job their fathers and grandfathers accepted in their day. The British learned a hundred years ago what the Romans learned over a thousand years ago: safety at home requires power abroad and that power depends on uncomfortable and bored centurions, Rome's in Parthia, Britain's in Malaya, ours in Korea, on duty and being killed. Whether you want it or not, world leadership seems to be something for which you are required to pay in the sacrifice of lives of your own young men.

From the jungle patrol, I drove back to Kuala Lumpur to explore why men were willing to live the wretched hunted lives of the Communists. In a secret psychological warfare office I spent a day talking with the most important Malay Communist who had thus far deserted, Lam Swee, formerly political commissar for the Fourth Communist Regiment in South Johore. Lam Swee was a small, mild, and shy man who had first fallen into communism because of his idealism and his drive to try to help his people to a better life.

With Lam Swee, the first appeal was the anti-Japanese work of the Malayan Communists. This was back in 1937 when the Japs had invaded China and Lam Swee, whose Chinese parents had recently emigrated from the homeland, joined up in Malaya to collect funds for the fight in China: "I admired the Communist Party as a gallant warrior ready to succor the weak. And I longed for a new order where everybody would have rice to eat and everybody would find employment." All Lam Swee wanted for himself was a job as a barber.

The war came, the Japanese conquered Malaya, the patriots like Lam Swee retreated to the hills, the familiar pattern repeated itself in one more Southeast Asian country. The hard-core Communists were already identified as anti-Japanese leaders and they had been prepared by Moscow or Mao to be tough effective guerrilla fighters. So they became the patriotic leaders against the Japanese invaders using the resistance movement to build up their following for Communist postwar control.

In Vietnam a Moscow-trained man of great ability, Ho Chi Minh, emerged; in Malaya it was Chang Peng, born in China and trained in Russia. In the years of jungle fighting, Chang Peng and Company now were able to give the Lam Swees of Malaya a thorough course in Communist dialectics: colonialism and the exploiting capitalist British must be thrown out of Malaya so a Communist state could give the peasants the tin and rubber plus food and freedom. In telling his story, Lam Swee never referred to Russia but only to the Chinese Communists. We in the West are wrong when we assume communism in Asia means the Soviet Union.

With the war over and the British back in control, Lam Swee and his fellow patriots came out of the jungle. Here was the point of no return in the Malay terrorist story. If there had been a Magsaysay on the spot to adopt the sweeping social measures that communism has since forced on Malaya, it could have eliminated the Communist threat in 1945. But the British continued their colonial free enterprise as they had before the war: "There were no jobs and we were wandering about unemployed after laying down our weapons. It was impossible to obtain two meals a day and a bed at night."

So Lam Swee joined a labor union to turn it communistic. When the British caught on to this he and his comrades fled into the hills to share in the vicious terrorism, the torturing of women and children to extract money, the killing of whites, the wrecking of Malaya. Nor was it British counterpropaganda that finally changed his mind. Only the corruption of the Malay Communist leaders, who suspected him of being a counterrevolutionary, finally led him to surrender.

The Communists never tried to "sell" Lam Swee their system or to make it easy for him to assimilate. Once they had him making common cause with them through his idealism, they started him on a long intellectual indoctrination. No three-month tour of Chinese or Russian Communist centers as we Americans do with our three-month Leadership Grants, which enable young Asians to take a quick hop, skip, and jump around a few American cities. The Communists deliberately make their indoctrination long, tough, and hard; they slowly unfold tested propaganda theses arranged to appeal to the young, and they have a group of rigidly trained teachers to put it over.

The British, under the magnificent leadership of Malaya's former High Commissioner and outstanding World War II intelligence general, Sir Gerald Templer, have succeeded for the present in putting down the Communist terror; and they believe Malaya's Politburo has been forced to flee across the Strait to hideouts in Sumatra. But the British know this is only chapter one in their fight. They must find ways to keep Malaya solvent and provide a gradually rising standard of living.

Hard as this will be to do, it is easy compared to their central problem. The days of colonial rule are over. If they wish to keep their investments in Malaya, they must turn over political control of the country to the people before the political situation explodes into another Indonesia, Burma, or Vietnam.

Such an assignment is a test for any power's wisdom; it is made difficult here by the combination of three incompatible races who make up the people of Malaya: the Indians, the Malayans, and the Overseas Chinese. Of the three, the Tamil Indians who have emigrated to Malaya are least important. But that does not mean they can be easily assimilated in a Malayan melting pot. The Tamils brought with them all their own lares and penates, their individual culture and gods, and one of the weirder but most illuminating sights on this peninsula is the great Indian fete of the year, a sort of Hindu Easter, when over thirty thousand Tamils gather at the Batu Caves in central Malaya to celebrate the birthday of their god Subramanya.

The high point of the day is when Subramanya is brought down to the river to be bathed. His cart is drawn by a team of sacred white bullocks and the god is enthroned on a great green-gilded peacock. On each side of him, attendants hold gold-fringed parasols, one of bright pink, one of verdigris-green. Right in front of the cart a number of priests wave visual *shashnik*, long brass rods dipped in flaming turpentine. Around Subramanya's juggernaut car with its crude wooden wheels, more priests blow frantic music through long wooden clarinet-like pipes about three feet long with wide wooden mouths, very similar to the old Hebrew trumpets. Other priests beat dark gourd-like drums, their fingers coated with sacred ashes so they seem to be beating time with ashen gloves. Subramanya is about four feet high, of copper painted a bright scarlet, and adorned with a gold sari covered with jewels. He has diadems on all six of his heads and bracelets and rings cover his twelve hands. The Hindus believe he was originally six children but that in an excess of maternal adoration, his mother squeezed all the children in her arms and thus this six-headed memento of Hindu Momism, Subramanya.

His priests pointed out exactly where the god would go down to the river for his bath and told me it would be a very colorful ceremony, so I set up tape recorders beside the steps leading down to the water. It is typical of today's civilizations that the steps built for the god's descent were faced with rusted pieces of iron emergency-landing strips left over from the war. When I heard the cart approaching, I turned on my recorders and started a description of the scene as the cart stopped some thirty feet away. While I was talking, a priest wandered down the steps with a little brass pot, dipped it full of water, and emptied it. This was the symbolic bath. Very different from what they had described.

When three Asians, or six, tell you definitely that something is going to happen at a given time and place, whether those Asians are Malays, or Chinese, or Indians, or Indonesians, or Japanese, you know no more than you did before: maybe the god will come down to the river when they say he will, maybe he will come another time or to another place, maybe he will never come, or maybe he will come to the river bank and then turn around and go back up to his cave, having been ceremoniously bathed by proxy in a little brass pot.

While Subramanya bathed, the Indians paid him little heed, most of them absorbed in their own trances. Along the shallow muddy river bed, worshipers performed ceremonial ablutions. No washing under sarongs here, they stood and scrubbed stark naked in the two feet of water. Only a yard or two away from some male bathers, a young woman, sedate in her own dream, sacred ash and sandalwood paste on her face, a diamond in one nostril, wound herself into her sari. She slowly pirouetted in toward an older woman who held the other end of the six yards of her pale rose-and-gold silk.

Up and down the river banks were knots of a few hundred people, each clique absorbed in its wild trance of exaltation, each with its own frantic tom-toms and wailing wood flutes, each intent on its own escapism, whirling, grimacing, jiggling up and down in short quick hops. In the centers of the little crowds, devotees were having long skewers plunged into their cheeks and arms, writhing, struggling against the friends who held them still while the blunt skewers were shoved in. These worshipers of Subramanya are one of the groups whom the British must fuse into a Malayan democracy.

The British are having almost as much trouble with the largest group in the federation, the Malays. They are a charming and friendly people living idyllic-seeming lives in their thatch villages in the jungles. The British are struggling to help the Malays and they spend a great deal of effort and money for little results. Unlike Westerners, the Malays are convinced they have everything they want.

The government wants them to become more ambitious and to raise their standard of health and living and to this end it has created an admirable project, RIDA, the Rural and Industrial Development Authority, to help teach the Malays. RIDA builds simple agricultural stations, each consisting of a few cheap roofed pavilions with big dormitory rooms above an open porch. Village leaders are invited to come here at the government's expense, to sleep in the dormitories, and to study better farming or study chicken raising, or learn to tend rubber trees. They even learn to build fishponds; fishponds in the jungle may sound absurd, but they can do an enormous amount for the underfed, protein-lacking Asians. Scoop out a hole, let rain fill it, throw in some weeds or garbage, get a few of the right fish; there is protein galore. If people cannot go to the sea for their fish, the technicians can bring the fish to the jungle.

The British who run the RIDA operations are proud of small accomplishments like a short foot bridge flung across a narrow stream. They find old pieces of junked cable from larger bridges, select some good lengths, supply a few bolts and a little wood and an engineer; the Malays build the bridges and take care of them. Unspectacular, but the peasants are saved ten mile walks to market with their latex or fruit. But there are not many RIDA projects, not because of lack of money but because of lack of requests for help from the Malays. They remain stubbornly contented. They need only a few sarongs a year; they can climb a tree or cultivate a small patch of land for their food; the climate is always warm and relaxing.

The Malays believe that if a thing is fun to do, it should be prolonged as long as possible, and so their wedding festivities run for four evenings. A Malay will happily spend the savings of five years on one of these weddings; in fact he would only consider saving money for some special occasion like this. The inside of a Malay house is usually one big room and this is decorated for the wedding by spreading a few oriental rugs on the floors and hanging some glittering paper streamers and flowers where they will be the most fun to watch. Most of the wedding ceremonies are general get-togethers with banquets where the members of the bridal party wear the most elaborate costumes they can afford. A bride may wear a Chinese costume in soft greens embroidered with gold dragons the first night, a deep red Indian sari the second night, and "fairy costume" of violet silk and variegated embroideries the third night. The groom will be as gaily dressed, but with no attempt to match his bride's costumes.

The final night the happy pair sit together on a bridal throne, admired by all their friends. Their throne is decorated with paper flowers and Christmas-tree lights twined around it. Behind them, special attendants fan them with green-and-red flowered fans embroidered with pearls. The groom in purple and gold stripes, with a gold necklace, half a dozen rings and a short gold kris; the bride in deep pink satin with a gold crown; the maid of honor in pale virginal colors; the best man in a bright blue blouse and a deep blue sarong bordered with gold. Everybody has a good time but the bride. Tradition puts her through an ordeal particularly demanding of a woman. During the four nights of ceremonies, she must sit impassively on the throne and never open her eyes or speak. An old woman stands behind her and if her head starts to slump to one side or the other, the old woman gives it a brisk push back to dead center.

The high point of the ceremony comes on the third night when the best man kneels in front of the bride and groom. He places some yellow rice in the groom's hand, and the groom, with a carefully aimed flick of the wrist, tosses the rice directly into his bride's face. If a grain should stick to her lips, it shows that he is going to be master of the household. The bride cannot open her eyes and dodge the rice, but the old woman is on the watch and throws her own hands forward to block the rice from the bride's face. Then the old woman turns over the bride's limp right hand and opens it. The best man drops some yellow rice into the bride's hand. With her eyes tightly closed, she tosses the rice toward her husband's mouth, while the best man tries to keep it from hitting its mark. The Malays do not seem to believe in complete equality of opportunity between the sexes.

If the Malays would work, the rice-production revenues of the country would rise. In order to earn more money, the Malays would want better educations and literacy would rise. To work longer hours, the Malays would need more strength and thus pay more attention to their diet and health. But much as the British try to coax these people to want more things, they will not. Malaya is short on rice, which must be imported at high prices from Thailand. When the British worked out a new way to fertilize rice paddies so the Malay farmers could increase their rice yield by one third, the Malays were delighted with the idea; but they then fertilized only two thirds of their acres, thus getting the same amount of rice as before for a third less work.

The British say that the Malays are "nice people, lovely people but not worth a damn. They won't take responsibility and they can't be trained as leaders." And in the competitive University examinations, only one Malay passes for every ten Chinese.

It may be partly the climate of Malaya, which stays around ninety degrees all the year; Templer said: "Oh, for ten degrees of frost a few months a year!" Where there is frost in Asia, the people are vigorous and full of drive. But climate will not explain the Malays because the Indonesians, of the same racial stock and living in the same kind of climate, have more drive; and living in the Malayan climate has not taken an ounce of drive out of the Chinese. Some blame everything on the Islamic religion of the Malays, with its fatalistic philosophy and its insistence that profits are evil. But there are other Islamic races that believe exactly the same thing and still have plenty of ambition. Or there is the pleasure of the Malays in sex: reputed par for the matrimonial course is at least one demonstration of affection every night of the week. This would keep the Malays relaxed, but no one has proved that any race has collapsed because of sexual enthusiasm.

Diet is certainly an important reason. The aborigines of Malaya get along much better; their basketwork has pride and precision while Malayan crafts have decayed. But the aborigines eat all sorts of wild herbs and hunt the animals of the jungles for meat. Since it is forbidden to them by the Koran, the Malays eat no pork, which would be their cheapest source of meat; they cannot afford beef, they must save their buffalo for field work, and their chickens are scrawny, so they get very little protein in their diet. They will not bother to grow green vegetables when there is cheap, hulled rice around, and so they get very few vitamins or minerals. Poor diet, in turn, may explain why they are such easy victims of malaria, worms, and a host of other infections that do not bother the Chinese or the aborigines.

But this is all guesswork. In economic and educational fields, the British work hard to help the Malays. But when you ask why the

Malays are the way they are, the British just repeat, "Custom, tradition, and a whole philosophy of life go far to determine the attitude which we loosely call indolence."

If the British have a problem of assimilation with the Indians in Malaya and a problem of stimulation with the Malays, they have a very different problem with the Chinese who are fast becoming the majority race on the peninsula. In the federation there are about three million Malays and about two and a half million Chinese. But then there are nearly another million Overseas Chinese down in Singapore.

Almost every one of the Communist terrorists has been Chinese, few Chinese have been willing to serve in the Home Guard against the Communists, and the chief source of support for the Communists came from the hundreds of thousands of Chinese squatters who had migrated to Malaya and set up living quarters in little settlements along the jungle's edges. As long as the government could not guarantee them protection, the Communists could extort money and food from them; as long as the government could not offer them a decent life, many would go along with the Communists.

So the Government of Malaya followed the example of the Edcor projects of the Philippines and embarked on a vast project for these squatters, moving them from the jungle's edges to resettlement camps near the bigger cities of Malaya and making available to each ex-squatter a small house and a sixth of an acre of land. He can own his own land and take twenty years to repay the government. Training centers are set up in dressmaking and cooking for the women, in mechanized trades for the men. Living near large towns, they can sell their produce or work at a trade; gathered together in one large subdivision camp, the Home Guard can protect them from Communist raids.

There are half a million Chinese in five hundred of these new towns and although the resettlement camps are expensive, they are less so than having the Malay Communists grow stronger. It is also less expensive than programs to improve the living conditions of the Chinese when they are strung out along the jungle. In addition, the Chinese in these camps write back about their new lives to relatives in Communist China and thus there is a side dividend, a positive anti-Communist propaganda.

The resettlement camps are just rows of the simplest, plainest houses, but the Chinese are really putting down roots here where they feel a pride of ownership. They have already built a movie house with their own money. These ignorant people who have never worked together in larger groups than their own families now elect their own local council to rule their settlement. In contrast to the reluctance of the Chinese of Malaya to enlist in the Home Guard, the settlement-camp Chinese volunteers have formed regiments and are training after work.

The flexibility of the Overseas Chinese is amazing. The ex-squatters are the lowest class of the Chinese immigrants, too ignorant to be able to find jobs in the cities of Malaya, yet they quickly become expert at any trade they are taught. Their more intelligent urban compatriots dominate the commercial life of the big cities. And Singapore, while it may have been founded by the British, is today the domain of the ambitious Chinese traders who run everything from auto agencies and printing presses to department stores and theaters.

In the entertainment category the Chinese entrepreneurs have invented a new variation of Coney Island, the "Worlds" of Singapore. They buy a few acres, surround it with any old kind of wooden fence, fill it with county fairs, stores, restaurants, bazaars, dance halls, and theaters. Admission to one of these, The Happy World, or the Great World, costs only a couple of cents. And in any one of these Worlds you can buy American sex-murder magazines, British woolens, or Chinese candy. And for about twenty-five cents, you can be entertained from 7 P.M. to 4 A.M. by a modern Chinese opera.

The opera performances are unique. The costumes are more dazzling than Ziegfeld or the Folies-Bergère, not a square inch unsequined; and the backgrounds are busy with sequined dragons, and potted palms fill up the interstices. Downstage left, an open frame window looks onto the stage from the wings and stagehands lounge behind it, keeping track of the action. With professional pride, and cigarettes stuck to their lower lips, they wander on stage, at the last split second but precisely on time, to move a chair behind an actor just before he sits down or to slip a cushion onto the floor just as the heroine starts an emphatic faint.

Downstage right, another open frame window with a drummer and an organist in a box. Sitting in front of them, right on the stage, tilted on the back legs of ancient Windsor chairs, a lackadaisical violinist and a saxophonist. With faces blanker than puppets, they play some kind of modern Chinese tune, if, when, and as long as they see fit. The cast intones the lines of the opera through the bridges of their noses. Theoretically, and if you have an ear for Cantonese singsong, the lines blend in with the music. But it is the drummer who really flies high, pointing up quarrels, narrations, love speeches, or just filling a three-second pause when there is no other noise.

In traditional Chinese style, the opera ends when the heroine, discarding her bright emerald sequined robe, slithers across the stage in scarlet silk-gauze pajamas and disappears behind the Chinese equivalent of a beaded curtain into a bedroom alcove. The drummer sits up straight on his stool, rolls his drum softly and clatters speculatively on its wooden rim. When the hero, after a six-minute nasal solo, gives a Nijinsky leap across the stage and dives through the curtain, the drummer's moment comes. For a solid three minutes of pure percussion, simultaneously and in combinations, he gives his all. The theater rocks with the noise as he does his artistic best to give an idea of the epic love-making going on behind the beaded curtain, and a stagehand stands at each end of the curtain, jiggling it to help the illusion along.

Near the opera houses of the Worlds are dance halls, again something special in Singapore. As everywhere else, the Chinese take what they like, give it a slight twist, and thereafter enjoy it. The Worlds have their own Chinese version of dime-a-dance girls. You pay the equivalent of a nickel for three minutes of dancing to samba rhythms ground out by a four-piece orchestra. But you and your partner never touch during the dance. You stand face to face, about six inches apart, and move back and forth across the floor, eyes intent on each other. Your partner follows your steps as if she were in your arms. To touch her or be touched by her would be just as bad as tripping up your partner in a Western ballroom. The women slide along the floor with a very sexy slouchiness and a bored look on their faces. Their trick, and it is a neat one, is to inspire their partners' libidos from a distance via slow stares of appraisal.

I watched a fat, middle-aged Indian, the pomade on his black hair perfuming the dance hall with attar of roses, dancing with not one girl but three. One fat, one tall, one short, in a row across from him, moving together in a single rhythm like refugees from the Radio City Rockettes; ebbing and flowing back and forth across the floor, driving the Indian into a corner of the ballroom, then fleeing, samba-wise, with him in hot pursuit. This with no movement above the hips by any of the four.

Substitute Asia for the three girls, the West for the man, and you have a good symbolic picture of the meeting of East and West. But if the symbol is to be an accurate reflection of today, the four would have to collide and blame each other for being out of step.

The Chinese of the Malay Peninsula are among the largest communities of the Overseas Chinese in Southeast Asia and the wealthiest. It is reassuring to discover how firmly they oppose Red China. They have not turned their primary allegiance to Formosa, but they have withdrawn their encouragement and their remittances from the present government of their old homeland. Instead, they are turning their focus toward Malaya as their permanent home. This is both a blessing and a curse for the British.

For a long time, as was true in the Philippines, these Chinese had no interest in the political setup and were not bothered because the British did not give them full rights of citizenship. They were here to make profits in this undeveloped land and then go home to China. Originally their most influential organization, the Malayan Chinese Association, was purely philanthropic. The British encouraged them to make it more political so as to offer an alternate standard to the Communists in Malaya. Having gone this far, the Malayan Chinese Association is now going considerably farther than the British wanted. Having turned into a powerful political organization, it has become the spearhead of Chinese pressure for complete political equality in Malaya.

For a time the association ran a huge lottery, the proceeds of which were used for resettlement help. Through this lottery and their donations, the Association built up so much political acceptance among the rest of the Chinese that the Federation government has had to step in and ban the lottery. Simultaneously, the Chinese of Singapore have been demanding a Chinese university to give their people a greater chance at higher education and to keep alive the flame of Chinese culture and civilization. The British do their best to block these signs of resurgent Chinese culture. They want to eliminate the Chinese vernacular schools and force the Chinese to learn English or Malay in the federation schools, most of the taxes for which are paid by the Chinese.

The chief strength and chief job of the British on the peninsula flows from the division between the Malays and the Chinese; since they are about equal in numbers, the British tend to side with the weaker and less vigorous Malays against the Chinese. The main reason that there has not been an amalgamation of the Federation and Singapore is that then the Chinese would outnumber the Malays and thus be able to control the Federation. The Malays are always fearful of this and the British do not want it.

There are many optimistic points about Malaya; few native Communists and a successful campaign against them; plenty of fertile land and a government working slowly but soundly to improve the people's lot with better agricultural methods, workers' pensions, hospitals, adult education at a village level. But basically, the future of Malaya rests on the ability of its rulers, the British, to turn it into a melting pot and then bring this melting pot to a boil, but not too much of a boil and not too fast. Although there are three races involved, only two make a problem. The Indians are a small and very quiet minority. But the Malays and Chinese, with about equal strength, coexist with a deep chasm of mutual contempt beneath their surface courtesies.

To explore these attitudes, I invited two young men, Mohammed Zain, a Malay, and Lim Loke Yin, a Chinese, to spend an evening explaining to me what their races wanted done next in Malaya and then record a broadcast with me. Since they were young, I thought they would be flexible, since both were intelligent and worked in broadcasting and had been exposed to Western thought and scientific techniques, I thought they would have much in common. In their answers to some of my questions, allow for the polite words of Asia, and perhaps you can hear the conviction and scorn of each race for the other's ideas.

"Mr. Zain, are you Malays determined you alone shall become the rulers of this country?"

"Certainly, Mr. Cooke. We don't want others, I mean aliens, Chinese and Indians, to administer the country. It is our right that this country should be returned to the Malays and ruled by us. . . ."

"Mr. Lim, what do you think about being an alien?"

"I was born here, Mr. Cooke. I have been here all my life. . . ."

"Mr. Zain, doesn't Mr. Lim have the right to have anything to do with the government?"

"Not directly. I mean, the Chinese can still live with us, trade in this country, but they would not be given high political posts. . . ."

"Then Mr. Lim, how would you feel if the British pulled out tomorrow and the Malays took over?"

"It would be a disaster because of the avarice and greed of most of the Malays, without enough education. You can't get independence just by wanting it. It needs many people with a high standard of education and thinking."

"Mr. Cooke, I don't agree with Lim Loke Yin. Let us run our country with what we have, with what resources we have. We must not wait until we are actually, as you Westerners say, educated and ready for it. . . ."

Between such antagonisms, the British must steer an adroit course that will not cause either race to become anti-British. The Federation is ruled by a British High Commissioner with the aid of an advisory legislative council appointed by him. In this council are seven Indians, sixteen Chinese, and thirty-two Malays. The allotment quiets the Malays, who get a theoretical majority, but it does not displease the Chinese because there are also twenty British members on the council and because twenty-four of the Malays on it are paid government officials, and thus controlled by the British. So the Chinese know the British can hold the theoretical Malay majority in check.

But from now on, the British are going to have to fight a rear-guard action against Chinese domination. The election laws have provided that while 90 per cent of the Malays born here could become full citizens, only 55 per cent of the Chinese had the same rights. The Chinese are demanding the ratio be changed and the British will have to gradually work out a fairer balance that will convulse neither race against the other nor against the British.

This is the short-range solution. For the long-range, the British are acting with wisdom and unselfishness. Of all the present-day colonial powers, they have the most right to be proud of their postwar record. They have made Singapore a city with as good a health record as any city in Britain. They are spending millions on education: in 1953 in spite of the four and a half years of fighting the terrorists, there were 780,000 children in Federation schools; in a few years they intend that all the young people shall be literate.

And while they try to bring material improvement to the peninsula, they have kept it at peace and out of civil war. On three sides of Malaya, national independence has been the order of the day. The Thais have always had their independent kingdom, the Burmese and the Indonesians have won their independence, the Vietnamese were fighting for theirs. The British see the inevitable and intend to keep ahead of it. They are struggling with the thankless task of training the races of this peninsula as quickly as possible in self-government, yet not allowing them to put the roof of national independence on Malaya before they build the foundations of local democracy. Local councils have already been elected, first in the big cities and resettled areas, now in all the other villages of the Federation. There is already legislation in each of the nine Malay states providing for the election of state legislatures. And, by 1955, the British have promised Malaya that there will be elections for a national legislature and a cabinet to take over the powers of the High Commissioner.

As the sequence of elections unfolds itself and as the British bestow fuller literacy on this peninsula, they hope that it will truly become a melting pot and that the younger generation, both Malays and Chinese, will forgo their mutual jealousies, dislikes, and misunderstandings. And the British are counting on education to show the people of the peninsula how to move forward and become fellow citizens of a new member of the Commonwealth, Free Malaya. Perhaps the British may be dragging their feet, seeking to preserve their power as long as possible. It is true that the British protect their own commercial interests here, but they also pay higher taxes on their profits than does the other important commercial group, the Chinese.

Meantime, while many leaders in the confused, faltering, new republics of Asia hurl the epithet of colonialism at the British, these shrewd and often idealistic mentors of a group of backward peoples in a confused tangle of races plod ahead with their thankless task and their farsighted hopeful prescription for freedom.

CONFUSION THRICE CONFOUNDED:

Indo-China

Just as the truce in the Korean War automatically elevated Indo-China into the most dangerous spot in Asia, so the truce in the Indo-Chinese war has automatically elevated Southeast Asia into the most dangerous spot in the entire free world.

Thanks to the terms of the Geneva Agreement, we have no more than a meager fifty-fifty chance—at the very optimistic best—of keeping South Vietnam out of Communist hands. But if, by infiltration, negotiation, or election, all of Vietnam becomes a Communist state, the likely consequences for the rest of Southeast Asia are predictable.

First, increasingly heavier guerrilla and political pressures upon the other two associated states of Indo-China, the little royal kingdom of Cambodia and the feudal chieftains of Laos. Once they are swallowed up, and the five million Laotians and Cambodians could not long stand up against the power of twenty-two million Vietnamese, the Chinese-Vietnam Communist bloc could turn its power, direct and indirect, on Burma and Thailand.

The United States, having refused to use its fullest strength to prevent the Communist absorption of Indo-China, would now be forced to support Thailand at any cost, desperately seeking to make it a bastion in the center of Southeast Asia against the victorious Communists. The present government of Thailand would support our efforts. But, given communism to the north and communism to the east, plus more and more of the fearful Overseas Chinese in Thailand secretly supporting their Chinese compatriots, some power group in Thailand's ruling class would heed the blandishments of the Communists and some kind of civil war would result. Sooner or later, we would be fighting the Vietnam war all over again in Thailand.

Simultaneously, the Communists would send more aid to the Malayan terrorists. Since a few thousand terrorists were almost able to convert rich Malaya into chaos, triple the contributions from nearby successful Communist revolutions and guess how long Malaya could be held.

Burma, hardly holding its own now, would be forced to change its policies; at best it would become pro-Communist, at worst its democratic government would be overthrown and a Communist government would replace it.

At that point the weak and divided new nation of Indonesia would not dare stand up against a Communist Southeast Asia. And, whatever her preferences, India would be forced to come to terms with this power facing her from the north and the east, a power which then would not find the creation of a Communist India an impossible task.

And the consequences of losing Indo-China and then Southeast Asia could have disastrous effects in North Asia. When the Japanese could find their desperately needed food and markets in Southeast Asia only by Communist sufferance, the best the West could hope for would be a neutral Japan. In time, unless the United States fought a war with China and won it, we would be forced back into the eastern Pacific behind Alaska and Hawaii, searching for safety in a new order where a Communist-controlled Asia was the ally of Russia.

So today Indo-China holds the potentialities for a catastrophe whose consequences could alter world history. And there can be no neat definitive solution to the problem because Indo-China, one of the least-known spots in the world, is also one of its most complicated and most confused areas.

Like "Asia," "Indo-China" is principally a word that describes a colored blob on a map, a geographical location, not a country or nation. It is three very different countries: Laos, a group of primitive tribes racially closer to the Thais than either of the other two Associated States; Cambodia, the ancient seat of the Khmer Empire, which received its original teachers from India and its religion from Buddha; Vietnam, which has been conquered over and over again by the Chinese who have given it Chinese patterns of culture and the Confucian religion. And the three countries use three different languages: Thai in Laos, Khmer in Cambodia, Annamite in Vietnam.

And the triple motif comes up again in Vietnam, which was conquered by the French and hates them most. No more a single nation than Indo-China was a single country, it was another French invention, made up of two French protectorates, Tonkin in the north and Annam in the center of the country, plus the French colony of Cochin China in the south. And if you want to go into history to get a little more confused, it was the warlike Tonkinese who drove the Cochin Chinese south who drove the Cambodians west.

With different kings and rulers, each country became a part of the French colonial empire of Indo-China at different times in different ways for different reasons: Vietnam by conquest, Laos by agreement, Cambodia for protection from Vietnam. And then in turn three foreign powers thrice confounded the Indo-Chinese confusion: the French colonials, the Chinese Communists, and the American mean-wellers.

Now, thanks to stupid French colonial policies in Indo-China compounded by indecisive American policies in Asia, the non-Communist world has suffered its worst defeat since Mao Tse-tung took over China. The partition of Vietnam is a far greater defeat than the partition of Korea, for South Korea was left with a firm anti-Communist government and an equally firm leader, while South Vietnam is left with no real leader, no real anti-Communist government, and no real indication that the tragedy of errors which gave the northern half of the country to the Communists will not be repeated in the south.

In the process of losing the Indo-Chinese War, the West committed every mistake its ingenuity could find, starting with colonialism and wavering through the whole gamut of dying empire from faint-heartedness to threats and fits of temper, from spasms of internal politics to orgies of external recrimination. When the war was over, it had cost over $8,000,000,000—at least half of which, one way or another, was put up by the United States—and the non-Communist world had suffered 250,000 casualties, including almost 100,000 French Union soldiers dead or missing.

When the truce was signed, 60,000 square miles of territory and 12,000,000 North Vietnamese were on the other side of the Bamboo Curtain. More important, we left the rest of Indo-China in a weakened position which will make further political victories easier for the Communists.

This holds especially true for Laos, the most vulnerable of the Associated States. Laos, Land of a Million Elephants, is a little larger than Utah, a colorful primitive country of jumbled mountains, jungles, and high plateaus. Ruled by King Sisavang Vong, Laos is technically a kingdom but the word is high-flown for this land of patriarchal villages ruled by headmen and possessing few intercommunications. For a thousand years Laos was a buffer state and feudal vassal of either Cambodia or Annam; it was not unified under one king until after World War II.

There are almost no roads in Laos and the twelve hundred miles of the Mekong River, winding along its western border, have always been its main thoroughfare. About one quarter of its people are tough, wiry mountain tribesmen, the other three quarters are gentle, fun-loving peasants of the same race as the Thais, living along the fertile banks of the Mekong where rice is easy to grow and fish are easy to catch. Most of the Laotian men wear black pajamas, skullcaps, and braids, and the women still wear their colorful native costumes with kiltlike skirts of many pleats. As easygoing as the Thais, the Laotians' favorite saying is "*bo pen whang* [never mind]," and they have never needed to mind about very much. There is no population pressure in this lucky, little-developed country of no industries, no cities, and no Army. Like the Thais, the Laotians are Buddhists of the gentle Little Vehicle faith.

Laos would be known only as an idyllic and charming country if it were not for its geographic location. It forms the eastern side of a little-known and rarely noticed Chinese wedge that is the free world's weakest point on the perimeter of communism. From the base of this inverted wedge, Yünnan Province pushes down from China to pry apart Laos and Burma so that it can reach toward rich Thailand on the way to Malaya and the East Indies. The country around this Chinese wedge is inaccessible and mountainous, difficult terrain for a modern power to defend and impossible for the weak and never unified tribes of upper Burma or Thailand or Laos to hold against the determined millions above it in China.

While South Vietnam is China's first objective, its chief political pressure is farther west. Spreading out from the Yünnan wedge, Red China hopes in time to set up a Communist Thai Federation. Centuries ago, millions of Thais once spilled down from the Yangtze Valley into Southwest China, and into Laos, Thailand, and the Shan States of Burma. Today their descendants live within and around the Yünnan wedge. As an opening gambit toward its Thai Federation, Peiping has already set apart a small autonomous Thai area in Yünnan with a provisional Thai capital at Cheli, has assigned a division or so of Chinese Thai troops there, has built a powerful radio station to broadcast in the Thai language to Laotians and the Burmese tribes bordering on the sides of the wedge.

Simultaneously with their attempts to seize Laos, Chinese agents are stirring up trouble and encouraging the Thais of the Shan tribes of Burma to continue rebellious against the weak central government. And one of the most famous of Thais, the author of Thailand's Constitution, its former Regent, Prime Minister, and leader of the pro-American underground during the Japanese war, Pridi Phanomyong, is now traveling back and forth between Cheli and Peiping, working toward the day when he can return to his country, overthrow the King of Thailand and become the head of a Communist state.

Not by warfare but by propaganda and by infiltration, the Communist Chinese hope gradually to win over the Laotians. It was to aid in this work, not to conquer Laos itself, that the Vietminh, the Communists of Vietnam, have several times flowed across the border into Laos. The old king of Laos, Sisavang Vong, did his best with the aid of a few French troops to push them back. But while they were fighting in Laos, the Communists established a puppet organization, Pathet Lao, the historic name of the country, to offer younger Laotians the heady beverage of "freedom and self-rule under the benign protection" of China. A prince of the royal house and half-brother of the Prime Minister, Souphaavong, is the head of this Communist-sponsored "Free Laos Government."

Thanks to the Geneva Agreements, the Chinese are now well on the way to absorbing Laos. Its two eastern provinces, Sameneua and Phongsaly, were turned over to the Communists. Since the northernmost of these, Phongsaly, is part of one side of the dangerous Yünnan wedge, China can extend her base of operations for the Thai Confederacy. The Laos Agreement limits to sixty-five hundred the number of French military permitted to garrison the country and train the Laotians. Geography will now make it costly and difficult for the French, or anybody else, to get into Laos to block Chinese agitators infiltrating from Yünnan. The French used to go directly across their northern Vietnam provinces and into Laos; from now on they must make their way up through the rugged mountainous land from the 17th parallel to the capital of Laos, Vientiane, far away on the Thailand border.

How long the weak royal government of Laos can oppose shrewd Communist political infiltration is anybody's guess. According to the Agreement, there must be a Laotian election in 1955. Even if they cannot win that election, it seems unlikely the Communists would give back Phongsaly and less likely the West would go to war over it. And the Chinese expect to win the election, for they believe that the French, the Americans, and the various Thai-peopled neighbors of Laos will be unable to find any adequate counterweapon to their insidious infiltration and implacable guerrilla warfare.

The second country of Indo-China, Cambodia, is in a much more fortunate and stable position than its Laotian neighbor. It has been a unified kingdom for a thousand years, since the days of the Khmer kings who spread its empire from Bangkok to Saigon. Occupying a flat fertile jungle plain about the size of Oklahoma, the Cambodians, although less sophisticated, are amazingly like their fellow Thais to the west in the kingdom of Thailand. They have enough land, enough to eat, and enough time to enjoy life.

The capital of the kingdom, Pnom Penh, is a lazy provincial town of less than four hundred thousand on the Mekong River. Typically Southeast Asian rickety thatch huts cluster around egg-yellow French stucco houses on broad, well-paved French boulevards. French cars, creaking oxcarts, rickshas, and ambling bonzes, the Buddhist priests, crowd the streets along with a few whites, many leisurely moving Cambodians and the inevitable bustling Chinese merchants. In flavor much like the old university city of Djokjakarta in Indonesia, Pnom Penh has its own exotic and colorful area, the compound of the Royal Palace and the Silver Pagoda.

Unimpressive from the outside, the Silver Pagoda is a storehouse of fabulous wealth. A gold Buddha about six feet high presides over its shadows. The Buddha, weighing about two hundred pounds, is said to be of solid gold and it has huge sparkling diamonds in each palm, its navel, and its forehead, plus many more glittering in an elaborate headdress and a shoulder piece of gold and diamonds. But the beauty of the pagoda is the floor. It is paved with engraved squares, seven inches by seven inches and about an inch thick, at least a thousand of them, and each one is of solid silver. The temple has small stained-glass windows, elaborate colored murals, and a red-and-gold ceiling; when the bright light of the tropical sun pours in through the stained glass and bounces off the ceiling and the murals, the colors are reflected in the cool pools of the silver tiles.

It was not as a tourist, but in the unexpected role of teacher that I viewed the temple. One of the United States Information Service men teaches a course in English for the most important bonzes of this temple, the Vatican of Cambodia, and I was asked to take over his class for a night. In a special classroom equipped with schoolroom wooden chairs with wide arms, twenty bonzes were waiting for me, all with freshly shaven heads, wearing sandals, rough saffron-gold robes wrapped around them like togas. The bonzes talked falteringly with me, appealingly childlike, mouthing their words with difficulty, gay and curious and shy, full of wrigglings and gigglings and blanknesses when they could not understand what I was saying. They appear at least fifteen to twenty years younger than their age and treated me with great respect because my lined Western face made them think I was a revered old man of at least sixty-five.

After the lesson, the Supreme Patriarch of Cambodia and my English class conducted me on a temple tour. We spread out like a long snake across the palace grounds. First came the High Bonze, his two chief assistants, and me. Within earshot, but never catching up with us, the chief dignitaries of the temple. Next, the elder priests. At suitably spaced distances the ordinary priests, the acolytes, the temple hangers-on, the lower servants. Looking down from the flat roof of the temple school, I could see these scrupulously separated groups sitting patiently in clusters across the courts, each waiting to move on in his proper sequence when we continued our way.

The young King of Cambodia, Norodom Sihanouk, is as colorful as his temple and bonzes. Fattish, with a handsome face and sharp brown eyes, he has the democratic air that only an absolute monarch acquires. A graduate of a French cavalry school who speaks fluent French, the King understands Western concepts, likes convertibles, race horses, and saxophones. He lives in a small orange-colored stucco palace, with air-conditioning, a royal golden throne under tiers of parasols, a private dancing troupe of his own, and a treasury full of jewels, including a great starburst of diamonds mounted on a black derby hat, which the kings of Cambodia used to wear when they went riding.

Dwelling in this exotic mixture of yesterday and today, Norodom Sihanouk is an astute politician who has taken shrewd advantage of the problems the French have been having with the Vietminh. The French colonials formerly ruled or controlled his foreign relations, finances, and Army; but when the civil war in Vietnam began to go against the French, Norodom gave them a choice between granting him almost full independence within the French Union or having him go into voluntary exile in Thailand while Cambodia fell to pieces without him as a rallying point. Having received the proper assurances from the French, the King in person successfully led his small army against Communist guerrillas who had crossed the border from Vietnam.

Long before the Geneva truce, the King, as a result of his actions, had established himself as the anti-colonial leader of his people against their enemies, for the guerrillas were Vietnamese and always considered foreigners and enemies of the Cambodians. And at Geneva it was King Norodom's negotiators who held up the signing of the Agreements, defying France, Britain, Russia, and China until they were given the right to enter foreign alliances and receive foreign aid if aggression threatened their country. Add to this the fact that Cambodia has no common border with the Communists—as long as Laos stays out of their hands—and it does not seem that the Communists have much chance of taking over Cambodia. The election in 1955, provided for in the Geneva Agreements, should be a thorough defeat for communism.

Slow infiltration and agitation against "the reactionary aristocracy" will have to be the Communist tactic. And for these purposes the farsighted Chinese Communists have already set up a Cambodian Communist guerrilla leader, Son Ngoc Tanh, and organized a puppet government, the "Khmer People's Liberation Provisional Committee"; by using the word Khmer the Communists play on the Cambodians' memories of their ancient kingdom. In time the Communists hope to merge this puppet Khmer Committee in a Thai Confederacy.

The King's position is made stronger and communism's weaker because Cambodians have enough land and enough food. Their villages are as simple as those of the Malays. Clear a spot in the jungle, fell a few tree trunks to serve as the stilts on which to build your houses so they are off the ground in the rainy season. Weave a few bamboo mats, cut a few bamboo poles, put them together on top of the piles with a rice-straw thatch roof. Cut a couple of more pieces of bamboo for steps up into your house and lug up a few flat stones to pile one on another for a hearth. Now raise enough rice for yourself and a little to trade for a few pieces of sturdy cotton for sarongs, save up a little more for feasts and weddings and funerals, have a few bananas and melons and roots growing near by, and there you are.

If you are especially industrious, cut a few more bamboo poles, build a little woven fence around your front yard, trade a little more rice for a few chickens and a goat. Most of the time you can sit and consider the universe, or whatever it is you want to consider, in the shade under your house.

Driving out from the pleasant provincial town of Siemreap to see the wonderful ancient rose-colored temple of Bantram Srei, we went hurtling along sand trails through the jungle past very small villages. There was one place where a bridge had fallen down and the jeep, going down a steep bank onto a dry river bed, could barely pull through the loose sand and up the other side. One little urchin watched us gravely from the top of the bank; there was no one else in sight. When we returned many hours later toward the fallen bridge, there seemed to be a flock of small brown crows perched on the riverbank; they were fifty small naked children. A rustle of anticipation ran through them when the jeep started down the steep sandy incline to the river bed. When the wheels sank in and the jeep stalled, the children screamed with joy; when the front-wheel drive took over and we slowly pulled our way out, there was a long-drawn sigh of disappointment; but when we careened victoriously up the other bank, they jumped up and down, cheering and waving us on.

Village life in Asia has been comfortable and stable. The death rates are always high, but that is "the immemorial will of God." Until Western knowledge begins to impinge on Asians. First your city cousins in Pnom Penh find out about Western benefits. Then you in turn will want vaccination for your baby or a better rice seed. These take more money which means more work. But you do not want to work any more; so already you begin to be discontented. Then other people buy medicines, and you see their babies, or the children of the French, do not die as yours do; so you begin to hate the white Frenchmen. And then the Communists come and say, "Take over your own country and all these benefits will be yours." Thus, the twentieth century comes to another Cambodian village.

In addition to placid villages, French-type capitals, and silver pagodas, Cambodia has one possession whose size and crumbled grandeur is without peer, the fabulous ruins of Angkor, the ancient capital of the Khmer kings from about 800–1400. Flying in toward Siemreap, suddenly in the midst of the monotonous scrawny palms, the blue sky is reflected in a moat coiled all by itself in the jungle; as you come nearer, from the middle of the moat, slowly rising into view come the immeasurable miles and tons of stone of the sunken shrine of Angkor Wat, the largest religious edifice ever built by man.

Around Angkor Wat (*Wat* means temple) are tons of different incredible parts of this city, which lay buried in the jungle for half a thousand years until the French raised it again to sight. Every one of its uncountable millions of stones had to be quarried and measured and cut and hauled to Angkor on bamboo rollers and then pulled up, set into place, and carved to fit the over-all design.

Exploring the ruins of Angkor, you come upon a trench, very much like a military trench but built of stone, on the walls are carved the figures of the Leper King with all his women, sitting cross-legged and private. Nearby is a reviewing stand of the Khmer kings, the Terrace of the Elephants, the pachyderms marching along in stone one behind the other, their massive shoulders supporting only space, for the terrace is gone these many centuries and the elephants are burdenless, trumpeting through the miasmas of time.

Oddly enough it is water that made the stone pile of Angkor possible. Nearby is a lake, the Great Lake, which gave the Khmers their wealth. Into this lake, the Mekong River, as large as the Mississippi, flowing down from Tibet, backs up in flood season. It quadruples the size of the Great Lake whose waters spread over, and whose fish feed on the submerged miles of jungle. The fish multiply; the fishermen catch a month's food in a few netfuls; and then, as the lake recedes to its normal size, myriads of fish die, and so fertilize the earth that it yields a year's crop for a few weeks' work. With food for everyone around them, the people of the Khmers might have raised a great civilization, but their kings ruled otherwise and preferred to turn their wealth into tombs, so millions of Khmers toiled and died to raise these piles of sandstone.

One of the innumerable wonders of Angkor Wat is the Gallery of the Inner Temple, which goes all around the inner court of the building, well over a mile long and twenty feet high. Every inch of it is a mural of thousands of carved figures moldering away in dry sandstone; in some places an elephant or a horse or a body has been in reach of the tourists, and from their hands a bit of oil has sunk into the dry sandstone and suddenly in the powdery dying lines of the ancient carving, one piece will stand out like translucent gray jade.

No one has ever counted the figures in the frieze of this gallery. There are battles by the hundreds, kings in chariots, processions, ceremonies, fish of the Great Lake leaping among stone waves and flowers, demons carrying the doomed to numberless infernos, stylized gods and goddesses on their clouds and in their heavens. And in between the damned and the blessed are long lines of the common people of the kingdom, laughing, juggling, eating, dancing. The kings and the gods might have been cut from the same stencil, but when the humble artisans came to chisel the figures of their own simple lives they needed to follow no rigorous pattern, so unintentionally they preserved for posterity a little of the life which all the Khmers might have enjoyed.

The Khmer kings must have marched along this gallery, proud that their monument would last forever. But an invasion descended on these stones of Angkor Wat and vanquished the empire by the simple expediency of wiping out the small group of aristocrats who ruled it. With the Khmer aristocracy dead, the mass of the people had no skills to hold the empire together.

Only their miles of temples remained, and the care of them would have absorbed all the work of the people. The Khmer peasants avoided this demand of their gods with village simplicity; they moved away from these cruel stones to a western part of the kingdom. The Khmer kings had brought their fate upon themselves: to preserve the stone of Cambodia for their temples, they had decreed that no house in the kingdom could be built of it; and so it was easy for the people to roll up their bamboo mats, move away from their stone past, and let the temples gradually sink forgotten into the green of the jungle as the white roots of the wild fig trees gradually toppled the towers of the Khmers.

No one remembers the name of Suryavarman, the Khmer king who drove his nameless multitudes to create no art or education or law or learning, but only to pile up and chisel out the massive empty tons of these temples of death. In the same centuries, halfway around the world at Chartres and Canterbury, other kings and their subjects reached out together to build temples of life, which they called cathedrals. And standing on the highest *prasad* of Angkor Wat, perhaps where Suryavarman himself once stood, following the sun as it dies behind the distant moat of the temple, watching the masses of bats come out into the dim light to tweet and swoop against the cold stones, which glow with a dark luminescence, your heart fills with compassion for the millions of Khmers, and even for their kings who never knew that only by building truth and love in the hearts of others can man build an enduring monument.

Coming back from the lost past, it is striking that Angkor, which is a variant of the Khmer word for city, is one of the very few great cities in the history of the East. South of Japan and China, almost all the cities of Asia were born in the nineteenth century and sired by Western fathers: Manila, a trading town on the Pasig River developed by the Spanish; Djakarta, administrative center of the Dutch in the East Indies; Singapore, Hong Kong, Rangoon, Calcutta, and Bombay, trading ports or business centers of Western man. What a contrast with our own civilization so inextricably bound in together with the palaces and the slums of our cities whence have come the economic sinews and the soaring ideas that have moved Western man ahead.

In Asia, it is not from the cities but from the villages that the heartbeat comes. Village life did not stimulate trade, for within reach were only more villages, producing similar goods. Tied down so closely to the slow rhythm of the cereal-growing seasons of the East, the Asian peasant has little conception of the drive and work the Western farmer gives to his acres. Speed and efficiency have entirely different meanings to a continent that has lived in villages for three thousand years from what they have in worlds shaped by the restless dissatisfied questing city drives.

We in the West, taking for granted our traditions and the educational systems that evolved in our cities, assume that every man is a potential leader. He is not unless he grows into one. The Asian villages may not give you ulcers; neither does their uneducated oligarchical village system produce many leaders.

In Cambodia, King Norodom complains that he must compose his cabinet of members of the royal family because he cannot find other intelligent leaders in the country; the United States State Department, seeking to bring promising young men of Asia to the United States for three months' study under its Leadership Grants, has as much difficulty finding young Cambodian recipients as the King has in forming a cabinet. The peasants pay little attention to king or country: "The writ of the Emperor ceases at the village gates." And freedom of thought or initiative have never been encouraged by the village elders who rule by seniority and acquire their power only after imagination has settled down.

The United States Information Service in many countries of Asia aims its efforts at "the people," trying to reach and propagandize whatever proportion of the peasantry can read its own language. In Cambodia this target group has comprised about ten thousand members of the so-called "upper classes" in the villages and towns, plus "maybe ninety thousand more villagers." But our sights are too broad and our propaganda loaded with BB shot. We try to speak to the peasants, but we are so many centuries away from what they know that our propaganda can only hope to get across a few very simple truths. And the peasants who can grasp these truths will not change the dynamics of our time, upon which our civilization must depend.

In the market bazaar of Pnom Penh is a bulletin board filled each week with American pictures and a text in Cambodian and French covering some piece of specific information in one of the pictures; one week there was a picture of the Jefferson Memorial and the text talked about "Thomas Jefferson, third President of the United States." The United States Information Service offered a prize to any reader of the bulletin board who could name our third president. About ten Cambodians came into the Information Service offices during the week; less than half of them could give the right answer.

It is the infinitesimal percentage of the literate and the trained, the earnest, determined, driving, and dedicated few, who must carry the burden of leadership. When they are committed, they can educate their people to follow. But we cannot go past them or around them. Even in the most westernized countries, like the Philippines and Japan, we must concentrate on the young intellectuals.

And the adjective and noun are equally important. It is the idealistic young who are selflessly searching for answers for their people. And they are intellectuals; otherwise they would not be concerned in the first place.

The young intellectuals of Asia are the equivalent of seminar students in our universities. But we use advertising techniques to present our case to Asia, and the advertising man has never had to consider an intellectual in his professional life, so he constructs our messages to appeal to the Asian equivalents of American comic-book readers and soap-opera devotees. Our information programs are glossy, easy-to-digest, pretty truisms about the American way.

Result: the young Asian intellectual rejects this pap and assumes it is typical of our system. He turns toward communism in his search for adult intellectual fare; it may be totalitarian, but to him it seems reasoned and designed for adults in an adult world.

If we do not wish to lose the only class who can help us in Asia, we must remember the serious young men and women in our college clubs and design our information to appeal at that level. That way we would automatically be searching out the best young brains in the Far

East. And it is these young men and women who are the seed corn of communism or democracy, the teachers or orators or editors or prime ministers or guerrilla leaders of tomorrow.

It is these young intellectuals who are the only available connective between the ideas of the West and the peoples of the East. And Asians will resist communism only if and when their young intellectuals lead the way. In the Cambodian villages it is going to be difficult to find these men; in French-educated South Vietnam there are many young intellectuals available, that is, if the French will allow them the freedom to act and allow us the freedom to help them.

Before the partition, the French pretended Vietnam was a full member of the French Union; actually it was a colony, pure and simple, under the unrelenting rule of a singularly obtuse Belle France which spent the profitable decades before World War II enjoying the fruits of colonialism: Frenchmen owned all the shipping and rubber of Vietnam, plus almost all its industry and its banks, plus a good two thirds of the rice yield of this country of twenty-two million conquered Asians.

Until the Geneva Agreements wrote finis to the shortsighted French policies, Vietnam could be best described as a pole carrying two trays of rice: the pole being the narrow mountainous little kingdom of Annam through the middle of which runs the 17th parallel; one rice tray being the rich delta of the Red River in Tonkin around Hanoi and Haiphong, now all in the new Communist state of North Vietnam; the other rice tray being the greater food-producing delta of the Mekong River, far down in the south of Cochin China around Saigon, now the capital of the new state of South Vietnam.

Two million people live in the Mekong delta in the twin cities, Saigon and Cholon. Cholon, one of the largest Chinese cities in Asia, is where the majority of the Overseas Chinese of South Vietnam live. It repeats the familiar Chinese pattern of zest and noise, of twenty-four-hour-long eating, talking, trading, gambling. And picking their way through the Chinese crowds on the sidewalks of Cholon stroll a wild mixture of French soldiers, Annamite nuns, Indians, priests, chic Parisiennes, and Vietnamese belles in black satin trousers and knee-length silk tunics slit up to the waist.

One of the most dangerous problems now facing South Vietnam is how to prevent its Overseas Chinese from becoming Communist supporters. Before the partition, some of the hua-chiao were secretly sending their sons to China for education and indoctrination. Now, looking ahead to the elections in 1956 which may reunite the whole country under the Communists, and having seen what happened in North Vietnam when the French pulled out, the Chinese of Cholon are going to be more anxious than ever to come to terms with the victorious Vietminh-Chinese power. Few of them will dare vote against the Vietminh in 1956 unless there has been a complete—and successful—new deal in South Vietnam. The French, who were conspicuously unsuccessful at detecting the difference between a Communist and a non-Communist Vietnamese, are going to have even more trouble trying to establish which Chinese are fifth columnists in the teeming city of Cholon.

In Saigon proper, a fresh variation is added to the multiple civilizations of Asia; here another great colonial power has recreated its home image in another sector of the Far East. If you could close your ears and nose to the sounds and smells, and your pores to the tropical heat, you could think you were in France. One of the sources of profits to a colonizing power has been its ability to levy prohibitive import duties on all products but those of its own factories. The French did an efficient job.

From your French hotel bed, looking out through French doors, you see the same low French iron balcony you would see in the *Septième Arrondissement* and the same kind of shutters, but instead of being wood, they are made of steel, protection against bombing or shooting. Beyond the balcony, trees like French chestnuts frame the window. On the other side of the street, a small French *libraire* has a window display of a new best seller, *Panorama du Comportement Sexuel.* Next to your bed, a French telephone; in the bathroom, a bidet. Below your windows, a little French café with the same kind of awnings you would see across from St.-Germain-des-Prés. In it, people speaking French as they sip their *fines* or *vin rouge.*

The French never paid high wages in Indo-China; a miner's prewar income was under twenty-five dollars a year. In addition to low labor costs and high import profits there also were the indirect profits of colonialism, opportunities for French overseers and French capital. Only in the Philippines under American tutelage has a white power in Asia not pursued this profiteering pattern. But in the Associated States of Indo-China the French added a layer of concern the Dutch never had: *la gloire et la France spirituelle.* They felt a responsibility to spread French civilization and they encouraged French learning and universities.

The French did not understand that by exposing the Vietnamese to the glorious French ideals of liberty and egalitarianism and by unifying these disparate kingdoms of Vietnam into a political entity, they were kindling the ideas of nationalism in the hearts of one more Asian people.

The Vietnamese are similar in general appearance to the Javanese, but they look more Chinese. Almost all of them wear black, a kind of shiny satiny black, which the sun gradually bleaches to a deep rusty charcoal. In this steaming climate the men wear only a brief pair of shorts, perhaps with an open shirt of black and the ever-present cone-shaped bamboo hat tied under the chin that you see from Formosa on south. The women relieve the monotonous black with a bright scarf.

Generally speaking, the peasants are Confucianists and there is great loyalty to the family or the joint family, that broadest sort of family clan that often includes most of a village. The joint family being a species of socialism, the peasants do not find things too different if their village is taken over by the Vietminh and communistically organized. There is ancestor worship, and Chinese shrines can be seen in the village huts. "Grandfather" is a title of great respect, used for the headman of the village or for an ambassador; less important whites bear the honorary degree of "Uncle." And this tradition-conscious people meticulously delineates the divisions of social status by dozens of other titles: Older Brother, Younger Brother, Youngest Brother's Second Wife, and so on.

The roads are busy with military traffic. There are machine guns mounted on the trucks. In each village guards patrol with loaded rifles in their hands. As is Java, Vietnam is a country where there are always at least thirty people in sight, working, playing, loafing, or just waiting along the road for the next bus. These Southeast Asian peoples never sit on the ground; they put their feet down flat and, lowering themselves from the knee joints, they sink their rumps as far down as they will go. Barely clearing the ground, they can sit, comfortable and relaxed, for an indefinite period. Maybe they have learned to do this because half of the year the ground would be too wet to sit on. The squatting Vietnamese eye Westerners impassively and incuriously, without hospitality.

Going through a small village, you often see a pile of rough-shaped burnt sienna pottery urns, each about the size of a grapefruit and piled in neat pyramids; in them is a special fish sauce loved by Asians. They pile fish in a mound and, letting them rot slowly, from time to time pile more fish on top. At the bottom they drain off the pressed juice. To this essence of fish they add the juice of their lemons, about the size and color of our limes but not as sour. This fish-lemon sauce is at once the salt and caviar of South Asia. As we drove through one village, a baby knocked down one of the empty urns and burst into tears at the crash; its mother straightened up from the sugar cane she was cutting with a big machete and turning it broadside, good-naturedly whacked his bare bottom with a resounding crash.

When a bus rattles by on the road, it is unbelievable how many people are jammed into it. At least four to each double seat, aisles packed, more on top of the bus, plus huge bulging bamboo baskets that make the bus as high above the roof as below it. Families drive along in little carts drawn by small pony-sized horses festooned with tinkling bells. The carts are about the width of card tables and half again as long, with roofs of wooden arches covered with bamboo matting to keep out the sun. The drivers sit cross-legged at the front of their carts, fourteen or fifteen people jammed in behind them.

One of the most fatuous assumptions of Westerners is that we are so much better mechanics than Easterners are. Away out on a country road in Annam, my army jeep broke down and none of us could fix it. We flagged down a rattletrap truck in the last stages of collapse. With gestures and a few French words, we asked the crowd inside if any of them could help us. They piled out and swarmed around the motor of the car, jabbering, poking, prying, and consulting with each other. Then they robbed their own truck of a piece of wire, stripped the insulation off with their front teeth, and patched the jeep up so it would run.

Asians can afford only the oldest and most decrepit of cars, which are always breaking down. They have never been trained to repair mechanisms and have no money for the expensive spare parts. But the Asian starts out with at least as much manual dexterity as we do. What he does not possess is the scientific approach. It is this lack of discipline that will so delay the growth in Asia of the complicated Western sciences, from mechanics to medicine. Doctors tell you they can never be certain, if they are not at hand, that nurses will properly sterilize hypodermic needles. Here is the gap of understanding between the science of the West and the performance of the East. The nurses can wipe off the hypodermic needles and see for themselves that there are no germs on them. Asia operates by common sense; the scientific approach has taught the West to give up this most misleading of man's guides.

The countryside around Saigon is flat, fertile country, but less fertile than the black earth of Java. Between the rice paddies are marshes clogged with water lilies. In the marshes people fish with baskets woven of stiff bamboo rods and shaped like large eggshells chopped in half. They plunge the wide, open end of these down into the mud and the fish are either impaled on the ends of the bamboo rods or trapped in the basket.

Every possible inch of the delta is farmed or fished by this overpopulated, underfed people. Their growth has doubled in the last thirty-six years and, civil war permitting, in 1980 it will double again. Ruled by the French since 1867, Vietnam, like the other two Associated States of Indo-China, was one of the most backward areas in Asia. Its 22,000,000 people scattered or squeezed in 127,000 square miles, about the size of New Mexico, have one of the lowest incomes and one of the poorest diets of the Far East. Eighty-five per cent of them are illiterate and 90 per cent suffer from tuberculosis, malaria, yaws, and other diseases. A few years ago there was one doctor for every 250 in the French communities; the Vietnamese themselves had only one doctor for every 40,000 human beings. The illiterate mothers follow ancient superstitions; they eat only rice and salt for the last four weeks of pregnancy and the combination of such folklore and lack of doctors means that up to half the babies of Vietnam die before they are a year old.

The French have not set up much better records in agriculture, for Vietnam has one of the lowest rice productions per acre in Asia. Even so, before World War II, this fertile land managed to export 1,500,000 tons of rice a year; now, because of the long war, only a third of this is available. Usury rates have been appallingly high, up to more than 100 per cent a year, and the sharecropper peasants paid up to half their yield to their landlords.

Once again, in Vietnam, bad land policies and a peasantry disenfranchised from much of the land have become one of the chief appeals of the Communists. The Vietnamese try to institute land-reform programs, but the familiar pattern tends to apply here again: the colonial power does not want to lose its investments and the wealthier landlords are one of its chief supports; while the few nationalist reformers are ill educated in economics and ill trained in the mechanics of land redistribution. On the other side, the Communist leaders are always well trained in Moscow or Peiping. When they take over, the results are immediate: they kill the landlords and present the peasants with an effective land-reform program. Ho Chi Minh has already done this in many areas of Vietnam under his control; as is happening in Communist China, the land is split up and all property of "French colonialists, reactionaries, and the cruel rich" is confiscated.

The French were no more liberal or farsighted in colonial politics than in colonial economics. When and as anti-French sentiment rose into violence—which was often—they suppressed it ruthlessly and learned nothing from it. They permitted no elections. They allowed the Vietnamese no voice in their own government. They granted the extraterritorial privileges of French citizenship to only twenty-six hundred of their most subservient stooges, about one in every nine thousand. Perhaps if history had meandered slowly along in Asia, the clarity of mind and egalitarian principles of French civilization might gradually have brought enlightenment even to the French colonials. But time did not wait. A world war and an extraordinary man changed the history of Vietnam.

In the prewar years, while the French were going along their happy way in Vietnam, the United States was struggling out of its Great Depression and paying no mind at all to Asia. During these same years a young Annamese patriot was being turned into the ablest revolutionary in Southeast Asia. His name was Nguyen Ai Quoc, but we know him better under the alias Ho Chi Minh. His story is a fine example of how communism, searching out the best young intellectuals for its future leaders and operating in terms of decades, and not by the starts and fits of a democracy, can come out ahead.

Reputedly the son of a mandarin, Ho Chi Minh is in appearance the typical Chinese scholar: slight, small-boned, spectacled, with a domed forehead, long nose, and the wisps of a Chinese beard and long thin mustaches; but his is the tireless spirit of a revolutionary who has fought against the French all his life. Forced to flee from Indo-China, in his early twenties he was in Paris, a photographer and a member of the French Communist Party. The Russians, searching always for the young men who might tomorrow convulse a world, recognized his ability and took him to Moscow in 1923 for advanced Communist training.

When his schooling was over, he began his agitating. For a while he was an adviser to Chiang Kai-shek before Chiang threw out his Communist advisers in 1927. He was a permanent delegate for colonized countries to the Comintern in Moscow. Then he worked for a while at the Russian Consulate in Canton. In 1930, in Hong Kong, he created the Indo-Chinese Communist Party and promptly organized an unsuccessful revolt in his homeland. There are many blanks in his history between 1930 and 1945. With the help of the Chinese and the Russian Communist parties, he was in and out of Indo-China secretly selecting his hard-core Communist assistants and preparing for guerrilla war, always presenting himself as the symbol of resistance to the French conquerors.

And a fact which assumes new meaning now that Ho's regime rules North Vietnam: he was not only the organizer of the Communist Party in Indo-China; for years he was in and out of Malaya and Thailand, doing the same job for the Communists there.

Act One of the tragedy of errors of Indo-China opened with World War II, when the Japanese seized Indo-China and the Vichy French ran it for them with no more freedom for the Vietnamese. Even the alternate French government, De Gaulle's Free French, trying to rally French areas to its standard, committed itself to nothing more than general statements about local autonomy being a desirable goal for Vietnam to look forward to, sometime in the vague future.

Under Japanese and Vichy auspices, young Bao Dai became the puppet Emperor of Annam, keeping himself well in the background. But after twenty-five years of study, struggle, planning, and rehearsals, the time of harvest had come to Nguyen Ai Quoc. He changed his name to Ho Chi Minh [He Who Shines], and he changed the façade of his party from a purely Communist organization to an anti-French, anti-Japanese, anti-Fascist setup called Vietnam Doc Lap Dong Minh Ho [The League for Vietnamese Independence], better known by its shorter title, Vietminh. Under this nationalist banner, "He Who Shines" and his Vietminh led the Indo-Chinese guerrillas against Vichy and Tokyo.

That Johnny-Come-Lately in Asian affairs, the United States, being interested only in military allies, considered Ho's Communist background less important than his willingness to fight the Japanese. So the American Office of Strategic Services backed him with guns and money, and by V-J Day Ho was firmly established in the minds of the Vietnamese as their symbol of national independence.

Supported by almost all Vietnamese nationalists, he established the "Free Democratic Republic of Vietnam." Ho's regime, never forgetting how much the Vietnamese fear things Chinese, has always carefully underplayed its Chinese support and has never admitted it is a Communist government. It was for this same propaganda purpose that, nine years after the Republic was proclaimed, in the 1954 truce talks at Trunggia the Vietminh negotiators again forced the French to call them representatives of the "Democratic Republic of Vietnam."

In 1945, having set up his new state, Ho established its capital at Hanoi, and Bao Dai added his prestige by becoming "Supreme Councilor." In March 1946 the French signed an agreement recognizing Ho's control in the north but leaving vague the future status of their prize colony, Cochin China. "Uncle Ho" journeyed to Paris and was received with full honors as the Provisional President of Vietnam.

The United States was conspicuous by its absence from the center of the stage while these crucial scenes were being played. In 1944 President Roosevelt had written Secretary of State Hull: "Indo-China should not go back to the French but be administered by international trusteeship. The French had Indo-China one hundred years and the people are worse off." But, like so much else, his prophetic letter was filed away when Roosevelt died. A new President of the United States had his hands full with postwar Russia and so the only power which might have influenced the history of Vietnam for the better carried water on both shoulders.

Washington recognized the regime of Ho but did nothing to restrain France when the French colonials and their army returned to Vietnam. Inevitably tensions rose toward an explosion. Bao Dai, never caught off base, piloted his private plane to refuge in Hong Kong. In a confused welter of events and countercharges, civil war broke out. The French re-established their regime in Cochin China and repudiated their agreements with Ho. In January 1947 the Provisional President of Vietnam returned to the hills as a guerrilla leader and the French started a "three months campaign" against the "rebels." Thus did the French enter into a war they did not recognize as a war, and the United States acquiesce in a decision we did not recognize as a decision. The majority of the people of Vietnam saw only a struggle between their new nationalist leader, Ho, and their old colonial master, France.

With the civil war, Act Two of Vietnam's tragedy swept on toward its dénouement. In the next seven years the war spread and Ho's forces snowballed until the French realized they must have some native Vietnamese symbol of nationalism. The only alternate leader to Ho was Bao Dai. He could be persuaded to return from Hong Kong only after he forced the French to yield on the main point which had precipitated their "three months campaign" against Ho. Cochin China was released from its status as a separate colony and the three parts of the country were combined into the new state of Vietnam. Then the Emperor Bao Dai became in theory the absolute power in Vietnam; as "Chief of State" he was "assisted by the president of the Council," but he appointed the cabinet and the president and he could dismiss them at will.

Bao Dai, only rival attraction so far to Ho Chi Minh, is a contradictory personality who walks with devious craft through the web of antithetical forces of his period, conceiving his role to be that of an aloof Chief of State, not a dynamic leader. Perhaps this is one of the important reasons Paris backed him; too good a leader would threaten its own power.

His own people seldom see Bao Dai for he lives up in the mountain fastnesses of Dalat about 150 miles away from Saigon in an ugly French, yellow stucco palace, a desolate parody of Versailles, with parks where dried up pink petunias and sparse clumps of orange calendulas in formal terraced flower beds spread out toward a lonely view over the mountains. Inside, the rooms of Bao Dai's palace are impersonally furnished in tasteless modern French furniture. There are only two touches of the East, a pair of magnificent carved ivory tusks over the fireplace and a fireplace screen of glass sculptured into a symbolic map of Vietnam.

Bao Dai, in the best oriental tradition, prides himself on showing no emotion. He is always aloof and regal. Whenever he appears before his people he is preceded by white-clad guards on roaring motorcycles; in the midst of them is a bright yellow Chevrolet convertible with the flag of Vietnam as a license plate, the Chief of State seated alone on the back seat. He is heavy-set, fattish, of medium height, indolent, with long slicked-down black hair and large black eyes, which are full of disillusionment except when he is looking at a beautiful woman. He never appears in Eastern clothes, always wearing a Western white shirt with dark tie, and sunglasses. Bao Dai stands passively or negligently while the national anthem is played. When he must, he moves through his part like an automaton, but he is a bored automaton, sharply contrasting with another Asian potentate, the young King of

Thailand, who holds himself rigid and goes through his paces with precision.

Yet this man is no soft puppet. He is a fearless hunter of tigers and elephants, an expert and hard-driving bridge player, an aviator who flies and services his own plane. In his own terms, he is also a leader; when you see him surrounded by the young officers of his Army he obviously dominates them, drawing them out, joking with them, yet keeping his dignity and their respect. And he has extracted more from the French than any of his countrymen have been able to. He is ruthless at power politics, playing his ministers off one against the other and in Vietnam permitting no other political personality to emerge. Most Machiavellian of his abilities is the way he has managed to keep aloof from the French who put him into power. No one can know how much he blocks them and they him.

It has been impossible to ascertain where Bao Dai stands on his rival, Ho Chi Minh. In my interview with him, the only radio interview he has ever granted, I asked him, "In Your Majesty's judgment, was Ho ever a patriot fighting for the independence of Vietnam, or has he always been a Communist?" Bao Dai answered me with no answer at all. "To my mind such discussions cannot have very great practical significance since in every country in the world the Communist Party is one of blind obedience to the foreigner."

Unfortunately for the French, Bao Dai's return did not reverse the course of events. While the new Chief of State was picking his way through the snares of Vietnamese political life, or hunting on his country estates in Dalat and vacationing on the Riviera, the French were sinking deeper and deeper into the quicksands of colonial war.

Then, as now, the very fact that the troops opposing them were French gave the Vietminh their greatest propaganda weapon, not love of communism but hatred of the French. An American mission, going into a small village during the civil war, saw this sign over an arch: "Communism No. Colonialism Never!!" And one of the young patriots of Hanoi explained why his countrymen do not fear the fire of communism: "When you are a bird in a cage in a room of a house which is on fire, you hate the cage more than the fire."

Right up to the time of the Geneva truce, the French kept all the bars on the cage and added a few more. The Vietnamese had no less than four secret police keeping watch over them: two secret police sections of the French Army—the Deuxieme Bureau and a special political arm—plus two secret police organizations of the Vietnamese government, like the other bureaus, controlled by the French. Undoubtedly secret police were needed to protect the country from Communists. But Vietnamese nationalists found that any anti-French agitation was treated as pro-Communist. And all this was going on at a time when every other colonial people in Asia—with the single exception of the unzealous Malays—had thrown off the yoke of colonialism and won national independence.

As the civil war in Vietnam dragged on and widened, the French began to yearn for more Vietnamese soldiers to take the strain off the French Union forces. And the Americans, by this time seriously alarmed about the catastrophe looming up over the horizon, were pouring billions of dollars into Indo-China and repeatedly pointing out to the French that if the war was to be won the first and most urgent task must be the creation of a large Vietnamese Army. By 1953–54, in theory the French were training such an Army and the Americans were equipping it. But the keystone of an army is a trained officer corps, efficient and resolute. This the French had no wish to create; it would have been too difficult to control "after the war" and so, in spite of intense American pressure, in the spring of 1954 they were only training some four thousand officers a year. They preferred to build an Army of privates to fight as the French directed and under French officers.

The French have complained that the Vietnamese Army does not show enough fighting spirit; the Army has seen clearly it was to fight for the French. This is not the way a guerrilla army is forged. The Vietnamese spirit is there if it is given motivation. Graduation exercises at the French training school at Dalat for Vietnamese officers showed me what is present and what is missing.

On the high gravel terrace of the school overlooking the mountains, two flags whipped in the cool air side by side, the Vietnamese and, in the place of honor, the tricolor. At Rawalpindi in Pakistan, where the British train the Pakistan troops, only the Pakistan green flag with its Moslem crescent flies over the training school and the British teach the Pakistani they are fighting for their own country and that the British, although members of the same union as the Pakistani, are only instructors. Not so at Dalat. During the impressive graduation ceremonies, Bao Dai sat in an armchair on the platform. On his right sat the French High Commissioner while in a lower seat on his left sat the actual executive head of the Vietnamese state, the President of the Council. The graduation class, conscious as are all Asians of status, did not miss this sequence of importance.

The maneuvers and ceremonies of the young Vietnamese officers were crisp and clean, ending in a moving ceremony that opened with a symbolic challenge of Vietnam to its enemies. First, the head of the cadets snapped to a salute in front of the Emperor, bowed, and took off his sword. In its place he picked up a bow and arrow. The cadet corps came to attention. The cadet captain with beautiful precision shot one arrow directly to the east, turned on his heel and shot a second to the west, then one to the south and the final one, flying high in the air, soared over the troops' heads toward the north.

Then as one man the graduating class knelt, and sang in deep solemn beat their "Hymn to the Dead," saluting their comrades who had died in battle. At the end of the hymn there was a long moment of silence, punctuated only by the snapping of the halyards against the flagpoles in the strong mountain wind. Then the entire two hundred cadets leaped from their knees straight up into the air, landed on their feet at attention and burst into the fierce war chant, *Xaug Quai*. At the end of the chant, saluting the Emperor, they marched off across the gravel and down the winding hill, a long white line headed for trains that would take them north to the battle front against the Vietminh.

As in Korea or Thailand or Malaya or Burma or Indonesia, the threat of outside aggression vanishes when these new countries have their own armies able and eager to defend themselves against all comers. The United States proved in Korea that such armies can be raised from raw Asian peasants at a fraction of the cost of maintaining a Western army, and when they are well trained they will fight for their own countries. As we did in Korea, we might have done in Vietnam, if the French had let us. But they would not. And so by 1953 they had created a Vietminh so powerful that France could barely keep control over the chief towns in South Vietnam. Beyond the city limits of Saigon there were elaborate sets of road blocks and barbed-wire passages so that no surprise raid of Communist jeeps or carts could crash through into the city. Overlooking the barriers were cement towers bristling with machine guns bearing on each car that filed through the barbed-wire maze and came to a stop to have its passengers checked.

In much of the country, once five o'clock came, the main highways were empty. Only armored cars and heavily armed jeeps dared travel them at night when most of the countryside was the province of the Vietminh. In the larger villages, the United States Information Service had put up bulletin boards or stocked little stores with American pamphlets, but few dared go in to read them because their names might be noted by the Vietminh. As the suppliers of the French and the Vietnamese, Americans were the enemies of the Vietminh who terrorized the villagers almost at will. The French could not tell when a man in a village group might be a Communist; the terrorists are people of the same country and they all look exactly alike. A Vietminh can come to a village at dawn, sink his greased gun in the mud of a rice paddy, and become a harmless Vietnam peasant. When the French tried to surround a Vietminh force, it melted away into the landscape.

Faced with this sort of threat from the Communists, some of the more powerful religious sects in this disunified land worked out their own security measures. The Catholics, the Buddhist Hoa Hao and the Cao Dai have each set up their own armies to protect their people. The most colorful of these sects is the fantastic cult of the Cao Dai, the Supreme Being, who live around their unbelievable holy city of Tayninh, spread out on a dusty plain at the base of their sacred Black Goddess Mountain in South Vietnam.

The Cao Dai, fervently anti-Communist, has its own armies to preserve order in its own way over its own land, and neither the French nor the Vietnamese Government interfere with it. A huge eye is its ever present symbol; even on the yellow flags of the Cao Dai in place of the stars on the American flag there is a small blue rectangle with a flaming red eye in the middle. These flags fly over their garrison posts, usually without any French or Vietnamese flag beside them.

The cathedral of Tayninh rises up out of a flat plain. It is a long building of pink and yellow stucco, undecided whether to be two or four stories high, ornate, and spouting with every sort of architecture and ornament known to man or nightmare. The walls have large open arches for windows, partly filled in with a design of huge pink formalized coral buds connected by cement rays to clusters of blue morning-glories connected by cement rays running into a great gaudily painted cement eye. The flights of steps leading into the cathedral are flanked with furious plaster lions with long tails. There are Gothic towers, Buddhist eaves, Victorian cupolas; in the center of the roof is a small dome capped with a rearing sea serpent on which, in 1926, the first Cao Dai pope reputedly rose out of the sea.

Inside the church, a quadruple row of pillars marches along to the nave, each one coiled around with stucco and gilt-scaled dragons, two unicorn horns on each dragon's head. The pale blue plaster ceiling, arched, vaulted, curved, and set with pieces of silver mirror for stars, looks down on the long nave rising in slow marble tiers toward the altar where priests in hooded silk robes, like Ku Klux Klanners, sit on thrones of vermilion and gold. Behind them are an assortment of altars covered with Chinese and Buddhist images, vases, and dragons. Behind the altars, half-drawn curtains of thin blue silk, with an appliquéd velvet overdesign in pink, veil a huge silk orb dotted with stars. In the very middle of it, another great eye peers out. Add to this pulpits in the pillars, fluorescent lighting, modern microphones.

And in the entrance to the cathedral itself there is a huge wall painting of the three great saints of the Cao Dai faith, inscribed, "Notice of the presence of trois saints: Binh Khiem, MASTER OF THE WHITE LODGE, Victor Hugo, and Sun Yat-sen, DISCIPLES OF THE WHITE LODGE." The founders of Cao Dai just happened to decide these three men were suitable founder saints. Each, clad in suitable costume, is depicted signing a sort of Ten Commandments stone piece.

The Cao Dai may sound silly to Westerners, but they have insured security in their lands and their people smile at you with friendly open faces. Somehow, their faith has short-circuited the hatreds of colonialism. If the French had taken heed of this successful cult which kept peace in and Communists out of its territories, they might have discovered how to persuade more Vietnamese to fight alongside French Union soldiers. But in the entire period from 1946 to 1954, the French could never seem to learn.

Everything the French have done has been too little and too late. Consistently, the growth of national Vietnamese consciousness has been faster than their recognition of it. Ignorantly, stupidly, intransigently, call it what you will, the French have consistently muffed their every chance to rescue the situation, thus persuading more and more Vietnamese to believe their only release from France is via the Vietminh. The first limited French declaration of independence for Vietnam did not come until July 1953, six years after the civil war started.

Perhaps the greatest indictment of French colonial rule is that it has never carried out a decent training program to teach self-rule to the Vietnamese. This was not only forced upon France by a minority clique of colonial industrial interests that had everything to lose from nationalism in Vietnam, but also by France's over-all colonial policy; if it granted more freedom in Indo-China, its North African colonies began to make more trouble. So they sat on the only safety valve in Vietnam, self-rule.

It was not until 1953 that the Vietnamese were permitted the first election in their history. It would have been hard to imagine a more restricted voting. Holding the election in the midst of a civil war drastically limited it. Only two thousand of the twelve thousand villages were considered sufficiently pro-Vietnamese to be allowed to vote; one million people out of twenty-four million; no women had the franchise. And the voting was only a symbol; the people were electing councilors who would "inform the authorities of the situation of the people."

The government announced that at some later, but unspecified date, these councilors in turn would elect district councilors who in turn at still another unspecified date would elect provincial councilors who in turn sometime would vote for a national legislature. Notice the gaucheness of the French as compared with the British; if this first, tentative, municipal election had been held in Malaya, the authorities would have specified the exact dates on which the later elections would be held.

It was apparent even to the politically untutored Vietnamese that the election mechanism provided an excellent device by which the French could keep control of any national assembly they ever permitted to be selected, since the whole pyramid of representative government would rest on the councilors elected only by the villagers the Franco-Vietnamese certified as dependable. Nonetheless, the imagination of the people was stirred by this their first step toward freedom, and of the eligible voters over 80 per cent voted.

A few months after the election, Bao Dai appointed a national congress to help him talk with the French about a revised place for Vietnam in the French Union. Bao Dai moved with his customary caution, selected two hundred men only eighty of whom represented political organizations, the rest being Bao Dai puppets. He convened the congress to meet for two days only and nominated a list of twenty people from whom he could select six to assist him in talks with the French. But when that congress met in late 1953, even these carefully housebroken appointees would not stay in line. They voted unanimously for freedom outside the French Union.

Moving every source of persuasion and pressure, the best the French and Bao Dai managed was to get the congress to say instead that it objected to join the French Union "in its present form." Then as it tried to propose a national union cabinet, it was hastily dismissed.

During these same years the United States was not distinguishing itself by its Indo-Chinese policies. Gradually as we saw the threat to the entire free world implicit in a Communist victory, we intervened in the Indo-Chinese mess, one toe at a time, too little, too late, and too ignorantly. First, in 1946, we allowed the situation to get under way when we might have persuaded France, prostrate and dependent on American funds, to grant independence to a non-Communist Vietnam. Second, in 1952, when the full dangers of Indo-China were apparent, we negotiated a truce in Korea whose foreseeable consequence was to allow the Red Chinese to shift more armaments and men to their allies in Tonkin. It was all part of the same war but we did not seem to have the international sense to know this. Third, although we financed the French Indo-Chinese War to the tune of more billions of dollars than the French had invested in prewar Indo-China, we could not—or would not—insist that the French bestow real freedom upon the Vietnamese.

And so, in mid-1954, after seven years of brave but stupid fighting against the Vietminh guerrillas in campaigns which, in the words of one French commander-in-chief, were "like trying to hit a swarm of flies with a hammer," the French went to Geneva and sought what terms they could from the victorious Vietminh and Red China.

The Geneva Agreement split Vietnam in two at the 17th parallel, approximately half of the land and population going to each side. "He Who Shines" and Company got North Vietnam, the Red River delta, and plenty of coal and iron for light industry; they also got the vigorous Tonkinese. The French were left with the South Vietnamese, the more indolent half of the people, plus the richer of the two rice bowls, the delta of the Mekong River. The south also has most of the military installations of the country, but the Agreement permits only replacements of miliary hardware now there. The north has the port of Haiphong, a most useful naval base for the Reds because it dominates the Gulf of Tonkin and much of the South China Sea.

Militarily, as a means to cease being killed in a war they no longer had the will to fight, the French negotiated a good bargain at Geneva. Since the 17th parallel runs through mountainous terrain, the French are left with an easily defended boundary, the narrow waist of

Annam. But to gain these military advantages, the French were forced to agree to elections in Vietnam within two years. At that time, July 1956, unless the Agreement is repudiated, the entire country will vote to decide under what kind of a government it will be reunited.

Theoretically, such a plebescite is a fair and democratic way to establish a legitimate government for all Vietnam; but, in fact, only a supreme effort can prevent South Vietnam from being lost to the non-Communist world in 1956. In the south is a demoralized, confused, civilian population and millions of *attentistes*—the fence-sitters—waiting to see which side is going to win and then cheer for it. If the French remain and try to teach the South Vietnamese, they will be hated as colonial rulers; if they leave, the country has literally no trained ruling class of its own.

Yet the government of South Vietnam must capture its people's support within two years in direct competition with North Vietnam, where sits the victorious, ruthless, well-organized, efficient regime of Ho's Vietminh. During the next two years, it seems certain, the North Vietnam regime will utilize all the customary methods of a police state—terrorism, suppression, brainwashing—to make certain its elections come out right.

And in addition there is the most potent of all the influences which will play upon the South Vietnamese, the same force that created the Vietminh power in the first place: the anti-colonial, pro-nationalist sentiment of the people and the young intellectuals. Ho, the first President of Vietnam, is again the head of a state and, in the eyes of many South Vietnamese, the real nationalist leader. If he dies, there are other Vietminh to step into his shoes: the Vice-President, Tham Van Dong, who handled the Geneva negotiations; or General Vo Nguyen Giap, who led his troops to victory against the French. The Secretary-General of the Vietminh, Truong Chin, who controls the party apparatus and takes orders from Peiping, will stay in the shadows, unseen by the Vietnamese peasants.

Of course, if he remains on the job, the French have the Chief of State, Bao Dai, on their side. But his influence is imponderable since he has never stepped out in front of events or sought to shape them. If he should at some point in the two-year interim step forward and oppose the French, he might become a potent rallying point. But only to the extent to which he becomes anti-French.

There is little cause to hope that the South Vietnamese will soon change their feelings about France. If anything, recent French acts have intensified their hatred. The French, failing to defend the country they insisted on bossing, signed away half of it. Vietnamese soldiers were good enough to be killed in the war, but in the truce talks at Trunggia, the Vietnamese representatives were permitted to raise points only when the French negotiator recognized them and he allowed them no voice.

Before the Geneva truce, there was a relatively cheap solution available in the Vietnam, a ménage à trois which could have saved the country. The French could have given Vietnam the independence it will now have to cede to them. The Americans could have quickly trained native Vietnamese armies eager to fight for their own nation. The third party to the ménage à trois, the Vietnamese people, would have been the citizens of a free and proud state. Then Ho Chi Minh would have been in trouble. For at least 80 per cent of his Vietminh were fighting only against French colonialism and they would have had no will to fight other Vietnamese defending the sovereignty of a free Vietnam. Ho and his Communists would then have been revealed in their true role as the puppets of the Chinese.

If this ménage à trois had been created in 1953, it is unlikely American troops would have been needed. And the strategy of the French could have been revised to save their man power. Their objective would not have been the costly one of driving out the Vietminh and the Chinese, but the limited one of interposing an allied army between the Vietminh and conquest until the Vietnamese Army and government could do the real job. But such a ménage à trois is now in the saddest of limbos, it might have been.

Today, if we are to have the least hope of helping South Vietnam stay out of Communist hands in 1956, there is one action which the United States and the rest of the free world have a right to require of the French: that they, in fact and with sincerity, grant the Vietnamese full independence.

This the French must do unhesitatingly, promptly, and so unhedgingly that the most suspicious young Vietnamese firebrand cannot be persuaded by Communist agitators that the French are up to another piece of political chicanery.

If the French will not do this, they should be left to lose the rest of Vietnam by themselves, for every cent we give without such an assurance will go down the drain and in the process irrevocably stamp us with the stigma of French colonialism.

If the French will grant true independence, then we can all buckle down to the real work, difficult, costly, urgent: in the short two years of grace before the elections somehow the non-Communist world must dramatically raise the living standard of the South Vietnamese and inspire them to understand, to want, and to choose some form of non-police-state democracy. For South Vietnam presents the free world with a great opportunity. There are only ten or eleven million people involved, and the rest of Asia knows that they are poor, uninstructed, ill trained. If the West will contribute enough of its skills and abilities and if the South Vietnamese can realize in time what freedom can mean and what it can do for them, the consequences will strike at the foundations of Communist strength in Southeast Asia. Aggression is only the minor part of the Communist dynamic. It gains its Asian friends principally because they believe it offers them plain and positive programs for a better life.

If we prove that democracy can do more for them, we will, for the first time, be fighting communism in the right place and at the right time. But it will cost a great deal, far more than the United States Congress has been willing to vote, per peasant, for Point Four and Technical Aid to any country. If we do not see the wisdom of paying such moneys in South Vietnam, we shall pay more later to try to protect ourselves from the consequences of the loss of Indo-China.

With the truce in Vietnam, Chinese communism is now at the same historical point of development reached by Russia after the coup in Czechoslovakia. From here on, direct Chinese military aggression against any spot in Asia but Formosa—that island being an intra-Chinese problem to most Asians—would convince the neutrals of Asia that communism is an armed aggression against their countries rather than a method to drive out colonials and improve standards of living. The most profitable future role for the Chinese Communists is to speak out for peace, for "Asia for Asians," for "all foreign military bases to be removed and all foreign armed forces withdrawn."

Even in Indo-China it was not a military war we lost but a struggle for the allegiance of the Vietnamese. The next phase in the struggle between communism and democracy in Asia is most likely to be a war of credos and propagandas, to make friends and influence neutrals. Moscow is today devoting five sixths of its government printing presses to turning out propaganda in Eastern languages. Peiping is following suit. It is expanding its training programs for agitators, opening up two new schools for Overseas Chinese, and adding more scholarships for those promising young hua-chiao whose parents cannot afford to send them to China for their education.

Not by arms but by arguments—this is communism's new strategy for victory, whether in South Vietnam, or Laos and Cambodia, or in the rest of Southeast Asia. First, infiltration via propaganda and the right schooling for the young intellectuals. Second, by means of these recruits, the strengthening of internal Communist parties. Third, accession to power via popular front governments with the liberals for the "common good"; or if this does not work, internal subversion and unrest. Finally, the creation of another "free regime."

Such is the course of maximum gain for China and Russia. We can never stop it by "massive retaliations." Nor by spending so much on military aid and so little on technical assistance and the war of ideas.

THE HAPPY PEOPLE:

Thailand

Every country of Asia is unique, and the differences between them are both wide and deep: the tropical-climated, Malay-settled Philippine Islands with their Spanish background and American enthusiasm; Japan with its Shinto religion, its Son of Heaven, its paper-screened houses, and its desperate economy; Korea with other gods and other customs; Formosa and China, differing in their ways from each other but both unlike the oriental cultures of Korea and Japan; Hong Kong and Singapore and Malaya with British buildings and British law and order and customs; Macao, that unforeseeable combination of South China and Portugal; Indonesia, another mad conglomeration, this time of ancient Javanese and Victorian Dutch; the mutual diversities of Laos, Cambodia, Vietnam, and Burma, adjacent countries in the same climate with many of the same races, yet differing in languages and customs, joining in nothing; the subcontinent of India, a turgid centrifuge of races and religions, a small universe in itself.

And until recently there was little intercommunication and less intercultural influences among the individual countries of Asia; far more connections between colonial areas and the European capitals of their conquering masters in Europe. The Burmese far more British than Thai; the Indonesians far more Dutch than Malayan; the Filipinos far more Spanish than Indonesian; the Vietnamese far more French than Chinese.

The kingdom of the Thais is one more of the bewildering patterns presented by the kaleidoscope of Asia. Supreme in tourist lore for peace and color, it has been for nine hundred years an oasis of security in the instability of Burma, Indo-China, and Malaya. Thailand, whose people object to its being called by its foreign name of Siam, means

Land of the Free. With about nineteen million people and two hundred thousand square miles, it is the oldest sovereign kingdom of South Asia, and along with Japan it is one of the two constitutional monarchies in the Far East. Ninety per cent of its people are farmers and have enough to eat. Whether or not because of this, Thailand is the most firmly anti-Communist nation of Southeast Asia and the best friend of the United Nations and the United States west of the Philippine Islands.

As you fly in toward Bangkok across quiescent islands in the molten sunset Gulf of Thailand, the flat fertile southern part of this kingdom resembles a much more lush and tropical Kansas. Its expanse of fertile land is less chopped into tiny holdings than the rest of Southeast Asia. Each thatched farmhouse nestles in a little grove of trees, again like an Asian Kansas, even to the clumps of trees along the winding river.

The great Bangkok airport of Don Muang is a transport hub through which passes all the air traffic from the Pacific to the Middle East; it is only forty-eight hours' flying time from the capitals of Europe, the New World, or Asia. The Thai officials at the airport are pleasant, relaxed, and relatively efficient. A reassuring sign, for you learn very quickly in traveling that there is no better index of the psychological balance of a country and its attitude toward the rest of the world than its customs officials: where they are drowned in red tape, as in India, or antagonistic toward the foreigner, as in Indonesia, the same biases are reflected in the attitude of the country's editors and government officials.

The familiar incongruities of yesterday and tomorrow are repeated again at Don Muang. A gasoline truck is parked in front of a building with a yellow tiled steep roof, its eaves ending in lightning-rod-like projections to prevent evil spirits from perching there. As I try to explain what a modern tape recorder is to a Thai inspector who can understand little English, he hears even less because a nearby radio speaker is blaring out "Slaughter on Tenth Avenue." A winking neon sign announces "Rita is back for her Affair in Trinidad."

The electric power fluctuates so much in Thailand that record players require special transformers, but the government is too busy building two TV stations to worry about modernizing its government-owned electric power and water plants. Editorials in the Bangkok press, with Thai humor, insist the inefficient electrical power and water supplies are a deliberate and wise plan of the government, proving that a Communist state would be impossible to bear, by showing how badly state ownership serves the people.

Bangkok, a city of nearly a million, is an acme of contrast even in its own terms: a drab, dingy collection of dirty hovels and arid reaches of slums exploding every so often into the glittering rainbow tiles and spires of palaces and temples, their contrasts addled further by the haphazard dropping in of stucco and concrete Western buildings. From a highway the amphitheater and the race track of the Sports Club are spread out across green turf, but between the highway and the club grounds is a canal with crude arched wooden bridges over it, and the canal is filled with six-foot-long sampans where coolie families live and die; on the other side of the street from the canal are luxurious mid-Victorian Saratoga Springs wooden houses.

The first thing that impresses you in steaming Bangkok is the bloodthirsty mosquitoes, which seem to bite only foreigners. Next comes the traffic. Nowhere else in Asia is it as difficult to get around; there are more cars per capita in Bangkok than in any other city in Asia—thirty thousand of them—and there is always a traffic jam. Besides cars and busses, the streets are filled with peasants pushing wooden-wheeled carts, and with slow bicycle rickshas. One ricksha can jam up a two-lane highway for eight or ten blocks, a good symbol of what happens when two civilizations so different in background and mechanisms try to proceed along the same road.

Bangkok's Rajadamnern Avenue, the Champs Elysées of Southeast Asia, is as wide as a four-lane highway, lined with trees, temples, and government buildings. At one end is the Ananta Samakom Throne Hall, at the other the Temple of the Emerald Buddha. In front of one of the government buildings a snake charmer plays with two cobras, selling snakebite medicine, and within two feet of the writhing cobras a motorized scooter chugs along, disturbing the cobras not a bit.

The canals of Bangkok, called *klongs* by the Thais, are dirtier than the canals of Djakarta and used for the same purposes, yet in Asia you soon learn to eliminate meaning from appearance and so find some beauty in sordidness. One of these klongs, about eight feet across, may be covered with stagnant slime, yet it is beautiful in the soft damp sunshine; the slime a shimmering neonistic yellow green, and a group of ducks sailing through it, the darker opalescent green of their feathers reflected in the little dark brown pools of water they clear as they move along; once in a while they veer off their course to circle a white lotus, which blends with their breast feathers.

A few blocks away from Rajadamnern Avenue is a typical market and bazaar street. A fortuneteller squats cross-legged on his bamboo mat in the shade of a tamarind tree, telling fortunes by palmistry, reckoning horoscopes by cards and trained birds. Typical of the Thai approach, he looks at your palm before he names you a price; if there is good fortune in it, he charges more. Pairs of Buddhist priests walk past the fortuneteller, their heads shaven, their lean bodies draped in saffron-yellow cotton robes, over their shoulders dainty shoulder bags lined in soft blues and rose. The priests step around mangy dogs, but the fortunetellers kick them away. Dogs are a sorry sight in Bangkok because the Buddhists do not believe in killing anything living, and the animals, diseased, enfeebled, dying, wander until they fall on the sidewalk or in a clump of bamboo. Above the fortuneteller's head, a modern mailbox with the royal arms of Thailand on it, but you learn not to mail letters there or even in the post office, for if your letter has expensive stamps on it government clerks may tear off the uncanceled stamps and throw your letter away; whenever you mail things in Southeast Asia or India, you make sure the stamps are canceled before your eyes.

Bangkok is the Venice of the Far East. And so neither Rajadamnern Avenue nor its chief commercial street, New Road, is its main thoroughfare. For hundreds of years a great river, the Chao Phraya, has spewed its flood silt into the Gulf of Thailand, and on this New Orleans-like delta the Thais built their capital city, spreading over onto new islands as the Chao Phraya built them. Today the main street of Bangkok is the Great River, and its smaller streets are the klongs around which most of the life of the Thai people is focused. One of the truisms of Asia is that you cannot know a country from the capital city and its westernized upper class. But from Bangkok there is no need to travel out into the countryside; half an hour away from the government buildings, along the market klong, the unwesternized life of the Thais goes on as it has for centuries.

Most of the selling and buying is done at dawn on the market klong, and so before the moon had set, I was climbing into a sampan at the Quai of the Rising Moon, poetic title but a dirty, dilapidated old wharf set against an equally old and dilapidated moon. We moved quietly along out into the Chao Phraya past small water trolleys chugging their passengers into the city. Anchored in front of the Temple of the Reclining Buddha were three old submarines, curiously like medieval monsters, their sides streaked with the red of rust above the gray-green scum and barnacles, their ancient superstructures rearing up with two rectangular holes against the dawning sky like the whites of monster eyes.

Next into view came the moldering boathouses of the royal barges. These barges are long canoes like those of the South Seas, their sides intricately wrought with inlaid brass and gold to catch the light, on their prows twelve-foot-high mythological birds, or seven dragons rearing up with open mouths painted bright red and fanged with glistening white ivory teeth. Once every year, enthroned on a flat platform fenced with gold, the King of Thailand goes down along the Chao Phraya, stopping at all the temple quais to award robes to the Buddhist priests at the end of the Buddhist Lent.

It was cool as we moved through the pearly light. A little later the day would be full of the humidity and heat of the Orient, yet the temperature rarely gets above 105 and you are not hemmed in with the heat by the structure of a large city. Moving along the river in the clear light, you can see the full horizon, for there are no high buildings and only a few palm trees against the sky.

The klongs of Bangkok flow around groups of islands, branching off and returning to the Chao Phraya. The market klong is flanked with ramshackle huts on stilts with wooden steps coming down to the water. The fronts of the houses are open to the river, and as you look through to the other end of many of them, you can see a glow of intense color, a small stained-glass window in the farther wall. People are kneeling on the bottom steps of their houses, taking their morning baths in the muddy water; like the other peoples of Southeast Asia, not believing in displaying the ugliness of flesh but washing themselves under their sarongs. A little farther on, a man standing waist-deep in the opalescent brown-green water scrubs his teeth; the white foam at the corners of his mouth is mirrored in the water and a baby splashes for the foam's reflection.

Bright potted plants in front of the dull brown-gray houses, which are sometimes vine-covered but never painted. Paint costs too much and lasts too short a time in this climate. A potter working on his bright orange clay. Men in white shirts and trousers waiting in a barbershop. Once in a while, curved bridges over the side canals leading to tiny white temples with curved roofs in golds and greens and vermilions. Every so often, pairs of Buddhist priests in their gold robes skim along on top of the water in their very light canoes like Adirondack guide boats, using their oars in perfect precision; beside them, their brass begging bowls in which they collect their daily food. The monks exist wholly on daily charity and they thank their benefactors by wishing them "old age, good health, and a good complexion of the skin."

The market klong itself is a small muddy canal filled with dozens upon dozens of sampan barges, floating grocery stores. Some are piled with tawny-amber bottles of beer, or glistening white ground lime, others with burnt-sienna rolls or bamboo urns filled with green palm leaves; a flower boat drifting by, heaped with small white flowers like gardenias or lilies of the valley and arm-wide clumps of pale lavender orchids.

Two river busses bump into each other, but no one complains as they are pushed gently apart. A sampan full of white clay saucers which are piled high with bright cerise-pink clams. Another of dark red roots. A sampan of meat, actually raw carcasses, but you see them as bright carmine-and-white splotches of color against the soft grays and browns of the klong and the sampans. A boat full of opalescent-scaled fish and one of round green watermelons. And a somber note but as beautiful as any of the rest, slipping quietly along, a sampan loaded with the dark blue-black of charcoal.

Now the bright scorching sun is pouring down on the klong and its hundreds of people paddling quietly along, selling their wares but not calling them or hawking them, waiting for a buyer's motion, no yapping, no bickering. From time to time a man sits relaxed in his sampan, ten or twelve fishlines stretched out around him, for even the fish are not disturbed by the marketing. The klongs are not only boulevards, washrooms, laundries, bathing pools, and shopping centers, but a prime source of food; if the rice paddies fail, the people of Bangkok can turn to their klongs.

The government of Thailand is putting much emphasis on food from the water. The Thais, along with the Cambodians and Formosans, are the only people of the Far East with an adequate diet; twenty-five million out of more than the billion people of Asia. But the Thai diet is deficient in proteins. And in the tropics not meat but fish must fill this need. So the government is stocking its rivers with fresh-water fish and is planning to develop deep-sea fishing along its thousands of miles of shore line. Thai scientists are expanding a new method to process a minute but plentiful animal life of the ocean called plankton into a paste full of proteins, vitamins, and minerals. If their methods can be passed on to the other nations that border on the oceans, a great and wholly unanticipated source of food supply could be opened up.

Since time immemorial, agriculture has been the chief occupation of the Thais. Over 90 per cent of the people work on the land. Today rice, rubber, tin, and teakwood are their chief exports, with rice accounting for 90 per cent of the economy and 95 per cent of their exports. Thailand has enough rice to feed itself and export over one and a half million tons of rice every year to less happy lands: one more reason why overpopulated starving Red China has designs on this tiny, weakly defended, and peaceful reservoir of rich land and surplus food. Before World War II, Indo-China exported as much rice as Thailand, and Burma twice as much; now, because of the civil wars in Burma and the disastrous eight-year Vietminh war in Indo-China, Thailand stands at the top of the rice-exporting countries of Asia.

Another thing that makes for economic and political stability in Thailand is that more than three out of every four peasants own their own land. The increasing population has not yet filled the vacant land. The government has passed laws that permit individual landlords to own only twenty acres of land. Thus the Thai farmer is sure of enough land to feed his family. This system makes the Thais, more than 60 per cent illiterate, the most contented people in Asia.

But for every blessing there is at least some curse. This warm climate and fertile country is the land of *mai pen rai*, "it does not matter"; the rice grows, the sun shines, you never get cold, why work hard, why drive yourself to be efficient? This has meant that the Thais have always avoided the arduous work of business or trade and left it to the industrious Overseas Chinese. Before World War II it was estimated that 90 per cent of the trade and commerce of Thailand was in Chinese hands, and today about 80 per cent is still in their hands. Most of the retail goods of Bangkok pass through the Sampeng, the Chinese quarter.

Historically, the Thai people came from the Yangtze Valley of China; many of their generals in their greatest period were full-blooded Chinese, and most high-ranking Thais today have some Chinese blood. In modern times, with so much unsettled land in Thailand and with the Thais so uninterested in business, the Overseas Chinese flooded in. Until 1900 they were welcomed because they were bachelors and married Thai women. But in this century the immigrants began bringing their families, setting up their own schools, and not blending into the country.

As is the case in Indonesia, everybody gives you a different estimate on how many Overseas Chinese immigrants there are in Thailand. Probably there are about three million, roughly the same number as are in the East Indies; but Thailand's situation becomes very different from Indonesia's because instead of being three million out of eighty million, the Overseas Chinese make up three million of the nineteen million Thais, over 15 per cent.

The Thai government bears down hard on the Overseas Chinese, but not principally out of resentment for the outlander. The Chinese Communists are a constant and growing threat to the Thais, and Bangkok takes the sternest measures against all things Communist. For a short period after the war it was forced to repeal its anti-Communist laws so that Russia would relax its veto and allow Thailand into the United Nations. Once there, it promptly re-outlawed the party, and in the UN supports all anti-Communist moves.

Thailand is lucky because, with enough to eat and no class hatreds, the peasants are not attracted to Communist propaganda. But the government is taking no chances of a fifth column emerging sometime from its Overseas Chinese inhabitants. When the president of the Chinese Chamber of Commerce, Chang Lan-ch'en, resigned because Communist elements had taken over and the secretary had pulled down the Kuomintang flag, the government stepped in, arrested the secretary, restored Chang's control over this most important point of Chinese influence within the country.

Recognizing these Chinese are a potential danger as long as they are Chinese-oriented, the men who run Thailand are determined to turn them into Thais whether they wish it or not. A new law limits immigrants from China to less than two hundred a year; no Chinese may own a business enterprise or rent land in a strategic area; he pays a special tax if his name in Chinese characters is over his shop; and the alien registration fee has been raised to about two thirds of a month's income. In the cultural field the government has stopped the importation of Chinese teachers from China; it decrees that only two hours a week of teaching in any Thai school can be devoted to Chinese language or subjects. And it is looking forward to the day when the Thai Chinese will have ceased to know the language of their homeland and will have ceased to think of themselves as anything but Thais.

But, whatever language and history their children may be learning, the Overseas Chinese in today's Thailand remain a cultural and community unit with strong emotional awareness of their Chinese background. Comprising about one sixth of the people, and far harder-working than the indolent Thais, inevitably they are going to increase, not decrease, in significance and influence. Ruling cliques can withhold political power from them, but their financial power interlocks with each cabal in the ruling class, and the economy of Thailand would fall apart without the Chinese industry and skill.

Therefore, each year unavoidably the Thai Chinese, like those of Malaya, will have more and more to say about their country's policies. The United States will not be able to reach directly into Thailand or Malaya to influence the Overseas Chinese—the governments would react to this as a new kind of colonialism—but it will be increasingly necessary for the United States to indicate a sympathy and an appreciation for things Chinese. The Overseas Chinese in Malaya and Thailand may not drag their feet at the idea of an Asian Defense Pact against Chinese Communist aggression, but they will not support an outright war against their homeland of China.

The Thais, always a let-live people, are primarily concerned with breaking the tie between the Overseas Chinese and the Communist regime to the north, leaving their compatriots to enjoy Chinese entertainments with little interference. Bangkok is one of the few places left, outside China, where a traveler can inspect typical Chinese opium dens operating with the government's permission. Much opium is grown in northern Thailand and a good deal of it finds its way into China.

The main room of a higher-class opium establishment is large and high-ceilinged. Along it are lines of wide ledge platforms broken up into stalls, about three feet off the floor, with walks in between them. The teakwood of the stalls gleams with a beautiful patina from the oils of the hundreds of bodies which have lain on it. There is room in each stall for one to four men in various stages of opium smoking, resting, talking, preparing their pipes, or asleep on their low porcelain headrests next to their little kerosene lamps.

From the proprietor a smoker buys a dollar's worth of opium sealed in a little aluminum holder shaped like the oil container for a typewriter. The sticky black raw opium looks like the chemical adhesives which join wood and glass together. The smoker settles down in his stall, rolls about a tenth of the opium on a long needle and holds it over the top of the glass chimney of the kerosene lamp, revolving it until the opium becomes soft. If it gets too runny, he cools it against a green palm leaf held in the other hand. He manipulates it for about five minutes, no point in hurrying; he is talking with his friends while he cooks the opium. When it is a round bead about the consistency of soft taffy, he pops it deftly down into a small hole on the side of his opium pipe.

Now he is ready for his smoke. He stretches out with his head on the porcelain headrest. Holding the pipe bowl over the flame of the lamp until the opium bead begins to smoke, he draws in a slow full breath of smoke, holding it as long as he can. Each bead of opium provides three or four lungfuls of smoke faintly woody and sweet, slightly oily and spicy, warmer and heavier than tobacco smoke, and with a slight sting.

The drug is destructive and habit-forming, but the Chinese have found in it a refuge from the pain and exhaustion of their hard work. As soon as their twelve- or fifteen-hour day is done, the coolies come for surcease, smoking the opium instead of spending the money for food. Since it kills appetite as well as takes away fatigue, each month they become more emaciated. After the opium has begun to relax his muscles, if the coolie can afford to, he hires a masseuse to stretch and ease his abused ligaments. These Thai masseuses never take up the opium habit, but they are an odd sight in the dens. One masseuse stood on the small of her client's back, treading sore muscles; another sat with the flat of her feet planted in the crotch of a coolie, his feet grasped in her hands as she pulled his legs firmly but gently toward her. Still another masseuse sat on her client's chest with both hands deep in his stomach, pushing it firmly down against his backbone; this was supposed to block off the pains of cancer.

A father sleeps in his stall; curled up against him, a little boy of eight, snoring. Other children wander in and out, paying no attention to the opium smoking. Sociability and quiet conversation all around in an atmosphere far more like an eighteenth-century English coffee-house than a den of iniquity.

The Thais themselves go in for little opium smoking. Although gentle and peace-loving, they are in no way effete. Sports are their favorite entertainment, especially boxing. You might call Siamese boxing the New One-Two, for it combines the mayhem of English boxing, French *savate*, Japanese jujitsu, and American commandos.

The fighters wear four-ounce gloves broken at the knuckles for harder punching. Their feet are bare, taped up about as far as a short sock would come but leaving the heels and toes free for action. Their trunks are very short, slashed at the sides to allow full leg freedom. By custom the champions wear red trunks and their opponents blue. In the bout I saw, the challenger wore the palest blue silk shorts imaginable; he was the "TERRIBLE STAR WHO WORSHIPS THE MOTTO 'DO OR DIE.' ONCE IN THE RING IT IS EITHER HIS OPPONENT IS CARRIED DOWN OR HE IS CARRIED OUT TO THE HOSPITAL." And Red, the champion, wore brilliant yellow chartreuse shorts with the narrowest of vermilion stripes; this "SUPER STAR IS FAST AND BRAINY IN ALL ACTIONS AND PREFERS TO USE DAMAGING PUNCH AND DANGEROUS KICK TO RUN OPPONENTS DOWN TO DREAMLAND."

During the rounds, a trio of triangle, oboe, and clarinet plays war music, slow or fast, depending on how the action is going. They get little chance to play slow tunes. In between rounds the fighters sit with their feet in pans of cold water to cool them off in this tropic climate, and their seconds pour pailfuls of water down the front of their trunks.

Practically the entire audience is in Western clothes. There are no respectable Thai women present, even in the gallery, but there are many Western women in ringside seats, and it is quite obvious what the Thais think of them. Unfortunately, in lands like Thailand which have seen so few Westerners, every American in the country is an ambassador by whose actions his whole homeland is judged. Before you can travel abroad you need a passport and health certificate. In these crucial years when the fate of freedom is being determined and so many Americans have already died for it, perhaps travelers should be required to study and pass a travelers' test in the customs and susceptibilities of a country in which they will travel or be stationed. The Thais say of the ignorance of our officials, "They mean well, poor things."

And wives should not be excluded from the briefing and tests. In Asia, even in our missions, they are far worse representatives than their husbands; rarely knowing much about the countries in which they live, seldom bothering to learn the language, they carry with them their make-up, cigarette smoking and promenading in slacks and halters. The inhabitants of the country judge us all by these few. And the Communists are delighted to watch us go right on repeating a mistake they have never made in Asia.

In Siamese boxing you can use hands, feet, arms, elbows, thighs, knees, heels, toes, and your head, in sequence or simultaneously. You cannot bite or hit below the belt, but that is an ill-defined region in this sport. When the fight starts, the contestants bow ceremoniously to each other and then launch themselves like guided missiles, colliding in mid-air, falling back on the canvas on their necks, bouncing up and going at it again. A favorite tactic is to sock hard at your opponent's face or solar plexus; he is forced to lean his upper torso back; you follow through in one lithe movement with your knee or the flat of your foot to his stomach, and when your foot lands, its thud can be heard all over the stadium. Another trick is to let your opponent swing his whole leg up in a kick aimed for your ear. You move your head slightly so he misses, and while he is in extended position you kick him with precision in the crotch.

After four rounds of these tricks interspersed with clubbing, fists in the Adam's apples, rabbit punches, and jujitsu chops, Red administered his coup de grâce. He turned his back on Blue, about a quarter turn away from him; then Red swung around in a three-quarter circle at full speed, with his elbow extended; at the end of the swing, with the full weight of his body behind it, he collided the point of his elbow with the solar plexus of his unfortunate opponent. Blue sat down abruptly and stayed down. There is no shame connected with being defeated; Siamese boxing is a match of skill, not brutality, and when a fighter is bloody or bowed, he stays down on the canvas and the audience applauds him for his wisdom as well as his fighting.

Besides boxing, the Rajadamnern stadium in Bangkok features track meets and other athletic events. There is horse racing twice a week and every year a nine-day beauty contest to select Miss Thailand. Their newspapers headline these beauty contests, sports news, and all the other items of American newspapers. Only the wording is different. Consider the press report of a beautiful young lady, Prasert Meegers, and her passionate suitor, Boonlue Chaisamak. After "trespassing upon Prasert's constitution and generally forcing her to do his filthy bidding," young Boonlue was arrested and testified, "I did not know how to show my love to her. I have done wrong but I have not yet spoiled her."

Wherever Western influence is freely accepted in Asia you get a press which may be venial in part and irresponsible in other parts, but a press full of inquiry, zest, and humor. In Thailand as in the Philippines, the English-language press is full of humor as well as serious subjects. One cartoon in a Bangkok paper dealt with the Thai proverb, "Don't play the fiddle to the buffalo." It pictured three faintly amused Thai water buffalo placidly listening to a frantically playing virtuoso in white tie and tails; one of the caribou is saying, "He's playing the allegro a little too fast, but then I've always preferred Brahms." Or the Thai press will with straight face propose new Thai dishes made from one of their most common animals, the water bugs: "Mince them well and pound furiously, more to bring out full flavor, then season with water and a little lime juice if desired." It is a sign of psychological stability when a people can take itself this lightly and parody itself in a newspaper any foreigner can read; there would not be such items in a newspaper of Indonesia or Japan or Burma or India.

The Thai press assumes as much political responsibility as it is permitted. Editorials argue very fluently for the setting up of an opposition party in the parliament and show why such a party is a necessary prerequisite to a working democracy. But the press's political commentaries are strictly limited because Thailand, although in theory a constitutional monarchy, in practice is a dictatorship. Such a word suggests suppression and secret police. So does the phrase "absolute monarchy." But neither tyranny nor political cruelty has ever been a political way of life in Thailand. Its Buddhism would have rejected it; its kings, benevolent despots, needed no police state apparatus to keep their power, and the present dictatorship tries to rule as ably as they did. In Europe, it was a long time after the French Revolution before France managed to set up any kind of a functioning democracy. Thailand abandoned the "*L'état, c'est moi*" method of government less than twenty-five years ago.

Today the people know and care little about democracy, but the ruling clique is trying gradually to teach the peasants the rudiments of democracy. Thailand has a parliament and holds elections. Most of the time the press is left free. But it and the government know that autocracy is going to remain in Thailand a long time, unless it gives way to the complete dictatorship of communism. Therefore, if need be, the government is perfectly willing to declare martial law in Bangkok and take over complete control of the press.

This control is used imperceptibly most of the time but can become implacable during a crisis or threatened coup d'état. And there have been many coups d'état in modern Thailand, more than anywhere else in Asia. A coup d'état overturned the absolute monarchy of the country in 1932 and set up a government of revolutionaries. There was another coup in 1933, two Revolts of the Princes were put down in the next two years, the King was forced to abdicate in 1935, and Marshal Pibul became dictator again via another coup in 1948. In all of these, only a couple of dozen men pulled the strings.

The political history of present-day Thailand has a unique theme: the rises and falls of two men, Pibul Songgram, the present dictator, and Pridi Phanomyong, now in Red China. Their story is a curiously interwoven illustration of the inevitable collision of the two kinds of political leadership when they are separated and vested in men of great abilities who become rivals and foes.

Back in the days of the absolute monarchy, young Pibul was an army officer who was sent to France to study in its military schools. In Paris he naturally met and became friends with other young Thais studying there. One of these was a brilliant young law student, Pridi. Pibul, the Army conservative and man of action, and Pridi, the scholar and intellectual liberal, became friends. Both were exposed to the liberating ideas of the West and, with other young Thai students, they carefully plotted a revolution to take away the absolute power of their King.

Pibul and Pridi returned to Thailand and for the next four or five years quietly went about their work as officer and lawyer while they prepared for the revolution. In 1932 they staged their bloodless coup; only about one hundred men were involved in a complete change in government. Power in their hands, the two men reacted in characteristic fashion; Pibul acted to get in his grasp the central power point, the control of the Army; Pridi went to King Prajahipok with the liberal constitution he had written. The wise King—Thai kings always come through when needed—gracefully accepted the inevitable, signed the constitution, and became a monarch revered by his people.

But once in power, Pibul and Pridi drifted apart in an ebb and flow of cabal struggles. In 1938 Pibul was the victor and became the Prime Minister of a regime dominated by the Army.

World War II opened a new chapter in their story. Prime Minister Pibul stayed in office and co-operated with the Japanese when they seized Thailand, while Pridi, contacting British Military Intelligence and the U. S. Office of Strategic Services, set up a Thai underground. Note the way, deliberately or otherwise, in which the Thai genius for the protection of their country works out: if the Japs win the war, Pibul, the Japanese associate, protects his country; if the Allies win, Pridi is standing by to take over power and protect Thailand from Allied retaliation.

When the war began to go against the Japanese, the King got sick and went to Europe. Prime Minister Pibul, undoubtedly aware of Pridi's anti-Japanese activities, appointed him Regent; Allied planes began to land at secret Thai airdromes. All the underground was run from the Regent's palace right under the noses of the Japanese, while the Prime Minister continued his collaboration and the Japanese occupation of Thailand remained a mild one.

Pibul and Pridi played the situation by ear, probably without ever discussing it, until the Japs had clearly lost; then the Prime Minister quietly retired from public life a year ahead of the actual defeat of Japan. The Thais never wait until the last minute to recognize coming international changes. The Regent Pridi, during the last year of the Japanese occupation, achieved the impossible, running both the pro-Japanese government and the anti-Japanese underground.

After the peace, at the Allies' insistence Pibul was jailed as a supporter of the Japanese; once the commotion died down, Pridi and the Thai Supreme Court discovered the law that sent him to jail was illegal, and he was released.

The next chapter is a tragic one with an unsolved mystery. In 1946, while Pridi was still Prime Minister, King Ananda Mahidol was found dead under suspicious circumstances, and it has never been established whether he committed suicide or was assassinated; whichever the answer, his death undermined the Pridi government, which was blamed by the people for the catastrophe, and so in 1947 there was another bloodless coup and back came Pibul.

In 1951 there was another operetta twist to the Pibul-Pridi story. By this time Pridi had fled the country, but his supporters in the government and in the Navy, most liberal of the three armed forces, tried to throw out Pibul. The Navy managed to kidnap Pibul and jailed him on its flagship, the *Sri Ayuthya*, to force the government to surrender. But the leaders of the Army and the police were not too concerned about what would happen to Pibul; the Air Force bombed the *Sri Ayuthya* and sank it. Pibul swam ashore, took back his position, put down the revolt.

Pibul Songgram is still Prime Minister but no longer dictator in his own right. He "rides two tigers," the two strong men of today's Thailand, the Director General of the Police, Phao Sriyandondh, and the Deputy Minister of Defense, General Sarit Dhanarat. Once they were tiger cubs and Pibul's henchmen; now his power lasts only so long as neither of the tigers believes he can safely take over with his own tanks and planes. As a direct aftermath of the Vietnam defeat and the hasty American build-up of Thailand's Army, it will be difficult for police boss Phao to keep up with Army boss Sarit.

Pibul's old rival, Pridi Phanomyong, having failed in the 1951 coup, was not heard from again until mid-1954. Then, on the heels of the Geneva truce, Pridi stepped back on the stage with an article which was broadcast and rebroadcast on every Chinese wave length that reaches Southeast Asia; writing in the *People's Daily*, official voice of the Chinese Communists, he urged the Thais to "rise against their rulers, American imperialism and its puppet, the Government of Thailand." This alliance of Pridi with Mao and Company casts an unpleasant shadow of events to come, for Pridi is the ideal figurehead to beckon his fellow Thais in Burma, Laos, and Thailand toward the Communist-backed Thai Confederacy already set up in China's Yünnan Province just above the weakly defended, mountainous, tribal areas of northern Thailand. If subversives begin to undermine Thailand from within, it is Pridi's name and skill which could best lure the Thais toward the Communist mirage of a "free" confederacy.

The position of the Army in Thailand emphasizes what different roles the military fills in different countries of Asia. In India or Pakistan the Army is unpolitical, a military organization to protect the countries from outside aggression; in the Philippines it has been an institution which in the later days of the Quirino regime protected the people from semi-illegal acts by politicians or selfish landlords. In Indo-China and in Burma it has fought for its country's life against revolts and Communists; in Indonesia the Army is an unpredictable force which may do anything or nothing. In Thailand, as on Formosa, it is the force which creates and keeps in power the vastly different dictatorships of Field Marshal Pibul and Generalissimo Chiang Kai-shek.

It would be erroneous to assume from the ups and downs of Thai politics that the country is in danger of coming apart at the seams. The people, well fed and content, are relatively uninterested in what happens in Bangkok, where about three hundred men do all the conniving and the ruling. And over and above the disunity of the small cabals of politicians and military leaders stands the King, who preserves continuity for and to the government. The Thai kings always having had many wives and more children, a very large percentage of the three hundred have royal blood in their veins and bear one of the three titles of nobility which descent from the King confers: Mom Chao, grandson of a king; Mom Rajawong, great-grandson of a king;

and Mom Luang, great-great-grandson. Thus the kings' blood and some of their traditional smartness have been spread through most of the ruling class.

The kings of Thailand have always been innovators. Chulalongkorn abolished slavery, and Mongkut, the king whose children Anna taught, set up the first printing press and the first medical school. Incidentally, the Thais detest *Anna and the King of Siam;* they consider it a parody on one of their wisest monarchs. And if the present King, Bhumibol Adulyadej, can do little, he wisely does just that, privately practicing on his jazz drums and writing his popular tunes in the privacy of his palace; in public he is punctilious in bearing and dignity.

Speaking of their King, the Thais do not say "our *King*" as a Britisher would; they lay the stress the other way: "*our* King"; and the common people, semi-feudal in their sentiments as well as in their village organization, remain firmly wedded to their kings, who govern by the "law of the heart."

In addition to affection for their King and the rich fertile land, there is a third foundation upon which Thailand's serenity is built, the Buddhist religion, which permeates the lives of all Thais, from the King in his palace to the child in a country village. The Buddhist monastery is the center of village life. As in the feudal period of Europe when the Christian monasteries were the repository of learning, so it is with Thailand's Buddhist monasteries: crafts, learning, medicine spring from them. Their feasts and their funerals take place in the compounds of these temples. In sickness, in distress, in joyful family events, the people go to the temples to consult the bonzes or give food and gifts to them for merit for themselves.

The very all-cohesiveness of family life in Thailand springs out of Buddhism. One of the precepts of the Lord Buddha was *matapitu-upatthana*, veneration for one's parents, the moral obligation to care for older relations. And so in Thailand, as long as this principle prevails, family life is stable and the old people, more fortunate than in Western cultures, have their place in the family, respected by the young.

Every Buddhist in Thailand spends three months as a young man in a monastery, living by its rigid ascetic discipline and studying the truths of his religion. As the monasteries and temple schools are the focal points in the countryside, in Bangkok the Buddhist temples are the city's greatest glory. Nowhere else in Asia can the Westerner see so much of the exotic and foreign and colorful as in the myriad temples of Bangkok.

There is the Wat Benjamabopit, a small pure-white marble temple glorious with gold-and-scarlet trim. There is the Wat Po with its Temple of the Reclining Buddha, filled with the largest Buddha in Thailand, who is over thirty feet long, covered with gold leaf, stretched out on a glittering bed, the soles of his feet the size of small shuffleboards, covered with designs in mother-of-pearl. There is the Wat Arun, the Temple of Dawn, with its thick, stubby phallus spires thrusting up very much like the temples of India or the buildings of Angkor Wat. The exterior of the Temple of Dawn, seen close at hand, is not imposing, being made of cement, and each of the towers is embedded with thousands of pieces of broken porcelain dishes rescued from a wrecked British ship; but from a distance it becomes a flashing design of enamels.

Also in Bangkok is one of the two most colorful monuments in all of the Far East, the Compound of the Grand Palace; only the frozen marble simplicity of the Taj Mahal equals the glittering, golden iridescent buildings of the Grand Palace. It is a small walled town, covering over a square mile, in which the kings of Thailand once lived. Here are their burial places and the little open pavilion where Anna taught the children of King Mongkut.

No imagination can equal the riot of Indian spires and Chinese turned-up eaves in the Compound of the Grand Palace. The roofs are tiled in glowing colors, usually a deep saffron gold. Every building is covered with designs in gilt, softened by the tropical climate. The columns of the temples are elaborately fretted with gold in small formal repeated designs set with pieces of colored mirror and then picked out with reds and greens and deep violets. Around the chief buildings are smaller monuments, fifteen-foot mythological guardians, inlaid with the same mirrors and colors, with fierce black or green faces and ivory teeth. Inconceivable profusion, blending in the play of light of the full sun, and when the sky turns dark and pearly and the heavy soft rain falls, through the crystal raindrops each building seems to glow with rose luminescence.

In the Compound of the Grand Palace is also the most beautiful Buddhist temple in the world, the Wat Phra Keo, the Temple of the Emerald Buddha. Around it is a covered gallery and on the walls is a frieze of a famous Indian religious epic, the *Ramayana,* dramatic in whites, pinks, greens, and gold, on a deep blue-gray background: a single archer with a single bow devastating an entire army complete with elephants and assorted beasties; a lovely mural of a god and goddess asleep in a temple, his seven hands caressing her as she sleeps; a fierce demon rising from the sea, an unfortunate fisherman impaled on one tusk; gods and goddesses floating in opalescent spheres; another god on his back with his tongue stuck out—it is so large it wraps itself around a whole palace.

The Temple of the Emerald Buddha is almost indescribable, a small building with square columns rising only thirty or forty feet. Its portals, as beautiful as the bronze doors of a Western cathedral, are of teakwood inlaid with a gentle, curving, almost dancing mosaic of dragons, formalized into flowing lines against the dark teak background and picked out in Thailand's unique soft pink mother-of-pearl.

Where the lines and the mood of a Western cathedral are a sharp, urgent, vertical supplication to the sky, Buddhist temples are gentle and serene. Their roofs are slightly concave, suggesting the gentle sagging of the thatched bamboo roofs of Southeast Asia. The turned-up curve of the eaves protects the building from sun and rain and contributes to the feeling of soft movement upward. Inside, all the vertical lines of the temples bend inward with a suppliant relaxedness.

The Emerald Buddha, sculptured from a translucent block of cloudy green jasper, is about the size of a small child and sits enthroned under a golden canopy in a veiled half-light at the top of a pyramid of golden tiers. The Buddha wears a huge diamond in its brow and has three sets of fabulously bejeweled raiments, one for each of the Thai seasons, cold, hot, and rainy; the King comes to the temple three times a year for the solemn ceremony of changing the vestments. High up in the temple eaves, just under the roof, hundreds of little silver and bronze bells are hanging, which every wisp of breeze stirs into soft tinklings. At the base of the altar are gold and silver trays which used to be sent as tribute by the Laos vassal princes and the Malay rajas to their overlords in Bangkok.

A soft and mild move upward toward a beneficent infinity is the keynote of the "Little Vehicle" Buddhism of Southeast Asia. There are no "thou shalt not" commandments, nothing harsh or forbidding. Instead, there are five precepts and you decide for yourself when you wish to follow them and for what period you wish them to be binding. During that period you are forbidden to kill anything living, to steal, to lie or slander, to "commit wrong sexual intercourse," and to take intoxicating liquor. If you wish to be still more strict, you may add three additional precepts: to eat no solid foods from noon until dawn, to indulge in no dancing or entertainment, and to lie on no soft beds. Sex enjoyment is not limited in Buddhism, except on the non-puritanical grounds that sex, like all the other pulls of the flesh, renders you less able to escape from the trap of the material.

Buddha teaches that greed, ill will, jealousy, and the other destructive forces of humanity are delusions of the self, springing from man's desires; the goal of Buddhism is to release man from these desires and drives of living so that he may join with the eternal and the all-blessed and attain Nirvana, the state of selflessness. Buddhism thus not only establishes a gentle, easily observed morality and ethics but also furnishes the best of man's rationalizations of the existence of suffering in this world, for Buddha's concept of karma explains away all sufferings and other inequalities or injustices in life.

In Buddhism, all willed actions, good and bad, have an effect upon you and those around you. The actions of all men create an interwoven chain, with no breaks. What we do in previous existences has made us what we are in this one. What we do here decides what kind of body and fate we shall have in our next existences. Through this Buddhist doctrine of incarnation we create our own karma, our fate, our miseries or our happinesses, as we move through the chain of incarnations. All willed actions are both causes and effects. Some sins you wear out in this life; others cause residual karma, which expresses itself in your next life.

Buddhism becomes a relaxing faith, for you sin only when you choose to, and then by your act you automatically have chosen your own less comfortable next reincarnation. What you, by yourself, do now creates your future. You can gather rosebuds, enjoy your sins, and reconcile yourself to suffering the consequences of them. Or you can work today for a better karma so that in a future life it is you who will be the most beautiful woman, or the richest man, or the holiest priest.

All of which adds up to a security and a stability in things religious and psychological. Nowhere in the concepts of Buddhism is there need to worry or fret or fear, no feeling of guilt to pursue you and torment you. The Thais are left carefree, not happy in the driving, positive sense in which we think of the world, but literally free of care. Theirs is a self-created happiness, achieved by "putting their troubles on the shelf and turning their backs on them."

A logical consequence of this attitude is that Bangkok is one of the dirtiest and most run-down cities in the Far East, one calculated to drive a foreigner crazy if he tries to do things in a Western manner. When the central telephone exchange will function or when someone is in his office at the other end of a telephone is unpredictable. The morning I was leaving Thailand, the Thai Air bus was supposed to pick me up at four-thirty in the morning, a time when there are no cars of any kind available in Bangkok. When by five-thirty no bus arrived, I frantically got the central operator on the telephone and tried to find some telephone where a Thai Air official might be located. She informed me indignantly that this was no time to be calling people, disconnected, and refused to answer the hotel number again. Result: I found a chauffeur asleep in his master's car—many of the chauffeurs here are very poor and have no place to live except in the car—woke him up and bribed him to drive me to the airport. He may have been poor but he had a flair for Western free enterprise: he charged me twenty-five American dollars for the fifteen-minute drive to the airport.

With these carefree undependabilities of the Thais in business, it will be a long time before Western business and Western efficiency take hold here. "We aren't interested in learning too much from you. We know the boon of contentment; we are not too anxious for the Western bone of discontentment."

Nursing their boon of contentment, the agile Thais have managed through hundreds of years to keep their relations with the rest of the world within a framework of reason. This, plus their extraordinary ability to bend with the winds of history, has kept Thailand an oasis of independence, unconquered, and uncolonialized by the Western powers who swept over all the other lands of Southeast Asia. Where there were insurrections or civil wars, the Europeans had the excuse of taking over to restore order; if a country would not open its borders to the foreign devils, imperialism campaigned under the banner of opening up trade. Greedy Europe offered little Thailand neither type of excuse. The Thais stayed unified, welcomed all foreigners to their country, happily traded with them, dissimulated when necessary with judicious skill. In one tense moment when a French gunboat steamed up the Great River to Bangkok, the Thai gunners, crack shots, fired on her, but they obeyed the King's command and carefully missed the gunboat.

An early French ecclesiastic said of the Thais, "They are dissimulators but they always make a great difference between doing harm to a man and not wishing him any good." And today they continue to conduct their international relations on the excellent principles of compromise and adjustment. Prince Wan Waithayakon, Foreign Minister, cousin of the King and first Prince of the Blood of Thailand, gave me a good example in practice of how the Thai mentality operates.

He came home from a UN meeting to find that the Thai parliament had not ratified a convention he had voted for in the UN. Calling in the lawyers of the People's Assembly, he demanded why the approval had been blocked. Lawyerwise, they explained that they had asked the question, "Is the United Nations a juridical person thus able legally to conclude a convention which can be ratified by our parliament?" And they explained somewhat anxiously to His Royal Highness that the UN was not a juridical person and therefore they could not ratify a UN act. Prince Wan made no attempt to force them to do his will. He explained gently that they had been asking the wrong question; the right question was, "Does the UN have a juridical personality?" The prince then easily proved that the UN had such a personality and the parliamentary lawyers happily ratified the act.

It is in this same benign way that the Thais approach their problems or anything new or foreign. In their language any foreigner is referred to by the pronoun "it," and in their own quiet way this sophisticated people undoubtedly feels elder-brotherish toward the rest of the world in general and Americans in particular. They think our best traits are "generosity, friendliness, and innocence," and our worst trait, "You've got nearly all the unpleasant qualities of the *nouveaux riches*," or "Some say the white man's burden is just a bag of gold he hopes to carry away when leaving our native countries."

Even when the color line comes in, they keep their equanimity. An editor described one of our Hollywood superproductions as showing "cruel hordes of fiendish yellow people being successfully thwarted by one superb white he-man: white remains forever good, and yellow, without any ill feeling toward us, is evil!" But if he was not disturbed by the movie, other friends of the United States were.

No matter where an American goes in this part of the world he sees queues of Asians lined up to see a Hollywood movie. There is no cause for smugness here, for if one American influence misinforms and antagonizes Asians more than any other, it is our movies. We spend millions a year trying to get Asians, who know so little about us, to understand us and like us; one "horde of fiendish yellow men thwarted by a superb white" undoes all the work and furnishes the Communists some of their finest propaganda.

In earlier days, when we were not fighting for our life, perhaps this would not have mattered too much. Today it does. In more than one Asian country, riots have followed the showing of particularly offensive American movies. If any American in these countries did one hundredth the harm one movie can do, he would be branded a traitor and pulled out of the country. Yet we go right on releasing such movies around the world.

This stricture applies to only a very few Hollywood movies, and it is easy to tell ahead of time which ones will do the harm. Within our own country the movie industry, by self-policing, has protected our most moralistic of peoples from the slightest tinge of sexual realism. Abroad, Hollywood operates with inexcusable irresponsibility. Films today are a medium of international communication. If Hollywood will not police its product and voluntarily hold certain films off the foreign market, then it is up to the people of the United States to protect their reputation through their government and set up a licensing system for film exports.

Free enterprise and private profit are respectable ends, but we are in a propaganda war to the death. It does not permit us to condone certain aspects of nineteenth-century the-public-be-damned operations when their results, no matter how unintentional, are at the very least a form of sabotage.

Fortunately such movies can do little harm in Thailand, the one place in Southeast Asia where there is no race supersensitivity and no anti-white complexes to arouse antagonism against us. Instead, this exotic, easygoing land co-operates with us as no other power but the Philippines does in all Asia. The Thais have always managed to stay neutral and safe by playing one side against another. Today, in the most dangerous world they have ever faced, they choose the way of the West. They are firm anti-Communist allies of the United States, willing and ready to join defense pacts, fight against communistic aggression, whether it be in Korea, Vietnam, or anywhere else in Asia. By so doing, they have put themselves in the direct path of the Chinese Communist juggernaut, for the rulers of Thailand believe that China's next aggression will come soon after the Vietnam elections of 1956 and will be directed against Thailand, using a dissident "free Thai" regime in the north exactly as was done with the Vietminh in Indo-China.

Thailand is strengthening all her border defenses, and half her budget goes into defense preparations. In the south she is conducting joint operations with the British against Communist guerrillas along the Malay border.

Geographically Thailand is like a balloon on a string. The string being the long Kra Peninsula which hangs down to Malaya. The balloon proper pushes up against weak neighbors and Communist threats: to the east and north for over a thousand miles, the Mekong River is the only barrier between Thailand and weak, Communist-threatened, defenseless Laos; where Laos leaves off, the rebellion-ridden eastern part of Burma begins; and just above the top of the balloon of Thailand presses down the dangerous weight of China's Yünnan Province, seat of the "free Thai" conspiracy.

Therefore Thailand is eager to join any and all Southeast Asian Treaty Organizations to protect herself from Chinese aggression, she is asking for extensive American military aid to build military highways fanning out from Bangkok toward her borders, and she will welcome white trainers and Western armaments to build up her army and a jet air force. Always a strong supporter of the UN, Thailand will demand that the UN live up to its commitments and keep a sharp eye on Chinese machinations along the Thai borders; at the first overt threat from the north, Thailand will appeal to the UN Assembly for help.

In the world ahead it is too early to tell what the next chapter will be. If the Communist Chinese, by armed aggression, internal machinations, or a Greater Thai Confederation, come flooding down and across from Indo-China, Thailand will become another Vietnam into which the United States will willingly rush hundreds of millions of dollars of military aid, but this time there will be one enormous difference: this time we will be aiding a free country fighting to preserve its freedom.

If the Thais continue to be a lucky people and war does not come to their borders, it is no less important that the United States continue to aid and strengthen this country. Our foreign policies in Asia must begin with our friends. In Southeast Asia the Thais like us the most and can adjust easiest to our Western values. For a few years it might take as much as a fraction of a cent out of each dollar in our budget to help this country raise its standard of living and gradually acquire more of the technologies of the West. It would be money well spent. We are lucky to have as our ally this self-reliant people who have never been conquered.

SOCIALISTIC PAGODA:

Burma

Burma, the Golden Earth, the Suvanni Bhumi of the ancient East, should be a small oasis of well-being in the desert of Asian misery. Instead, it has more problems, and more different ones, than any of its neighbors with the exception of Indo-China. To the Western world its similarities to Indo-China are not reassuring.

There are only three ways the Sino-Russian axis could move down from the heart of Asia into South and Southeast Asia. One is far to the west of Burma through the Khyber Pass, where the Pakistan Army stands guard. The second and easiest path is the traditional coastal road of conquest from Southeast China and Tonkin to Cochin China, then west to Thailand, Burma, and India. Ho Chi Minh and the Vietminh Communists of Indo-China have successfully blasted open this route. The third way is down through the valleys of weak and divided Burma to the Gulf of Thailand. Once there, Communist forces and infiltration could spread east to overrun the rest of the peninsula, south to overrun Malaya and the East Indies, and west to their ultimate goal, the wretched hundreds of millions of people on the Indian subcontinent.

So far, communism has not moved in force onto the Burma road. But second only to the terrible urgencies of Indo-China is the West's need to keep an unstable Burma from slipping into the Communist orbit. Today there is frustratingly little the democracies can do to aid the isolationist and suspicious Burmese Government. It has been impossible in recent years to persuade this government to accept even as an outright gift American armaments to strengthen its police force and Army.

As in Indonesia, Burma's leaders are Marxists who have led their country to freedom from a colonial power, and as in Indonesia, that struggle has left Burma's leaders full of psychological insecurity, with an almost psychotic distrust of the white man and his capitalism.

Like Thailand, Burma is a land sprouting with the good green rice and enriched by the good gentle faith of Little Vehicle Buddhism. Like Malaya, it has the transportation and buildings and training of a former British colony. Like the Philippine Islands up at the other end of the arc of Southeast Asia, the Burmese Government has firmly supported democracy and political freedom, and like the Philippines, Burma suffered the ravages of a long seesaw of war between the Japanese and the Allies.

Like Indo-China, its borders touch directly on those of the bursting imperialism of Communist China. And again like Indo-China, "Burma" is a better way to describe a colored segment on a map rather than a nation in the Western sense of the word. As Indonesia was the administrative entity set up by the Dutch colonials, and Indo-China by the French, so Burma is the geographically contiguous pieces of territory formerly ruled by the British; an unstabilized assemblage of mutually unaffectionate tribes and races of differing backgrounds and beliefs. It is no compliment to any of the three colonial powers that their years of rule left in the three countries no sense of unity. Today the results of their divide-and-conquer policy work against the three powers in particular and Western democracy in general.

The geography of this land of about nineteen million people makes the problem harder for everybody but the Chinese Communists, who could, if they chose, capture it piecemeal, valley by valley. Burma is about the size of Texas, a hot and humid land of mountain ranges and jungle valleys which run down from the Chinese border south to the great delta of the Irrawaddy River at Rangoon. Thus a country almost impossible to defend, Burma is surrounded by unstable, unfriendly, or powerful neighbors who, in the words of her Prime Minister, hem her in "like a tender gourd among cacti."

Only on the narrow far southern tip of her peninsula does she have a safe neighbor, Malaya. On the west is an India five times her size. All along her northwest and northeast frontiers, like a strong rubber nipple over a baby's bottle, is Red China. On the east is the feeble land of Laos, from where communism is already menacing Burma and from where the propaganda of the Greater Thai Confederation is beamed to Burma's revolting tribes of Thai ancestry, the Shans. And where Laos ends, Burma's borders join those of her ancient enemy, Thailand.

Roughly speaking, three main groups make up the people of Burma: the foreign-born Indians and Chinese, about 8 per cent of the country; the Burmans, about 60 per cent; and the hill tribes, the Karens, the Shans, the Kachins, and the Chins, who make up around 30 per cent.

The Burmese flag of red has a blue rectangle in its upper left-hand corner; in it, a large white star surrounded by five smaller stars symbolizing "the union of the Burmans, the Karens, the Shans, the Kachins, and the Chins." A symbol, yes; but a union, not yet.

The Burmans are the people who live in the rice-growing area around Rangoon; the largest race in the country, they control the central government and are trying to persuade or force the other tribes into unity.

The eight hundred thousand Indians and the three hundred thousand Overseas Chinese, in whose hands is well over 50 per cent of the business of the country, give the Burmans no trouble. But the hill tribes have been fighting the Burmese Army for most of the history of the new republic.

The passionately anti-Burman Christian Karens, who revolted against the central government in 1949, still manage to have a semi-autonomous state of their own spread out in southeastern Burma. The other three tribal units equally dislike the Burmans and make what trouble they can. The Kachins, who live in the extreme north between India and upper Yünnan Province of China, are beginning to look to Peiping for support and are sending many of their young men to Yünnan for Communist training.

Still more of a threat are the Buddhist Shans, the hillmen of Thai descent whom the Red Chinese are blandishing with the Greater Thai Confederation. The Shans live up along the Burmese side of the wedge of Chinese territory coming down from Yünnan Province between Laos and Burma. There the Chinese are garrisoning Thai Chinese troops and building roads and airports up to their side of the border. It is probably at this point, via a Communist-inspired and -backed Shan Thai revolt against Rangoon that civil war and Chinese infiltration would come down into Burma.

The history of Burma has been one of consistent instability, a description which still holds true today. She won her national freedom in 1947 after years of guerrilla warfare, first against the Japanese and then against the British, and so her fighters, especially the young men, have grown up in a tradition of violence and revolt. Her great revolutionary leader, General Bogyoke Aung San, was assassinated by rival politicians before the Republic of Burma was created. His successor, U Thakin Nu ("U" in Burmese stands for Uncle and is the equivalent of "Sir" or "The Honorable"), has managed to keep from being assassinated, but the first seven years of this new republic have been a long succession of revolts and civil wars. Often the government and its very small Army have been fighting for the life of their new state against as many as nine different and mutually antagonistic armed factions and warring tribes who had in common only their refusal to recognize the existence of a central Burmese government.

But these warring tribes, nuisance though they are and delay though they may make for the peaceful development of Burma, are not dangerous unless China directly supports them, for the government is slowly establishing control and order over more and more of the territory these hillmen dominate. When we read in our papers of a new revolt of minority groups in Burma or Indonesia, we are assuming this unrest is a new twentieth-century condition we must eliminate or see it push these countries into communism. But tribal unrest and banditry have been part of the pattern of these feudal societies for centuries.

The British did little to reduce tribal tensions while they ruled Burma. Instead they helped keep the tribes separated by enlisting the hillmen in their Army and the Burmans in their civil service. Religion also helped. Buddhism is surprisingly resistant to Christianity; few Buddhists give it up for the harsher religion of the West. But the hill tribes had only a crude animism of their own plus a prejudice against Buddhism because the Burmans followed it. The Karens welcomed the Baptist missionaries from the United States who taught a Christian religion that helped them look down on the Buddhism of the Burmans. During the civil wars of 1949–50 the hillmen went into battle against the Burmese Army, or the Burman's Army as they would describe it, singing "Onward, Christian Soldiers."

The Burmans are very fond of paralleling the troubles of the first years of their republic with those we had in the first years of the United States. It is fair to point out that five years after our own independence we had not yet adopted a constitution. Both Burma and Indonesia have. But the similarity stops there. In the first place, the fights for independence of most of these new countries of Asia have been purely negative revolutions against a hated colonial conqueror.

We Americans were luckier; quite aside from the difference in initiative and drive which may come from a cooler climate, we were Overseas Britons permitted to learn to govern our country for ourselves. Even after the Revolutionary War we never hated the British with the self-destructive emotions which colonialism instilled in much of Asia.

And second, one of the greatest boons of the nascent American system, we agreed upon a Declaration of Independence before we fought for freedom, and thus we possessed a moral and political pattern of the future to which every fractional group in our new republic was committed. This had much to do with our ability to function together as a nation after independence. The new republics of Burma and Indonesia and Vietnam have not had such an ideological blueprint, and this lack has had much to do with their instability.

It is a measure of the narrow margin of safety which the Burmese Government has possessed that a small number, less than fifteen thousand Kuomintang Chinese troops, could engage almost the whole available military power of Burma. After the Communist victory in China, some of Chiang Kai-shek's troops fled from South China into the Shan states of Burma and lived quietly near the borders of Thailand until 1952. Then they broke loose from the rough *cordon sanitaire* which the Burmese Army set up around them. The Burmese could not have encountered a more serious threat to their national unity than this revolt; it forced them to shift their Army from the campaigns against the revolting hill tribes, and it offered Communist China a logical pretext for intervening in Burma to prevent these Kuomintang troops from later reinvading China.

Burma knew the Formosan Government was aiding these KMT troops, and she was convinced her old enemy, Thailand, was helping too. This brought the United States in to the mess. Since both Formosa and Thailand are our close allies, there were many charges in Rangoon that the United States was behind the KMT troops. No Burmese official with whom I talked could give me one good reason why the United States would want to support a small group of KMT soldiers in Burma and so chance throwing the country into China's lap, but the suspicion continued.

Finally, with UN and American help, Chiang agreed to repatriate some of his men, and the United States paid part of the cost of airlifting them out, although we had no obligation whatsoever to do so. Then the Burmese Government, objecting because only about one sixth of the Chinese had departed, announced that if the Americans were really sincere in wanting to solve this problem they could easily do so by demanding Chiang force all these soldiers out or stop all aid to Formosa. Futile for an American to point out that we could not so dictate to Chiang or so antagonize and weaken an ally against communism.

Quite aside from the grave threats to Burmese unity which come from the Kuomintang troops still in Burma and from the hill tribes, the new republic faces the most serious internal threat of all from its own Communists. This is a triple threat, for there are three Burmese Communist parties. The strongest is the BCP, the White Flag Communists, supporters of the Stalinist doctrine; their stronghold is the central jungles of Burma and, well trained and disciplined, they are busy stirring up trouble among the Shan tribes. Next in line are the CPB, the Red Flag Communists, who follow a Trotsky doctrine; they are principally a nuisance value, a few thousand guerrilla bandits disrupting communications or raiding plantations and villages. But in a country of mountainous jungles a very few determined Communists can keep a whole area in ferment, as the Malayan Communists are still proving. In addition to the two underground Communist parties is one aboveground, the BWPP, the Burma Workers and Peasants Party. It holds a very small percentage of the seats in the Parliament and the BWPP leaders were once members of the dominant party in Burmese politics, the AFPFL, the Anti-Fascist People's Freedom League.

However anti-Western and anti-capitalist the Burmese Government may be, it is not a friend or admirer of its own Communists. The present rulers of Burma know them from the days of the Japanese occupation and the revolt against Britain, when they and the Burmese Communists were part of a single guerrilla movement. They have fought the armed revolts of their Communists as firmly as they have those of the hill tribes, and Rangoon has foiled several Red coups. But the government is not anti-Communist in any broader ideological sense. Like the Vietnamese, the Burmese would instantly choose native communism to foreign colonialism; they were prepared after World War II to fight the British power in Burma with the Communists as their allies.

Fortunately the Communists have not acted very shrewdly in crucial, rich, and easy-to-grab Burma. Their underground has been inefficient and their leaders have never gone through the international training schools of Moscow because the Kremlin handled Burmese affairs as a subdivision of the Indian Communist Party and thus, ironically, Burmese Communists have been a colonial Communist party. Until they find a better leader than Thakin Than Tun, they will not be a serious threat.

Nor will they, unless China's power waxes in Vietnam and they receive much more support from the Overseas Chinese of Burma. There are only about a third of a million of these and they have followed the familiar sequence from support of the Chinese Communists to recoiling against them. As far as an outsider can learn, Burma's Chinese are not pro-Communist today, but even the ranking anti-Communist Chinese in Rangoon refused to go to the 1952 Formosa meeting of the Overseas Chinese. Burma's future is too obscure to bring attention to themselves, either from the government or the native Communist terrorists. Learning Burmese and hoping to become members of the Burmese community, the Chinese remain terrified of a serious Burmese outbreak against them, either as an aftermath of the Kuomintang troubles or because of Chinese communism.

However, it would be optimistic to assume that internal communism cannot become more threatening in Burma. Communist China is taking over the direction of these Southeast Asian Communist parties and will give them a more coherent program. There is a large and powerful pro-Communist sentiment in Burma. And the Communists have the immeasurable advantage of being a yellow, Burmese party instead of a white, foreign party. Compare this with the weakness of the Western democracies in Burma or Indonesia, where there are no indigenous organizations dedicated to spreading Western ideals. While I was in Rangoon there was a Chinese-Burmese fair celebrating the Chinese New Year, attended by tens of thousands of Burmese to whom clever leaflets of Communist propaganda were passed out. There was not a single foreigner in evidence at this rally; Burmese did all the work. If the democracies staged such a fair, we would have to hire people to pass out our pamphlets and we would have to be on hand to be sure they did it right.

When we are forced to take the initiative in South Asia, being white Easterners, what we do redounds far more against us than for us. If we could only retire from the arena and let time take its course until some of the wiser men in these neutral countries, beginning to comprehend the virtues in our form of democracy, would form their own pro-West parties to carry, in their own ways and according to their own thinking, the burden of information. But of course we cannot withdraw today because of the threat to these neutral countries and to us from the looming power of Burma's northern neighbor, Communist China.

Any day of any week the Chinese Communists could invade Burma. Opinions vary on why they do not: some say it is because China is too busy elsewhere; others say Peiping is afraid the UN would step in and make of her aggression another Korea. Also, Burma is close, in every sense, to India. If China seized Burma, India would be very, very unhappy and much less neutral toward China and Russia. But perhaps the most important reason is a less optimistic one: with a Burma so weak and made up of so many dissident minorities ready to fight and able to be exploited, plus the bias of the Burmese against the West, China may well feel that in the long run Burma will fall into her clutches.

Given the massive and ever-present power of China just across her borders, add the Burmese distrust and fear of the West, and Burma's foreign policy could not possibly be anything but blatantly neutral. She was one of the first nations to recognize Communist China and she has remained on the friendliest terms ever since. She loathes the Kuomintang on Formosa as fascistic, militaristic, and anti-Marxist, three deadly insults in the Burmese vocabulary; in the UN, Burma agitates to have the island of Formosa returned to "its rightful owners" in Peiping. She dislikes Thailand almost as much as Formosa, first because of her jealousy of her neighbor, whom she treats as if Thailand were of no international importance although it is just as large and far more stable than she, and second because she considers Thailand a stooge of the Americans.

Burma, viewing any Pacific Pact or Southeast Asian Pact as a disguised maneuver to ensnare her in an alliance against China, is determined to tread the middle path of neutrality between "the slaveries of communism and the capitalistic West." She believes she is carrying out her policy of complete neutrality when on the one hand she refuses to accept American technical aid with no military strings attached, and on the other hand sells rubber to Peiping in spite of a UN resolution labeling rubber a strategic material. True, this was done via private concerns and after the Korean truce; true, rubber is not a top-priority strategic material; but it is one more evidence of a foreign policy more anti-Western than neutral in its acts.

Burmese officialdom is reluctant to discuss publicly this foreign policy with Westerners. As compared with radio interviews in every capital in Asia, I was unable in Rangoon to persuade any cabinet minister or any leading editor to explain his country's official position. It is difficult to believe Burmese are sincere when they say that, if the democratic bloc wins out, freedom is as much threatened as if the Russian-Chinese bloc wins. But as long as Red China remains powerful and communism works as well as it is doing today, neutrality is the best we can expect, and Burma will continue to boast that she is an equal among equals who will not "lift our fingers or nod our heads at a signal from anyone."

Burma viewed the Vietnamese war purely as an anti-colonial uprising against the French and she hailed the Geneva Agreement. But if and as Communist infiltration develops in Laos or more Chinese support goes to the rebellious tribes of Burma, Rangoon will be forced for her own self-protection to become less neutralistic and more interested in defensive pacts, even with the West; we can only hope that she protects herself in time. In the meantime, however much Burma fears either China or the West, Premier U Nu allots his praise with what he considers an impartial hand: "The United States saved the world from the scourges of Nazism and Fascism during two world wars at huge sacrifices of man power and materials; the Communist leaders of China have abolished foreign economic exploitation and wiped out bribery and corruption for the first time. They are building a new world for their masses."

All decisions on foreign policy and every other aspect of the government of Burma are made in Rangoon. The capital and largest city of Burma, Rangoon, like Manila or Djakarta or Bangkok, is the nerve center of the country. As in Kuala Lumpur and Singapore, the British have left a strong imprint on the city, which is filled with British architecture and divided by broad British-built highways. But there are as many Buddhist pagodas as British buildings, rearing their gilded, bulbous spires above the flat roofs. And where the Burmese have had anything to say about it, as in the City Hall, the white cement walls of the West are capped by exotic peaked roofs of Burmese design.

Chinese, Indians, and Burmans all mingle together in Rangoon, still jammed with refugees and shanty-town shacks as a result of the civil war which made so much of the countryside unsafe. In Rangoon you realize you are nearing India when you see pavements splotched with scarlet patches, spit from betel-nut chewing. In the wet season the patches become pools of iridescent liquid red on the dun-colored cement. Remove the refugees and the pagodas, and you might think this city were in Malaya or over in India, until you noticed the costumes the people wear. Most of educated Asia today has given in to the impractical suits and hot leather shoes of the West. Not so the Burmese; they continue to wear their national costume, the becoming and highly practical *longyi*.

The men's longyi is a completely uneffeminate skirt. Usually of scintillating Burmese silk, it is a piece of cloth about two yards long and one and a half yards wide, its two ends sewed together to form a long tube. You step into it, wind it around you, and tie the top at your waist. If you tie it properly—and every Burmese has a different ritual—the longyi stays anchored around you while you are walking or running or bicycling. My own premonitions of becoming pantsless in Rangoon were realized only once. I was making an entrance at a formal reception; the assembled guests were waiting for me in a room on the second floor. When I came to the top step leading into the drawing room, I forgot to lift the hem of my longyi.

With the longyi, you wear an open-collar sport shirt and a pair of sandals. The ebullient Burmese do not go in for dull colors. A man striding along Sule Pagoda Road may be wearing a bright raspberry-pink silk longyi and a nile-green shirt, sandals on his bare feet, a cigar in his mouth, and an old fedora on his head.

If you are a dignified elder, instead of the fedora you wear a *guangbaung*. These are little wicker baskets, relics of the days when Burman headmen wore topknots and tucked them into the baskets. Over the guangbaungs is wrapped very pale and gauzy material, usually pale rose or orchid, with a flowing Windsor knot down on one side. To be fashionably dressed, you may add a Chinese frogged jacket of thin wool and a set of diamond or emerald studs in your shirt, always real jewels and as large as you can afford, indicating prosperity, not ostentation.

The women you see on the streets, and you see more women by themselves in public here than anywhere else in Asia, wear a feminine version of the longyi, an *aingyi*. It is usually of a flowered material; above it a wide bra band, tightly wrapped, and a sheer waist of white or cream net demurely buttoned at the throat and wrists. No hat, but flowers or jewels in the hair. Because there is no place for pockets in these clothes, both sexes wear bags of embroidered materials hanging from their shoulders; the men's plain, the women's with swaying silken tassels. Custom decrees that the woman's aingyi is never hung to dry above the man's longyi, and no decorous wife would fling her aingyi over the side of the bed in which her husband sleeps.

Rangoon, built on low swampy land like Calcutta or Saigon or Bangkok or New Orleans, is one of the hottest and dampest places in the world. With a minimum of a hundred inches of rain a year and four months of steaming heat, the longyi is an ideal costume. If it gets wet, you can whip off the soaked skirt, step into another one, and be dressed again. If you are hot, you unlash it in one motion and fan yourself with a swift back-and-forth movement of its folds, or you can raise it from your toes to your knees and fan yourself at that end.

The Burmese are as distinctive in their character and psychology as they are in their costume. The Irish of the East, impressionable and happy-go-lucky, they are famous for quick ardors and sudden coolings. Perhaps naïve is the best single adjective for them; naïve in their approach to life and naïve in what they expect from others. This quality is especially noticeable when you contrast them with their equally easygoing neighbors, the sophisticated and worldly Thais. I suspect that some of the red tape which enmeshed me in Thailand was fairly deliberate, a non-malicious but quietly superior toying with the brash Westerner; somehow I do not think a Burmese would do this.

Both the Thais and Burmese flash you friendly smiles, but it is impossible to guess what a Thai may be thinking, while the Burmese seem to wear their emotions on the surface. Even their history is a naïve one; everyone else is an ogre whom the Fairy Prince, Burma, drives howling from the stage of history; according to their Maha Yazawn, the Great Chronicle of Kings, they thoroughly trounce everyone in sight in a series of glorious victories which leave them masters of the world. They are even naïve about the present-day threat of Communist China: "China is too busy to come in here."

As individuals, they meet the world gaily and openly; as the Thais do, they let joy come spontaneously. Perhaps because these two peoples have never known starvation, both are insouciant about the troubles of the morrow. In sharp contrast to the apathy of the ordinary Indo-Chinese or Indonesian or Indian, the Burmese are full of animation and never sullen. As neat and clean as the Chinese, they are equally addicted to gambling and they have many Confucian sayings, like: "If a cock ruffles up his feathers, it is easy to pluck him." On the subject of roosters, the Burmese will tell you that a long time ago religious fanatics burned the Indian Veda books of astronomy. Some roosters pecked at the ashes of the sacred book, and thus Burmese roosters have, to this day, the miraculous and exclusive accomplishment of being able to crow in unison, exactly at midnight.

The Burmese are proud of their ability to laugh at trouble, even their own. Prime Minister U Nu tells how some villagers went out with garlands and gifts to greet the Japanese invaders but came back to their village in twos and threes, very depressed because the Japanese had taken their gifts, slapped them, and made them work all day. Then as they thought over their predicament, its ludicrousness hit them and they howled with laughter at their plight and were cheerful again.

There is a Burmese version of our Western "Saturday's children," with an animal to go with your disposition, depending on what day of the week you were born: Monday's children are jealous and like tigers; Tuesday's are honest and like lions; Wednesday's, short-tempered but soon calm, and like elephants with tusks; Yahu's (from noon to midnight on Wednesday and a separate day in Burmese reckoning) are strong-tempered and like elephants with no tusks; Thursday's, mild and like rats, a not unpopular animal in Burma; Friday's children, talkative and like guinea pigs, which evidently have a different characteristic in a tropical clime; Saturday's, hot-tempered and like dragons; Sunday's, stingy and like garudas, the legendary half birds-half goddesses.

The women of Burma are uniquely fortunate, for in all Asia, only in Burma are women the equal of men. In this country "equal" is almost too weak a word; Burmese women have the status which New York career women work for, yearn for, and never quite acquire. They boss their husbands, smoke cigars on the street—dainty ones but unmistakably cheroots—and still remain exceedingly attractive and feminine. Often the more ambitious half of the marriage partnership, the wives have always shouldered equal responsibilities, and no Burmese husband would consider buying a house or investing in a business without his wife's consent. In the bazaars and in the market places the women handle the retail business; even in the names of the shops, both the husband's and the wife's names appear on the signboards, and not "John Doe and Wife," but "John Doe and Mary Smith," her maiden name. If a husband is a Foreign Minister, his wife receives the title "Mrs. Foreign Minister."

Since prehistoric times Burmese women have enjoyed this equality. Under the Burmese kings they often served as headwomen, and in folk tales dealing with the problems of Burmese Solomons the judge becomes a Solomonia, a "Princess-Learned-in-the-Law." Today all professions are open to women, and they number more than a quarter of the students in the University of Rangoon. The laws of marriage, divorce, and inheritance give woman as much freedom as she has in California. Marriage in Burmese law is a civil contract stating that the man and woman have agreed to "eat and live together" openly.

Buddhism, the religion of the country, is not involved in marriage or in sexual relationships of any kind, except that it is contrary to Buddhist law to force a woman; she must be enticed and satisfied. In most of Asia the male philanders as he pleases; here he is rather restricted because his wife can divorce him any time she pleases and take a substantial share of their estate with her.

Also, in the Burmese Buddhist system marriage is a partnership for joint happiness and development of husband and wife, not a method of adding more lives to society or to the support of the religion; therefore, birth control is recognized and large families are the exception. This life-limiting factor has had much to do, here and in Thailand, with the fact that there has been enough land and enough food to go around.

Family life is happy, well balanced, and gregarious. Relatives are always visiting or dropping in: "You don't invite people for parties here; they just come." Burmese children are rarely disciplined and seldom need to be; they entertain themselves and they are very fond of singing and dancing. Whatever material things a Westerner may feel Burmese families lack, they appear to enjoy each other much more than do our families in the West.

Like the houses of Cambodia or Malaya, Burmese houses are built up on stilts to capture the breeze and provide a shady yard beneath. Unless they have learned to live in Western style, even the well-to-do live in amazingly simple homes of plain dark-stained planks. The upstairs part of the house is a long narrow room with no windows except at the front. There are sleeping rooms on each side of it with only a casually hung piece of cheap cretonne in the doorways for privacy. Everyone sits on mats and sleeps on mats, and there is very little furniture. In the main room, only a radio, a few books, and a few dishes in a closed cabinet; almost no ornaments and usually no pictures on the unpainted wood wall, except perhaps a calendar or a newspaper picture pinned up.

But the Burmese live this easily and simply because they wish to, not because they cannot afford more material comforts; a woman who lives in such a simple house may own a dazzling collection of rubies or emeralds. For the Burmese look upon jewelry not only as an ornamentation but as the only dependable kind of investment; in an unstable country, they learned hundreds of years ago that jewels were easy to take with you if you suddenly had to run.

Burmese food, too, is unlike anything with which we in the West are familiar. You sit on mats at a table only about eight inches above the floor, of course with your shoes off; you never keep your shoes on in any Southeast Asian home or temple. The first course is *tali*, a tepid drink which resembles diluted coconut milk and has a tangy, slightly fermented taste. Next comes rice cooked with coconut and a little fat. Then there are large prawns fried with garlic, red pepper, and other hot spices. With this, a relish the Burmese love, shredded shrimp fried in garlic-saturated oil until almost black. Then *hilse*, a white fish which has been fried in another hot sauce. To our Western palates all these sauces burn alike; to the Burmese each is enormously different, a subtle blend of a dozen spices and saffron and curry, which will occupy a Burmese cook for half a day. Next comes a course of fish salad and sliced cucumber with lots of vinegar and herbs, very refreshing in hot weather, but unsafe for a Westerner to eat; even watermelon is dangerous because the water in it has come out of the contaminated ground of Asia.

There are no knives or forks; you eat everything with your fingers, including the sticky rice, and when the meal is over you are brought a washing bowl and then a rinsing bowl for your greasy hands. Dessert is *jaggry*, a Burmese confection tasting like maple sugar and made from the same palm tree that furnished the palm juice which began the meal. The final course is a famous Burmese treat, pickled tea. This is just what it sounds like, only more so: fermented green tea leaves, thoroughly pickled with slices of garlic, sesame seeds, and other unimaginably peculiar Asian spices. Pickled tea is like a thousand English savories all treasured up in musty velvet for a couple of years. A sampling half the size of your fingernail is delicious; any more and the taste sinks into your inlays. After the pickled tea, you finish off with betel-nut chewing and cheroots.

Every house in Burma has its Buddhist shrine, where flowers and food are offered to their gods. Although a gentle and not demanding creed, their religion is very important to the Burmese. They will spend their last pennies on candles to be burnt or on a small pagoda to be built to acquire merit in the eyes of Buddha and a better karma in their next life. Disease and death are met calmly and without bitterness, since they are part of your karma, and how you face them will help determine whether your next life will be a happier one.

Just as Buddhism contributes to the easygoing mode of life in Burma, it is also responsible for the truly democratic character of the new republic. With 90 per cent of the people Buddhist, it is said the time for declaring their independence was fixed by Buddhist astrologers, and Burmese democracy faithfully carries out the Buddhist teaching of complete human equality without class or caste consciousness.

In contrast to its external policies, the government of Burma consistently lives up to the Western idea of what a free government should be. Burma has a democratic constitution, free elections, free speech, a free parliament, and, a much more important test, it has no secret police. When the AFPFL assumed leadership, it commanded 85 per cent of the seats in the Parliament. In a country close to collapse from civil war, U Thakin Nu and his associates had a perfect excuse to declare a national emergency and rule the new nation to suit themselves. This they refused to do, and theirs has been an admirable unbroken record of democratic political processes at work.

Like all the cabinet ministers, the Prime Minister is a devout Buddhist. When he can, U Nu lives as a hermit and his hobby is to go on pilgrimages to Buddhist shrines. But when some Buddhist monks demonstrated against the Moslem slaughtering of animals for food, he fasted to demonstrate his support of this small minority's right to its own practices. In his public speeches he exhorts Burma to remember that the basis of national judgment and action is the *mingala sutta*, the Buddhist beatitudes: "Not to follow after fools . . . The support of mother and father, the cherishing of child and wife . . . Patience, the soft answer. The sight of those controlled . . . To do deeds that bring no blame . . . A heart untouched by worldly things, passionless, secure . . . this is the greatest blessing."

As in Thailand, the evidences of Buddhism are always around you in Burma. Nothing glows more in the heat of midday than a Buddhist priest clad in his saffron robes and carrying a big parasol of oiled paper in deep magenta-tangerine. Here the bonzes go into politics and smoke or chew gum, material indulgences which would horrify the traditional Thai priests. As ever-present as the bonzes are the temples in this land of pagodas, and dominating Rangoon is the most famous Buddhist shrine in Asia, the Shwedagon Pagoda.

Legend has it that in this shrine are some hairs from his head which Buddha bestowed upon two brothers from Rangoon, or Dagon, as it was then called. They decided a great pagoda must house their gift and Sakka, the Lord of the Heavens, came down to earth and with the aid of four *nats*, or spirits, selected the site. When the sacred hairs were taken out of their casket to be placed in the vault, "Eight Hairs flew up to a height of seven palm trees, emitting rays of variegated hues with such a dazzle that the dumb could speak, the deaf could hear, the lame could walk, and a rain of jewels fell knee-deep."

The glittering golden Shwedagon Pagoda sits on a leveled-off terrace at the top of a high hill, its base surrounded by assorted religious monuments, sixty-four small pagodas, sphinxes, figures of elephants, lions, serpents, and various spirits, including beloos, yogis, nats, and *wathundari*, recording angels. The pagoda itself presents a unique silhouette, a cone-shaped bulbous bell composed of seven shapes piled one on the other. Its base is a huge bell, topped by an inverted begging bowl, topped by a twisted turban, all three levels covered with gold leaf. From here on up each level is covered with solid-gold plates. Above the turban is a bulbous spire shaped like a plaintain bud and over seventy feet in circumference; on top of this an open umbrella shape, topped with a vane, topped with the *seinbu*, or diamond bud, a globe of gold ten inches in diameter inlaid with diamonds and other precious stones. Buried inside the pagoda, according to the legend, is an inestimable additional treasure. When I asked my guide how much he thought there might be there he said, "Nobody knows, but the Communists will find out when they take over."

The gold of the Shwedagon Pagoda, flashing its fine show over the city of Rangoon, is a symbol of Burmese piety and of practical waste. Buddhism, stressing the quality of living and of kindness to your fellow beings, pays little attention to man's material welfare. Buddhists do not believe in accumulating money; the miser inhabits the lowest hell in Buddhist theology, and Buddhists save their money only to give a big feast or to acquire merit by plastering gold leaf on pagodas.

The consequence of this Buddhist teaching has been that Burma lacks an indigenous business class; its traders have been principally British or Indian or Chinese. Almost no educated Burman goes into business; he becomes a lawyer or a professor or a government employee and he never learns about, is interested in, or has any comprehension of the private-enterprise system. The direct result is Burma's weak economy with its lack of capital and, even worse, its complete lack of understanding of the role of capital in developing a higher standard of living. Moreover, the same forces that turned President Soekarno and the Indonesian leaders into confirmed Marxists have operated in Burma. In reaction to the colonial British rulers in Burma and to the capitalist white system which they represented, U Nu and his associates turned to Karl Marx for justification and guidance. They are unrescuable Marxists, and *Das Kapital* is their economic Bible. Therefore, they are deeply suspicious of every act of a capitalistic system and will heed none of its advice or avail themselves of its proffered aid.

With this background, it was inevitable that when Burma won her freedom, her leaders would set up a socialistic state. And they have their Pyidawtha, the most sweeping and deliberate planned welfare system outside the Communist orbit. Their Constitution states as a fundamental law: "Private monopolist organizations are forbidden"; and as state policy: "There is a general tendency toward large-scale planning, support of co-operative organizations and collective farming."

The government has made itself responsible not only for all the usual functions of a democratic government in the West, from health and justice to police and education, but for the entire economy of the country. It receives the land revenues, liquor taxes, forest revenue, motor-vehicle duties, court fees. It also buys at prices it sets, and sells at prices it sets, all the exportable produce of Burma. All factories built in Burma are owned and operated by the government. And so far in its Pyidawtha, good intentions of the Burmese Government have been far more conspicuous than its ability to improve the lot of its people.

Burma started out with serious burdens, thanks to the British colonial system and the burnt-earth policies of the Japanese war. The country has little electrical power, the base of an industrial system; only 3 per cent as much as is available to an American, 20 per cent as much as to a Japanese, and 60 per cent as much as to a poverty-stricken Indian. With a small population on a rich land, yet its diet is one of Asia's lowest in fats, minerals, and proteins. With only 1100 doctors for 19,000,000 people, 20 per cent of its babies die before they are one year old—one of the highest infant mortality rates in Asia—and 50 per cent die before they are ten years old.

Rice is the staple crop of the country and its real capital. The sale of rice is the principal source of revenue for the government, over one half of its yearly revenue. The government maintains a monopoly on rice exports, paying a farmer one fourth of what it receives from the sale of his rice, keeping the other 75 per cent for itself. Before the war Burma sold its less fortunate neighbors about four million tons of rice a year, twice the yield of Thailand or Indo-China; today, in spite of all the government's efforts, it has not been able to raise its rice production to prewar levels.

In a shortsighted effort to hold up a high price of rice, the government recently was left with an export surplus on its hands. The Marxist-minded editors of Rangoon did not condemn the government's inefficiency or its socialist system. Instead, the English-language *New Times* of Rangoon looked around for a capitalistic ogre and editorially suspected the United States of being behind insidious planning "to break down the price of rice and thus render our government unstable."

Men who understand economics could help the well-meaning Burmese Government if it would listen. They know that the most constructive thing Rangoon could do would be to put its principal emphasis on, and all its resources behind, increasing rice production. If this were accomplished, it would have two constructive consequences: South Asia would become a more stable area because more food would be available; from the sale of her rice Burma would receive more capital with which to build up her economy. But very few speeches of the government deal with rice production, while yards and yards of rhetoric are devoted to their grandiose plans for creating an industrial state.

Again, this is a consequence of Marxism and colonialism. Marx preached the necessity of a government creating its own industrial state to protect its people from exploitation by capitalism. The Burmese Government intends to do this. But the Burmese leaders have no clear idea of what is really involved in an industrial state, nor how to go about achieving it. A few years ago Burma negotiated to buy a steel rolling mill; one week's operation of it would have filled all her needs for a year. She lacked both coal and coke, she had no skilled labor to operate the mill, but she still wanted to buy the mill to become industrialized and "protect ourselves from exploitation."

Where they understand their problem, the men who rule Burma do a creditable job, as in their program of land socialization, which has become a positive anti-communism force. Before the revolution, over half of the usable land was in the hands of absentee, principally foreign, landlords who charged exorbitant rents. When Burma became a republic, its government, trained in the Marxist theory of the evil of landlords and aware that a nation of peasants would not long support any government which did not give them land, passed the Land Nationalization Act of 1948, which eliminated the large tracts of the landlords, with due compensation, and distributed it in small holdings to be farmed by the peasants.

However, this is only step one in Burma's welfare state. The land is now owned by the government, which intends to proceed with socialization. The Ministry of Democratic Local Administration is providing the capital for farm collectives to be directed from Rangoon. Into these collectives the peasants would be amalgamated under arrangements similar to those of the Russian collective farms. The government's motive is not to acquire more power over its peasants but to help them. A coincidental activity of the same ministry is the development of democratic self-government in the thirty thousand villages of Burma, whose people are illiterate and ruled by local headmen. Such plans raise two big questions: Can the small group of educated men in Rangoon adequately direct such an apparatus, and can the ends of their democratic welfare state be achieved without eventually trapping both the peasant and the well-meaning central government in a dictatorship?

The land program and village democratization is part of a grandiose Burmese Plan of economic development running until 1960 and designed to double the income per Burmese. The hopeful statements of the government about the plan read beautifully: "All we need to do is exploit our natural resources; once it is done, Burma will be flowing with milk and honey, the welfare state in fact and in truth." But the disparity between published statements and actual achievements is large.

Consider the rehabilitation brigades which the government has established. The purpose is admirable, to rehabilitate the ex-guerrillas of Burma and in so doing to train thousands of men and women to become skilled workers in Burma's program of industrialization. I went on an inspection trip at the brigade headquarters at Aung Sen Myo, where four thousand people were being trained. From the enthusiastic government publications, I had expected the project would be full of machinery and people learning to operate them; but when I got to Aung Sen Myo I found only a few small brick factory buildings. In them was a little machinery, small lathes, presses, which had been sitting in the factories for many months; most of them were still not assembled. The government representative who showed me around was very proud of the existence of the crated machinery; it demonstrated that his country was industrializing.

In the simple carpentry shop and bricklaying shops of Aung Sen Myo tangible progress was being made. Here the men were taught how to use the simplest tools, the kind they could afford back in their villages. First they learn to build rough benches and desks to be used on the project; next they lay small brick walls and tear them down again; and later they go out to build projects for the state.

This is the kind of industrialization which Burma should attempt on a large scale now. The local director of the project had a wise prescription from which his cabinet bosses could profit: "We concentrate on the building trades because we need to learn to do first things first. We shall train them to take apart and put together and oil and tend the machines long before we operate them." Such a prescription is a long way from the idea of Pyidawtha, the planned welfare state, making the unrealizable promise that it will double the income of every citizen in eight years and turn Burma into a modern industrial paradise.

Intrinsically Burma is economically strong. She has rice and teak, copper, tungsten, silver, gold, tin, nickel, amber, jade, rubies, and oil. Since in good years she sells more than she must buy, she can afford to begin the purchase of light industry for her people. But crated machines in the shops are not enough. Like Indonesia, and because of the same kind of colonial bias, Burma is delaying her own future. In the capitalistic Western world are the available technicians, managers, and skilled supervisors to come in and teach her how to do a twentieth-century job, the same kind of personnel who have done so much in the co-operative Philippines and are now helping Burma's neighbor, Thailand. But, again like the Indonesian leaders, the rulers of Burma believe capitalism is a devil from which their country must be protected at any cost.

The government wants to pull its countrymen out of their illiteracy and is devoting a great deal of effort to this admirable end. It is as hard a job for them as it is for the Indonesians. The British educated few Burmese, and the government has few teachers available. But the West has many technicians experienced in the techniques of organizing a curriculum and teaching system. If they were used in Burma, they could not possibly be capitalist agents, since the government would dictate and supervise the contents of the textbooks and courses they arranged.

Technicians must come from the West; we are the principal repository of these knowledges and we alone have more trained personnel than we need at home. But Burma will not give herself a break. And while she will not utilize our teachers, in her Chinese schools Burma permits Chinese teachers who frequently subtly influence their pupils toward communism. The government refuses to see this as dangerous: the rules are always different in this part of the world if Westerners are involved.

In spite of pretenses made by some of the American government personnel in Burma, the fact stands out today that in an ex-colonial Southeast Asia where we are not popular, the high point of our unpopularity is Burma. It is not that the man in the street seems to resent us. No American meets many Burmese when he is in their country because few speak English, and even fewer Americans speak Burmese, but those ordinary Burmese with whom you come in contact seem friendly, open, and hospitable. Not one of these adjectives describes Burmese officialdom. The far from friendly or co-operative government of the present seems to feel Americans get in the way, criticize them, or are conniving against their country. And a final test of anti-American bias: while it has been difficult to do business in Indonesia, it has been almost impossible in Burma.

When you probe beneath the surface you come reluctantly to the conclusion that if the men who rule Burma were forced to choose between American democracy and Russian communism, or, as they would put it, American capitalism and Russian economic democracy, it is more likely the leaders of Burma would choose communism. They would insist that this is untrue, but their refusal to recognize the existence of the totalitarian state in Russia while they exaggerate every destructive aspect of capitalism shows their bias, not caused by the Communists but triggered by the old hurts and psychoses of colonialism. The Prime Minister of Burma puts himself on record: "You will recognize there is hardly any difference between the three-year-old Burma and the three-year-old Russia." The Minister of Land Democratization talks about his ideals for local freedom in a Burmese village and cites as his goal "the freedom which now exists in a Russian village."

The plain truth is that in most of Asia the only conceivable economic choice is communism or socialism. Capitalism is not in the running; too many Asians hate it and they could not set up a capitalistic system if they wanted to. They have almost no capital. The peasants cannot possibly save up money to invest; their problem is to keep from starving to death. It is only the governments who, from their taxes, are able to get together capital to build factories. If we cannot offer these governments a non-Communist and a non-capitalistic economic system, they will throw out the baby of freedom with the bath water of private capitalism.

Yet all the time we have the answer they are seeking. It is the name, not the game, that is making the trouble. For today the actual system under which the United States operates bears no resemblance to the capitalism Karl Marx wrote about and these people hate. One of the greatest accomplishments of the twentieth-century West is our present system of social capitalism. Our income taxes are higher than those in any so-called Socialist country of Asia. Both major American political parties, our Congress, and our people believe that, wherever the welfare of all the people demands it, it is the duty of the national government to take whatever economic steps are necessary to protect them.

These are tenets very similar to those held by the free, democratic socialistic governments of Asia. They would be dumfounded if they heard our government transmitters preaching them as the American way. If we could make common economic ground with the Asian Socialists—Socialist parties who are up to now anti-West because they are anti-capitalistic—we could automatically create for ourselves powerful domestic supporters in every country in Southeast Asia willing to fight their own internal Communists.

Once the common meeting ground of economics was established, these now antagonistic countries could, at their own tempi and in their own ways, take over more of what they could understand, relate to themselves, and use of the knowledges of the West.

The old cultures of Burma and the other nations of Southeast Asia are running down. This is not a tactful statement and one which each of these civilizations would resent as another example of stupid Westerners who cannot understand their values. Nevertheless, while they were once great civilizations with much to give the world, today much of their architecture or music or literature or handicraft are relics of their outlived past. You hear about Thai silver, Japanese batiks,

Burma silks; when you go to buy them or see them made, you are not impressed. At best the craftsmen work as their ancestors did, with the same old tools and the same old patterns, except that their hand is not as skillful and they are only copyists.

Perhaps it was colonialism that robbed these civilizations of their old power and drive. The fact remains that today Africans have more vigor and ping in their old arts than many Asians. Every year the glorious past of these civilizations dies a little more; fewer and fewer Asians learn, practice, or appreciate the ancient disciplines. In Thailand only two or three women perform the old dances; in Java only a few old men can perform the shadow plays.

This is not to imply for a second that these peoples are any less gifted or artistic than those of the West; perhaps they are more so because they are closer to nature and spend more time in contemplation and their own inner expansion. But today, of their own choice and without propaganda pressures or Western salesmanship, they are shifting over to Western arts and then adapting and altering them to their own patterns. The most dramatic example of this deep wide swing in values is in music. Everywhere in Asia the young are repudiating their traditional cadences for jazz: a vivid proof that Asia is gradually moving into vibration with the twentieth century, for nothing could be more foreign to the past of Asia than jazz.

The Burma Broadcasting Service arranged an evening of modern music for me to record for American listeners. It was a unique experience. Burmese jazz is played by a semi-Western orchestra with saxophones, clarinets, electrical guitars, and a bass viol consisting of a long waxed string tied down in a square box and giving out a good solid thump-thump. The songs I heard had Burmese words set to American tunes. One, called "Tyew Pia" told of a girl whose beauty was like white light reflected off a pale blue-green wall, ethereal coolness being a prime attribute of beauty in this steaming climate. The poetry of "Tyew Pia" was sung to a hopped-up version of our tune, "Buttons and Bows." Burmese musicians play this music the way our first masters of jazz did, playing a simple melody over and over, ad-libbing as they go. Improvisation plus the Burmese wailing cadences is an incredible fusion; I would never have thought I could hear twelve choruses of "Buttons and Bows" before I recognized the tune.

If we tried to broadcast American music only a few Asians would listen to it. But the Burma radio broadcasts "Tyew Pia" at the wish of, and for the enjoyment of, Burmese listeners. Similarly, when you hear "The Lambeth Walk" in Bangkok, or a Japanese "Floating Down the Mississippi," or a Chinese voice shrieking "Begin the Beguine," each in its own way is getting hep to our kind of civilization.

Pwe, the famous Burmese entertainment, is a more startling example of how Asians can take and use what they want of Western techniques when left to do it of their volition and at their speed. I saw a pwe, a theatrical performance featuring Burma's most famous dancer, Kenneth Sein. You go in the evening to a large temporary building, like an American circus tent, but built of bamboo-mat walls and a bamboo-mat roof in three sections, the center section higher and a vertical gap of about four feet between it and the two side roofs, for ventilation. Inside, the orchestra seats are mats placed on the floor, each one numbered; behind them are the loges, a triple row of deck chairs, more elegant, but you can hardly see the stage from them.

The pwe starts around nine o'clock and lasts until dawn. You see respectable women unescorted here, something that happens nowhere else in Asia. Families bring their babies and small children to sit or sleep through the whole night, and to interrupt the entertainment constantly as they are escorted outside and back in. Most of the care of the children is done by their fond fathers.

The pwe stage is hung with a resplendent deep blue velvet curtain, and below it is a pit full of a percussion-instrument orchestra similar to a Chinese orchestra and used in the same way, for punctuation and a general filling in of silent moments. The play begins traditionally, the actors in beautiful old costumes, against a set representing Buddha under the banyan tree, singing a traditional chant. The chorus does a temple dance in tight brocade skirts with long trains. There is another religious song something like a Gregorian chant. The percussion section has a medium-sized seizure. And we are ready to get down to business.

The curtain rises on an orange velvet drop, and a man in Western dress with an accordion sings a pop tune in jazz rhythm, wishing health and happiness to the audience. All this is piped to you on a big loud-speaker faultily wired and overmodulated, the combination of Eastern nasalties and Western sound distortion filing your eardrums into shreds.

By now it is ten o'clock and time for the play proper. It opens with a scene in the dark: three beds covered with mosquito nettings on a dark set. You see a phosphorescent derby enter, sneak under one net, pause, and then exit. A minute later there is a piercing shriek, followed by Western police sirens in the background; the lights come up, and you discover a girl has been murdered.

Cut to a street-scene backdrop like an American vaudeville stage. A newsboy peddling papers sings a topical song about Burmese current events; in the paper is the report of the murder. Cut to a police-station backdrop, via a black-out, and a sergeant comes rolling in on a coaster platform which carries his police desk. Long cross-examination scene, going into a fade-back to before the crime. The sergeant and police station are pulled out by a rope attached to the platform, the backdrop goes up, and the lights dim down as we fade back to the night before the girl was killed.

The next scene is a bare stage full of dancing girls in costumes painted with phosphorescent flowers. They do a traditional dance, "Flowers in the Dark." And then in comes the star; in contrast to their beautiful old Burmese costumes, he wears bright blue satin Western trousers and a wide-shouldered mess jacket. Kenneth Sein goes through a Western tap ballet routine, weaving in and out among the flower dancers. Now he is joined by the murdered girl, in a beautiful yellow antique costume, who performs an exotic temple dance. Then they both come downstage and go into a rousing buck-and-wing soft-shoe clog. By then it was twelve-thirty and I left while my head was still on my shoulders. The play would go on until morning and end with another old ceremonial Buddhist dance.

The pwe, like Burmese jazz, may sound ludicrous. But it has a lesson for Westerners. The Burmese have selectively taken over what they wanted of our culture and integrated it into an entertainment which appeals to their own ordinary people. The varieties of Western stage devices the pwe employed and the magnificently tight way the Burmese playwright wove them into his own native story show how these people can use the West when they want to. Our economics is certainly no more complicated than our entertainment. Gradually, with patience and skill on our part, we can help them understand and want for themselves more of our techniques in other fields, but only if we do not proceed too fast and try to force upon them things they do not realize can fit their patterns.

Up to now our propaganda ineptitude has been glaring, and much of the money we have given away has been wasted. We gave Burma a quarter of a million dollars to save more of her stored rice by killing insects and rats which preyed upon it; the insecticides worked, but the Buddhists were horrified; living things had been killed, perhaps their own grandfathers in their latest karmas. We planned an efficient sawmill, but since it would have put twelve hundred workers out of jobs it was not used. We showed the Burmese how to raise tomatoes, but they did not like the taste of them and would not eat them. We introduced deep plowing and broke up the hard pan under their rice paddies which held in the water without which the rice could not be grown.

And even when we do the right things, they are not appreciated in Burma. We persuaded them to let us rebuild the war-devastated port of Rangoon with American funds so their rice crops could be exported. When I was in Rangoon I heard us accused of having repaired the port so we would be able to move in our warships and dominate the country. The end result of all our well-meaning charity has been that the Burmese Government, suspicious of us and fearful that Communist China would assume that they were inclining to the West, canceled all aid funds which the American government had been pressing on it.

American foreign policy in Asia has been hindered by inferior personnel. Many of these diplomatic posts are hardship posts, where because of disease, discomfort, and inhospitality, the State Department has not been able to persuade its most gifted people to serve.

Here in Southeast Asia, where everything is done on a person-to-person basis, our ambassadors exert far more influence than they do in Europe or South America. What we have least of is realistic and tough-minded Americans who can be tactful and courteous but clear and firm. Do-gooders in some touchy spots like Burma feel conditions are so delicate that true facts, if reported home, would prejudice Americans against giving more money to the countries, and they believe people like the Burmese are too touchy and psychotic to be asked honest questions.

Such diplomats grossly underestimate the Burmese. Prejudiced against us or not, the Burmese are a courageous people of intellectual toughness. We render them much more suspicious by pussyfooting around issues and mealymouthing generalities than we would by straightforward American reactions. While we need to put our best foot forward, still it must be our own foot, not someone else's. Nations must coexist as they are, not as a few men may pretend they are. We overrate the subjective element in Asians; in the long run their practical gain or loss will determine their policies and their relations with us. A nation will be on our side because it believes as we do or because we can do more for it than our enemies can.

Only where colonialism is involved is this untrue. There, always, is an unreasonable, explosive, emotional bias in Southeast Asians, and actions that put the United States in a posture of colonialism do us more harm than anything else we could possibly do.

I found such a posture existing in Burma. None of the Embassy people told me about it. It was only after many hours of conversation that the polite Burmese brought it up and told me how they felt about the Kokine Swimming Club. In British colonial days no Burmese had been permitted membership in the club. In 1953 many of its members were Americans, including a considerable proportion of the top officials of the Embassy, but even in the free republic of Burma no Burmese was permitted to belong to Kokine.

As the Burmese told me, the result "outweighs all your aid programs or any fifteen million dollars you have given us." However, the American Ambassador told me it was none of my business to inquire about this and none of his business to suggest to members of his staff that they should not belong to such a club.

Within the United States minor provisions of some of our laws, like the McCarran Immigration Act, do as much damage. The most famous woman in Burma, Dow Mya Sein, the president of the National Council of Women of Burma, told me she would never again come to the United States because "I couldn't admit the truth of how I make a living, and your McCarran Act requires I state whether or not I ever earned a living through prostitution." She was making a joke of it, but every woman in Asia who comes to the United States and must answer such a question will be deeply offended and influenced against us.

Certainly the Asian has a legitimate cause of resentment in these outcroppings of colonialism. On the other hand, we Westerners have equally legitimate cause to complain of the double standard as applied to us by the ex-colonials. If you have an appointment, your Asian guest may be an hour late and will feel he needs no excuse, but if you are late you are demonstrating that you, the white man, feel superior to the yellow man. In all these ex-colonies, if and when you find anything less than perfect in the ways they are conducting their affairs, you are promptly told this imperfection is a direct result of the way they were held down for centuries by the British or the French or the Dutch and not allowed to learn to do anything for themselves.

It might be fair, without any implication of condescension, to call the Burmese and their Southeast Asian cousins the adolescents of the twentieth century. Adolescent because they are several centuries younger than the West in experience with freedom and the social responsibilities of adult nationhood. Adolescent because they are deeply suspicious of their democratic elders of the West, deeply resentful of imagined slights to their newly achieved dignities. This adolescence has been rendered far more emotional by the inferiority complexes left by colonialism. Only Thailand and the Philippines, of all these countries, do not have this background. And only Thailand and the Philippines do not react against Americans because they are white.

This part of the world is racing down the corridors of history from pre-Christian or feudal times to the twentieth century. We took a thousand years for the transitions we expect them to make in a lifetime. Their forced evolution sets up a terrible turmoil, external and subjective, in these nations. To paraphrase Newton's law, two tempi of life, two philosophies of life, cannot occupy the same space at the same time. We cannot prevent the explosions which accompany Asia's effort to do this, but we must avoid adding to the critical mass.

Since it is so difficult to help these people, it would be so much easier for them and for us if we could only leave them alone until they wanted to learn. But because of communism we cannot. If the men who rule Burma and Indonesia cannot make their welfare state work, they will lose to communism. Therefore, no matter how trying these people may be to us, we must help them in spite of themselves to make a success of their Socialist states. It does us no good to have tantrums because they will not like our capitalism. The only choice for Burma or Indonesia is their democratic socialism or China's communism.

Therefore, Americans must go on in this part of Asia, unappreciated and hindered, fighting an uphill battle to aid these peoples in spite of themselves, working and giving without appreciation from these adolescents for what we are doing. If the West gives aid, we are feared for our imperialism; if we do not give it, we are accused of wanting these countries to collapse so that we can take them over again. If we use troops to stop aggression in Asia, we are accused of being the aggressors; if we do not interefere militarily and a country is lost, we are accused of being unwilling to fight for freedom. If we do not take a position on the political parties in these countries, we are accused by our friends of being for the most reactionary fascist groups; if we support groups more along the lines of our own way of life, we are accused of intervening in the domestic affairs of another country.

Nevertheless, if we do not help these countries, they will fall to the Communists and they will lose their own future. Therefore, our future course is clear. For our own sake and for theirs we must have patience and fortitude, or, in a word, understanding.

SUPINE CIVILIZATION:

India

An American is as far from home as he will ever be when he reaches India. Half the globe and a thousand centuries away, India is the largest neutral country in the world, a place where true understanding between East and West is still impossible, yet where day-by-day functioning between the two is very possible. Perhaps through our common aspirations we can build here a counterblock to China. Second to China, India has the largest land mass and the largest population in the world and, like the Chinese, the Indians are proud possessors of one of the two greatest cultures in all Asia. If the 370,000,000 Indians ever join the 500,000,000 Chinese against the West, Asia is lost to the free world and the United States will face the greatest danger in its history.

India covers approximately one and a quarter million square miles, one fifteenth of the world's land surface. One seventh of the human race lives in its twenty-nine states, more than in North and South America combined. India is not a country; it is a subcontinent. Had it broken up, as did Southeast Asia, it would have made over twenty different countries each larger than Burma or Thailand, Korea or the Philippines. Separated from the mainland of Asia by the towering barriers of the Himalayas, it is blessed in the north with its own super-enormous Ukraine, a scimitar of deep fertile soil two hundred miles wide and twelve hundred miles long, curving across the country from the Bay of Bengal to the Punjab. Below this belt are the deserts, the jungles, and the vast plateaus of southern India. Half in the Temperate and half in the Tropic zones, India lies supine and dependent on the monsoons, the unpredictable winds that bear the rain for her crops.

This subcontinent has myriad immensities and incredible contradictions piled and jammed and jumbled together. You can travel for a year and not cover half the country. You can study for a lifetime and not comprehend one tenth of its philosophies. To begin to understand it, you do not move about, you sit still somewhere and contemplate India until gradually its differences cancel each other out and the inchoate maze of facts gradually coalesces into a pattern of meanings.

India has over half a million villages, where 80 per cent of its people live, yet Calcutta and Bombay were two of the three largest cities the British Empire possessed. Its climate ranges from some of the clearest, coolest mountain air in the world to some of the stickiest, stuffiest swamp mists. Its peoples speak fifteen major languages and over seven hundred dialects, including Hindi, written from left to right and spoken by more people than speak English in the United States, and Urdu, which combines Persian and some Arabic with the Hindi and is written from right to left with an entirely different set of characters.

One of India's hundreds of princes is reputedly worth more than a billion dollars; he could "lay a carpet of pearls from Charing Cross to Oxford Circus." Yet over 65 per cent of the people of India go to bed hungry, over 75 per cent cannot read or write, and over 25 per cent of the babies die before they are a year old. India's conquerors have bequeathed an architecture that ranges from wooden Hindu temples crawling with sculptures of explicit sexual joys to Moslem mosques soaring in abstract marble; from mud huts unchanged since the birth of Christ to British imperial buildings as stately as any in Westminster. Their religions include more Hindus than there are Protestants or Catholics in the world, plus more Moslems than there are in the neighboring Moslem state of West Pakistan, plus more Buddhists than in any country in Southeast Asia, plus Christians, Fire Worshipers, and other assorted small minorities with only five to ten million members each. It would be astonishing enough if all these diversities had existed at different periods of India's history; it is miraculous that they can all coexist today, and coexist peaceably.

The first thing that hits you as you enter India via its largest city, Calcutta, is not diversities; instead it is dinginess and dirtiness and the degradation of the human spirit that comes from desperate, everyday hunger. In North Asia I was told, "For the rest of your journey you will be going downhill and you won't hit bottom until you reach

India." Calcutta is that bottom, and Indians, too, recoil from these, their worst slums.

The big central railroad station of Calcutta, the red brick Howrah Station, is on the west side of the Hooghly River. From a distance it looked as if the wide arches leading inside were hung with black bead curtains. But when you got to the entrance, you found they were not beads but flies, which you literally pushed aside with your hands as you went in. Except for a few narrow aisles, the interior of Howrah Station was filled with hundreds of squatters, refugees who fled penniless from eastern Pakistan to Bengal. To get out to the trains you threaded your way along a couple of narrow passageways. The rest of the cement floor could not be seen because refugee families had covered the floor with their mats, pots, and rags and were sleeping, eating, cooking, dying, begetting new life, or just sitting in a confusion of flies and dirt. The more enterprising families set up a tiny stall in their little piece of the station to sell single cigarettes or betel nuts or some fried foods. And these squatters are only a token of the refugee problem which has faced the overburdened government of India—far greater than the problem faced by the Allies in Germany at the end of World War II. Without a cent of outside help this poverty-stricken country has absorbed over six million refugees who came to India from Pakistan when Partition, the Great Division of the subcontinent, occurred in 1947.

The costume of the Calcutta male, the *dhoti,* is typical of much that is different, or rather indifferent, in the Indian character. Yards of some loosely woven cheap material, three or four feet wide, are wrapped around the waist like a voluminous skirt. Then the free end is looped down between the legs and tied up at the back of the waist. The result is a pantaloon around each leg, bagging and sagging down, with none of the crisp precision of the Burmese longyi. With the dhoti, the men wear an open-necked Western-style shirt with a collar band but no collar. And the shirts, usually of a dingy narrow-striped material, have much longer tails than our shirts and are worn outside the pantaloons.

The dhotis are cool but they rarely look clean. There is water available at hydrants on the streets of Calcutta. Sometimes people bathe under these. Taught by their religion to look upon the body with indifference, they may bathe naked on a public street. Or they take a small brass pot full of water and pour it over their hands. Much of India is dry and dusty. Water is not plentiful, and Hinduism would label as grossly materialistic the idea that cleanliness is next to godliness.

The burning ghats of Calcutta show another side of the Indian character. Quite small by comparison with the great funeral places of Benares, the ghats are on bare ground just above the riverbank. The mourners, a few friends in clean white, bring the corpse to the ghats on a stretcher, the dead face lolling in the hot sun, a few flowers around it, some more flowers or fruits carried ahead on a round bamboo platter. Other mourners follow behind with a drum and small brass cymbals. In the Hindu religions, at death the spirit abandons the body and takes on a new incarnation, perhaps a far happier one. Therefore, to a Hindu, a funeral is not sad and the corpse is an empty shell, signifying nothing.

At the ghat, firewood is laid out on the bottom of a trough scooped out of the hard ground to ensure a good draught; the body is laid on top, more wood is piled in a tentlike triangle over it, and the flames rise up through the shimmering haze of the midday heat, the wood burning fiercely and cleanly. The ashes are swept together and thrown into the river; thus sanitation is preserved in a hot country.

Calcutta is full of odd juxtapositions. Not far from the ghats are large, insipid statues of British viceroys or Victoria, solid reminders of the imprint the British have left on India.

In the center of the city, on its busiest highways, men sleep on mats on the sidewalk. You get used to walking around them just as you get used to turning your car out around the various cows meandering on the main boulevards or munching away at the contents of trash cans. One sign at a street corner would be a wise admonition for Indian foreign policy: "No infiltration left."

Juxtaposed contradictions until you are dazed. A beautiful girl, dignified in dark magenta silk sari heavily embroidered in gold, riding sedately on the handle bars of a bicycle pedaled by a boy friend; an Indian in a white suit watching her through the window of his air-conditioned Cadillac. Beyond his car is a cart loaded with lead ingots; it has two huge wooden wheels, and two emaciated old Indians painfully drag it along.

Contradictions and color and dirt are with you always as you travel into central India, up through the dirt and religious fervor of Benares to the imperial city of Delhi, the old Delhi of history with its bazaars and its squalor, New Delhi of the British with its miles of parks and wide roads and spacious houses.

Old Delhi's Diljit bazaar swarms with people in as many costumes as your head is full of impressions. Girls walk by with cymbals on their ankles, making a lovely sound. You see turbans, trousers, pajamas, every sort of garb. The Punjabi dress is called a *salwar*, a loose kind of pajama with a long shirt coming down to the knees, and whenever you see a lady who looks as though she had borrowed her husband's pajama coat you know she is a Punjabi. Everything is sold here. The favorite drink, churned while you wait, is a curd made from buttermilk and costing about ten cents for an earthenware jarful. My guide, an Indian member of Parliament, whispered with a grin, "Don't touch it, it's full of germs. But, oh my, I will have to drink some. Oh, oh my, oh my!"

A ragged peddler sells sugar-cane juice which he mashes from the cane with a little roller like a clothes wringer. Near by, another man earns his living a harder way. He binds up his forearm as firmly as possible with a piece of old khaki linen and picks up a stout heavy stick of hard wood about three inches in diameter. Then, bracing himself, he takes the stick and beats himself on the tensed muscles until the hard wood cracks and breaks across his arm, which turns black and blue with hemorrhaged blood vessels. For this you pay him two rupees, about fifty cents, enough to feed his family for a day. Near him is a holy fakir with long needles jammed through his cheeks and a needle through his tongue; walking past the fakir, an elegant Brahmin woman with a pendent diamond, like an earring, dangling from the side of her nose; on the other side of the street, beyond a low Western brick wall, an English garden of larkspur, hollyhocks, roses, and masses of summer phlox; looming up in silhouette, the great Red Fort of Moslem India which once housed a peacock throne of solid gold.

And in our time the kaleidoscope of history has superimposed a new pattern, the Republic of India, on this diversity of mores, races, climates, languages, and peoples. Its existence compliments equally the aspirations of the Indian people for freedom and self-rule, and the rule of the British, who left behind them Indians sufficiently well trained to be able to create a working democracy. The Republic of India started out with nine partially self-governing provinces, four centrally administered provinces, and over five hundred princely states, plus the crushing problems of the partition with Pakistan and little experience in self-government.

In 1952, five years after independence, it held its first election. India had one of the most illiterate electorates in Asia. Over 80 per cent of her people could neither read nor write, but they flocked to the polls on foot, on crutches, by bullock, by automobile. In an election in which there was no violence and complete freedom of speech, over 107,000,000 men and women, the largest number ever to vote anywhere, proudly took up for themselves the power that formerly had been wielded by the kings of England and their viceroys.

The elections also tangibly proved to the 45,000,000 Untouchables of India that their country was now a democracy. In the old days, if even the shadow of an Untouchable fell across a high-caste Indian, he had to perform purification rites. During the campaign the Untouchables, in spite of assurances of constitutional equality, were afraid to come and join the rest of a village to hear an election speech; they sat carefully by themselves on the outskirts of the circle. But on polling day, for the first time in their lives, they stood in the same queue with high-caste Brahmins. Now when there is a political meeting the Untouchables sit with the rest of the town or village.

When the ballots were counted, thanks to the personality of Jawaharlal Nehru, heir to the prestige of Gandhi, the Congress Party had won an overwhelming victory and 74 per cent of the seats in Parliament. Unlike most of the other new republics of Asia, with their welters of splinter parties all dickering and conniving among themselves, India now has a single party which commands sufficient votes to put through an integrated legislative program. Even the tragedy of Partition had a lucky side result: it removed from the Indian Parliament the Moslem League, second largest party in pre-Partition India and the fervent enemy of the Hindu Congress Party.

But in dealing with the diversified complexities which are India, facts can be very misleading: every Indian "either" has an equally important "or." The Congress Party won most of the seats in Parliament; but, even with the great prestige of Nehru and with no rival candidate of equal stature and no rival major party challenging him, Nehru and his Congress Party could not win half the ballots. Only 45 per cent of the Indian electorate voted for them. Therefore, this first period of unified Congress Party rule and reform is only a prologue to the main play. India is another of the new nations which have been united on the negative aim of throwing out the colonial master. It remains to be seen whether she can develop a positive feeling of national unity.

There are two momentous questions about its future which cannot be answered today. First, in the long run, will a wretched India be able to withstand the blandishments of her own Communist Party? And second, with so many races, creeds, and castes and a background of national serfdom under one conqueror after another, will the free peoples of India be able to resist their own divisive forces?

So far the chief divisive danger comes from language. The British drew their provincial boundaries for administrative efficiency and cut across the main language units of the country. Today peoples who speak the same language want to become citizens of the same province, but although language is a powerful unifying force for those who speak the same dialect, a large language state tends to separate its citizens from all who cannot speak their tongue.

Down on the southern coast of India many people speak only the language called Telegu. Nehru has had to yield to the pressures of these people and give them a language state of their own as large as Thailand or Burma. Eleven districts have been separated from Madras State to create the new state of Andhra, seventh largest in India, with about twenty million Telegu-speaking people. Since they have been Indians only in the sense that they were ruled by whatever foreign conqueror controlled the whole subcontinent called India, it remains to be seen whether the citizens of this new state will gradually develop a group-consciousness as Indians or as Telegu-speaking Andhrans, set apart from the other hundreds of millions of Indians.

A greater danger that faces India is the long-range danger from her Communists. Today they are not a significant force; they polled only about 5 per cent of the votes in the 1952 elections. Nehru and his associates have no intention of becoming fellow travelers or tools of the Indian Communists. Repudiating violence as a way of life, the Congress Party is still ready to crack down on Communists and has already jailed some eight thousand.

The Communist Party of India is concentrating its efforts not on the peasants alone, but on the unemployed intellectuals, women as well as men. And so far education has been their best ally. The first Communist success in India has occurred down on the southwestern tip of the country in the state of Travancore-Cochin. This state, the size of New Hampshire, is the most Christian state in India and the most literate; where the average literacy in India is one out of six, in Travancore half the people can read and write.

In 1954 the Congress Party lost the Travancore state elections to the Socialists and the Communists. The election was a protest against the failure of the Congress Party to do enough fast enough to decrease economic want in the province. The victorious Communists, whose leaders are young, efficient, and able, do not plan to try to take over Travancore. They are pursuing a much more subtle policy, the popular-front tactics that have proved so successful in Europe. Wherever they can, they join with the well-intentioned, non-Communist parties of social protest like the Socialists, and then gradually their hard-core bloc infiltrates the youth organizations, the labor unions, and key government positions.

The secretary general of the Indian Communist Party, Ajoy Kumar Ghosh, and his followers have no hope of gobbling up India soon; it is too big a bite and Nehru is alive. But the Communists are going to work, via united fronts in weak provinces and via every possible divisive propaganda, from stirring up religious intolerance to demanding more language states. Their long-range hope is that the Congress Party will be able to make so little headway against the general misery of India that in the next general election, in 1957, it will lose control of Parliament.

But there is a deep influence in India that works against communism. It is Hinduism, that whole complex of faith and convictions and social behavior patterns which his religion has instilled in the Hindu peasant. A Westerner would assume that, as the Indian peasants move into today's world and realize that they need not starve and that their children need not die, they might turn to communism. So far they have not.

The tenets of communism violate basic religious tenets of Hinduism. Poverty, which communism is exploiting so well in so much of the rest of Asia, does not have the same meaning in India. Deep in their moral and religious background is a respect for poverty; no man of wealth has even been a national hero in India. And since their religion teaches that you live through a chain of reincarnations, whatever misery you are in today is only one turn on the wheel of your evolution.

Also, no creed more thoroughly violates the Hindu Gandhian doctrine of non-violence than communism does. Gandhi taught, and Hinduism teaches, that evil means will never bring a good end; this runs diametrically against the Communist teaching that any means and any violences are justifiable to achieve the end of the Communist state.

Communism urges workers and peasants to raise themselves from their miserable lot, but Hinduism teaches that such actions are irreligious; you go against the gods if you do not remain in your allotted caste, and if you try to change your lot the only result will be a worse karma in your next incarnation.

Hinduism is by all odds the most important force in India. We Westerners think of India's choices as communism or democracy. But democracy as such is not a leading protagonist. Hinduism is communism's greatest enemy and India's all-important force of gravitation, the centrifugal force, and the only one, which can hold together the gyrating planets and rings and moons of the disparate subcontinent.

Hinduism is as significant in politics as it is in religion, for it is the drive which powers India's nationalism. Every new republic of Asia won its independence because of a revolution against colonial rule. Westerners often call this Asian drive nationalism. It is, but not in the European sense which associates the word so closely with geography and race.

India's nationalism is far more social and religious, a way of life intuitively accepted by most Indians and all Hindus: in one word, Hinduism. The country's westernized leaders and its illiterate peasants are amazingly devout; essentially they believe alike and they share a usually unvoiced but unshakable conviction of superiority to other civilizations.

India's nationalism, now waxing hotter and more jingoistic, is a logical development of Hinduism and it seems likely India will become more isolationist and more intransigently neutral than it is now. But although Hinduism may trample on many of our pet notions, the Western democracies had better keep in mind that, since this same Hinduism violently rejects communism, the annoyances of Hindu superiority are far less troublesome than a Communist India would be.

Nehru, the Hindu, is thoroughly aware of the challenge and the peril as well as the power and the glory which are his as the all-powerful leader of India. He has commanded the necessary votes in Parliament to put through his sweeping reform bills and his revolutionary Five-Year Plan. And, Foreign Minister as well as Prime Minister, he is the unchallenged architect of the policy of Hindu neutralism which has the overwhelming support of his countrymen.

There is an Indian proverb: "One should keep oneself five yards from a carriage, ten yards from a horse, a hundred yards from an elephant, but the distance one must keep from a wicked man cannot be measured." Although the Indians will not say so in public, they consider both the Sino-Russian bloc and the American-European bloc wicked men. They intend to join neither.

The leaders of India view the existence of a powerful Communist China on their northern borders as the most compelling fact of present-day Asia. They push consistently for its admission to the UN; they refuse to endorse any acts that could be interpreted by China, or her friends, as inimical. They sent no troops into the Korean War and they refused to recognize any Chinese aggression in the Vietnamese war, which they labeled as a struggle between Asian nationalism and French colonialism. Unwilling by philosophy, and unable because of their economic weaknesses, to meet China's force with force, they persist in the public conviction that peaceful coexistence will reform the dynamics of communism. Therefore India and China embrace each other as friendly Asian neighbors, reaffirming their joint faith in the principles they wrote into their Tibetan treaty: "non-aggression, mutual respect, mutual benefit . . ."

But Delhi is no credulous Djakarta; in private, many Indian leaders quote the proverb, "He who lives on the riverbank must make peace with the crocodile," and they are exceedingly apprehensive of the long teeth of Peiping. If the next step of Communist infiltration undermines the Laos government or encroaches on India's close neighbor and protégé, Burma, India's attitude toward neutralism and the UN will undergo a considerable change.

India has always been a loyal supporter of the UN but values it as a world forum, imposing no military obligations on its members, offering a way to live in harmony with nations "whose religion, politics, and ways of thought are foreign to our own." The Indians view some American actions in the UN as almost immoral because, by our insisting that the UN settle disputes by general rules of justice, they believe we are embittering the relationships between the power blocs. When we point out to Asian neutrals like the Indians, the Burmese, or the Indonesians that we ask only what is fair, they answer, "Your obligation is to find a modus vivendi with your enemies." Abstract concepts of justice are not important to them. In the Hindu, Buddhist, and Chinese philosophies the moral man is the peacemaker, not the man who stands on his rights.

There are many factors, moral and political, selfish and idealistic, which, joined together, create Indian neutrality. There is the implicit spiritual superiority of Hinduism and its central conviction that, force being evil, its use will lead to evil results; thus neutrality becomes a species of passive resistance to the evils of the two force blocks in the world.

Also, India is a new nation, with little strength and few resources, rent by partitions, overburdened by illiteracy and disease and starvation. Delhi is very fond of drawing a parallel between its position and that of the infant United States in 1790 or 1850, when we were a confirmed neutral vis-à-vis European power blocs of that day. A more accurate parallel with India might be the United States' position in 1913 or 1939, when the British Navy protected us from aggression and Britain could not persuade us to abandon neutrality until we were attacked. Today, with our naval and air power balancing out China and Russia, we in turn will not be able to reason with India any more successfully than Britain could with us.

Some well-meaning friends of India believe that if a war came India would be on our side. That is wishful thinking. The dreams of India's leaders for a better life for their people would have to be abandoned if their country, which already imports food and painfully supports a small army, should have to carry the burdens of modern war. India would come into a war only if forced in. Her borders join those of Russia and China for twelve hundred miles. If an aggression is committed upon them, she would not stay on the sidelines; otherwise she will remain neutral. Should war come and the West be winning, neutrality would have paid off in saved Indian lives and won Indian exports; if we should be losing, all the more reason not to have been on the losing side.

But the Indian leaders recognize the terrible danger to the world and to themselves from a world war with hydrogen and biological weapons. Utilizing their position as neutrals, they will continue, snubbed or unsnubbed, to do everything they can to find some negotiable common ground to reduce the absolute danger of civilization's destruction.

There is also a world power factor in India's neutrality. The second largest nation in the world, she has ambitions to become the third focus in that world and the arbiter of all Asia. She hopes gradually to attract all the smaller nations of Asia into her orbit through the appeals of peace and Asia for the Asians. Next, she would extend this Asian entente to the underprivileged nations of Africa. Holding the balance of power in Asia and commanding so many votes in the UN, India, the third focus, would become an effective influence for world peace and persuade the other two blocs to give more aid to the non-white, underdeveloped nations.

Indians believe that if they cannot create this third focus, communism will slowly absorb the non-white world. Be that as it may, nations go where they benefit most, and India, underdeveloped herself, has not the industry, wealth, and extra goods to shore up or raise up the economies of the countries she would like to attract to her third force.

But since India is always a contradiction, in her foreign policy, too, there is bound to be paradox. Her neutrality, her non-violence, her reasonableness, her emphasis upon mediation as a method of settling disputes—all these go by the board when Pakistan is brought up. The intensity of the hatred between the nations of India and Pakistan is appalling. Partition was a tragedy for both. Pakistan was left with all the jute and no jute mills; India was left with the jute mills and no jute; Pakistan, with raw cotton and no textiles; India, with textiles and little cotton. Each must bear unnecessarily heavy defense budgets because of fear of the other.

In little things and big things the two neighbors distort each other's position. One of the leading plane lines, Indian National Airways, gives out fans to its passengers. On the fans is a map of the cities to which the air line flies. Karachi, the chief port of West Pakistan, is on the Arabian Sea; but on this fan map it is placed about a hundred miles inland. At the time I planned to fly from Delhi to Lahore, the ancient city of Pakistan, there was some rioting there. The Pakistani said it was perfectly safe to come, but the Indian plane refused to fly because "it's too dangerous, there may be a revolution tomorrow." Conversely, the last afternoon I was in Delhi I watched a small student demonstration in Gloucester Square; the next morning, in Karachi, I read headlines about "Major Riots in Bharat," Bharat being the Hindi name Pakistani use for India.

The man who is responsible for India's policies, internal and international, is her Prime Minister, Jawaharlal Nehru, one of the most complex leaders in the world. A high-caste Brahmin and a leader in the revolution against Britain, an Indian trained in Western universities, Nehru is the most valuable living Asian to the West. His words, his actions, and his leadership are the most powerful forces for stability on the Indian scene.

The approaches to the Prime Minister's office in Delhi's Parliament Building are imposing. Outside, a great pile of red sandstone circled with classic columns; inside, the Parliament Building has long wide corridors handsomely paneled in polished wood. In front of the doors of the important offices are bearers in special Indian costumes: immaculate white trousers, white turbans, and long red coats down to their knees and heavily embroidered in gold. Into the wide gold sashes of their tunics are stuck heavy gold daggers. While I was waiting in Nehru's anteroom, his secretary rang a bell. One of these men strode in with magnificent bearing, stood in front of the secretary, reached into his sash beside his ornate dagger, and brought out a folder of American matches to light the secretary's cigarette.

The westernized offices of most of the important statesmen of Asia look as if they had been furnished with secondhand prewar modern furniture. In Nehru's waiting room there was an old red carpet, light yellow wood walls, a couple of indifferent photographs of old Indian carvings not well framed, two or three overstuffed chairs and a sofa in ugly blue brocade shot with pink; green brocade drapes at the windows and doors, two huge electric bulbs with ugly glass shades hanging by wires from the ceiling, a couple of unmatched wooden chairs, a wooden desk, and a Victorian hatrack.

About twenty feet from the Prime Minister's reception room, across a green-turfed sunny inner court, is his private entrance into the lower house of Parliament, the House of the People. Suddenly, here in a part of the world where no one hurries, that door burst open and a slight figure in a long buttoned coat strode across the lawn. His screen door opened, his sandals slapped across the stone floor, and his secretary in the waiting room sprang to the interoffice phone just in time to answer Nehru's ring. In less than forty seconds the Prime Minister had left Parliament and arrived for his first appointment.

When I was ushered into Nehru's office, a large quiet room furnished in plain blue with a plain polished desk and one picture of Gandhi on the wall, I expected to meet a typical jittery, overworked head of state. Nehru was clad all in white, and his hair is snow-white. His face is as flexible as an actor's, always reacting to his fast switches in mood. His motions have an easy, graceful flow and his voice is poised and relaxed, not used for effect but as an instrument to express his thoughts.

The thing you remember most about him is his eyes. They are large, dark, and liquid, and when he is thinking of some question he has been asked, he gazes into a remote distance, not as if he were self-hypnotized, but searchingly. The adjective that best describes him is "patrician," for he has the fine bones and delicate features of the high-caste Brahmins, who in the civilizations of India have always been the priests and the thinkers.

Nehru is often represented as a Hamlet sicklied o'er with the contradictions of East and West, caught between them and unable to decide to which he belongs. He is not. He is thoroughly Hindu, thoroughly relaxed in his own set of values. Some people see him caught between the antithetical values of communism and the free world. He sees his civilization as superior to either of these cruder and more barbaric powers; wisdom flows in one direction only, down from India to the Russians and the Chinese, the Americans and the Europeans.

Reaching out beyond the immediate for broader frames of reference, Nehru looks for states of mind, not events, to explain the present world situation. He believes that most of the troubles in the world arise from fear of someone else: "Associate yourself with a man, no longer will you be afraid." That does not mean Nehru underrates the dangerous consequences of existing fears: "Today the world is full of apprehension, fear, and dislike. They govern events. If we can reduce that bad psychology we will make a great gain. If only we could have some assurance of peace for the next ten or fifteen years, there would be a number of adjustments which could lead to permanent peace. But for the moment one lives from hand to mouth with danger."

Meantime he knows where he wants India to go and he is leading her forward. With his death will come India's testing period. The men most likely to succeed him are about his age, in their late sixties. This whole set of men who rule India are dedicated patriots, carrying a crushing sixteen-hour-a-day burden of responsibility. And they are all products of the period of British rule, trained and inculcated by British overseers or in British universities. It remains to be seen whether the educational and social system of the Republic of India will be able to produce comparable leaders. The same question waits to be answered at each layer down through the British-created Indian Civil Service, for a few people must do all leading and ruling in this new democracy.

Western efficiency does not exist among the common people; they must depend on the genius of a Nehru and the British-educated group which serves with him.

No country in Asia has a more cumbersome bureaucracy than India; like Indonesia, she has preserved many of the worst features of a nineteenth-century colonial system. Customs and immigration are small cogs in the over-all operation of a government machine, but they are revealing ones and, incidentally, Asians find many of our American immigration officials benighted and inefficient. In India the customs officials push their pens courteously but interminably. Much of this can be blamed on the old colonial system. The British trained the Indians when in the least doubt to refer everything back up the echelons. Today, not only does the petty Indian bureaucrat go on performing as he was taught, but the Indian cabinet officer at the top seems to demand the same rigid subservience his British predecessor enjoyed. Result: interminable red tape and unbelievable time wasting.

When you enter most countries by air you receive long forms to fill in while you are still on the plane, and then officials at the airport double-check your answers. When you arrive by plane in India, it takes longer to get through these details than anywhere else in the world, even longer than in Indonesia. Different men at different desks, writing in languages with which they are not too familiar, laboriously fill in the long forms for Westerners, one after another writing in your passport number, misspelling your name, and correcting it over and over again. Each official enters this data in similar ledgers. A detail, but typical of the way the wheels of the Indian Government revolve.

I brought my tape recorders to India under exactly the same arrangements I had made with twelve other Asian governments, but, after receiving assurances from Delhi and from the Indian Embassy in Washington that I would have no trouble bringing them in, India gave me a far worse time than all the other countries put together. The Indian Customs refused to allow the tape recorders in the country for two weeks without a very high duty paid in advance. After several days of exasperated telephoning from Calcutta to Delhi, the Indian Information Ministry finally forced through a clearance from the Central Customs office. But Calcutta did not receive the official release, and so I had to start over again.

Finally, the head of the Indian customs in Delhi telephoned to the director of the Calcutta customhouse and ordered him to release my tape recorders into my custody. The Calcutta director hung up and said, "I haven't any instructions in writing. He might die, and then how could I justify having released the recorders to you?"

At the end of my visit to India I had to have my visa extended forty-eight hours in order to talk with Prime Minister Nehru. To get this visa extension took me two and a half hours, three taxis, forms signed and witnessed by at least ten different people, plus—and without the plus, heaven knows how long it would have taken—a couple of calls to Nehru's private secretary.

Such is the daily operating inflexibility of the Indian administrative machine. If decisions on other details involved in the governing of 370,000,000 people scattered over a subcontinent are as difficult to pass from a cabinet minister to a small bureaucrat halfway across India, and if they are administered with such slavish punctilio, it is hard to see how enough can be accomplished soon enough. The words "soon" and "enough" have little meaning for the Indians. As one of the MPs said, "In the eyes of government, years do not matter and months do not occur." But with communism setting itself up as a competing system to India's government, "soon" and "enough" have great meaning for us who are anxiously watching from the West.

In the long run, whether or not India's democratic government can become efficient enough to run this vast country depends on how fast and how far the people will become westernized. Up to now India has not gone through this process. Not more than 1 or 2 per cent, the elite, have become acquainted with Western values. Yet even this is a tremendous accomplishment in a country like India. Only fifty years ago, when a high-caste Brahmin returned from a trip to the West he had to go through lengthy religious ceremonies to erase the pollution of his visit.

Today these shibboleths of the past are fast disappearing from the upper classes of the cities, and they in turn are bound to lead the next lower social stratum in the same direction, and so on, ad peasantum. In many parts of the world the twentieth century is closer than we realize. India has also undergone a social revolution which has opened up a new life for the young people in the cities; in Delhi or Bombay or Madras the magazines angle many articles toward the "girl in the white sari," the emancipated career girl who goes off to work every day dressed in her white sari. This never would have been possible a few years ago.

But the old ways are still followed by most of the country, and family obligations are still the chief loyalties in this ancient land. A short while ago a prominent high-class Brahmin family in Bombay had a son who was about to go to England to school. The mother wanted her son to marry a girl of his own caste before he left because "if he goes to England unmarried he may bring back a white wife, which would never do here. Or when he comes back he may be so changed that he selects a wife who would not feel loyalty to us but only to him. He must marry now, for this way we will have a daughter-in-law."

This land of India, one of the first pockets of civilization in the primitive world, was old when the Filipinos and the Thais and the Japanese were young. Geologically, too, its central plains are old, with small eroded bits of hills standing a few dozen feet high above the flat landscape, and slow, silt-filled meandering rivers. The countryside is a little like western Nebraska or Texas or Arizona, but with goats everywhere, and often a group of monkeys silhouetted against the sky.

The land, fertile when irrigated, looks farmed to exhaustion, for here on the central plains the earth is a light-colored dun gray with none of the black, rich-earth look of Southeast Asia. The dun-colored huts seem to have sat there for centuries and often they lean up against the ruins of some old Mogul or Persian building. Most of them are of an adobe clay and the ever-present cow dung. In India, floors or walls of a peasant's hut may be made of dung, and in any village you can watch old women crouching around a dung pile, molding flat round slabs, their fuel for warmth or cooking. There is almost no wocd anywhere on these central plains, and paper is exorbitantly expensive for the peasants.

Through the country, highways are well cared for, but when traveling by car across India you must allow extra time spent at train crossings, for the gatekeepers lower their barriers across the road fifteen minutes or half an hour before a train is due to pass. No one minds, for Indians are used to waiting by the hour or by the day for everything. Southeast Asians resent Western attempts to rush them and they go in the opposite way, but the Indians have a purely negative approach; they do not seem to react against your efforts to rush them, they just go on as they were, or rather they do not go on.

Water is precious in much of India, and the well is the chief gathering place in the village. For sanitation the government has built six-foot-high concrete platforms around the wells and the people cling with their toes to the rims of these platforms, washing or bathing themselves as they have for thousands of years. The rigid system of India's villages has changed little, and the villagers, 80 per cent of the Indians, have never learned to function together above the level of the joint family or the small community. Therefore, it is hard for them to understand an impersonal institution. A businessman told me he envied our big department stores of the West, and when I asked him why, he said, "We can't get enough honest men to run a good department store." And as for the government, "Every minister and everyone else is preparing his son for a good job in the government." But this does not indicate a different sort of people; it is an example of a different period of history. Ancient Greece and Rome were like much of Asia today, countries which responded not as unified national units to the world around them, but as patriarchal joint families with their chief loyalties to their own small groups and very little to the state; even in the flowering of Greece there was little larger community loyalty beyond the extended family group called the city-state.

In the Indian village the principal loyalty is not even to the whole village but to your own caste, for it is as a member of a particular caste that you find your place and responsibilities. By the Hindu rules of religion as well as society you live in that caste from birth to death and you do not expect to marry outside of it. The system is so tightly put together that it is even difficult to marry someone of your own caste who lives in another province. When a high-caste Brahmin guitarist in Delhi fell in love with a high-caste Brahmin singer in the nearby United Provinces, although both were Brahmins of high caste and both musicians, there was a huge uproar in their families because "your wife's ways will differ so much from ours."

But the Indian caste system is not the unadulterated evil so many Americans picture it. Each caste has clearly defined privileges as well as restrictions, and the system works to reduce social frictions. Since each man's position is determined at birth, there is no point in struggling to better himself socially, so he can relax and enjoy his own stable position. Having been accustomed from birth to living side by side with other castes who are almost as remote from him as foreigners, the Indian is automatically conditioned in social coexistence. Reinforce this with the religious teaching that there is no absolute good or evil, and you can begin to see why there has been so little intolerance in the Indian social system.

A Parsee is a fire worshiper, a materialist, and a trader, while a Hindu rejects all three values; yet they could live side by side in the same village without friction, each recognizing that the other has the right, without criticism or evangelization, to go his own way, practice his own customs, and believe in his own gods. Indian life is based on this mutual respect. It has had to be in order to avoid the consequences of overpopulation.

Indians say, "The only way we can work together is to agree; if we cannot, then we must agree anyway, agree to respect each other." Thus India becomes a melting pot in the sense we of the evangelizing West do not know, and the Indians believe much of the frictions of Western life would be eliminated if we would grant others this right of coexistence.

The concept of coexistence is both a strength and a weakness, for it prevents Indians from flying at each other's throats, but it is another passive virtue. It does not give them the mutual understanding which in turn would provide the basis for working together in larger groups. The Indians have the negative ability to allow political or social groups to go their way. They have not developed the deeper understanding and sympathy which come from positive acceptance of those around you. It is precisely because Americans positively and actively accept other men of other castes, economic and social, that we have been able to work out our system of mass production and nationwide co-operation.

Because of their gentleness, their courtesy, and their indirection so characteristic of Asians, we too often assume that they admire us more than they do. In most of Asia it is the inferiority feelings of once colonial peoples that create the antagonisms toward Americans, but Indians do not seem to have much of an inferiority complex. When they write of their music, they explain why Westerners rarely like it: "If melody of this kind sounds exotic to the Western ear, it is probably because the West has lost the sense of pure melody." If the Hindu Indians suffer from any complex, although it may be the result of a deeper and inverted inferiority, it appears as a superiority complex.

Yet Indians do not reject; they only turn away from. Through the centuries they have never reacted against any conqueror; they are adjusted to being conquered. "Supine," "passive," and "feminine" in all their good and bad senses are words that describe the Indian civilization. Virile conqueror after virile conqueror has attacked her; the Aryan or the Greek, the Arab or the Mongol, the Persian or the British. She has passively accepted their embraces and borne them children, the long line of Indian civilizations. And femalewise, India has taken unto herself some of the best of each of her spouses.

The building that Westerners consider the very essence of India is a perfect symbol of this. The incomparable Taj Mahal has nothing to do with the chief culture of India, the Hindu values; it was not built of typical Indian materials nor designed according to Hindu

Indian architectural rules nor built by a Hindu. A Moslem creation, designed by a descendant of Genghis Khan, and then placed on the flat plains of central India, it remains a geographical accident, but an artistic miracle.

Traveling around the world, you are disappointed by a great many famous monuments whose photographs often display more beauty than the originals possess. But seeing cannot stale and pictures cannot convey the mirage of unbelievable loveliness which is the Taj Mahal. Approaching it through the dust of Agra and the blinding harsh midday sun of India, you come through a ponderous arch of red sandstone, and suddenly the Taj Mahal is in front of you, floating amid its pools and its gardens.

Everyone in the West has seen pictures of the stately rows of evergreens and the long rectangular pools of limpid water and the white marble paths that lead your eyes to the Taj Mahal. But if you have not been there, you do not realize that this is surrounded by high trees and a high wall. And you do not realize that the green of the grass and the trees is something you seldom see on the sere plains of central India. The pure white of the Taj Mahal is unique. Because of dirt, dust, economics, and lack of interest in cleanliness, almost nothing in India is white. Light clothes are unbleached cream-colored cotton, and the buildings are of red brick or dun adobe, or red or yellow sandstone. But the Taj Mahal is white, white marble blazing in the midday sun.

And photographs have not shown you that on each side of the eight-sided building with its domes and its four slender minarets is a smaller building of red sandstone, complementary in designs and motif to the Taj itself, balancing and making even more ethereal the central building which Shah Jehan raised as a tomb for his beloved wife, Mumtaz Mahal, the Beauty of the Palace. The little building on the left of the Taj was to be a mosque in which continuous Moslem services were to be held for Mumtaz, and its twin on the right was to be a guest house for the devout and learned Moslems who were to come to Agra for the services.

Perhaps pictures do not capture the beauty of this building because they cannot show its three-dimensional symmetry. No flat picture could convey the balance of shapes and sizes and planes that creates the serenity of the Taj Mahal, the Crown of the Palace. Take a good-sized picture of the Taj and with your hand block out any small piece or pieces of the building, a minaret, or one of the smaller domes, or the high marble foundation upon which the building stands; instantaneously the design will fall out of balance. Take out the tiny spire at the top of the central dome, and the dome is too big; take out a minaret, and the building is squat. Every part of the Taj Mahal works and pulls against every other part, creating the perfectly balanced tension of true symmetry.

Every moment of the day or night the shadows of the Taj present fresh beauty: blazing in the midday sun, dying away into the dusk, faintly silhouetted against the evening sky with its darker reflection in the long pool, and finally, as the rim of the full moon slowly rises above the trees. Shah Jehan, a great architect in his own right, placed the Taj on a plateau high above a river and oriented it so that the sun and moon would rise and fall in a long sweeping arc across the width of the buildings.

In contrast to the teeming ornateness of Hindu sculpture, everything inside the Taj Mahal is white marble, cool and plain. Lining the octagonal gallery around the central hall are its only ornaments, large plaques of marble which were carved by Chinese artists into single formalized flowers, a tiger lily or a lotus ready to bloom. In the center of the building under the high arched dome, a marble screen about six feet high and over four inches thick encloses the tomb area. The tons of marble have been chiseled out to leave only a delicate, simple filigree design. Inside the screen are the replicas of the tombs of Shah Jehan and his Beauty of the Palace. They are plain white sarcophagi simply inlaid with bits of dark orange and green and yellow marble in designs of columbines and chrysanthemums and poppies. This work was done by some Italian artists the Shah imported, yet, Chinese or Italian, the same cool, clean classical feeling is carried out in every detail.

The central dome of the Taj is eighty feet high, and when you stand under it an attendant gives a single mourning cry which falls away in the hollowness of the room, and then from the top of this five-thousand-ton edifice, which took twenty years to build, the cry suddenly reverberates back to you in soft overlapping echoes, first from one part of the dome and then from another.

Down in a low crypt under the floor of the central gallery are the real tombs of Jehan and Mumtaz. He had planned originally to build a tomb of his own on the other side of the river, a "palace like the white Taj but of black marble and connected by an arched bridge of marble." It is one of the ironies of history that the son who caused

Mumtaz' death when she was giving birth to him should grow up, seize the empire from his father, and imprison him before Shah Jehan could build his own black marble tomb.

Before I went away from the vaulted room of the Taj Mahal I left a tiny candle burning on the replica of Mumtaz' tomb. When I had walked the hundreds of feet down past the long pools and marble terraces I came again into the high red sandstone arch of the entrance building. In the distance the Taj Mahal shimmered under the moon, and in its vaulted central arch was the smaller arch of the tomb room, and in the middle of that arch my tiny candle flickered. And I thought of the description Tagore had given to the Taj Mahal, a description only an Indian could have conceived: "A drop of tear on the cheek of time."

The real India, the India of the three hundred million people who follow the Hindu religion, ethics, and culture, is not comprehensible to Western and Christian values as is the Moslem Taj. Hinduism is no bridge between East and West. The Hindu religion is a religion of complete acceptance, not only of good but of evil, while our Western religion, like that of Islam, is exclusive, leaving out or rejecting what it does not believe is good. The attitude of Hinduism to sex is an example of this acceptance.

The sculptured gods in the temples of South India shock all but the most sexually realistic and anthropologically wise Westerners. Hindu gods and goddesses are portrayed in stone explicitly enjoying the pleasures of the flesh. These pictures, to Hindus, are erotic but never pornographic. All forms of life, including sexual activity, are manifestations of God and His creativity. Every Hindu god or goddess is married; there are no bachelors and no virgins. One of the manifestations of the Lord Siva is as a phallus, and the President of India presides at festivals worshiping that stone manifestation.

Although the Hindus thus take certain aspects of the flesh in their stride, renunciation of the flesh is one of Hinduism's basic teachings. The Hindu conviction that life is an illusion enables them to move unperturbed through the unlovely sides of life; by supine acceptance of the ugliness of the world you learn to withdraw from its material distractions and so achieve spiritual equanimity.

Here again the passive side of Hinduism comes out: you do not get excited about or react against, you relax and you ignore. The contemplative Indian goes further. In one of the great Indian poems, the *Bhagavad-Gita*, the hero poses this problem to the god Krishna: If I act, evil may be the result, so shall I act? And Krishna replies that the good is not to act at all. Krishna's teachings lead Hindus to their doctrine of non-violence, the thesis of not breaking out of a trap but enduring it until it fades away. Emotionally you can do this only if you practice *moksha*, putting behind you all material things and the violences that go with them.

But moksha does not necessarily jibe with the twentieth-century material improvements. India's westernized leaders, with the aid of hundreds of millions of American dollars, are trying to build a twentieth-century technology; but we cannot assume that old India is convinced that these material improvements are worth the profound struggles they require. The Horatio Alger concept would be utterly unintelligible to an Indian.

It is lucky for Indians that they have believed in withdrawing from the flesh and its needs, for in few countries in the world have people had as many intolerable material conditions to ignore as here. The problem of moving forward from substarvation to medium starvation is, for India, an enormous one. To begin with, like most of the other backward countries of the world, she faces the deadly specter of overpopulation. But even if her population should be held at present levels, the problem is appalling.

Statistics speak for themselves: over 80 per cent illiteracy, less than one doctor per ten thousand patients, dozens of diseases which kill hundreds of thousands of people a year, one of the highest infant mortality rates in the world, twenty-five dollars' worth of capital equipment for each Indian as compared with over fifteen hundred dollars' worth for each American, a population density six times that of the United States. In any other country but passively resistant, supine India, such facts of life would long ago have resulted in bloody revolution.

Nehru and his associates have mapped out a five-year plan of sweeping state socialist action to raise their prostrate nation. But, unlike the grandiose and unrealistic national plans of the Indonesians and the Burmese, the Indian plan has been blueprinted by men who know how economic forces operate. One of the greatest tributes to English training is the appreciation for private enterprise in today's India. Unlike the rest of Southeast Asia, India's stores and businesses are run by the people of the country, not foreigners. Whatever his religious ideals are about material things, the Indian has learned to develop an accountant's eye for an extra penny.

India has the closest thing to a Western economic machine south of the Philippines. She has the largest steel mills and the second largest industrial system in Asia. She has a movie industry second only to Hollywood, and India's private producers make commercial films and sell them to private theater owners.

The leaders of the government of India have been trained in economics at the best British universities; in Parliament and throughout the country they are backed by millions of private shopkeepers who also understand the mechanics of the market place. This gives India a tremendous advantage over her neighbors in Southeast Asia, who have the same economic wishes she has and at least as large a raw-material potential but who have no understanding of how the economic wheels go around. Her Five-Year Plan is based on technical know-how and what can be achieved, not on political rhetoric and what they would like to accomplish. Burma announces she will double her national income in eight years; India hopes she may be able to raise her income as much as 10 or 11 per cent in five years. The Burmese chase the will-o'-the-wisp of industrial production instead of raising rice production; India's plan will only double pig-iron production in the next five years, but it will increase by at least ten times the production of agricultural fertilizers. Urgently as she needs hospital beds, the plan concentrates on first things first; it provides for only a 17 per cent increase in hospital beds, but it will increase by at least 75 per cent the number of training schools for doctors and nurses.

India understands how invaluable a help private enterprise, with its great storehouses of capital and know-how, can be to a young nation. Instead of mistrusting foreign capitalism, she is gambling the success of her all-important Five-Year Plan on foreign financial aid. Without billions from abroad she cannot carry it through, and she is counting on getting about 25 per cent of the money from the United States.

The plan covers every aspect of Indian life: industrial development, trade development, research programs for industry and agriculture, hospitals, social services, universities. But the primary emphases are on village rehabilitation and higher food production. Food is the most urgent need of India. Her land is even less productive than that of China.

Nobody has ever counted the villages of India; there are well over half a million of them, connected to the outside world only by bullock trails. Over 80 per cent of the people live in these villages, and 75 per cent of them work in agriculture. Sixty per cent farm less than two acres and 50 per cent are sharecroppers working for absentee landlords, often at exorbitant rental fees—up to 50 or 75 per cent of their crops—and so land-reform laws were one of the first acts of the Nehru administration.

But, whoever owns the land, a great deal more food must be raised on it. At this point the national plan goes to work on a hundred different fronts. First of all, the monsoon land of India has had a history of drought upon drought. Therefore, she plans to construct dams to irrigate her droughtland and turn it into food-producing areas. One dam, the Bhakra-Nangal Dam, larger than the Grand Coulee, will be built at the foot of the Himalayas and will irrigate more than six and a half million acres in the driest part of the country.

The principal attack of the Five-Year Plan upon India's problems is at the village level. Supported by direct aid and planning assistance from private and public American institutions, India has launched the most comprehensive and dramatic community-development program in the history of the world, its Community Development Projects, which include agriculture, sanitation, health, diet, and cottage industries. First by pilot-plant experiments, next in selected areas which have already embraced thirty-nine thousand villages, and then finally extending over the entire subcontinent, India plans to educate her villages out of feudal times and into modern times. To do the educating, the plan employs radio, traveling caravans, films, mobile stages for instructive dramatic productions, exhibitions, and teams of all kinds of specialists.

When you talk to the men who run the plan, their emphasis again is not on the big and the glittering, but on the small. They tell you about the work being done to show the villagers how to construct brick kilns so they can have better housing; they demonstrate how a very small amount of money invested in digging a deeper village well or a channel to bring water from canals already existing can raise crop yields. They show you the manure piles lying out in the sun in most villages; if pits were dug for the manure, its nitrogen would not evaporate, and if such better use could be made of all the compost heaps of India, this seemingly trivial improvement could increase food production by almost 10 per cent. So simple, all you have to do is teach people how; so difficult when you have three hundred million illiterate peasants to teach.

The Five-Year Plan will determine whether India drifts into more misery and chaos. However, its success or failure has even broader connotations for the free world. We talk about how valuable India would be in a war with China. This is questionable; she could easily be more of a liability than an asset. In cold fact, India is more important to us if there is not a war than if there is one. We in the West think of the choice in the world today as between the United States and Russia. This is not the way Asians see it; for most of them, the choice seems to be between China and India.

Both civilizations are of great antiquity and possess great prestige in Asia; both are peasant civilizations; in their very different ways both are trying to raise the economic lot of vast and wretched populations. Asia is watching to see which will do the better job. If India can develop free and democratic state socialism that works, the true Asian antidote to communism will have been found. If India fails and turns to communism, it is difficult to visualize any of Asia south of the Philippines holding out against a Sino-Indian bloc. Then Asia will be lost and a new and infinitely perilous future will be faced by the democracies.

The odds are now roughly 60–40 in our favor, and if we are to avoid a debacle greater than the loss of China, we are going to have to give, and give generously, to help a neutral India win this struggle. It will cost us billions. And we shall have to give the money, not because the Indians will love us afterward; they will not. We must give it as a form of life insurance for our own children.

We are going to have to continue to show Asians, practically and socially, how our system pays off better than communism. This means the more powerful we are the more we must give. When our granaries are bulging with wheat and the Indians are starving and we do not give them some of that wheat, the Communists distribute a cartoon entitled "Sermon on the Mount," showing a starving Indian peasant with a dying baby in her arms standing at the foot of a mountain of U.S. wheat, on top of which a fat Uncle Sam sits smoking a cigar and saying, "You don't get anything for nothing in this world, pal."

If we will not give enough and do our part, we lose India. If we will do what we can afford to, and with consideration and integrity, we have a good chance of winning, for in one sense time is on our side in the struggle for India and for Asia. Time is needed for these new nations to learn to govern themselves, and time is needed for the uncommitted and the partially committed of Asia to see for themselves how the Russian and Chinese systems really work out. Gradually, if they can gain time, these nations may become adjusted to us and to the twentieth century.

Yet in a terrible way, through man's deepest drive, time works for the Communists and against us. Implacably, inescapably, every hour of every day, communism's best ally grows a little more powerful. And it is a threat to which, so far, we have not even tried to find an answer.

It is population growth, the fact that men and women beget children, that in Asia they beget more children than food can be found for.

In the past, death alone has saved the world from death. Today Western technology is staying death's hand and keeping alive in Asia more and more people to consume less and less.

In India, barely able to keep above starvation today, there will be four hundred million people by 1960 and five hundred million by 1985. This increase will not be the result of special Eastern zest, for Asia is not increasing its population as fast as the West, and no country in Asia, including India, has increased its population as fast as the United States. But Americans have plenty of land and food. India has neither. As in the rest of Asia, her population is far ahead of production.

The most alarming fact about today's Asia is not that it is poor and starving but that, based upon actuarial figures, it is going to be poorer and more starving tomorrow in spite of anything and everything the West can do. Every twelve months the equivalent of an Indo-China is added to the world's population. Each day there are seventy thousand more mouths to be fed than the day before, most of them in Asia.

From 1938 to 1950 the populations of South and Southeast Asia went up 15 per cent, but cereal production, their main foodstuff, went up only 4 per cent. Or, put another way, in spite of all the money and all the effort which these countries and the West have together invested in Asia, starvation is gaining, for in 1954 only 86 per cent as much food was available to an Asian as in 1938.

Most of the countries of Asia are ignoring this statistic, but India is facing up to her problem. We in the West read about the two hundred million cattle of India that because of Hindu teachings cannot be killed for food. And we cite this as an example of India's stubborn refusal to face facts. But since Hinduism imposes no religious restrictions on birth control, India is able to tackle her population problem directly. Large and influential groups in the country are pushing for birth-control laws, and the government has set up a research program to find cheap contraceptives for its peasants.

The West must face the fact that every health measure we take in the Far East can be a potential Frankenstein. It creates more people to eat the food there is, to starve on it, and to begin to wonder whether communism might not fill their bellies better.

The real handwriting on the wall of the free world is the rising curve of babies who live and the descending curve of adults who die at an early age.

Since Western science has decreased the dynamics of death, ours is the responsibility for supplying some other counterbalance to the consequences of overpopulation. There are only two alternatives to too many people and too little food: less people or more food. The discovery by Western science of a really cheap contraceptive for the peasants of the Far East would do more to help the health and welfare of Asia than billions upon billions spent any other way. And it would do more to stop the spread of communism.

If this violates the basic religious convictions of the West, then we must face up to a harder job: finding immediately more food for Asia. What we can spare from what we grow is not enough. It will take synthetics, by the billions of tons, supplied every year, to keep Asia alive. This we should be able to accomplish if we are determined. An international program to find synthetic foods, costing as much as the atomic-energy program, could surely discover the answer to our problem.

This is a very costly solution. Worse, it is a very unlikely solution. But those who cannot countenance the easier material and scientific method of birth control had better push with spirited fervor for the much more difficult alternative of food synthetics. Otherwise, no matter what India does and no matter what the other countries of Asia do, there can be no long-range stability for them. And no long-range safety for us.

IF FAITH REMAINS:

Pakistan

Pakistan, the farthest west of the brave new countries of Asia, became a nation for an entirely different reason from any the world has seen. In the other republics of Asia, their unity, if any, is a nationalism grounded on hatred of colonial masters; Pakistan's unity is that of religion. It came into being against every tenet of reason or practicality, and it cannot endure unless the ideals of a Moslem state are at least as important to its 76,000,000 people as language, climate, and economics.

Most people can name the five largest nations in the world: China with 500,000,000, India with 370,000,000, Russia with 200,000,000, the United States with 160,000,000, and Japan with more than 86,000,000. Few people realize that the sixth and seventh largest countries are also in Asia, and they are also the two largest Moslem nations in the world. Indonesia with almost 80,000,000, and Pakistan with more than 76,000,000.

But Indonesia is weak and confused, Marxist and neutralist, anti-white and anti-capitalistic, while Pakistan has one of the finest armies in Asia, is pro-capitalistic and a friend and ally of the United States. One of the two largest Moslem nations in the world, it is already a leader in the Moslem world. Therefore, Pakistan can be a valuable ally of the free world. It is an ally against communism and it is an ally for better international understanding because it can serve as a bridge between the Christian world of the Western democracies and the crescent world of the Moslems which flings its long arc across the Indian Ocean from Indonesia to North Africa.

The two parts of the subcontinent, Pakistan and India, can be characterized by the two elements in Chinese philosophy, the *yang*, or masculine element, and the *yin,* or feminine element; Pakistan is forceful where India is philosophical, determined where it is lackadaisical, intolerant where it is patient.

Pakistan is not really one nation but two countries separated by the entire twelve-hundred-mile width of its worst enemy and old allegiance, India. When Partition came in 1947, two large and wholly non-contiguous pieces of Moslem India formed the new religious state of Pakistan. One piece is East Pakistan, as far east as you can go in India, reaching up between India's Bengal Province and Burma. The other is West Pakistan, as far west as you can go in India, looking south onto the Arabian Sea, west onto Iran and Afghanistan, and north past Kashmir to the Khyber Pass, Russia, and China. Thus Pakistan has one foot in each of the huge and otherwise unconnected geographies of the Middle East and the Far East.

This is a fact of usefulness to the West, but to the Pakistani it is an unending national headache and ominous threat. Unless you placed half of Pakistan on the Arctic Circle and the other half on the Amazon River, it would be impossible to find two sections of the world more dissimilar than the halves of Pakistan. Heat and the Moslem faith are literally all this nation have in common. The 42,000,000 people of East Pakistan speak Bengali and live in a hot, humid, swampy land which gets from fifty to two hundred inches of rain every year. There are about a thousand Bengalis jammed in every steaming square mile of their province. The 34,000,000 people of West Pakistan speak Urdu and live in a hot, dry desert. They are spread out from three to a hundred per square mile.

East Pakistan, on the Ganges and Brahmaputra rivers, with limitless swamps, plantations, palm trees, heat haze, and mosquitoes, grows rice, tea, and the vegetable gold of Pakistan, jute; its people are Southeast Asians, eating rice, looking and acting like Burmese or Thais. West Pakistan, on the Indus River, with rugged mountains, sprawling plains, and barren deserts, sits astride the great caravan routes from East to West; its people are Middle Easterners, growing cotton and wool, eating wheat and meat, looking like Arabs.

From the air there is no way of telling where India leaves off and West Pakistan begins. Both have vast Texan plains, barren deserts, and dry river beds dotted with sagebrush and stunted palm trees. As the dry plains blend into Karachi, the capital of Pakistan, its suburbs seem Texan subdivisions with hundreds of modern concrete ranch-type houses, some begun, some half built, some completed. As one drives in from the airport at dusk with the sun below the dusty horizon, the light has an eerie, opalescent quality, as if it were being reflected off mother-of-pearl instead of bouncing off the corrugated aluminum of the workers' quarters. Across the highway is another Asian incongruity, a huge, empty zeppelin hangar left over from the war.

Since 1947 the Pakistani have turned Karachi from a sleepy fishing village and provincial center into the capital city of their new country. It has wide, smooth modern roads and miles of modern concrete buildings. Bunder Road, which runs straight across the city from east to west for eleven miles, is something like a main street in any big western Texas city, and people stride along with Texan energy. I realized how close Karachi is to the Arab world when I saw the many camels on Bunder Road swaying alongside the motorcars, drawing long flat carts with auto tires on their wheels. The camels wear bells on their knobby knees, and one driver had tied a bunch of artificial sweet peas on his camel's receding forehead above its querulous dowager face. On the camel's cart were a group of modernistic pieces of furniture, arcs and angles and inlays of ebony wood on bleached mahogany.

Roads are jammed with autos, tricabs, bicycles, camels, and pedestrians, none paying the least attention to where anyone else is going, no one giving way to anyone else. Therefore, everybody makes as much noise as he can: drivers keep their palms on their horns; if you have no horn, you ring your bicycle bell; if you have no bell, you shout. The camel, his sweet peas and his furniture, had no sooner been left behind than we stopped for a Moslem wedding procession. First came men playing piercing oboes and clashing cymbals; behind them, four men carried a kind of festive stretcher decorated with two or three arches and trimmed with flowers and crepe-paper streamers. Friends of the bridal couple escorted the stretcher, the bells and bracelets on their ankles sounding contrapuntal rhythms as their bare feet danced on the macadam pavement. Behind the flowered stretcher, the happy couple rode in a low-slung modern American car glistening with chromium plate.

But the characteristic sound of Karachi is not traffic horns or Persian cymbals; it is hammering, for houses and government buildings are springing up in every vacant lot. There are as many women construction workers as men in Karachi, filling the baskets of bricks by hand, digging in the baked clay, breaking stones. The women used to wear the Moslem *burkas,* veils that showed only their eyes. In Pakistan today, wherever custom interferes with progress, it is abandoned; instead of a burka, the women workers wear a detachable veil, tied back over their hair instead of over their faces. Although they are very poor and working for a few cents a day, almost every woman has silver bracelets on her ankles and wrists, and some of them have gold studs in the sides of their noses, since there are few banks in Asia.

In Pakistan the costumes of the people show the influence of the Middle East. As the longyi of Burma gave way to the sari of India, now the sari yields to the *Arabian Nights'* dress of the Moslem world. On formal occasions the women wear *gharara,* the ceremonial dress once worn at the Moslem court of Delhi, pajama trousers and long tunic and shawl of silk or brocade, glittering with gold and silver flowers, fishes, and figures. For everyday wear most women wear the practical *shalwar kamez* over baggy ankle-length trousers and a long tunic shirt that comes down to the knees and is made of a light material like chiffon. Wearing their cool and neat shalwar kamez, the Pakistani women can stride along, ride a bicycle, or carry a load of bricks.

Most of the year the desert air of Karachi is bright and clear under a brilliant blue sky. Often you can see a black design spreading across that sky—flocks of kites with widespread black wings—below them, crowds of gray crows, both groups cawing and swooping down for garbage. They are the real sanitary guardians of West Asia; without them disease would be even more widespread. There are very few beggars on the street; they ask once for alms and then leave you alone, a wonderful change from the whining and pestering of the Indian beggars.

Yet Karachi is a desperately poor city and, like Calcutta, it has been inundated with refugees. In 1947, when Pakistan was born, Karachi had less than 250,000 people and its water supply was barely adequate. Since then over 1,000,000 Moslem refugees have come to this city, most of them penniless and starving. The 40 per cent who came from the cities of India had no training in farm work or heavy manual labor, and there was no urban work available. Old men squat on the dirt floor of a half-finished building of concrete blocks, working at crude plank benches, sweating and panting as they shape crude locks with heavy iron files.

It is no wonder, with this piling up of people in an unprepared city, that Karachi today is neither beautiful nor healthful. If you miss dysentery in Saigon, you will get it in Bangkok, which ignores germs, and if you miss it there, it will catch up with you here in Karachi, whose doctors say, "So many souls are washed away by dirt and tubercular bacilli." Physical health may be poor in Karachi, but the capital's psychological health is very good, reassuring in its bustling conviction. The people and the government are too busy building their country to take time off to look for imagined slights. When you enter Pakistan, your reception is flabbergasting. Gone is the sullen hostility of Indonesia, the beaming inefficiency of Thailand, the suspicious courtesy of Burma, and the ponderous bureaucracy of India. You might be back in the Philippines or in a British colony when you land at Malir Airport.

Brisk and well-trained officials welcome you and, instead of the interminable waits of India, the Pakistan entrance machinery can clear a full planeload of fifty-five passengers in less than one third of the time it takes ten people to get through any division of the Indian mechanism. The post offices of Pakistan are another contrast. Where those of Southeast Asia or India are dirty and crowded, full of people behind the counters, wandering around indifferent as to whether or not they wait on you, here a Moslem in an immaculate costume waits behind the grille ready to help you. When you mail a letter in India you buy a stamp at one window, stick it on yourself, and go to another window to have it canceled; in Pakistan you buy a stamp, the clerk sticks it on the envelope and flips it into a bag.

Small points, but good indications of the way a government is working: customs inspectors, army trainers, national-plan architects, each is a part of the same governmental procedure and spirit; a bad job from one group means a bad job from all.

I got another surprise when I came to deal with the Pakistan Government Information officials. In various Asian capitals, in my negotiations to select famous people of the country for broadcasts, it was a constant problem to try tactfully to find good broadcasters in English. In sensitive Southeast Asia and India this took hours of delicate circling around the point. The Karachi official interrupted my first sentence: "Oh, you mean is the Minister a good speaker? Maybe he isn't. Let's find a better man." In most of Asia government spokesmen mention only what their countries have accomplished or what they hope to do. In Pakistan an official discussing his problems with you analyzes them objectively and includes where he has fallen short of what he intended to do, and how he intends to straighten it out.

Until the partition of the subcontinent, the only difference between a Pakistani and an Indian was that the former was a Moslem, the latter a Hindu; otherwise, they had the same backgrounds. The present Pakistan Civil Service was created by the few Moslems who had been in the British-trained Indian Civil Service. There were not five typewriters when they arrived in their new capital of Karachi; they dragged in packing cases to use for desks and they paid for their own chairs and supplies.

The Pakistan bureaucracy had every excuse to be as cumbersome as that of India. When you ask them why they are so much more efficient, they answer, "We had to be." Mohammed's emphasis on practicality and on action in this world helped them, but the chief reason for the dynamic change lies in the word "necessity." A few years ago the Pakistani leaders were "fogged in by colonialism and suspicious of the West." But a new country with no past to lean on had to take help where it could be found. They had to do first things first and directly.

Given their will to achieve "their own nation based on their own religion," it took them a very short time to discover that the Western ways are often the shortest distance between two points when you want to get things done. Instead of saying, like their brother Asians, "Westerners ought to come here and help us on our terms," they found out what Westerners wanted in order to come and help, and then worked out methods to make them reasonably happy.

What Pakistan has done, any other government and people of Asia could do if they had the wish and will to change. Except where communism forces us to do otherwise, American foreign policy and technical aid should stick to a cardinal principle: help people to get only what they already desperately want; only then will they use our help and like us better for the resources we have spent to help them.

In the period from 1947 to 1954, Pakistan was a one-party state ruled by an all-powerful Moslem League. In the first years of their separated political lives, Pakistan and India have each been controlled by a single party commanding three quarters of the seats in the parliaments and 80 per cent of the voters: in India the predominantly Hindu Congress Party, and in Pakistan the Moslem League. But the Indian constitution is a secular one which guarantees equal rights to all citizens regardless of religion, while Pakistan intends to have an Islamic republic in which no law can be passed that is repugnant to the Koran, and only a Moslem will be able to be the figurehead President or the chief executive, the Prime Minister.

Pakistan has been a long time writing a constitution. When it seceded from India, the Moslem League members of the old Indian Assembly, who had been elected in India, came over to Pakistan and dominated the new nation, whose people are only about 16 per cent literate and not much over one per cent concerned with politics. Since it is this group that comprises the National Constituent Assembly and is writing a constitution, no Pakistani in this supposedly democratic country has had a chance to express his will on this constitution. And, as in any group that holds unchallenged power, some of the Moslem League became arbitrary and corrupt. They enjoyed their power and were in no hurry to write a constitution.

Meantime, resentment in East Pakistan had been building up to an explosion. Economically it was much the poorer part of the country, suffering a constant rice deficit, able to earn only about one third as much income per capita as anything-but-rich West Pakistan; politically it was convinced that Karachi wanted to make it a virtual colony because West Pakistan controlled the Assembly and was proposing clauses for the constitution which would have given East Pakistan, where a majority of the people live, only the barest of equality in the parliament. Finally, in March 1954, the East Pakistani went to the polls in a provincial election, shattered the uneasy status quo, and overthrew the power of the Moslem League in the east. A new United Front Party gained 213 seats in the provincial legislature and the Moslem League was left with only 9; even the president of the eastern Moslem League was swept out of office.

Thus the free elections seemed to have destroyed the curious anomaly of a Moslem state controlled by a West Pakistan with fewer Moslems living in it than lived in either East Pakistan or India. With a majority of the seats in the Constituent Assembly, 45 of the 72, to be filled by United Front nominees, it seemed that grievances could be eliminated. And the Karachi government, well aware of the divisive strains between its parts, was doing what it could: the majority of its meager economic strength was going into projects to help the east, and the Assembly had voted that Bengali, the language of the east, should become a second official language, equal in standing to Urdu, the language of the west.

But tensions kept on rising, thanks to the United Front provincial government. Separatist-minded, it proved itself inexperienced and inept. Result: increasing strikes, riots, threats of secession, and bloodshed until the Prime Minister of Pakistan, Mohammed Ali, former ambassador to the United States and an East Pakistani himself, intervened. He accused Communist plotters of being behind the unrest, deposed the United Front government for "treasonable activities," declared martial law, and sent the Pakistan Minister of Defense to restore law and order.

However, since the majority of Pakistani, even in the eastern province, are Moslems, such grave political divisions do not necessarily help the divide-and-conquer Communists. Unlike the Communist parties in neighboring India and Burma, the East Pakistan Communists are weak and underground. There were only two Communists elected in the provincial election; both were Hindus. There are no Communists in the Moslem League. Moslems believe that "to put every citizen at the mercy of the state, possessing all political and economic power and all means of living, is totally opposed to the spirit of Islam."

If you argue that communism outside of Russia thrives only where the people are miserable, when you look at the terrible want and misery of Pakistan and the illiteracy of its people you should assume it is a fertile climate for communism. But Pakistani hold that "communism is bred in spiritual poverty, not economic poverty." Confronted with a deeper and more fervent faith, communism fails; and Islam supplies its people with that kind of spiritual conviction. "If it were not for our religion we would be on the side of communism, because there are so many things we want that we have not and that you of the non-Communist world have. But not with our religion and our belief in the All Mighty."

The other nations of Asia whose borders touch on Russia or China walk and talk circumspectly; neutral and pacifistic. Not so Pakistan; its leaders denounce communism as "an instrument of Russian foreign policy dedicated to the interest of Russia as a Great Power." And, recognizing the aggressive threat of communism, the Pakistani put their first national emphasis on security. Poor as they are, desperately needing every cent to build their country, rehabilitate their refugees, feed their starving, and nurse their ill, they spend 70 per cent of their national budget on their Army, a quarter of a million volunteer fighting men.

Over half of the old Indian Army were Moslems, and they made up over three quarters of its front-line troops. Today these physically tough and superb fighters compose the Pakistan Army. Possessing no cash to buy modern weapons and having only one small factory to make rifles and small arms, until 1954 the Army struggled along with equipment raked together from the relics of the first two world wars, obsolete but still formidable in the hands of men who knew how to use guns and were willing to. Then the United States, seeking to extend a Middle Eastern alliance against Russian moves south and realizing that the Khyber Pass is the only good land approach from the steppes of middle Asia down into India, came to Pakistan's aid with a military pact similar to the one we signed with Turkey. It is designed eventually to furnish the armaments and roads and bases to turn Pakistan into another Turkey, able to stand up against any aggression.

If security is the first pillar of Pakistan foreign policy, its second pillar is much less satisfying to American foreign-policy makers. In the UN Pakistan is demanding that all free countries support the principle of international self-determination. This brings her into collision with the United States in the Near East and the Middle East. The Pakistan Government fights the French policies in North Africa and sharply criticizes us for supporting French colonial policies in Tunisia and Morocco contrary to "your tradition, your history, and your instincts for self-determination." She was sharply critical of the French in Vietnam, insisting, as did most Americans, that if France in 1948 had granted Vietnam the autonomy it offered in 1953, there would not have been an Indo-Chinese war.

We will find the Pakistani a thorn in our sides whenever we vote with the British or the French against the Arabs and the Egyptians and other subject peoples. As one Communist-fighter to another, they warn us that there are two gigantic struggles going on in the world today. One is the contest for the mastery of the world between the capitalist countries headed by the U.S.A., and the Communist countries headed by the U.S.S.R.; the second is the struggle of the nations of Asia and Africa against the "political domination and economic exploitation of the West." The Pakistani, as do most of our non-European friends, urgently want the United States to support more self-determination and economic freedom for the small and newer countries, which would then begin to see reasons why they should take a stand against communism.

There is one area where Pakistan's foreign policy is as thoroughly intransigent: in its relations with India. The two countries hate and fear each other. Each bears the terrible scars of Partition, the heartbreak of the uprooted twelve million refugees, and the massacre of another two million in religious riots on both sides of the border. Superficially the attitudes of the two countries are different, but underneath they are similar; the Indian press is patronizing, sweetly reasonable, and self-righteous, while the Pakistan press is inflexible, arrogant, and aggressive.

Kashmir is the magnifying glass that focuses the hatred on both sides to a burning point. Pages and footnotes galore could be used to list some of the complicated wrangles of the Kashmir incident, the most abrasive and acerbated point of disagreement in the cold war being waged between the two countries. The Pakistani are determined to fight to the bitter end on the Kashmir issue, and the Indians have an equally mulish determination not to yield one semicolon. Behind all the other frictions over who shall have how much of this great and fertile province of Northwest India is water, for Kashmir controls the sources of the great rivers that water the granary of West Pakistan, the Punjab. These rivers, like the ribs of an open fan, flow southwestward until they empty into the Arabian Sea at Karachi. Without them the granary of Pakistan would become a desert, and so the Pakistani say, "We could not hesitate between a waterless Punjab and war; we might just as well die quickly as starve slowly."

And of course another force working toward the mutual antipathy of the two countries is the incompatible religious convictions which forced Partition. Every aspect of modern Pakistan—its Western drive, its political setup, its stand on communism, or its culture—starts with the shaping cause of this country, Islam. Erected upon a sense of religious identity rather than a national identity, this country regards itself as the twentieth-century disciple of the prophet Mohammed. If you ask a Pakistani what he is, he does not say he is a man or a Pakistani or a merchant; he says, "I am a Moslem." When he has wished someone badly he adds, "*Tauba, tauba* [God forgive me]"; when he says he will or will not do something, he adds, "*Insha Allah* [God willing]"; and every time he begins an effort, he says, "*Bismallah* [In God's name]." And he thinks of his own country, in the words of the founder of Pakistan, Quaid-i-Azam, as "the laboratory of practical Islam," which will lead the Moslem world ahead.

This is the only religion of the religions of Asia that is close in beliefs and practice to Christianity. The followers of Mohammed accept the Old Testament and, although they are convinced Mohammed was the last and greatest prophet, they still believe Jesus was a great prophet. Thus accepting so much of our ethical and religious background, it is not surprising that they act so often as we would.

Believing in the unity of God and the brotherhood of man, they carry the brotherhood idea farther than we Americans have; Moslems have never known color or race prejudice or privileges. A man is judged on the righteousnes of his conduct and life, how he measures up to the Koran. And democracy is inextricably woven into the teachings of Islam. "Consensus of opinion" was one of the most important ideas Mohammed taught his followers—in all important matters the Prophet consulted his companions before he acted—and Moslems are enjoined by the Koran to decide by consultation.

From a Westerner's point of view, Christianity and Islam have certain useful virtues in common which the religions of the East do not value as highly. There is a powerful and fructifying interrelation between Christian teachings and the development of man's material betterment and the evolution of social behavior pattern whereby larger groups of people will want to function together. No reasoning man of the West believes that his responsibilities stop at the farther edges of the development of serenity in his own personality or in the material protection of his own family and relatives. The men of the East are not led by their religions to this conclusion.

Like Christianity, the religions of Asia start with the recognition that evil and destruction spring from selfishness, self-absorption, and self-desires. In Christianity these forces are associated with the devil and balanced out by the injunction to "do unto others"; that is, you are urged to recognize how much you would hate it if others act selfishly unto you, and thus by thinking outwardly, toward others, you limit your selfishness and desires. From our basic Golden Rule it is an easy step to recognize that this "do good unto others" applies not only to the people around us but more broadly to our national community and even to the nascent world community.

The religions of the East, although starting from the same central concept of the destructive force of the selfish drive, like everything important in the East, stay focused on the individual, the subjective, the unique. And therefore, these religions have not led out toward wider social responsibilities. Buddhism says that for your own sake, so that you may achieve nirvana, you must conquer your selfish drive. Religiously and ethically many steps must be taken before the deeper truths of the Eastern religions are correlated with the practical facts and mechanisms of twentieth-century technology, God's newest gift to His children.

We do not develop our inner spirituality enough, and we, as individuals, are the poorer for it; they do not develop their outer cooperation enough, and they, as democracies, are the poorer for it.

The Pakistani, although living in the East, live by the convictions of a variant of practical Christianity, and therefore it has been easy for them to accept Western efficiency and practice the mutual cooperations which can help them in their time of crisis. The Hindus are practical and efficient in spite of a religion that deems both virtues trivial. The Pakistani, like Americans, are practical and efficient because of a religion that deems these things all-important. And the Pakistani see many other similarities between themselves and Americans as well as some better and some worse traits. They believe they are far more God-fearing and God-obeying than Americans, pointing out that many of us do not pay much attention to the precepts of our religion, while few of them will even take a drink because the Koran forbids it; they feel more self-confident than Americans and are surprised that we are afraid and they are not, although their situation is worse than ours has been since Valley Forge.

On negatives in their character, they point first to what they call *radpak*, self-indulgence; they do not cut their coat according to their cloth until well after they are running out of cloth. They also have a lack of proportion, an intensity that goes too far, whether it be in interpreting the Koran or in exacting work from laborers or animals. Since these were the only two weaknesses the Pakistani could find for me and since they had much difficulty digging these up, it would seem safe to assume they are not without national pride or even conceit.

To the Pakistani, the greatest virtues in the American system are friendliness, love of work, and adaptability. Recognizing their own attachment to the past and its traditions, they envy us our openness to new ideas. Those who come to the United States are startled because we are so much less materialistic than they thought; they find us as God-fearing and as aware as they of the social responsibility of money. The Koran, forbidding usury, teaches them that private property and private enterprise are a moral trust to be used in the service of mankind, and they are dumfounded at the amount of private money in the United States that goes into social services.

If the United States is to do a better job in making friends around the world, we must emphasize in each country the values of the American system which fit in best with the values appreciated by that country. In Pakistan much more should be done to underline our God-fearing characteristics and our mutual consultation methods. In India and in Burma we need to stress the developments of the American Government in national planning and the amount of coexistence and tolerance in the American system. In Japan we need to underline how the American is able to remain a functioning member of his society, subordinating himself to it when necessary, yet is able to expand his own personal expression.

We do such a bad job in our information programs because of our obsession that Asians can be handled in a single way and because our government and our representatives abroad know so little about the backgrounds, the ethics, and the values of these other peoples of the world. Although university study centers, Russian or African or Middle Eastern or Southeast Asian, are beginning to fill in some of the gaps, it is a dangerously blank area in American foreign policy.

As of today there is no adequate briefing material available for American representatives going to countries of the Far East. What is needed are not Asian variations on the wartime booklet that explained Britain to American GIs. The American foreign or economic officer desperately needs much deeper and broader evaluations of the psychological motivations and the fundamental values of these Asian civilizations which he must attempt to appraise accurately and to influence sympathetically for the United States.

The Pakistani, when they criticize us, find two big drawbacks in American life. They accuse us of a lack of balance, of insisting that everything must be all good or all bad and thus easily becoming victims of our own propaganda campaigns. And they criticize us for our lack of respect for the past, a condemnation with which all Asia agrees. It believes Americans are unwilling to learn from the past and want to interpret the present without reference to it; this seems especially shallow and stupid to Asians because they put so much stock in the past.

And this, in turn, shows how two right points of view can make a misunderstanding. Since Asians are so much a part of their own past and so regulated by it, we come to wrong conclusions if we do not consider their past as prime data when we try to figure them out. Conversely, Asians think we are childish in our attitude toward the past because they do not understand what a short past we have had and how little it has determined what we do today. We call them hidebound; they call us superficial.

But the attitude of the Pakistani today toward their own women is neither hidebound nor superficial. Women in Islam have always had certain rights granted to few other women in Asia. They can hold property and they have always had the right of divorce; but, wishing to protect women from their genius at changing their own minds, Islamic law requires them to make three declarations of divorce, a month apart, before it becomes final. Possessing the rights of divorce, Moslem women tend not to use them. They feel that American women "make their beds and then want to jump right out of them," and that by demanding too much respect they do not get enough from their husbands.

Before Partition, the marriage systems of India did not recognize the stroke of lightning between two people which we call romantic love. Moslem parents, like other Asian parents, looked around in their own circle for a husband or wife for their children, talked their choice over with the other parents concerned, and then arranged that the couple meet. Nowadays the Pakistani women envy the American teen-agers' freedom and yearn to have their husbands wipe the dishes as in the United States. But Pakistani husbands say, "Our women have grown very froward since independence."

Only in the remoter provinces do you still see women in purdah, completely concealed in tents of material with a slit at eye level so they can see out without being seen. At the frontier "they are very strict and they would shoot a woman if she be seen without." Most women have thrown their veils aside as well as their homebody approach to life. Today Pakistani women by the thousands are in the armed forces; ciphering, decoding, nursing, learning to shoot or to put radios together, studying all the sciences of the West, and enjoying fully as much freedom as American women have.

It has been necessary for the women to shoulder many burdens because their country has been in a time of grave economic crisis, tottering on the edge of financial insolvency and starvation. Pakistan, like all the other countries of Asia except Japan, is an agricultural country, with 80 to 90 per cent of its people on the land, earning about sixty cents a day. Jute and cotton make up 85 per cent of her exports and furnish most of the foreign exchange upon which she must depend for her industrialization, for all her finished goods, and even for such simple necessities as textiles.

Pakistan had a very favorable economic break when the country was born, and most of her new buildings and small industrial plants are the result of it. The Korean War broke out soon after Partition, and raw-material prices went soaring up on the world exchanges. Jute and cotton became worth more money every month, and simultaneously fine weather produced bumper crops. Assuming prosperity was here to stay, and desperately needing textile mills to process her cotton so that she would not have to buy cloth at a high price from India, Pakistan embarked on an expensive program, building textile mills, fertilizer plants, irrigation canals. It is an example of the economic senselessness of Partition that at the time she was straining to build textile plants, right across the border India was struggling to plant cotton so she would not have to buy the raw material from Pakistan.

For the first few years all went well in Pakistan as the money from her golden exports poured in. Then with the Korean truce, world prices fell, until jute was down two thirds and cotton one half. Result, an economic crisis which has forced Pakistan to stop most of her projects for her future and institute strict rationing and compulsory savings. In the same period another disaster struck at the new country, which in good seasons raises barely enough food to avoid actual famine, the average East Pakistani diet of eighteen hundred calories a day being close to a starvation level. In 1952 a two-year drought hit Pakistan and forced her, during the same period of falling income, to spend much more of her foreign exchange to import wheat.

To help Pakistan in this extremity, the United States donated close to a million tons of its huge wheat surplus. This gift of wheat exemplifies a potent instrument of foreign policy available to the United States. We produce far more food than we consume, and if we cannot sell that food, our farm income would fall and in turn push our economy into a recession. To prevent this, the government takes over our farm surpluses. But if it cannot get rid of them, there is trouble, and if we burn them or let them rot, we allow people to starve to death.

We are also spending billions abroad for our safety and world stability. Our food surplus should be viewed as a part of that expenditure and be used to help our friends around the world. The American Congress should cease to think of food surpluses as a problem and begin to regard them as an opportunity.

The Pakistan food crisis highlights another general point of Asian economics. If Pakistan could have sold its jute and cotton at adequate prices, it would not have been starving and it would not have become an economic invalid. Every raw-material country in Asia, in lesser degree, has had a similar experience. Indonesia has not been able to dispose of its rubber; Malaya has seen its tin piling up; Thailand and Burma have been unable to move enough rice; Japan has not been able to sell enough of her factory products. The economic pressures of self-preservation will force these countries to sell their produce to whomever they can, including the Communists. For Americans, well fed and comfortable, to expect that the desperate countries of Asia will not trade with China and Russia is to fool themselves. When it becomes a choice between not trading with the Communist blocs and starving, or exchanging products with Russia and China and thus improving her own sad economic lot, no country will choose suicide. Even Pakistan has had to increase its trade with Russia around 300 per cent in two years.

Like India, Pakistan has established a national plan to strengthen her economic position and raise her standard of living and, like India, her chief emphasis is on land reform, irrigation, food production, more fertilizers, better seeds and farming methods and crop yields. Like her neighbor, she is attacking her problems via the same kind of realistic appraisals and practical solutions, taking aid where she can get it and welcoming it. The Pakistani are building one cement plant with Canadian aid, another with New Zealand help; they are doing rural rehabilitation and land reclamation through World Bank loans; with America's help they are embarking on village-aid programs and building light industrial plants. They are constructing the Sukkur Barrage, the largest single irrigation work of its kind in the whole world, and another almost as large and also in the Sind, the Kotri Barrage. And, like India, Pakistan is attempting to attract foreign capital; the Pakistani permit capital to be remitted from the country without restriction; they offer concessions to foreign investments in the form of exemptions from state taxes, abolition of import duties, and special depreciation.

They also use socialistic measures where they need to. In overcrowded Karachi, the government officers badly needed housing, but the government did not have the money for building. So the officers formed the Pakistan Government Housing Society, open to anyone who works for the government, from office boy to cabinet minister; the government gave land to the society and advanced eighteen months' salary to help its employees finance their houses.

Risk capital is the hardest thing to find in Asia, and so Pakistan has established an Industrial Finance Corporation, something like our RFC, to provide loans to existing industries for expansion; businessmen, not government functionaries, serve on its board of directors. After Partition the country did not have a single spindle to convert its jute into bags and, although there was a demonstrable market for bags, the backward private capital of this part of the world would not come forward to finance the needed factories. So the government stepped in to help the construction of the world's largest jute mills on the shores of the Kalshy River in East Pakistan, but the IFC makes no effort to interfere in the plant's operation.

The Pakistan Industrial Finance Corporation, searching, as are the other Asian countries, for American investors, has a sound formula. It sets up a joint America-Pakistan-owned company. In it the American concern provides machinery as its part of the ownership, while Pakistan finances the local expenditures but leaves the management of the mill in the hands of the skilled foreigners.

As in the case of food production, by the dynamics of its own economy and of world geopolitics, the United States is going to be forced into more foreign investments. Just as we produce more food than we can consume, we produce more industrial goods and capital equipment than we can possibly use at home. The only times we have been truly prosperous have been times when we were exporting capital to the rest of the world. In the past, these periods were primarily periods of war or war crisis: 1914–18, 1938–45, 1950–51.

What war has forced us to do in the past, the preservation of peace will force us to do in the future. When you are the leader in the world, you either lead or are trampled down. American businessmen must now lead abroad as well as at home. Business is at least as much the creator of world leadership as anything in the American idea of democracy or in our military power. American business must familiarize itself with the problems of South Asia, where it is so urgently needed and where, by sound investigation and shrewd choice, it can defend the private-enterprise system in which it so fervently and belligerently believes.

In Pakistan today, an American company has invested fifty thousand dollars in shrimp fishing. If the project is successful, it will furnish both a new financial support for this country and a new food supply. The government has set up a monopoly on oyster growing and is sowing beds from which it will be able to export oysters to all of

Western Europe. The United States has granted three quarters of a million dollars to the port of Karachi for the expansion of harbor facilities and refrigeration, storage, and processing plants.

If the plans work out, these Pakistan ventures will become pilot plants for the rest of the starving nations of Asia. Most of them, with so few proteins now available, have seacoasts. In the warm southeast coastal seas of Asia there is an immeasurable treasure, far more fabulous than Aladdin's, of high-protein food and exports for foreign exchange. But the fish will stay in these waters until the know-how of the West shows these peoples how to fish their seas and furnishes them the money with which to preserve and process the yield.

Meantime, as in India and almost all of the rest of Asia, the most appalling Pakistan statistic is her population increase. In spite of a life expectancy today of only twenty-five years as compared with sixty years in England, she adds about six million new food consumers each year.

But whether we do anything about population growths in and with Pakistan, there are a great many things the United States can do. In the first place, economic crisis in Pakistan, as in India, does not mean economic collapse. The country will be in business as long as the people keep their will. The worst thing that could happen in Pakistan would be an eventual breaking in two of the country's disparate east and west. This could happen only if the Islamic ideal ceases to burn in Pakistani breasts.

The largest newspaper in the country, *Dawn,* bears the admonition "Faith Remains and will bring errant Duty and Discipline to heel." If it should not, there would be a second partition on the subcontinent: East Pakistan would either return to the Bengali fold and become again a province of India, or it would become another new republic, the weakest and most vulnerable to communism in all Asia.

If the worst came to pass, East Pakistan, sitting between a neutral India and a neutral Burma, might turn away from American co-operation and military aid to join the neutral bloc. That would still leave West Pakistan, a firmly anti-Communist state with more people in it than has Burma or Thailand, Malaya, the Philippines, Korea, Formosa, or Indo-China. And geographically speaking, the combination of West Pakistan on one side of the Middle East and Turkey on the other presents a very strong deterrent to any Russian drive down toward the Persian Gulf.

And at home on her own subcontinent, Pakistan, the present seventh largest nation in the world, or West Pakistan alone, works as a powerful damper on Communist aggression. If necessary, even a West Pakistan could raise an army of a million. Her airfields, modern and numerous, could place the industrial centers of Soviet Central Asia within reach of American strategic bombers. Two of the most important airports of the world are near Karachi, geographically an unavoidable hub of world aviation crossing from the Middle East to Asia. Its civilian airport, Malir, is the largest of its kind in Asia. Near by is Maunpur, the military airport built by the British and the Americans in World War II and kept in good repair by the farsighted Pakistani. Maunpur is one of the largest military airports in the world and able to handle any aircraft.

A militarily strong Pakistan fills the dangerous vacuum of military power on the teeming subcontinent and provides a base from which to defend India if she should not be willing to abandon a policy of neutrality until too late. And if India should gradually drift into the Communist orbit, a strong Pakistan would help delay that drift and serve as a counterbalance to it. India, furiously inimical to Pakistan, will make every conceivable trouble over each step taken by the United States to arm Pakistan. Afraid of a strong Pakistan army, she also fears its presence would bring the cold war closer to her borders. Also, Pakistan, increasing her economic strength and developing a powerful modern army and air force, begins to shape up as an equal and challenger to India in the councils of South Asia.

India rejects the concept of force to confront force and believes neutrality is the answer in South Asia; choosing the policy of nonviolence, she hopes the Communists will not fill this vacuum with their own power. Pakistan would block by force any attempt of Russia and China to do so. The vast region of the Middle East, the Indian subcontinent, and Southeast Asia of itself has neither military power nor the industrial base for it. There are only two ways this vacuum will be filled. One is via the Communist man power of China plus the Communist industrial power of Russia. The only counterbalance to this is the man power of free Asia plus the industrial power of the United States.

Unless we give this area over to the Communists, we must continue military support to our allies like Pakistan. But if Americans are willing to lift their vision beyond the frustrating, costly, and dangerous necessities of power politics, there is a broader reason for supporting this new nation. Being the largest Moslem nation on the earth, Pakistan is looking forward to the time when her example can lead the rest of the Moslem world, "decadent, corrupt, poor, and in economic chaos," toward the same kind of decent future she hopes to gain for her own people.

As we strengthen her and help her to understand ways and benefits of the Christian West, we simultaneously build for ourselves a bridge across to the three hundred million Moslems of the world. As Christians we cannot be a prime influence on these peoples and their countries, but Pakistan, with encouragement, might become the architect of a Christian-Moslem world-wide co-operation. If she could establish an alliance of Moslem powers and by her example help the backward Moslem world to progress, Pakistan could help create another great bloc of nations which communism could not threaten.

But with no derogation of Pakistan intended, this vision, like so many other hopes for the world's future, must begin in the heart and in the head of the United States. Before Pakistan can do anything, she must become strong and we must make her strong. The United States is in for a long, costly, and painful pull if it is to fulfill its responsibilities in the Far East and interpose the shield of its strength between the growing aggressive might of the Russo-Chinese axis and the struggling new nations of Asia. Many Americans assume that, if we will, we are able to decide where Asia will go. We cannot. We have neither the power nor the prestige to swing the billion Asians where we choose. We can only help and influence their decision.

Even this will take a lot of doing. It is going to have to be done slowly. And it can be done only with the help of our friends.

We have many obligations in Asia. For Christianity's sweet charity we must do what we can to help the starving to live; for our own protection we must give money and aid to countries that do not admire us, so that they will not drift into communism's hands. But we cannot afford to give all the aid each of the nations of Asia wants or needs. Our first obligation must be to our friends and allies who want to go along the same road we do to the same kind of future.

There are four questions which the United States has a right to ask of any Asian people and its leaders before we decide how much aid to grant that country. The questions might be described as the four F's: fear, force, freedom, friendship. One: Do you fear the results of a Communist government of your country? Two: Will you join us in using force, if necessary, to stop Communist aggression in Asia? Three: Are you proving by your policies in your own country that you are for freedom and a democratic way of life? Four: Since any country's best and most dependable allies are friends, are you a friend of the United States?

Any nation and people who can answer yes to these four F's is entitled to first priority from us, economic, military, or psychological. Malaya, as a ward of Britain, receives her aid from Britain, therefore she does not belong in this questionnaire.

Country	*Fear of communism*	*Willingness to use force*	*Freedom at home*	*Friend of U.S.A.*
BURMA	yes?	no!	yes!	no!
CAMBODIA	yes!	yes!	no	?
FORMOSA	yes!	yes!	no!	yes
INDIA	yes?	no!	yes!	no
INDONESIA	no	no!	yes?	no!
JAPAN	yes	yes	yes?	no?
KOREA	yes!	yes!	yes?	yes!
LAOS	yes?	?	no?	?
PAKISTAN	yes!	yes!	yes?	yes
PHILIPPINES	yes!	yes!	yes!	yes!
SOUTH VIETNAM	yes!	yes?	no!	yes?
THAILAND	yes!	yes!	no?	yes!

Unfortunately, only Korea, Pakistan, and the Philippines can give some kind of a yes to all four questions; quite possibly Thailand, because of her benevolent dictatorship and her efforts to teach democracy to her people, should be included with the other three. Even so, none of the four is now powerful or influential. It is up to us to find ways and pay money to help them become both.

Below this category of indisputable friends and allies, who deserve far more help than we have given them, Americans may rank Asian nations differently, depending on how urgent is the threat of Communist aggression and depending on what they think is the best way to improve the world around us. Take the difference between the answers on Japan and India and Formosa. If you believe that freedom at home is all-important and force will not help the world, you rate India high. If you believe that internal freedom is nobody's business but the country involved, you rate Formosa high. If you believe it does not matter how a country feels about the United States if it is willing to fight and has some form of democratic government, then Japan gets a higher priority.

As the internal situation varies in a country, or as external dangers wax or wane, ratings shift. And each man adds or takes away his question marks according to his own judgment.

But we must always remember that, without our friends in Asia, we can achieve nothing. We need to help Asia and we need Asia's help. Both of these noble objectives are possible. But not by ourselves. A nation that does not help its friends and fellow believers ends up without ideals, at the mercy of its enemies. To depend on friendship is to depend on a fire that burns without being consumed.

But in addition to strengthening our friends, we must encourage them by adopting a wiser Asian policy. We must get on the side of the angels. We must prove that we really believe in the things we profess to live by. We are for peace. We must prove it by making common cause with the UN and with every neutral in every kind of friendship pact or non-aggression pact. We are against colonialism. We must prove it by demonstrating, as we never have, that nowhere in the world will we support colonialism or the subjugation of backward peoples. And then we must help them to be free and prove by our own acts that they are equal.

Asians are not inscrutable Orientals, they are starving Orientals, starving for food and for freedom. We believe in progress. We must become identified with it and depended upon for it. Technical aid is our forte. We must begin to exploit it.

Above all, we must provide a clear and convincing answer to the question uppermost in Asian minds: "Why will I get more out of democracy than out of communism?" The very way this question must be phrased shows how little we have done to answer it for Asians. And how much is left for us to do.

950
C772t 34276

COOKE

There is no Asia

SINKIANG
C H I N
AKISTAN
RAWALPINDI
DELHI
AGRA
INDIA
GANGES R.
PAKISTAN
CALCUTTA
HOOGHLY RIVER
BURMA
IRRAWADDY RIVER
MANDALAY
YUNNAN PROVINCE
CHELI
TONKIN
HANOI
LAOS
MEKONG RIVER
RANGOON
THAILAND
BANGKOK
ANGKOR
SIEMREAP
PNOMPENH
CAMBODIA
SAI
COCHIN
BAY OF BENGAL
TRAVANCORE-COCHIN
MALAY PEN.
MALAYA
KUALA LUMPUR
SINGAPORE
STRAIT OF MALACCA
SUMATRA
INDIAN OCEAN
DJAKA
JAV